Literary Manuscript Culture in Romantic Britain

Edinburgh Critical Studies in Romanticism
Series Editors: Ian Duncan and Penny Fielding

Available Titles
A Feminine Enlightenment: British Women Writers and the Philosophy of Progress, 1759–1820
JoEllen DeLucia
Reinventing Liberty: Nation, Commerce and the Historical Novel from Walpole to Scott
Fiona Price
The Politics of Romanticism: The Social Contract and Literature
Zoe Beenstock
Radical Romantics: Prophets, Pirates, and the Space Beyond Nation
Talissa J. Ford
Literature and Medicine in the Nineteenth-Century Periodical Press: Blackwood's Edinburgh Magazine, 1817–1858
Megan Coyer
Discovering the Footsteps of Time: Geological Travel Writing in Scotland, 1700–1820
Tom Furniss
The Dissolution of Character in Late Romanticism
Jonas Cope
Commemorating Peterloo: Violence, Resilience, and Claim-making during the Romantic Era
Michael Demson and Regina Hewitt
Dialectics of Improvement: Scottish Romanticism, 1786–1829
Gerard Lee McKeever
Literary Manuscript Culture in Romantic Britain
Michelle Levy

Forthcoming Titles
Towards Romantic Periodical Studies: 12 Case Studies from Blackwood's Edinburgh Magazine
Nicholas Mason and Tom Mole
Romantic Environmental Sensibility: Nature, Class and Empire
Ve-Yin Tee
Scottish Romanticism and the Making of Collective Memory in the British Atlantic
Kenneth McNeil

Visit our website at: www.edinburghuniversitypress.com/series/ECSR

Literary Manuscript Culture in Romantic Britain

Michelle Levy

EDINBURGH
University Press

Edinburgh University Press is one of the leading university presses in the UK. We publish academic books and journals in our selected subject areas across the humanities and social sciences, combining cutting-edge scholarship with high editorial and production values to produce academic works of lasting importance. For more information visit our website: edinburghuniversitypress.com

© Michelle Levy, 2020, 2021

Edinburgh University Press Ltd
The Tun – Holyrood Road
12(2f) Jackson's Entry
Edinburgh EH8 8PJ

First published in hardback by Edinburgh University Press 2020

Typeset in 11/14 Adobe Sabon by
IDSUK (DataConnection) Ltd

A CIP record for this book is available from the British Library

ISBN 978 1 4744 5706 4 (hardback)
ISBN 978 1 4744 5707 1 (paperback)
ISBN 978 1 4744 5708 8 (webready PDF)
ISBN 978 1 4744 5709 5 (epub)

The right of Michelle Levy to be identified as the author of this work has been asserted in accordance with the Copyright, Designs and Patents Act 1988, and the Copyright and Related Rights Regulations 2003 (SI No. 2498).

Contents

List of Illustrations	vi
Acknowledgements	viii
Introduction	1
1. Intentionality and the Romantic Literary Manuscript	28
2. Literary Reviews and the Reception of Manuscript Culture	64
3. Anna Barbauld's Poetic Career in Script and Print	101
4. Lord Byron, Manuscript Poet	140
5. Jane Austen's Fiction in Manuscript	182
6. Script's Afterlives	214
Afterword: Blake's Digitised Printed Script	259
References	268
Index	290

List of Illustrations

The figures and colour plates may be viewed at: https://edinburghuniversitypress.com/book-literary-manuscript-culture-in-romantic-britain-hb.html by clicking on the resources tab.

Figure

I.1	Robert Darnton, 'The Communications Circuit'	9

Tables

1.1	Entries in Dorothy Wordsworth's *Grasmere Journals* with corresponding poems by William Wordsworth	50
1.2	Comparison of opening entries in Dorothy Wordsworth's *Recollections of a Tour in Scotland* (DCMS 50, 54, 97)	54
4.1	Poems removed from and added to Byron's four early verse collections	144
4.2	Comparison of different versions of Canto I, stanza 7B/viii, *Childe Harold's Pilgrimage*	156
4.3	Comparison of manuscript and print versions of Canto I, stanza 87, *Childe Harold's Pilgrimage*	160
4.4	Unauthorised poems published during Byron's lifetime, published from manuscript or private print sources	168
5.1	Inventory of Austen's surviving fiction manuscripts	184
5.2	Comparison of Austen's letters from J. S. Clarke and her 'Plan of a Novel'	190
6.1	Major scholarly critical editions of Romantic authors	233

Plates

1. John Keats, 'This living hand, now warm and capable', MS Keats 2.29.2, Houghton Library, Harvard University
2. Dorothy Wordsworth, title page of *Recollections of a Tour in Scotland*, illustrated by George Hutchinson (DCMS 55.i)
3. Dorothy Wordsworth, title page of *Recollections of a Tour in Scotland*, illustrated by George Hutchinson (DCMS 55.ii)
4. Dorothy Wordsworth, first page of 'A Winter's Ramble in Grasmere Vale' (DCMS 120)
5. Dorothy Wordsworth, last page of 'Irregular Stanzas: Holiday at Gwerndovennant' (DCMS 120)
6. Barbauld's poetry, by publication status, by decade
7. Byron's poetic output, by poem and page length, by year
8. Byron's poetic output, short and long poems, by date
9. Byron's poems, long/short, unprinted/printed
10. Byron's poems, printed/unprinted, short/long, by year
11. Byron's short poems, printed/unprinted, by title of first publication
12. Fair copies of Byron's printed/unprinted and short/long poems
13. Jane Austen, 'Plan of a Novel according to hints from various quarters', MA 1034, Pierpont Morgan Library, New York
14. Engraved letter from Anna Seward to Archibald Constable, tipped into volume 1 of *The Letters of Anna Seward. Written between the years 1784 and 1807* (1811), 2003J-EC372, Houghton Library, Harvard University
15. Frontispiece, *The Works of Anna Laetitia Barbauld. With a Memoir by Lucy Aikin* (1825)
16. William Blake, 'The Little Boy Lost', *Songs of Innocence and Songs of Experience*, British Museum, copy T, object 13
17. William Blake, 'Infant Joy', *Songs of Innocence and Songs of Experience*, British Museum, copy T, object 25

Acknowledgements

In a book that examines how writing is transformed for print, and that emphasises the sociable and collaborative nature of the process, an acknowledgements section presents an opportunity to reflect upon the many people and institutions that have supported my research. I am supremely fortunate to work in the English Department at Simon Fraser University, with an exceptional community of scholars working in the fields of print culture and book history. I have the incredible good fortune to be colleagues with Betty Schellenberg, one of the leading scholars of eighteenth-century manuscript culture, whose research, happily enough for me, ends just before the Romantic period. We often half-jokingly discussed issuing our books in two parts, and it is my fondest hope that this book may be found to be a worthy follower to her *Literary Coteries and the Making of Modern Print Culture 1740–1790*. I am also grateful to Colette Colligan, who has provided me with conceptual and organisational suggestions, ongoing moral support, and more working titles than I care to recall. Leith Davis has also been an enthusiastic reader of parts of the draft. Manuscript culture is a subject that has been well plumbed by early modern scholars, and I owe a special debt of gratitude to Margaret Ezell, for her inspirational writing on women's manuscript culture, and for her support of my work. Many years ago, in the doctoral programme at UCLA, Anne Mellor hooked me on the Romantic period and the contributions of its incredible women writers, and that influence has been potent and persistent. During the period I have been working on this project, I have received support from the Social Sciences Humanities Council of Canada (SSHRC); I am grateful for their support. I have also worked closely with the Interacting with Print group, based at McGill University, and it has been a privilege to learn about intermediality with its fearless leaders, Tom Mole, Andrew Piper, Jonathan Sachs and other members of the Multigraph Collective.

As the author of a study that examines several well-known Romantic authors, two of whom (Austen and Byron) have been studied intensely and all of whom have been studied well, I am indebted to the literary and textual scholars who have laid the foundation for my own research. Without the work of Dorothy Wordsworth's editors, Ernest de Selincourt and Pamela Woof, much of what I have to say about her manuscripts would be impossible. I am also deeply indebted to the curator of her manuscripts held at the Wordsworth Trust, Jeff Cowton, and his staff, especially Becky Turner, for their kindness, patience and expertise. William McCarthy has been an invaluable source of information and support in my research on Anna Barbauld. I was fortunate to have an earlier version of Chapter 3, 'Anna Barbauld's Poetic Career in Script and Print', appear in 'Anna Barbauld in Script and Print', in William McCarthy and Olivia Murphy (eds), *Anna Barbauld: New Perspectives* (Lewisburg, PA: Bucknell University Press, 2014), pp. 59–96. I am grateful to the publisher for permission to reproduce a revised version of this essay.

My research on Byron rests on the foundational textual scholarship of Jerome McGann. His remarkable seven-volume *Complete Poetical Works* has been a constant companion while working on Chapter 4, and it has been my privilege to mine its contents to support my analysis. The editorial work of Alice Levine has also been of great assistance, as has the scholarship and support of colleagues and friends who study Byron, especially Gary Dyer, Tom Mole, Jane Stabler and Andy Stauffer, friendly compatriots on many Byron-manuscript-themed conference papers over the years.

On Austen, the analysis that appears in this book is indebted to the groundbreaking digital edition, *Jane Austen's Fiction Manuscripts*, and scholarship by its editor, Kathryn Sutherland, as well the other editors and scholars of Austen's manuscript works, particularly Linda Bree, Margaret Doody, Peter Sabor and Janet Todd. Chapter 5, 'Jane Austen's Fiction in Manuscript', is an amalgamation, expansion and reconsideration of two articles: 'Austen's Manuscripts and the Publicity of Print', *ELH* 77.4 (Winter 2010): 1015–40 and '*Sanditon* as fragmentary draft manuscript', *Persuasions Online* 83(2) (Spring 2018), *Special Issue on Sanditon*, co-edited Susan Allen Ford and Anne Toner. I thank the editors of those issues/journals and the anonymous reviewers for helping see those publications into the press. The Afterword's analysis of Blake is indebted to the pioneering editorial, curatorial, bibliographical and digital work of the editors of the *William Blake Archive*, Morris Eaves, Robert Essick and Joseph Viscomi, and I have also greatly benefited from the scholarship of Luisa Calè.

Many libraries and collections were visited to gather the research necessary for this project, a book that recounts (and celebrates) the preservation and custodianship of the literary manuscript record. I owe special thanks to the following institutions and their curators and staff: the British Library, Chawton House Library, Houghton Library, Harvard University, King's College Cambridge, the National Library of Scotland, the Wordsworth Trust and the Manuscript and Print Studies Collections at Senate House Library, University of London. I was permitted to examine Byron's manuscript of Cantos I and II of *Childe Harold's Pilgrimage* (known as 'Manuscript M', for 'Murray'), which remains in the possession of John and Virginia Murray. I am grateful to them for providing me with access.

Teaching the literary manuscripts of the Romantic has been an enormous source of both pleasure and knowledge. There are too many students to mention by name, but I owe a great deal to Kendal Crawford, Alex Grammatikos, Kate Moffatt, Ashley Morford and Reese Irwin for their enthusiasm and for showing me what is now possible in terms of manuscript study even without access to the original documents. Several students have helped with research and copy-editing, and to them, Sarah Bull, Brenna Duperron and Kandice Sharren, I feel deep appreciation. Martin Boyne also assisted with copy-editing, and I am very thankful for his help. I would also like to thank the Edinburgh Critical Studies in Romanticism series editors, Ian Duncan and Penny Fielding, and my editors at Edinburgh University Press, Michelle Houston, Ersev Ersoy and Eliza Wright, for the care, speed and kindness with which they have seen this book through the press. I'd also like to thank Catherine Hookway for her assistance in the preparation of the index.

To the curators and editors of Romantic literary
manuscripts, past and present

Introduction

We possess more surviving literary manuscripts from the Romantic era than from any previous literary period.[1] This abundance of literary manuscripts has been a boon to the period's textual scholars, many of whom – Jerome McGann, Jack Stillinger, Kathryn Sutherland, to name just a few – have introduced major innovations in their editorial work on Lord Byron, John Keats and Jane Austen. To date, the period's literary manuscripts have been largely the province of these scholarly editors, and have been consulted chiefly for the textual evidence they provide. Literary manuscripts can, however, tell us much more: as Mark Bland contends, 'manuscripts are always witnesses to something other than the texts they preserve'.[2] *Literary Manuscript Culture in Romantic Britain* begins the work of unearthing these alternative stories: describing the practices by which handwritten documents were composed, shared, altered and preserved; reconstructing the social networks these practices sustained; and uncovering the expressive freedom and constraints of literary manuscript culture. The study of Romantic literary manuscripts is also, inevitably, the study of print, and of its contentious nature during a moment of extraordinary political, social, and economic change. Using the extensive archival manuscript record we possess for the period, this book reconstructs the cultural practices that co-evolved between handwritten culture and a rapidly expanding print marketplace. Offering the first expanded analysis of the practices and values ascribed to literary manuscripts of the period, this book illuminates the complex interdependencies and entanglements between the media of script and print.

Drawing upon recent work in the disparate fields of book history, literary and media studies, textual scholarship and digital humanities, this study advances the fundamental thesis of early modern scholars – that manuscript production and circulation continued long after the advent of print – and of media historians – that newer media (such as print) did not overtake and subsume older media forms (such as manuscript). Repudiating a 'decline and rise' or 'succession' model of technological change, this book instead posits a model characterised by media interaction and exchange.[3] Early modern scholars now understand that the coming of print did not replace or render manuscript obsolete: as David McKitterick notes, 'the boundary between manuscript and print is as untidy chronologically as it is commercially, materially or socially'.[4] 'Print', as Mark Bland writes, 'did not replace manuscript: the two existed in conjunction with each other as complementary forms of mediations'.[5] Margaret Ezell, Harold Love, Arthur Marotti, and others have demonstrated the ongoing vitality of manuscript culture throughout the early modern period, with Marotti contending that 'the interaction of print culture with an overlapping manuscript culture shaped the construction of literature itself, and the status of authors, texts, and readers within it'.[6] Although scholars of the early modern period have acknowledged 'the intermixture and hybridity of these two media as a keynote of the culture of communication of the period', an assumption nevertheless persists that these were separate cultures that, at some point in time (usually during the eighteenth century), diverged.[7] According to William St Clair, speaking about the late eighteenth century, 'the public and private spheres increasingly came to be separated by the two text-copying technologies, print for publicly available texts sold commercially, manuscript for personal domestic documents kept privately within a household'.[8] Harold Love frames it somewhat differently, stating that by the eighteenth century, '[w]hat was kept in manuscript was increasingly what lacked the quality required for print publication', the assumption being that print was readily available to writers worthy of it.[9] In both cases, the eighteenth century is the period when script and print become divided realms of activity, with different cultural meanings attached to each.

Recent scholarship in the eighteenth and early nineteenth centuries has resisted these narratives, countering the assumptions that print replaced manuscript and that the two can be easily separated from one another. Andrew Piper has called attention to the '*simultaneity* of various writing technologies within what we have traditionally called "print culture"'.[10] *Interacting with Print: Elements of Reading in the Era of Print Saturation* (2018) examines the broader media ecology of the eighteenth and nineteenth centuries to contest the belief that print stood apart from, and dominated, other media.[11] Scholars of the period have also examined print's assimilation of orality, as traced through major Romantic genres like the ballad, lyric and conversation poem, as well as oral-print genres associated with particular authors, such as Coleridge's 'table talk', Blake's *Songs*, and Barbauld's 'familiar chit-chat'.[12] Likewise, scholars of Romantic-era drama have called our attention to performative activities that intermingled with print, from mental theatre to literary tourism. Most recently, Betty Schellenberg's *Literary Coteries and the Making of Modern Print Culture 1740–1790* (2016) makes an important contribution in her account of manuscript-producing coteries as an integral element of eighteenth-century British literary print culture.[13] She corrects the assumption of print dominance by persuasively demonstrating that, for her period of study, 1740 to 1790,

> [s]cribal culture, with its appeals of intimacy and authenticity, was not in fact gone; a more accurate description, from the perspective of the mid-eighteenth-century person of letters, would have been that this was a culture in which the media of script and print, with their distinctive practices and priorities, were nevertheless in close conversation, sometimes interdependent, sometimes mutually antagonistic, but between them offering a rich array of options for literary expression, exchange, and preservation.[14]

Literary Manuscript Culture in Romantic Britain supports many of Schellenberg's findings about the persistence of manuscript culture and its ongoing uses in relation to print, though it does so by shifting attention to a differently configured period, examining a distinct set of authors, living within an altered literary and political landscape.

This book draws inspiration from John Keats's short lyric 'This living hand, now warm and capable', a poem that conspicuously calls attention to itself as something in the process of being made by a 'living hand', as the poet handwrites individual letters and words, one after the other, and then imagines presenting the page to its intended reader: 'see here it is / I hold it towards you'.[15] The poem, which survives in a single authorial copy reproduced in Plate 1, insists upon the materiality of the literary manuscript and the embodied act of creating it.[16] It asserts an indissoluble connection between the creator's body and the handwritten page. And it portends the forceful impact of handwritten documents when seen, held and felt by readers. Although not a book about handwriting per se, like Aileen Douglas's *Work in Hand: Script, Print and Writing, 1690–1840* (2017) – an exhaustive account of the diffusion of practices associated with what she terms manual handwriting – this study does draw our attention to the living hands writing, sharing and otherwise using manuscripts during the period.[17] It contends that a careful study of the manuscript record can uncover the Romantic-era practices of composing, revising, exchanging, reading, copying, embellishing and preserving, all essential components of the period's literary culture that are often overlooked. It addresses the everyday work of literary production and circulation, the sociable nature of manuscript culture, and the expressive freedom of manuscript exchange.

In many respects, the motivations for circulating literary manuscripts are continuous with traditions dating back many centuries, as writers composed poetry and prose to mark important private and public occasions, to entertain friends and family, and to express dissent. Keats, like many writers of the day, wrote many poems that he did not print such as 'This living hand' – a poem drafted or copied on the flipped folded sheet that contained the draft of *The Jealousies*, another unpublished poem, as may be seen in Plate 1. Some of the major examples drawn from this study evidence the sociable nature of the period's manuscript writing: there is Anna Barbauld's occasional verse, written to celebrate domestic and national events; Jane Austen's juvenile fiction, written to amuse and shock her domestic circle; and Lord Byron's satirical lyrics, written to expose his literary and political foes to his coterie readers. Often, the content of these works made them unsuited to or inappropriate for print: literary works were often withheld from or rejected for print for a wide variety of reasons, such as that they were deemed to be of little interest beyond the writer's social circle, or too risky to print.

Even if we consider the so-called 'big six' male Romantic poets' use of manuscript dissemination – an approach to British Romanticism that this book resolutely does not adopt – we find that all six poets elected, or were compelled, to control access to some of their literary writing through manuscript circulation. One of the period's great poems, William Wordsworth's (1770–1850) *The Prelude*, circulated in various manuscript versions for over half a century before it was posthumously printed; and one of Samuel Taylor Coleridge's (1772–1834) most famous poems, 'Christabel', rejected by Wordsworth from inclusion in the second edition of *Lyrical Ballads*, enjoyed a dynamic existence during its nineteen-year manuscript life, so much so that Coleridge would boast in the *Biographia Literaria* that '[d]uring the many years which intervened between the composition and the publication of the Christabel, it became almost as well known among literary men as if it had been on common sale'.[18] Thirteen separate manuscript versions (both autographs and transcriptions) survive from the period between 1797 and 1816; and Coleridge kept revising even after publication, annotating no less than five copies of the 1816 print edition.[19] Political and personal controversies resulted in many poems of the second generation of male Romantic poets – Lord Byron (1788–1824), Percy Shelley (1792–1822) and John Keats (1795–1821) – being circulated exclusively in manuscript during their lifetimes. Keats, much like Coleridge, was a profligate epistolary versifier, with many of his best-known poems first transmitted by correspondence, and some only through that medium. Because of the confidential, radical, or scandalous nature of so much of their poetry, many of Byron's and Shelley's lyrics appeared only in manuscript or were privately printed in very small print runs. Of the big six, this study addresses only Byron at length, the poet who, given his success as a print author and cultural celebrity, seems an unlikely choice but who rewards attention given his extensive use of manuscript throughout his career. This study ends with a brief afterword on William Blake (1757–1827) – the last of the big six – whose development of an experimental process of illuminated printing essentially guaranteed a circumscribed readership for his books, like those of the illuminated manuscripts they evoked. At the same time, Blake's illuminated books were not private documents but were shown, sold, circulated, read and seen by many others, even though they had not been produced by a printing house and their sale was neither financed nor promoted by a publisher. By bringing into view how authors of the period used a variety of copying technologies to circulate their writing, from commercial and private print to handwritten documents and Blake's invention of 'printed script', a fuller picture of the period's literary history and practices emerges.

This study also devotes considerable attention to women writers of the period. Early modern feminist scholars have demonstrated the need to study women's literary manuscripts as an instrument of recovery: as Margaret Ezell and others have shown, many seventeenth- and early eighteenth-century literary texts by women circulated in manuscript, often because they preferred to share their writing in this way.[20] By privileging print, even implicitly, scholarship of this earlier period had overlooked a large body of women's writing that was highly valued and influential in its day.[21] Even into the nineteenth century, men and women often *chose* manuscript circulation for some of their writing, for reasons similar to their predecessors, as explored in Timothy Whelans's *Other British Voices: Women, Poetry, and Religion, 1766–1840* (2015). Whelan's study provides an invaluable supplement to this book, demonstrating how women's nonconformist religious writing 'embraced a collaborative, sociable model of manuscript culture'.[22] Likewise, *Literary Manuscript Culture in Romantic Britain* is invested in articulating how and why women used script, and finds considerable evidence for the sociable aims and activities that Whelan describes. Whelan focuses on four women (Mary Steele, Mary Scott, Jane Attwater and Elizabeth Coltman) who circulated most of their writing in manuscript during their lifetimes. With three of these women, however, at least some of their writing appeared in print, exemplifying how closely intertwined the cultures of script and print were during this period.

My study takes a different approach to reach a similar conclusion, emphasising the importance of scribal practices to Jane Austen (1775–1817), Anna Barbauld (1743–1825), Charlotte Smith (1749–1806), and Dorothy Wordsworth (1771–1855), four canonical women writers who engaged fully with print but whose engagements with manuscript culture have either been overlooked or undervalued, or both, a consequence of our tendency to overestimate the importance of print as the primary vehicle for the circulation of literary writing. The study of women's manuscript writing and practices offers a corrective to print-centric accounts of individual female authorship, accounts that persist in women's literary history from the eighteenth century onward.[23] At the same time, it is important to observe the unique pressures that late eighteenth- and early nineteenth-century print culture imposed on women, and their responses to these pressures. Charlotte Smith objected strenuously when her poems were published without her consent, robbing her of much-needed income. Anna Barbauld likewise declined to publish many of her poems herself, preferring to circulate them in manuscript, but tolerated their appearance in print.

Dorothy Wordsworth allowed her brother to print some of her poems and adapt prose from her journals and travel narratives for his publications, though most of her written output, which was considerable, was shared within her social circle in handwritten form. Manuscript writing produces genres unique to it, often indicative of an expected intimacy between writer and reader; Whelan observes many of these genres in his study, and nearly all of the case studies to follow offer similar examples, ranging from Dorothy Wordsworth's daily journal entries to Jane Austen's satirical lampoons. Exploring the complex nature of women's relationship to script is one of the chief objects of this study.

Taking Romantic-era literary manuscript culture and its inevitable entanglement with print as its central subject, the subsequent six chapters examine the literary manuscripts and writing practices of several central Romantic authors, and the shifting set of cultural and political conditions they faced. In doing so, this study presents a new account of literary Romanticism, one that recalibrates accounts of individual authors' works, careers and practices; reconstructs networks of authors, editors, publishers and readers; and reconfigures concepts of privacy, sociability and publicity. It also addresses how the expanding print culture of the late eighteenth century impacted both the practices and the values ascribed to manuscript culture. It seems likely that new opportunities in print drove the superabundance of manuscripts being produced. In 1817, the publisher John Murray memorably describes how he was inundated with manuscripts: 'I am constantly harassed by shoals of MSS. Poems – two, three, or four a day. I require a porter to carry, an author to read, and a secretary to answer them.'[24] Inevitably, some of these poetic manuscripts stalled en route to print (as publishers like Murray were unable to keep up with the supply, let alone publish them all), and many re-entered scribal culture as a result. Still others were never submitted for print, but were shared in handwritten form. The rise in printed matter also seems to have generated new affection for and interest in manuscripts, as increasingly, owners of literary manuscripts, particularly of unprinted material, assumed the responsibility of rescuing, preserving and protecting these sources – whether from unwanted publication, benign neglect or outright destruction. Handwriting itself also inspired interest, even devotion, for what it could reveal about the character and creative processes of the creator, and for how it could connect the possessor with the hand and body of the creator.

This study does not claim that literary manuscript culture in itself rivalled print as a means by which literary texts were circulated and literary reputations were formed. Rather, it addresses the ongoing role that manuscripts played in the literary culture of the period, seeking to understand why so many authors, and so many individual literary works, enjoyed a double life, moving between script and print in recognisable but also unusual patterns. It is obvious that, during this period, 'every printed book was first a manuscript', but this does not mean that all manuscripts ended up as printed books, nor that the process from script to print, even for those works that were published, should be only the province of textual editors.[25] Manuscript circulation was in many cases critically important to the work's development and submission for print in the first place. The collective processes that transformed literary manuscripts into print-ready texts deserve greater attention, as they demonstrate the labour, sometimes painstaking and difficult, other times pleasant and easy, that transformed manuscript into print. Even when literary works were printed, they were often still hand-copied, from both manuscript or print copies, for a variety of reasons: the print version could be rare or ephemeral; hand-copying could be an act of devotion, scholarship or preservation. Copying from print could, in some cases, be as extensive as copying from script.[26] Thus many texts circulated in script *and* print, sometimes sequentially, but also, and far more often than is acknowledged, concurrently. Finally, notwithstanding the seeming ubiquity of print in the period, many writers shared their work in manuscript alone, whether by choice or by necessity. Romantic literary culture transpired within multiple, overlapping media realms.

In describing the interactions between these two media realms, *Literary Manuscript Culture in Romantic Britain* also seeks to overcome the conceptual separation of print and script as autonomous realms of activity. In many accounts, scribal culture remains sharply differentiated from print. Scribal culture has been described as a 'medium of social intercourse', with a lack of clear divisions between authors and readers, editors and compilers.[27] It has been characterised as less hierarchical than print, as works are read, annotated, amended and answered by others as they circulate within a defined community.

Manuscript production and circulation has also been understood as being more subject to the direct control of the author:

> Authorship in the scribal medium was in every sense more intimate [than print]. Writers would have written to be read in their own hands or in those of close friends and associates: as the example of Sidney's 'Old' *Arcadia* demonstrates, their readers would have been present to their imagination as they wrote in a way that was difficult if not impossible for the print-publishing author.[28]

Overall, manuscript culture has been defined as decentralised, non-hierarchal, collaborative and multi-directional. Print culture, by contrast, has been understood as an arena marked by specialisation, driven by market forces and shaped by innovation. Robert Darnton's 'communications circuit' (Figure I.1) presents an influential model for the study of the history of printed books, one that posits cooperation within a defined structure: the nodes along the circuit are discrete and separate, thus indicative of a high degree of specialisation (for example, publishers are not printers, shippers are not booksellers, and so on).[29] The circuit describes a sequential process that isolates certain groups from one another – authors and publishers interact, whereas authors and printers do not – and that divides various forms of labour, the intellectual from the commercial, the commercial from

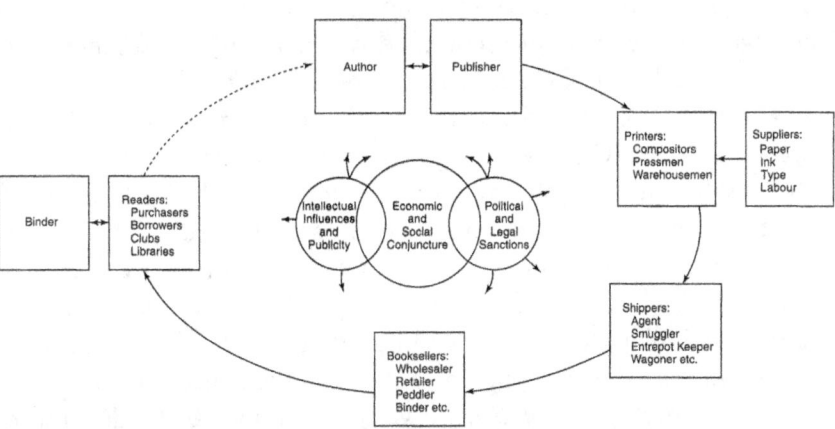

Figure I.1 Robert Darnton, 'The Communications Circuit'. 'What is the History of Books?', Daedalus, 111:3 (Summer, 1982), pp. 6583. © 1982 by the American Academy of Arts and Sciences.

the mechanical. Furthermore, whereas manuscript culture operates outside of a market economy, its motivations being those of friendship, kinship and social allegiance, print culture is based in the market and its imperatives. According to Arthur Marotti and Harold Love, in the early modern period, 'Authorship for the press was public, supervised and divorced from any sense of personal contact from the reader.'[30] Notably, neither of these models accounts for the role of other available media.

Even if we accept that these divergent understandings of print and manuscript culture describe the early modern period, they seem far less convincing when applied to the Romantic period. Examples from across the period suggest the problems of assuming that manuscript culture can be easily separated from print. In 1796, S. T. Coleridge collaborated with his friend, the printer Tom Poole, on a sixteen-page sonnet collection. Here Coleridge was actively and directly involved in the production process, and he sought to use print as an intimate medium:

> I amused myself the other day (having some paper at the Printer's which I could employ no other way) in selecting 28 Sonnets, to bind up with Bowles's – I charge sixpence for them, and have sent you five to dispose of. – I have only printed two hundred, as my paper held out to no more; and dispose of them privately, just enough to pay the printing.[31]

Sonnets from Various Authors, although printed, was not a commercial object; it was neither a commodity nor a gift, but something in between. Further, as Coleridge makes plain, print did not imply universal distribution to a so-called public – Coleridge 'dispose[s]' of the copies 'privately'. Only seven copies of the work survive, six of which belonged to individuals known to Coleridge, and three of which are bound up with Bowles's sonnets, as he had intended.[32] In an age of private print (of small print runs whose circulation was directed by the author, such as Coleridge's *Sonnets*), print could serve as an instrument of sociability to nearly the same extent as handwritten copies.

Coleridge's print pamphlet also disrupts the concept of print as a fixed medium. With *Sonnets from Various Authors*, Coleridge improvised, collecting poems from print sources without regard to copyright or other commercial concerns. Although in theory manuscript is easier to amend than print, in practice, especially in this period, print could also be a highly malleable medium. Printed books of the period were subject to correction, personalisation and customisation by hand, via practices of editing, inscription[33] and annotation.[34] The use of moveable type, and the small edition sizes of most published books (since most publishers were unwilling to risk large quantities of paper unless sales were assured, and they rarely were), meant that print itself was subject to considerable and, indeed, for some authors, constant emendation over time. Printing a literary text rarely fixed it, with print technology being in some ways comparable to the technology of handwriting in accommodating a literary culture of revision. Although the print run of 200 for Coleridge's pamphlet was low, it was not that much lower than many commercially printed works;[35] indeed, many authors like Coleridge resorted to private print, printing small editions entirely at their own expense (Byron did so on numerous occasions, as we will see in Chapter 4).

If Coleridge's privately printed pamphlet *Sonnets from Various Authors* challenges the association of print with the public and the commercial, the manuscript transmission of Anna Barbauld's short poem 'A Thought on Death' refutes the assumption of an intimate connection between writer and reader, and the understanding of scribal networks as being subject to authorial control.[36] The transatlantic migration of Barbauld's poem will be considered in more detail in Chapter 3; for now, it is salient to note that the poem, which does not survive in a single authorial manuscript, was printed without Barbauld's authorisation (or knowledge) three times in the United States (once in New York and twice in Boston) before its publication was brought to her attention, when it was published for the first time in England, having been copied from the Boston periodical. Upon learning of the first English printing, in 1822, Barbauld expressed astonishment at its journey across the Atlantic: 'how it got there', she wrote, 'I know not'.[37] In this example, Barbauld's manuscript poem enjoyed a wide circulation, and was even admiringly quoted in correspondence between Thomas Jefferson and John Adams, without her involvement. This example seems to confirm William St Clair's claim that, by the end of the eighteenth century,

> those authors who wished to select their readerships by sending manuscript copies to chosen readers, 'scribal publication,' could no longer do so with confidence. For it was often then impossible to prevent a

manuscript copy falling into the hands of a printer who would print it, assume the intellectual property rights, sell copies to the general public, and frustrate the author's wish to restrict access.[38]

Unauthorised publication was merely surprising to Barbauld, but it was maddening to an author like Charlotte Smith, who lamented the appearance of her poems in what she termed 'the prints of the day'.[39] For Smith, unauthorised publication resulted in a loss of earnings that she desperately need to support herself and her family. Once again, the orderly and equitable operation of the communications circuit (in which authors initiated publication and were compensated for their work) cannot be assumed. The print explosion of the last quarter of the eighteenth century did not obviate the need for and desire to circulate literary works in manuscript, but it complicated the effort to do so as manuscript works could more easily find their way into print, through accident, greed, or malfeasance.[40]

There are many other examples of the ease with which manuscripts (or portions of them) could be reproduced without authorial consent, indicative of the contested and unstable boundaries between script and print. In 1817, the same year John Murray bemoaned the shoals of manuscripts appearing at his doorstep, another errant manuscript, this one by the then poet laureate Robert Southey, was deliberately printed without the author's consent: *Wat Tyler*, an early, republican work, dating from 1794, was printed in an effort humiliate Southey for betraying his early political ideals.[41] Literary works could be printed not only from manuscript copies, but even from those who had heard recitations and remembered the contents. More than twenty years after *Wat Tyler* appeared, in February 1839, *Tait's Edinburgh Magazine* published a lengthy essay by Thomas De Quincey (1785–1859) that quoted and paraphrased at length and apparently from memory Wordsworth's *Prelude*, the epic poem that Wordsworth had purposefully shown and read only to a handful of readers, for nearly four decades.[42] Suppressed or delayed publication could cause other problems to authors. When 'Christabel' was finally printed in 1816, Coleridge felt it necessary to pre-empt any charge that *he* had plagiarised Walter Scott's *Lay of the Last Minstrel* (1805), which had appeared in print *before* Coleridge's poem, though it was Scott who heard, memorised and imitated aspects of 'Christabel' as he had come to know it from scribal copies and oral recitations. Coleridge also had to confront William Hazlitt's criticism, in his review in the *Examiner*, that Coleridge had inexplicably omitted a line in the poem about Geraldine; a line which Hazlitt knew from a manuscript version and which was, according to him, 'the keystone that makes up the arch'.[43] Mary Shelley faced a similar set of challenges when she was finally allowed to publish an authorised edition of her late husband's *Poetical Works* in 1839: friends and admirers of Percy Shelley objected to her excisions from the published poems, removals which they could identify based on their familiarity with the poems in manuscript.

It would seem, then, that fears that a manuscript could be reconstructed from memory, or that a copy could reach the printers without authorial involvement, were not exaggerated. In 1797, Jane Austen, perhaps only half-facetiously, remarked to her sister that she 'would not let Martha [Lloyd] read First Impressions [the earlier version of *Pride and Prejudice*] again upon any account . . . – She is very cunning, but I see through her design; – she means to publish it from Memory, & one more perusal must enable her to do it.'[44] Two decades before that, in 1777, Hannah More (1745–1833) explained with exasperation that, 'though I have never given, or suffered to be given but two copies of the little Ode to Dragon, yet I have received within these few days five or six letters from my friends in Town, earnestly requesting to have it published, for that so many people can repeat several of the stanzas that I shall certainly have a mutilated copy get into print'.[45] Thus it was that authors throughout the period had legitimate reasons to anticipate that their manuscripts might be circulated in ways that they did not approve of; allowing others to copy or even read their manuscripts, a mark of favour and intimate friendship, could invite disobedience, even treachery. By historicising manuscript culture in a later age of print, we find that the assumptions of control over handwritten documents and of the supposed congeniality of manuscript culture no longer necessarily hold, since recipients of manuscripts were not always trustworthy and manuscripts could travel far beyond their intended reach. At the same time, three of the authors discussed in this study, Austen, Barbauld and Byron, could rely on the discretion of their intimate readers, and their confidence was not misplaced.

The foregoing examples caution us to be wary of assuming that at some point 'the public and private spheres of the book separated'.

Print was never inevitably commercial and public, manuscript non-commercial and private; print did not necessarily serve as a proxy for quality, manuscript for mediocrity; and literary works in both script and print could defy the control of their creators.[46] Adrian Johns's scholarship on the values ascribed to early print is relevant here, for he too has found that print did not arrive with its qualities intact; rather, 'the very identity of print itself has had to be *made* ... by virtue of hard work, exercised over generations and nations'.[47] This book seeks to demonstrate that 'the very identity of print' was still being made in the late eighteenth century, impacted by the expansion of the print market and the cataclysms of political upheaval. More than three centuries after the arrival of the printing press, both print and script retained the contested and unstable character that Johns has argued they held in a much earlier period.[48]

The subsequent chapters explore how authors participated in these controversies, surrendering and resisting, adapting to and negotiating with one another over fundamental questions about the nature of print and script. When Byron was admonished for printing poems that the *Edinburgh Review* declared would have been better left in manuscript, he both retaliated (in penning his acrid 1809 satire *English Bards and Scotch Reviewers*) and relented (in shifting towards other, more socially sanctioned forms of poetic expression). When Jane Austen was coerced by the Prince Regent's librarian into dedicating *Emma* to the Prince, she took her revenge by writing a scribal lampoon of the librarian and by secreting hidden barbs at the sovereign within the novel itself. Anna Barbauld took up her pen to chide male poets, including Coleridge and Byron, and to give vent to her disagreements with women writers, including Hannah More and Mary Wollstonecraft, but printed none of these poems, instead reserving for print a small selection of her early occasional verse and domestic poetry that had been much admired by friends, and a handful of intense critiques of governmental policy, one of which (*Eighteen Hundred and Eleven*) earned her almost universal scorn as the misguided, unwanted, and unpatriotic 'intervention of a lady-author'.[49] These are just some of the fundamental debates about what was allowable in print.

Over the next six chapters and Afterword, this book deploys a range of methodological approaches to present a detailed investigation of literary manuscripts and the practices associated with their creation and use. It considers both literary manuscripts of texts that went unprinted during the lifetimes of their creators as well as those that were, presenting a capacious account of how handwritten literary documents were shared, copied, read and valued. It describes the material processes that brought these manuscripts to confined and extensive audiences, as authors, editors and publishers transformed manuscripts for print. By studying how manuscripts were altered as they transitioned to print, and excavating the motivations behind such revisions, the book opens up larger questions about conceptions of print (and script) as they were being formulated. Given that this book attempts to reconfigure our understanding of the period's literary culture through a targeted examination of its media history, it supplements close readings of literary texts and case studies of individual authors with distant reading strategies (in Chapters 2 and 6, which provide a synoptic view of the reception and remediation of literary manuscripts both historically and contemporarily) and quantitative methods (in Chapters 3 and 4, which establish the pervasive use of manuscript exchange of Anna Barbauld and Lord Byron). By yoking traditional methods of literary analysis (such as close reading and collation) to innovative distant reading methods, this book participates in the quantitative turn in literary studies, an approach that accounts for the large number of graphs and tables included within the pages to come.

The next chapter, 'Intentionality and the Romantic Literary Manuscript', supplies an essential description of manuscript and print cultures in the Romantic period. It probes the attempts by book historians, manuscript scholars and textual editors to establish guidelines for understanding modern literary manuscripts, that is, manuscripts created in the age of print. It questions conceptions of scribal culture that rest upon the scholar's capacity to discern authorial intention, and that exclude from consideration those manuscripts intended for print. Donald Reiman, in his categorisation of modern manuscripts into three groups – private, confidential or social, and public – relies upon an editor's ability to determine the intended audience of any given manuscript. However, as this chapter demonstrates, intention is rarely discernible. In Keats's 'This Living Hand', for example, the addressee remains unstated, frustrating our attempts to understand Keats's intentions regarding publication: is Keats addressing Fanny Brawne, suggesting that the poem is a private document? Is he addressing members of his coterie who regularly transcribed and copied his poems, implying that the poem is a confidential manuscript? Or is he addressing his future, posthumous readers, hinting that the poem is a public document? Uncertainty can also arise because manuscripts are often produced, revised and preserved over time, such that intentionality can often shift. Many of the literary manuscripts described in the pages to come have at best uncertain or shifting intentionality with respect to publication. It is this condition of uncertainty that defines many if not most literary manuscripts of the period. In fact, one of the most interesting features of literary manuscripts of the period is that even when intentionality can be inferred it is often unstable, reflecting the uncertainties and challenges authors faced in seeking to identify, and address, different audiences.

This chapter grounds its theoretical analysis in a detailed survey of the literary writing and material practices of Charlotte Smith and Dorothy Wordsworth, two authors who have long been regarded as belonging, respectively and exclusively, to the divided worlds of print and script. Smith represents print authorship, as a writer who, after her earliest sonnets were printed from manuscript copies, appears never to have circulated her poetry in handwritten form again and who destroyed all of her literary manuscripts before her death; Wordsworth, on the other hand, has long been regarded as the period's quintessential manuscript writer, and her manuscripts survive in profusion.[50] The comparative method undertaken in this chapter demonstrates that neither author could work in one medium without an inescapable consciousness of, and participation in, the other. With Wordsworth, we find that even her most private texts are suffused with a consciousness of print; conversely, with Smith we find that her verse, though oriented towards a print public, is nevertheless permeated by an implied audience of knowing readers, and thus draws upon scribal habits and audiences.

In Chapter 2, 'Literary Reviews and the Reception of Manuscript Culture', the focus shifts to the literary reviews, specifically to debates within them about what should appear in print. As reviewers encountered large quantities of published literary writing, some of which was clearly written for the market and some of which had identifiable origins in manuscript culture, they faced both a practical problem – how to keep up with the rising tide of new publications – and an ethical dilemma – how to respond to the proliferation of print. Did the large increases in literary print publication (and the increasing number of authors entering print) signal a decline in taste and a degeneration of literary standards? Or did it suggest the opposite, the enlightened progress of society and the improvement of literary taste?[51] Within Jane Austen's famous defence of the novel, voiced by her narrator in *Northanger Abbey*, the clash between these positions is articulated: 'Let us leave it to the reviewers to abuse such effusions of fancy at their leisure, and over every new novel to talk in threadbare strains of the trash with which the press now groans.' Many reviewers believed, as Austen notes, that the presses were groaning with trash, but others (including Austen) found this position 'threadbare'. In proceeding to offer her famous defence of the novel, Austen threw her lot in with those who believed in the ameliorative effects of printed fiction.

Although the reviews were themselves powerless to stem the tide of print, they adopted contrasting opinions about whether it was their role to act as gatekeepers and disciplinarians. Reviews debated whether print required certain fixed standards of value, whether it was the proper medium for writing unlikely to survive beyond the current season, and whether it should only be used to address a larger public, and engage with universal themes.[52] This chapter focuses in particular on reviews of works that had identifiable origins in manuscript culture, as a species of writing subject to particular scrutiny by the reviews. The *Monthly Review*'s attack on Coleridge's *Sibylline Leaves* (1817) provides one example of this antagonism towards the publication of seemingly confidential writing:

> several of the *Copies of Verses* that follow are, in our opinion, more adapted to the silence and the privacy of domestic enjoyment, than to glaring and repulsive publication. The author's sympathies with his family are surely too sacred for general notice.[53]

This chapter compares the reviewing practices and editorial policies of two journals: the *Edinburgh Review*, the journal the most outspoken in its criticism of the publication of manuscript writing, and the *Annual Review*, the journal the most tolerant of all literary productions. By comparing a large quantity of reviews, many of the identical publication, between 1802 (when both journals were founded) through to 1809, when the *Annual* ceased publication, we find the *Edinburgh* promoting their authority as cultural tastemakers, laying down pronouncements about what was worthy of print and boldly asserting that some forms of writing were better left in manuscript. Conversely, we find the *Annual* embracing most writing, even if destined to please only a few, for a short duration. This chapter examines how reviewers at the *Edinburgh* constructed print as a public medium and, by necessary contrast, manuscript as a private one, a division that is understood to be intrinsic to script and print rather than a product of the ideological dispute that was fought in part in the pages of the literary reviews.[54]

Chapters 3–5 are case studies of the literary manuscripts of three individual writers, Anna Barbauld, Lord Byron and Jane Austen, who exemplify different manifestations of the tension between script and print during the period. Each author presents unique methodological challenges due to the state of their surviving archives; for Barbauld, a very small number of manuscripts survive; for Byron, we have manuscripts for nearly all of his verse (printed and unprinted during his lifetime); and for Austen, we have extant manuscripts of some, and perhaps most of her unpublished material, but, with one small exception (the cancelled chapters of *Persuasion*), no manuscript witnesses from the print novels. The varying nature of these archives is itself revealing of another issue this book addresses: the practices of preservation and the status that literary manuscripts were accorded during the period. Byron's celebrity, as well as his longstanding relationship with John Murray, ensured the preservation of many of his manuscripts, including drafts and press copies rarely retained by publishers.[55] Few other writers of the period were as fortunate; whereas the potential literary and even economic value of Byron's working drafts and fair copies was recognised during his lifetime, the preservation of Austen's and Barbauld's manuscripts owed itself to the sentimental importance attached to them by their heirs. Cassandra Austen carefully preserved her sister's unpublished material after her death – her juvenilia as well as the complete *Lady Susan* and the unfinished *The Watsons* and *Sanditon*. As family mementos, the manuscripts were divided up after her death, resulting in the dispersal of the archive. As with Austen, Barbauld's nephew and niece inherited her manuscripts (the basis for Lucy Aikin's posthumous printing of the two-volume *Works* in 1825), but the decline in Barbauld's reputation throughout the nineteenth century meant that, by 1943, none of her remaining unpublished writing had been collected, printed or acquired by an archive, such that her papers were left to perish in a flat in central London during the Blitz. Authors themselves also made decisions about what to keep and what to destroy: Charlotte Smith destroyed all of her literary manuscripts, whereas Dorothy Wordsworth kept almost all of hers, with an understanding that eventually some of them would be published.[56]

Chapter 3, 'Anna Barbauld's Poetic Career in Script and Print', adapts to the minimal archival record in part by taking the long view of Barbauld's career as a dynamic example of the interactions between media, gender, and genre over a period of nearly seven decades, from the 1760s, when she began composing verse, to the 1820s, when she died and a significant quantity of her unpublished writing came to light. Barbauld's considerable fame as a poet rested on the social verse she published in the 1770s – poems she had written a decade earlier for her domestic circle and that retained their sociable origins, even when she reluctantly published them. For reasons we only imperfectly understand, Barbauld resisted the publication of most of her verse even after the enormous success of her 1773 volume *Poems*, reviews of which compared her favourably to both Milton and Shakespeare. Barbauld never printed another collection of her poems, although she talked about the possibility of doing so, and continued to write poetry for the next five decades of her life. Some of these poems Barbauld strategically printed in magazines, and the others she circulated in manuscript. This chapter points to the sociable and political nature of many of Barbauld's poems, as well as to the satiric vein that runs throughout. It seeks to understand her reluctance to publish her poems and her willingness to publish in other genres, from political and religious tracts to educational and children's books. Barbauld needed convincing that her social poetry was of interest to a wider audience than those to whom it was originally addressed; yet it is not the case that Barbauld upheld a distinction between the public and the private, insisting that activities of the domestic sphere, such as child-rearing, education and religious observance, were at the heart of national politics.[57]

Chapter 4, 'Lord Byron, Manuscript Poet', engages with the most popular and commercially successful of the English Romantic poets. Byron's poetic career was so public, and so enmeshed in print, as to have blinded us to his continuous and deep engagement with manuscript culture. This chapter begins by offering a quantitative assessment of Byron's poetic output during his career, in order to address basic questions about his use of both media and to trace patterns of publication and manuscript dissemination. Throughout, from his earliest poetic efforts to his last, we find the surprising degree of difficulty that Byron encountered in preparing his verse for print and the ongoing reliance he had on manuscript to circulate his poetry, his short verse in particular. The chapter begins with a consideration of his earliest four verse collections, printed between 1806 and 1808, analysing the removals and additions of individual poems from one collection to the next as part of Byron's ongoing struggle to transition from narrower to wider audiences without compromising his poetic candour. A similar set of difficulties emerge in the manuscript revisions to the poem that launched his fame – Cantos I and II of *Childe Harold's Pilgrimage*. Here, a study of the revisions to the manuscript offers direct insight into how he addresses both the confidential readers whom he could trust with the more dangerous aspects of the poem and the wider audience whom he sought to court in print. After *Childe Harold's Pilgrimage*, Byron seems to have avoided the difficult and lengthy process of revision and rearrangement by separating his writing into different categories: the handwritten short poems he entrusted to members of his coterie and the longer poems he wrote for the public (which nevertheless passed through the hands of his literary advisers on their way to print). Taken as a whole, this chapter provides evidence of Byron's use of manuscript at all stages of his career, confounding the notion that he can be regarded exclusively as a print author and elucidating the sources of his discomfort with print.

Chapter 5, 'Jane Austen's Fiction in Manuscript', examines the novelist's scribal practices through a study of her surviving manuscripts. As with the previous chapters, it deconstructs the separation that has been assumed between her early fiction in manuscript and her later novels in print, demonstrating how elements of and impulses from the early writing survive into print. Austen presents a provocative case of a novelist, now amongst the most revered in the language, whose fiction manuscripts languished en route to print, as she laboured to conform to the demands of the print novel. As with Barbauld, we are largely prevented from comparing script and print versions of the same work given the lack of surviving manuscripts. However, the nature of Austen's confrontation with print can be discerned through other means, by examining her later manuscripts – those written near the end of her life and at the height of her career in print. Here we discover the pleasure she took in her confidential manuscript writing and infer the challenges she faced in transitioning her fiction into print. A common thread that runs throughout these case study chapters is the extensive accommodations that had to be made by authors before their writing conformed to the requirements of print, as they understood them. Nevertheless, by bringing into print culture some of the confidentiality more easily expressed by them in manuscript, these authors challenged the rigid conceptions of print propriety under which they laboured.

Chapter 6, 'Script's Afterlives', draws my consideration of Romantic literary manuscripts forward to the present moment, examining their shifting cultural status from the late eighteenth century onward, including their preservation and dissemination in print and now in digital form. Significant changes to the treatment and valuation of literary manuscripts began in the late eighteenth century, as they began to be preserved and collected as never before; indeed, this book depends upon the wealth of literary manuscripts that survive from this period, as well as the work of editors of both print and digital editions of the period's authors. The attention to contemporary manuscripts arose in part from a growing scholarly and public interest in ancient scripts and manuscripts, as antiquarians, linguists and palaeographers were confronted with scripts brought to Britain from across the globe; the Rosetta Stone, discovered by the French during their military campaigns in Egypt in 1799, being only the best-known example. The invention of lithography around 1800 allowed for script to be reproduced more easily than by engraving, thereby enabling the reproduction of scripts, like hieroglyphics, for which metal type fonts did not exist. The discovery of ancient scripts, and encounters with indigenous peoples who did not possess written language, also prompted reflections on the history of writing. Thomas Astle's highly regarded *The Origin and Progress of Writing* first appeared in 1775, and it reflected the preoccupations of Britons with lost civilisations, piquing interest in the ways cultures marked their existence and history through writing.[58] These encounters also contributed to a valorisation of writing and written cultures that drove demands for the preservation of written documents of national and cultural significance.

These new collecting practices and copying technologies were accompanied by a new devotion to handwriting and to handwritten manuscripts: autograph collecting began in earnest, with autograph hunters using both polite tactics and cunning ploys to procure samples of handwriting, especially signatures, with the resulting disfigurement of many nineteenth-century letters. New technologies such as lithography were soon invented and put to use to feed a growing appetite for reproducing handwriting in print, particularly autographs of historical figures and celebrities. All of these developments combined to prompt greater public interest in Britain's own historical record, fuelling efforts to discover and conserve important manuscripts and calling attention to their lamentable destruction. The widespread nature of this fascination with such discoveries – an early version of an 'antiques roadshow' that no doubt led many to seek out old treasures, and some, like Thomas Chatterton (1752–70), to forge them – may be found in the many anecdotal accounts that found their way into local papers and bibliophilic narratives, as well as workaday fictional conventions like the found manuscript, a trope so commonplace by the 1790s that Austen parodies it, mercilessly, in her account of Catherine Morland's deluded attempt to recover an ancient manuscript in *Northanger Abbey*. This chapter thus traces a number of developments that impacted the preservation of and attitudes towards literary manuscripts – all of which reflect an awareness of the proliferation of print; just as many now fear the vanishing of cursive script and, indeed, of all forms of writing by hand under the pressure of machine writing, the Romantic period experienced a nostalgia for handwriting and handwritten documents.

The second half of this chapter turns to critical treatments of the period's manuscripts in its textual scholarship. It interrogates Jerome McGann's assessment that '[t]extual and editorial theory has heretofore concerned itself almost exclusively with the linguistic codes', asking how the privileging of the textual has impacted our engagements with the period's literary manuscripts.[59] It investigates the major scholarly critical editions of the last five decades to understand how editorial practice has grappled with the period's literary manuscripts and the literary culture in which they were embedded. It examines how recent digital editions of the period's manuscripts have improved our access to and revived our interest in literary manuscripts as bearers of cultural meaning beyond the textual. Examining digital collections of Romantic manuscripts, the chapter concludes by asking how this newest medium might enable different understandings of scribal culture, at the same time it asserts that the digital will never supplant earlier print critical editions, nor the original manuscripts themselves.

'Afterword: Blake's Digitised Printed Script' brings this study to a close with a brief consideration of the unique method of printed script developed by Blake in his attempt to fuse the media of script and print, drawing and engraving, and thereby collapse the divide between handwriting and typography, word and image. Blake's attempt to unite script and print aligns with one of the chief objectives of this study and inspires its methodological attempt to deconstruct the problematic separation between the two media, a division that owes itself at least in part to Romantic-era debates. All of the examples provided in this book – the separate models of script and print that have been theorised by textual scholars and book historians (Chapter 1), the ideological constructions of script and print in literary periodicals (Chapter 2), the careers of individual authors in script and print (Chapters 3, 4 and 5), and the strategies for remediating and evaluating Romantic literary manuscripts (Chapter 6) – work to destabilise these divisions and replace them with more fluid, contingent, and permeable boundaries, ones that reflect the actual conditions and experiences of the period's writers. By describing the material artefacts and cultural practices that occupy the space of written culture, this study aims to contribute a more capacious account of Romantic literary and media history.

Notes

1. According to Erick Kelemen, 'Not until the nineteenth century did rough drafts and journals begin to attain a status that encourages careful preservation after an author's death': *Textual Editing and Criticism*, p. 45. See also Dana Gioia, 'The Magical Value of Manuscripts', pp. 9–10; the *Norton Anthology of English Literature*, 7th edn, II: 2859; and Donald Reiman, *The Study of Modern Manuscripts*, pp. 10–17, 36.
2. Mark Bland, *A Guide to Early Printed Books and Manuscripts*, p. 9.
3. Paul Duguid describes the 'rhetoric of supercession' as the assumption that 'each new technological type vanquishes or subsumes its predecessors', in 'Material Matters', p. 495.
4. David McKitterick, *Print, Manuscript and the Search for Order, 1450–1830*, p. 12.
5. Bland, *A Guide to Early Printed Books*, p. 17.

6. Arthur Marotti, *Manuscript, Print, and the English Renaissance*, p. xii.
7. Julia C. Crick and Alexandra Walsham (eds), *The Uses of Script and Print, 1300–1700*, p. 12. The year 1700 is treated as the outer limit of manuscript culture in that collection's title, in the annual *English Manuscript Studies 1100–1700*, and in McKitterick's *Print, Manuscript and the Search for Order*, which claims that although script and print 'intermingled' far more than was previously thought, they were finally 'divorced' in the late seventeenth century (pp. 13–17). See also George Justice, 'Introduction' and 'Suppression and Circulation in Late Manuscript Culture: Frances Burney's Unperformed *The Witlings*', pp. 1–16, 201–22.
8. William St Clair, *The Reading Nation*, p. 48.
9. Harold Love, *The Culture and Commerce of Texts*, p. 288. For similar arguments that suggest the demise of manuscript culture, see Moyra Haslett, *Pope to Burney, 1714–1779*; George L. Justice and Nathan Tinker (eds), *Women's Writing and the Circulation of Ideas*; and Linda Zionkowski, *Men's Work*.
10. Andrew Piper, *Dreaming in Books*, p. 135.
11. Multigraph Collective, *Interacting with Print*. My book *Family Authorship and Romantic Print Culture* also examined the collaborative nature of family literary production and circulation in the period.
12. See, for example, David Fairer, *Organising Poetry*; and Maureen McLane, *Balladeering, Minstrelsy, and the Making of British Romantic Poetry*. Jon Mee has made an important contribution in *Conversable Worlds*, an examination of the impact of conversational paradigms on literary culture and public debate more generally. Julia S. Carlson, in *Romantic Marks and Measures*, likewise expands the field by examining the discourses surrounding elocution and prosody.
13. Betty Schellenberg, *Literary Coteries and the Making of Modern Print Culture 1740–1790*.
14. Ibid. p. 2.
15. *The Poems of John Keats*, p. 38.
16. All coloured illustrations, identified as plates, may be viewed at <https://edinburghuniversitypress.com/book-michelle-levy.html>.
17. Douglas examines transformations in the use of different scripts (round, italic), the teaching of handwriting and the materiality of handwritten practices more generally: *Work in Hand: Script, Print and Writing, 1690–1840*.
18. S. T. Coleridge, *Biographia Literaria*, 7: 238. Jack Stillinger's textual scholarship on Coleridge's poems has demonstrated their widespread manuscript circulation in multiple versions: *Coleridge and Textual Instability*.

19. Stillinger, *Coleridge and Textual Instability*, p. 79.
20. Margaret J. M. Ezell, *Social Authorship and the Advent of Print*.
21. Margaret Ezell has been central to this project, as have other feminist scholars of the period, particularly Julie Crawford, Helen Smith and Gillian Wright.
22. Timothy Whelan, *Other British Voices*, p. 3.
23. Most of the extensive, groundbreaking work that has been done on women's literary history of the period has been focused largely on print: see Paula Backscheider, *Eighteenth-Century Women Poets and their Poetry* (2008); Jennie Batchelor, *Women's Work* (2010); Stephen Behrendt, *British Women Poets* (2009); Catherine Gallagher, *Nobody's Story* (1995); Anne Mellor, *Mothers of the Nation* (2000) and *Romanticism and Gender* (1993); and Susan Staves, *A Literary History of Women's Writing in Britain, 1660–1789* (2006). There has been extensive research on the Bluestocking circle, as one of the last significant female coteries to circulate many of their texts in handwritten form: Betty Schellenberg, 'Bluestocking Women', pp. 63–83.
24. Samuel Smiles, *A Publisher and his Friends*, I: 370.
25. Bland, *Guide to Early Printed Books*, p. 83. All printed books began as manuscripts until the introduction of the typewriter in the 1860s, to be followed by other mechanised forms of writing.
26. In his *Biographia Literaria*, Coleridge recalled his earlier efforts as a scribe, when, flushed with his admiration for the sonnets of William Bowles (1762–1850), he was led, 'within less than a year and a half, [to make] more than forty transcriptions, as the best presents he could offer to his friends'. In Coleridge's hands, print enjoyed the kind of personalised circulation thought endemic to manuscript: I: 15.
27. Harold Love and Arthur Marotti, 'Manuscript Transmission and Circulation', p. 63.
28. Ibid. p. 58.
29. Robert Darnton, 'What is the History of Books?', p. 67. Figure I.1 is found on p. 68.
30. Love and Marotti, 'Manuscript Transmission and Circulation', p. 58.
31. *Collected Letters of Samuel Taylor Coleridge*, 1: 252.
32. David Fairer, 'Coleridge's Sonnets from Various Authors (1796)'.
33. Piper, *Dreaming in Books*, pp. 128–38; and 'The *Art of Sharing*'.
34. Heather Jackson, *Marginalia*; Andrew Stauffer, 'Hemans by the Book'.
35. Small print runs were the norm, and most editions did not sell out. Although edition size and actual readership cannot be conflated, we know that many books were read by only a handful of readers, with most copies remaindered or otherwise recycled: see St Clair, *Reading Nation*, pp. 175, 320.

36. Love and Marotti, 'Manuscript Transmission and Circulation', p. 58.
37. *Monthly Repository* 17 (November 1822): 679.
38. St Clair, *Reading Nation*, p. 49.
39. From the Preface to the first and second editions of *Elegiac Sonnets*: C. Smith, *Poems*, p. 3.
40. James Raven, *The Business of Books*, p. 8. Periodical and newspaper publications were frequently venues for manuscript material. The number of London newspapers sent to the provinces nearly tripled between 1782 and 1796, from 3 million to 8.6 million; and, during the same period, the number of provincial newspapers mailed to the capital more than quadrupled, from 46,000 to 200,000. By 1800, more than seventy provincial publications appeared each week: see Hannah Barker, 'England, 1760–1815', p. 103.
41. The story of how this manuscript was retained by the original publisher-to-be, and ultimately printed twenty-three years later, is a fascinating one in itself, testifying to the value that resided in unpublished manuscripts. Composed in 1794, a manuscript copy was shortly thereafter entrusted to the radical publisher Samuel Ridgeway, who was then imprisoned. There are several accounts of how the poem came to be printed, without Southey's consent, by Sherwood, Neeley and Jones: that the poem was given by Ridgeway to H. D. Symonds (who was imprisoned with Ridgeway) and then to Sherwood; that the poem was given by Southey to William Winterbottom after Ridgeway refused it; and that Winterbottom either stole the manuscript from Ridgeway in prison, or unauthorised copies were taken by Winterbottom's friends. See Robert Southey, '*Wat Tyler*'. The temptation towards unauthorised publication arguably grew stronger after the ruling of Lord Chancellor Eldon in 1817, which denied Southey an injunction to suppress the publication of *Wat Tyler*, on the basis that no publicly libellous work was entitled to legal protection. Of course, the publishers would still run the risk of being prosecuted for public libel if the work was seditious, obscene or blasphemous, but radical publishers had many ways of evading legal punishment for their publications.
42. Thomas De Quincey, 'William Wordsworth', pp. 119–206, and especially pp. 406–80. First published in *Tait's Edinburgh Magazine*, January, February and April 1839. For a detailed account of De Quincey's recollection of the *Prelude*, see John Edwin Wells, 'De Quincey and *The Prelude* in 1839'.
43. [William Hazlitt], 'Review of "Christabel; Kubla Khan, a Vision; The Pains of Sleep"', pp. 348–9.
44. Deirdre Le Faye (ed.), *Jane Austen's Letters*, p. 44. Martha Lloyd (1765–1843) was one of Austen's closest friends.
45. Nicholas D. Smith, *The Literary Manuscripts and Letters of Hannah More*, p. 17.

46. Bland, *Guide to Early Printed Books*, p. 16.
47. Johns, *The Nature of the Book: Print and Knowledge in the Making* (1998), p. 2.
48. Ibid. p. 2.
49. [John Wilson Croker,] 'Mrs. Barbauld's *Eighteen Hundred and Eleven*', p. 309.
50. *Journals of Dorothy Wordsworth*, I: v.
51. For a full investigation of this issue, see the chapter on 'Proliferation' in Multigraph Collective's *Interacting with Print: Elements of Reading in the Era of Print Saturation*, pp. 243–59.
52. See Betty Schellenberg, 'The Second Coming of the Book, 1740–1770', p. 36, on Samuel Johnson's discussion of how texts may achieve permanence and become 'often read' by writing 'upon general principles, or deliver[ing] universal truths'.
53. 'Review of *Sibylline Leaves*', *Monthly Review*, p. 33.
54. Such assumptions are beginning to be called into doubt again, in our digital age, when to publish a blog online does not make it 'public' in any real sense: the overwhelming majority of the hundreds of millions of blogs are read by very few individuals, if at all.
55. A similar fate was enjoyed by many other major writers of the period, all of whom had devoted family and friends: Percy had Mary Shelley; Keats, a devoted coterie; Wordsworth, his sister and wife; Coleridge, his daughter and son-in-law, and later his nephew. The rising reputation of these authors during the nineteenth century also accounts for the care taken with their physical manuscripts.
56. See Chapter 1 for a discussion of Smith's and Wordsworth's manuscripts. For another female author who similarly preserved her writing in manuscript for posthumous publication, see Teresa Barnard, *Anna Seward*, Chapters 2 and 6.
57. See Michelle Levy, 'The Radical Education of *Evenings at Home*'.
58. Thomas Astle, *The Origin and Progress of Writing*.
59. Jerome McGann, *The Textual Condition*, p. 43.

Chapter 1

Intentionality and the Romantic Literary Manuscript

Literary manuscripts have always been central to the stories we have told about literary authorship. As witnesses to the processes of creative composition, they have long been used to support theories of original genius.[1] One of the earliest examples may be found in John Heminge and Henrie Condell's address to the reader, in the First Folio of William Shakespeare. There, they contend that Shakespeare, in drafting his plays, never blotted a line: 'his mind and hand went together: and what he thought, he uttered with that easiness, that we have scarce received from him a blot in his papers'.[2] Almost two hundred years later, in 1807, Isaac Disraeli repeated the analogy, bestowing high praise upon the handwritten manuscripts of Thomas Moore: 'a specimen of a full mind, not in the habit of correction or alteration; so that he appears to be printing down his thoughts, without a solitary erasure'.[3] The conceit has been applied to many Romantic authors and their manuscripts. Keats's manuscript of 'Ode to a Nightingale', showing virtually no cancels or substitutions, has been interpreted in like terms, as a first draft and near final copy, demonstrating the poet's natural genius.[4] Wordsworth is believed to have composed poetry aloud, while walking, later copying his words down from memory.[5] Jane Austen's brother declared that 'everything came finished from her pen; for on all subjects she had ideas as clear as her expressions were well chosen'.[6] The list of examples could go on.

If an unblotted page signified a clear mind, what might a blotted page imply? This is the question taken up, with comic overstatement, by Charles Lamb (1775–1834) in his magazine essay 'Oxford in the Vacation'. Here, he recounts his horror upon being presented with the draft manuscript of Milton's poetic masterpiece, 'Lycidas':

> There is something to me repugnant, at any time, in the written hand. The text never seems determinate. Print settles it. I had thought of the Lycidas as of a full-grown beauty – as springing up with all its parts absolute – till, in evil hour, I was shown the original written copy of it, together with the other minor poems of its author, in the Library of Trinity, kept like some treasure to be proud of. I wish they had thrown them in the Cam, or sent them, after the latter cantos of Spenser, into the Irish Channel. How it staggered me to see the fine things in their ore! interlined, corrected! as if their words were mortal, alterable, displaceable at pleasure! as if they might have been otherwise, and just as good! as if inspiration were made up of parts, and those fluctuating, successive, indifferent![7]

The draft manuscript destroys, for Lamb, the illusion of poetic inspiration, of poetry 'springing up with all its parts absolute'; rather, poetry is the outcome of a laborious mental effort, involving uncertainty and indecision, the product of chaos, even chance. The draft provides evidence not of poetic genius, for Lamb, but of creation as 'mortal, alterable, displaceable', of a poem being 'made up of parts . . . fluctuating, successive, indifferent!' To Lamb, these literary manuscripts are not 'treasure[s] to be proud of'; and he expresses the half-facetious wish that Milton's manuscript had been better 'thrown . . . in the Cam'. His disgust in seeing Milton's revisions stems from their capacity to disrupt the mythology of original genius, in which poetry (and even fiction) comes unbidden, fully formed, and without the need to be 'interlined, corrected!' Lamb's valorisation of the imagination as a visionary capacity aligns with emergent understandings of authorial, and especially poetic, genius.[8] It reflects a conception of poetic inspiration associated with Romantic poetry (Wordsworth: 'all good poetry is the spontaneous overflow of powerful feelings'; Keats: 'if *poetry comes* not as *naturally* as the leaves to a tree, it had better not *come* at all'), though is not exclusive to it, as we have seen in Henry Austen's remarks on Jane Austen's fiction.[9] For Lamb, poetic manuscripts, particularly drafts, are dangerous in their capacity to reveal 'the work-shop' in which great art is produced.[10]

Lamb expresses his antagonism to viewing a poet's foul papers, even to seeing handwriting, and his desire for witnessing the settling effects of print. For Lamb, print fixes the contingent and fluid nature of manuscript textuality. According to this line of thought, print should subsume and replace the handwritten documents upon which it is based, much in the same way that many literary manuscripts, at least press copies, were routinely destroyed after printing. Lamb's preference for print also echoes a model of media change, in which a newer medium (in this case print) is seen as replacing, if not improving upon, an older one (in this case manuscript). Lamb is troubled by the capacity of the draft to unmask the work of writing; at the same time, however, he participates (albeit unwittingly) in the process by which such artefacts came to be preserved and displayed, 'like some treasure to be proud of'. That is, even though Lamb objects to the conservation and presentation of such manuscripts, and to the celebration of them implicit in such activities, he nevertheless participates in (and writes and publishes about) this species of literary tourism.

In the same essay in which Lamb describes his aversion to Milton's draft, he also describes his own material writing practices, for him an activity undertaken to escape the drudgery of his employment as a clerk at the East India Company. At his place of work, he describes how he would use readily available writing material, the 'outside sheets, and waste wrappers of foolscap', as surfaces that 'do receive in them, most kindly and naturally, the impression of sonnets, epigrams, *essays* – so that the very parings of a counting-house, are, in some sort, the setting up of an author'.[11] In this account, literary writing is inevitably destined for print ('the setting up of an author'), manuscripts for the printing shop, as he invokes the language of presswork ('receiv[ing] ... the impression') to describe the process of writing by hand (much like Moore 'printing down his thoughts'). The scraps upon which he writes are not to be kept and shown to others, but are instead way-stations, temporary containers for texts as they journey to the more permanent and stable medium of print. In describing his own literary manuscripts, then, Lamb's essay disputes that any meaning or value should be attached to them as material or textual artefacts.

Recent scholarship has reflected upon the impact of literary manuscripts very differently from Lamb; Anna Chen has explored 'the cultural perception of handwriting as an inherently unique and authentic embodiment of its writer', whereas Marta Werner has addressed '[t]he allure of the draft'.[12] For Werner, writing about Emily Dickinson's manuscripts, the draft draws us in because it issues 'from the erring hand, from its labor, its risks, its inhabitation of time and history, from, that is, its very perishability'.[13] Werner notes that in early and uncritical accounts of the draft manuscript, much like we find in Lamb or Disraeli, the draft 'was imagined as a reflecting glass by which we might see directly into the mind of the writer and the creative process': with, as we have seen, a lucid mind projecting itself as a clean page, a tentative or confused mind as a soiled one. Werner contends that, rather than imagining the manuscript as a mirror, scholars should 'traverse its surface and decipher the traces inscribed upon it' to find 'the passage of writing traced through time, the multiple, contradictory decisions made during the process of composition and registered in part in the spatial play of the hand across the paper'.[14] Although she questions the rhetoric of inspiration and genius, and even distances herself from an account of authorial agency, Werner nevertheless interprets the draft as revealing an intimate and poignant scene of writing. Ultimately, for Werner, the draft 'belongs most essentially to the realm of the private, offering a living record of "the writer at grips with his or her own traces"'; it documents 'the "secret [life] of writing, the back and forth of the text in the process of creating itself"'.[15] Although Lamb wishes to keep this secret life of writing hidden, and Werner wishes to probe it, both share a belief that the literary manuscript is a site of profound meaning.

For Lamb, Milton's draft of 'Lycidas' and his own papers of 'sonnets, epigrams, *essays*', as manuscripts intended for print publication, are, as he would have it, of little value compared to the settled print version. Many textual scholars would agree, treating the authorised print versions as authoritative. Similarly, scholars who study literary manuscript culture, and who have attempted to categorise modern literary manuscripts – that is, handwritten literary documents produced in the age of print – have tended to consider literary manuscripts intended for print as not belonging to manuscript culture, and even as not being properly characterised as modern manuscripts. Of course, few if any scholars would agree that draft literary manuscripts are unworthy of attention and preservation, thereby taking a different view than Lamb. But Romantic-era literary manuscripts of printed works have generally been the province of textual scholars alone.

Publication and Intentionality

Literary and textual scholars are only too familiar with the problems associated with divining authorial intention. As W. K. Wimsatt and Monroe Beardsley wrote in their famous essay 'The Intentional Fallacy', 'the design or intention of the author is neither available nor desirable as a standard for judging the success of a work of literary art'; and the same applies, they claim, for any act of interpretation.[16] Textual scholars, however, regularly seek to discern an author's final intention in editing a text, although it too is a task fraught with challenges. Intention has also been considered relevant to the study of modern manuscripts, with scholars suggesting that it is possible to draw a line between manuscripts the author intended to print and those she intended to keep in manuscript. In his study of early modern scribal culture, Harold Love goes so far as to remove from consideration all manuscripts prepared with print in mind, arguing that they belong to the realm of print (not scribal) culture.[17] This position relies upon the assumption that manuscript and print culture occupy essentially disparate fields: 'to be an author or a reader in one medium or the other was a significantly different activity'.[18] Although primarily addressing literary culture of the early modern period, Love and Arthur Marotti suggest that, if anything, this division becomes even more absolute in subsequent centuries, as they imagine there being no essential difference between a nineteenth-century printed poem and its manuscript copy, since the manuscript was 'never intended to be read except by the author, the publisher, and the compositor'.[19] Marta Werner largely adopts this position, claiming that modern manuscripts 'designate only a general category of documents – i.e., documents that do not attain printed form'.[20] In other words, a literary manuscript of a work that was in fact printed (presumably during the author's lifetime, though this is not made explicit) is not a modern manuscript at all, but rather a document belonging to the world of print.

Donald Reiman, in his account of modern manuscripts, helpfully broadens this narrow account of what counts as a modern manuscript. He identifies three categories of modern manuscripts: private, confidential and public. Reiman defines private manuscripts as those intended for the eyes of the author alone or for only a very select few, a category that essentially aligns with Werner's understanding of modern manuscripts. He defines public manuscripts as those designed expressly for a large, indiscriminate audience, a category that essentially aligns with Love and Marotti's understanding of modern manuscripts. But Reiman adds to the private and public a third category, that of the confidential manuscript, describing those manuscripts intended for a social readership. This category proves remarkably helpful for understanding a great number of literary manuscripts produced in the Romantic period. As an editor of the works of Percy Shelley, Reiman has adapted this model to account for what he terms Shelley's 'released' manuscripts – that is, those that were circulated in manuscript to the poet's friends and associates. By naming this category of 'released' manuscripts, Reiman acknowledges that they circulated and were meant for consumption even though they were not printed in the poet's lifetime.[21] Reiman's nuanced understanding of audience and his intermediary designation of the confidential offer an important insight for this study.

At the same time, although Reiman does propose a more capacious and useful understanding of modern manuscripts, he remains committed to the concept of intentionality: 'the primary fact that categorises a manuscript as *private*, *confidential*, or *public* . . . is the nature and extent of the writer's intended audience'.[22] Assigning authorial intent regarding publication to any given literary manuscript, however, is in many if not most cases a difficult if not impossible endeavour. Authors rarely leave explicit statements of their intentions for their manuscripts. Intention can sometimes be discerned from the content of the manuscript itself or from extraneous material, but it is an inherently unstable concept, particularly in the Romantic period when print was so ubiquitous that most writers could not help but contemplate publication, even as a distant possibility. In such circumstances, intention regarding publication (like authorial attention) is rarely available to scholars. Furthermore, even if intention regarding publication was fixed early on in the writing process and can be recovered, it was often shifting, or frustrated. This slipperiness of intentionality is perhaps most evident in the middle category of the 'confidential manuscript', where the precise scope of dissemination is not known or, in most cases, knowable. According to Reiman, confidential manuscripts are destined for those either personally known to the author or situated as a group of like-minded readers. This description of the intended audience opens up both an indeterminacy (as readers could and did easily share copies) and an ambiguity, for a writer could use *either* script or print to reach such readers. Many writers intended their handwritten documents to be circulated amongst readers within this sociable zone, with no thought of print at first, only to change their minds later. Others used manuscript as a deliberate testing ground, seeking advice and approbation before taking the next step towards print. Still others sought to reach a confidential audience via print, a possibility in an age of small print runs and self-financed publication 'by the author'. Thus even a manuscript properly described as confidential could be intended for manuscript alone, or print alone, or both. Fundamentally, the assumption that intention respecting audience is fixed and ascertainable is flawed. Many literary manuscripts were created and shared without any certain idea, in the mind of the writer, as to whether and how the work would ultimately be disseminated. Although the classificatory dilemma might be most acute in relation to this intermediary category of confidential manuscripts, it occurs with private and public manuscripts as well: private manuscript forms like letters and journals were regularly published, and manuscripts intended for print failed to find publication venues, hence becoming, by default, confidential or private documents.

In the period under review, manuscript and print presented authors with multiple and overlapping cultural spaces for which they could write and in which they could be read. Even manuscripts unambiguously destined for print were *intended* to be (and usually were in fact) read by a far larger circle than 'the author, the publisher, and the compositor' – including friends and family, advisers and editors, and often a much wider social circle. As Mark Bland reminds us, 'the printed book is the consequence of a complex process of manuscript activity', and by excluding from consideration (as belong to the realm of print culture) all manuscripts that were ultimately printed (as Love and Werner suggest is appropriate), a wide range of literary practices, from copying and editing to collecting and preserving, to say nothing of actual textual composition and revision, remain unexamined.[23] In this period, even the most 'social and non-competitive' forms of manuscript writing could be read by many and subject to the draw of print, with the movement of private or confidential manuscripts into print representing a commonplace phenomenon.[24]

The histories of two famous Romantic-era poems that circulated for decades in manuscript, both discussed in the previous chapter, reveal how slippery the assignment of intentionality can be in practice. Wordsworth's 'Poem (title not yet fixed upon) to Coleridge' was described by the poet as, at once, a private poem, written for and addressed to a single person, and 'a sort of *portico*' to a larger, public work (*The Recluse*).[25] After early drafts of the poem were completed and revised, Wordsworth read it to others and thus allowed the poem to circulate in oral form amongst his friends and admirers. Thus, during his lifetime, he treated the poem as if it were a confidential manuscript, deliberately withholding it from print; but he also treated it as a public poem, a piece of intellectual property in need of the copyright protection he engineered by delaying publication. It circulated and portions of it were printed from memory during his lifetime; but it was not published in full, in accordance with his wishes, until his wife printed it as *The Prelude*, shortly after his death.[26] Given this history, how should we define Wordsworth's intentions regarding the manuscript? The poem was simultaneously intended for manuscript and print circulation. It fulfilled a sociable function for decades, yet Wordsworth withheld it from print, in part to increase its commercial value to his heirs. While intentionality (where it can be ascertained) may be a relevant marker in the assessment of a manuscript, this example proves that the 'intentional fallacy' also exists in relation to an intention to publish.

Coleridge's 'Christabel', another poem that remained unprinted for many years, directs attention to the opposite phenomenon: as a poem that the author intended to publicise immediately, but which, for a variety of reasons (none of which had to do with Coleridge's intentions) remained unpublished for years. After 'Christabel' was rejected by Wordsworth for inclusion in the 1800 edition of *Lyrical Ballads*, it circulated widely, in at least thirteen manuscript copies (and almost certainly more that have not survived), as well as through unknown numbers of oral recitations.[27] 'Christabel' was thus more widely read and less subject to Coleridge's control than *The Prelude* (in part because the latter was a very long poem drafted and copied in several large notebooks kept within the Wordsworth household). Literary manuscripts could thus be published in a limited sense, with the text being 'designed to please a reasonably extensive audience'.[28] The example of 'Christabel' again points to the difficulties of assigning intentionality to any given manuscript: are the manuscripts that circulated before the poem's appearance in print in 1816 public because Coleridge originally intended the poem to be published? Or are they public because they in fact circulated very widely? Or are they better characterised as confidential manuscripts because they were not in fact published?

These examples point to the instability of the categories of private, confidential and public manuscripts. Intention is not always fulfilled: a poem meant for print might not be printed; a poem not intended for print could be printed without authorisation; a poem could be intended for both print and manuscript at once; and so on. There is a further slippage between these audience categories and the medium associated with each, particularly with the confidential. As we have seen, print could be used to reach a confidential audience (as with Coleridge's *Sonnets from Various Authors*) and manuscript copies could reach a very extensive audience (as with Barbauld's 'A Thought on Death'). That is, a literary work that circulated in manuscript could be much more widely read than a printed work. Given these complexities, it seems (once again, like authorial intention) that intention regarding audience 'is neither available nor desirable' as a means of categorising, describing and understanding modern manuscripts. Instead of relying on these categories, this study posits a method that is grounded not in discerning authorial intention but in ascertaining determinable facts about how individual manuscripts were made, used and shared.

Other classificatory schemes for modern literary manuscripts have been devised, and these must be briefly addressed as they can present other concerns. Manuscripts can be described according to the hand that wrote them and the level of polish and finality they reflect. *Authorial manuscripts*, known as *holographs* or *autographs*, are those written in the hand of the creator of the text; *drafts* reveal a higher degree of revision or correction than *fair copies*, which usually show few or no visible corrections. *Draft authorial manuscripts*, like the one Lamb is shown at Trinity College, represent the most highly valued forms of literary manuscripts because they emanate from the body of the author and capture the author in the act of creation. For this reason, collectors (both private and institutional) have been drawn to them, as have readers. *Authorial fair or presentation or press copies*, particularly of printed works, have been deemed to be of less value, as they do not reveal (or reveal less of) the creative process. They are often of limited utility for editorial purposes as well; *fair and presentation copies*, if they reflect writing already published, and *press copies* were rarely preserved in any case, and when they are their contents are often thought to be reflected in the final print versions. *Authorial fair copies* of unprinted works hold more scholarly value, though they are chiefly consulted by textual editors to establish a copy text. *Non-authorial fair copies* are perhaps the least valued, as they do not invoke the creator; unless no other version of a work exists, they are usually deemed unimportant to textual scholars, as very often the copies are based on more authoritative witnesses. Both authorial and non-authorial fair copies, even of unpublished material, have been generally under-studied. In part, this neglect relates to the devotion to the draft, whether as a site of literary creativity or labour or, as is usually the case, both; in part, this disregard reflects the assumption that most literary culture was transacted through print. Examination of both drafts and fair copies can, however, provide a fuller account of literary culture: scrutiny of drafts reminds us of the many challenges authors faced, and the considerable assistance they received in readying their works for a public audience; whereas attention to fair copies can break down monolithic understandings of authorship by drawing out the practices of making and circulating handwritten documents, and the networks through which they passed.

In this chapter and throughout this book, I pay attention to literary manuscripts that can be classified as drafts and fair copies, authorial and non-authorial. Drafts are chiefly examined for what they tell us about the practices of textual composition and in particular how authors shaped their works for different audiences. Drafts and fair copies are important in revealing the sociable realm of literary creation, which is rarely secret or solitary (though it is often presented as such). Fair copies are useful to the aims of this study in that they provide a strong evidentiary basis for understanding the extent to which literary texts were copied and disseminated in handwritten form. However, categorisation of literary manuscripts as drafts or fair is vexed, as many manuscripts occupy multiple designations at once. As a practical test of these categories, this chapter now turns to the writing practices and literary writing of Charlotte Smith and Dorothy Wordsworth. Smith and Wordsworth are two authors whose literary careers appear to occupy divergent positions on the script–print continuum, yet their experience as writers demonstrates the need to reimagine the cultures of script and print, to conceive of them not as separate media realms but as entangled fields of literary endeavour. This analysis treats the period's literary manuscripts as potential sites of recovery, not only of textual histories and creative processes, but of the material, social and embodied practices by which literary culture was transacted.

Charlotte Smith's *Elegiac Sonnets* and Manuscript Culture

Charlotte Smith first entered print in 1784 with her privately published collection of sixteen poems, *Elegiac Sonnets, and other Essays*. In her preface, she insists that she composed the sonnets neither for the market nor for a social audience, but for the consolation it brought – in other words, she insists they are private manuscripts: 'Some very melancholy moments have been beguiled by expressing in verse the sensations those moments brought.'[29] Smith thus creates an origin myth for her poetry that is not dissimilar to Percy Shelley's later formulation, comparing a poet to 'a nightingale, who sits in darkness and *sings* to cheer its own solitude with sweet sounds'.[30] At the same time, in this preface to the first edition, she describes the social circulation of her manuscripts, suggesting that in fact they were confidential manuscripts through copies being taken or procured. She explains how friends to whom she had given copies made further copies, by which the poems first entered print:

> Some of my friends, with partial indiscretion, have multiplied the copies they procured of several of these attempts, till they found their way into the prints of the day in a mutilated state; which, concurring with other circumstances, determined me to put them into their present form.[31]

According to Smith, then, her private and/or confidential manuscripts rapidly became, without her consent, public manuscripts; as a result of the 'mutilated state' of the copies in circulation, she was compelled to 'put them in their present form' and print them. As we can readily observe, Smith's narrative demonstrates the multiple, shifting and even contradictory positions she held respecting the intended audiences for her poetic manuscripts.

As it turns out, 'Mrs Smith left no posthumous works whatever' such that it is impossible to scrutinise her poetic manuscripts to determine intentionality. Her sister explains that 'The sweepings of her closet were, without exception, committed to the flames.'[32] Although many of her letters were preserved, only two poems survive in authorial manuscript: 'Evening' and 'Hope', both sent to Smith's friend Sarah Rose on 30 July 30 1805.[33] Without literary manuscripts, it would seem that Smith's poetry (and her fiction) has been entirely subsumed and settled by print. The lack of surviving authorial manuscripts renders it difficult, if not impossible, to ascertain whether poems (other than the two sent to Rose) circulated prior to print, presenting a prime example of one of the ways in which, in Mark Bland's words, 'print obscures manuscript'.[34] But even though Smith's (and, and we may presume, her publisher's) destruction of her literary manuscripts prevents our recovering Smith's actual practices of manuscript production and circulation, her printed poetry, particularly the prefaces to the nine editions of *Elegiac Sonnets*, provide considerable insight into her attitudes towards manuscript composition and circulation.[35] Although from the surviving record it appears that Smith was almost exclusively a print author, a study of her published writing demonstrates how she both associated herself with and distanced herself from manuscript culture.

In her preface to the first edition of *Elegiac Sonnets*, Smith provides a disdainful account of manuscript culture, protesting her loss of control, reproaching her friends for their 'partial indiscretion' in circulating 'mutilated' copies of her poems and thereby making them available to the press. Thus Smith invokes manuscript culture only to critique it. Her statement further implies that, inevitably, print will absorb and overtake manuscript. In her narrative, print culture also comes under attack, as her poems are printed without authorisation and remuneration. In 1784, Smith was an unknown woman of the landed class, living in the provinces, with minimal connections to London or literary circles, not the sort of individual we might think of as being an obvious target for publication in 'the prints of the day'. Smith's paratextual statement challenges the notion that manuscript exchange emerges from sociability and that authors possessed physical control over their manuscripts. Her narrative describes a late-eighteenth-century manuscript culture impinged upon, arguably even corrupted by, market forces.

The print culture that Smith participated in, at least originally, departed in other respects from the commercial norms associated with print publication. When Smith printed the first edition of *Elegiac Sonnets*, she did so at her own expense, with the third and fifth editions published by subscription.[36] Both methods of publication demanded that she adopt the roles of publisher, shipper and bookseller, thus replicating the amalgamation of roles that exists within manuscript culture.[37] Moreover, throughout her career, Smith courted the aid of patrons, suggesting that, even decades after Samuel Johnson's 'Letter to Chesterfield'. in which Johnson had pronounced patronage dead, authors still very much depended on it.[38] The journey of Smith's sonnets from manuscript to print adheres neither to the received model of manuscript transmission nor to that of print culture, with the nine editions of the *Elegiac Sonnets* indicating just how unstable the medium of print could be. Issued over a sixteen-year period, Smith's sonnets were presented to the public with different prefaces and subscriber lists, by different publishers, with and without illustrations, in various formats and prices, and with the sonnets arranged in various combinations. Much in the same way a manuscript notebook could be filled over time (as we will see in the discussion of Dorothy Wordsworth's manuscript notebooks), Smith's constant enlargement of this collection suggests print had a capaciousness and adaptability that could rival manuscript.

Although print obscures Smith's actual practices of manuscript circulation, it reveals what she thought about it, for she plainly believed that her poetry would be more acceptable to the public if she claimed it was *not* written for it. Smith's poetic enterprise rests upon a model of sensibility and a representation of interiority that had great resonance through the period. In the untitled first sonnet in the collection, Smith locates the origins of her poetry in her suffering, as she laments, 'how dear the Muse's favours cost, / *If those paint sorrow best – who feel it most!*'[39] Here, Smith elucidates a concept of the poet that had great force in the period. William Wordsworth, who greatly admired Smith, echoes her in his now famous declaration (in the preface to *Lyrical Ballads*) that the poet is one who is 'endowed with more lively sensibility, more enthusiasm and tenderness, who has a greater knowledge of human nature, and a more comprehensive soul, than are supposed to be common among mankind'.[40] It is this capacity for feeling, for self-exploration, that becomes the *sine qua non* of Romantic poetic consciousness. Although Smith's conception of the poet was by no means new, it resonated strongly with poets of her own and the next generation. Her influence may be felt not only amongst her nearest contemporaries (such as Wordsworth and Coleridge) but also perhaps even more strongly in the next generation: in Keats, whose most famous ode begins with an utterance of pain ('My heart aches'[41]), and in Shelley, whose unpublished 'Stanzas Written in Dejection, Near Naples' also echoes Smith's articulation of isolated suffering ('Alas! I have nor hope nor health, / Nor peace within nor calm around'[42]).

Byron also shares with Smith the experience of 'interiorized exile' ('I have not loved the world, nor the world me'), as well as that of actual exile, as both, for different reasons, were forced to flee to the Continent.[43] Curran neatly summarises the point: 'Charlotte Smith was the first poet in England whom in retrospect we would call Romantic.'[44]

Smith's development of this poetic persona was vexed, however, given her deliberate and profit-driven use of the medium of print to publicise her suffering. For Smith's '[t]urn[] inward' – to borrow Anna Barbauld's formulation in her lyric poem, 'Summer Evening's Meditation'[45] – is simultaneously self-regarding and audience-oriented. In publicising private feeling, Smith set a potent if self-contradictory example for subsequent poets. Her poems also demonstrate how intentionality could be deliberately manipulated: almost immediately after the first edition, Smith began to write more sonnets for print, though she continued to attempt to portray herself as Shelley's nightingale, as one who recorded her private utterances for herself alone.

Smith dedicated the first two editions of *Elegiac Sonnets* to the poet William Hayley (1745–1820), a writer who exemplifies how manuscript exchange could quickly transition to print and could even be instigated with the ultimate objective of print.[46] From the 1760s, Hayley had sent occasional verse and dedicatory sonnets in private letters to friends, hoping to incite a poetic exchange within a sociable context *and* at some point to print the poetry that resulted. As such, his poems, as Reggie Allen argues, may be sited within both a gift and a market economy, simultaneously belonging to scribal and print culture. In a new preface to the enlarged third edition of *Elegiac Sonnets*, Smith continues to adopt the posture of one who writes poems casually and without thought of their monetary potential, explaining that the new poems were 'recovered from my acquaintance, to whom I had given them without thinking well enough of them at the time to preserve any copies myself'.[47] However, her claim that her sonnets were produced within and for manuscript circulation alone became increasingly strained as the number of poems increased greatly, from sixteen in 1784 to ninety-two in 1800. And yet the need to posit a realm of writing and exchange free from a consciousness of print and insulated from the market economy remained a necessary fiction for her and others throughout the period.

As her *Elegiac Sonnets* expanded, both the narrative she told about her poetic practices and her poetic utterances themselves became subject to increased scrutiny. In her 1792 preface to the sixth edition, she reports an exchange with an unnamed friend, who suggested she include some new poems 'of a more lively cast [as] might be better liked by the Public'.[48] Smith again rehearses the origin story about her poetry, that it was written for herself alone:

> *You know* that when in the Beech Woods of Hampshire, I first struck the chords of the melancholy lyre, its notes were never intended for the public ear! It was unaffected sorrows drew them forth: I wrote mournfully because I was unhappy – And I have unfortunately no reason yet, though nine years have since elapsed, to *change my tone*.[49]

Her defensiveness arises from public suspicion about the authenticity of her feelings, increasingly demanded of lyric verse: so she submits 'an apology for that apparent despondence, which, when it is observed for a long series of years, may look like affectation'.[50] Proofs of authenticity of feeling were widely demanded during a period overflowing with the verse of pain and suffering: one of Jane Austen's most ordinary heroines, Charlotte Heywood, admits that her enjoyment of Robert Burns's love poetry is lessened by his infidelity: 'He felt and he wrote and he forgot.'[51] The common reader as much as the professional one sought assurances that expressions of feeling were genuine. Whereas with manuscript exchange in a coterie such feelings could be more readily assumed or confirmed, in print, assurances were required.

With her husband's dissipation and abuse not matters of public knowledge, Smith had trouble establishing her claim on the public's sympathy. Therefore, beginning in her preface of 1792 and more fully in her 'Preface to Volume II' in 1797, Smith began to divulge details of her personal circumstances. In 1792, she calls out the unfulfilled promises of '"the Honourable Men" who, *nine years ago*, undertook to see that my family obtained the provision their grandfather designed for them', as a justification for her perpetual melancholy.[52] In her 1797 'Preface to Volume II' she aggressively defends herself from the charge that her suffering is feigned, an allegation from which she contends herself 'unhappily exempt' given her ongoing private misfortunes.[53] She exposes 'the men, who have withheld my family property', and are therefore responsible for unjustly depriving her children of their inheritance.[54] Here Smith articulates the source of her pain, which had hitherto been only vaguely hinted at. In other words, in 1797, Smith's paratextual additions introduce both a personal and a political edge to her poetry. Her sufferings are particularised and her oppressors are identified, by gender if not by name. In this way, Smith's feminist poetics invoke another touchstone of Romanticism: what Curran calls the 'interweaving of the public and private, the political and the personal'.[55]

In Smith's dedication of her 1793 poem *The Emigrants* to William Cowper (1731–1800), she 'takes the risk of using distinctly politicised diction when she asks [her readers] to "vindicate" herself from the faults of poetic design'.[56] By invoking Wollstonecraft's *Vindication of the Rights of Women* (1792), Smith situates her oppression within a political, rather than simply a domestic sphere. However, it was precisely this politicisation of her situation that began to turn readers against her: 'As the years ground on', Antje Blank observes, 'Smith's desire to reclaim through her literary works a voice denied her in contemporary legal discourse alienated more and more readers.'[57] According to Sarah Zimmerman, 'Smith's growing frankness about the details of her autobiographical lyric speaker's melancholy in the prefaces to her later works, combined with her increasing willingness to treat social issues, made her a less universally sympathetic figure.'[58] The weakened sales of *Elegiac Sonnets* (the number of subscribers fell from 815, for the fifth edition in 1789, to 283, for Volume II in 1797) may have suggested to her that she had overplayed her hand. Hence she withdrew the 'Preface to Volume II' for the next edition, in 1800. Clearly, Smith perceived that public tolerance had been exhausted.

In addition to the nine lifetime editions of *Elegiac Sonnets*, Smith also published ten novels, several volumes of writing for children, translations of French novels, and a drama. Her embrace of print was needful: her father's profligacy compelled her to marry at age fifteen, and soon after her husband was placed in debtors' prison, forcing Smith to fend for herself and her growing family. In fact, many of the poems that first appeared in early editions of *Elegiac Sonnets* were composed in prison, where she had joined her husband, and where she had almost certainly written them with a view to print. A gift economy was untenable for Smith as a woman who had to support herself and her large family. Participation in sociable manuscript culture could not, for her, occur alongside of commercial print, as manuscript exchange was rapidly overtaken by unauthorised (and uncompensated) print. As she printed more writing in different genres and venues, and continued to add more poems to *Elegiac Sonnets*, her claim that she wrote to soothe her own sorrows became unconvincing. Yet Smith apparently felt compelled to construct an audienceless poetic space, one that was separate from the market. Smith presents as a prime example of the inadequacy of separate models of print and manuscript culture, insofar as her sonnets, though printed and known to us exclusively through print, invoke (even if factitiously) a private sphere of manuscript activity. Having begun with the posture of composing sonnets for herself alone, Smith struggled when it became increasingly clear that her effusions were commodities, written for the market, and her difficulties intensified when she named the source of her suffering as a woman. In describing how her sonnets came to be printed, she narrates a common fiction, one in which she sought to relieve herself of authorial intention and agency. Although feigned, this account was far more palatable to many of her readers than the truth. The destruction, apparently at her hands, of all of her literary manuscripts may also reflect her understanding that manuscripts had to be printed to be monetised, destroyed to be controlled.

If Smith's example suggests how print can obscure manuscript, Dorothy Wordsworth's illustrates how manuscript can obscure print. Unlike Smith, Wordsworth left behind a large archive of manuscript material, and she is known to us today almost exclusively through her manuscripts and as a manuscript writer. As Jared Curtis observes, Wordsworth's practices of manuscript retention were a family habit:

> [William] Wordsworth and his amanuenses were 'hoarders,' savers of paper generally, of notebooks, both commercial and handmade, and of loose manuscripts of the poet's writings, and were reluctant to let it escape from their hands even after a work they contained had been published. To this material Wordsworth returned again and again as he revised his poems tirelessly, whether or not they had reached print.[59]

However, a careful study of the Wordsworths' practices of manuscript production, dissemination and preservation make apparent the interlocking nature of the spheres of print and script. Within Dorothy Wordsworth's manuscript notebooks, the subject of the rest of this chapter, we find a pervasive consciousness of print. The lengthy discussion that follows is enabled by the significant manuscript record that survives; it is motivated by the pressing need to confront misconceptions about her writing – and about authorship and media in the period more generally.

Dorothy Wordsworth's Consciousness of Print

Ernest de Selincourt offers an essential description of Wordsworth as a manuscript writer, stating that she is 'the most distinguished of English prose writers who never wrote a line for the general public'.[60] This view, based on his perception that she had no intention to print any of her writing, has been influential: the *Norton Anthology of English Literature*, for example, has similarly claimed that Wordsworth 'has an enduring place in English literature even though she wrote almost no word for publication'.[61] The remainder of this chapter undertakes a study of the manuscript and print record to undermine these definitive statements of intentionality. Wordsworth did in fact revise some of her writing with the intention of printing it, and she lived to see several of her poems and prose narratives in print. These statements (that Wordsworth 'never wrote a line for the general public' and 'wrote almost no word for publication') are problematic not only because they ignore her printed output. First, these statements commit the critical error of assuming that there was something odd or paradoxical in a talented writer not submitting her work to the public. Second, these statements, in their (erroneous) claims about her lack of print publication, ignore her use of manuscript culture, and thus fail to acknowledge that much of what Wordsworth wrote did in fact circulate, sometimes widely.

Statements like de Selincourt's and the *Norton Anthology*'s rhetorically imply a contradiction, in Wordsworth being a distinguished writer who did not publish her work in print. These assessments are founded on several misapprehensions about the nature of manuscript writing and its importance. Implicit in these statements is an assumption that works that were unprinted were private and unvalued. But, as we will see, Wordsworth's works were widely known in her domestic circle and beyond and were highly esteemed by those who read (and copied and illustrated) them. Even in those instances when her social audience is recognised, the lack of a public audience has been interpreted as odd, a sort of failure. Wordsworth's supposed absence from print and her lack of a public readership have thus long been lingering sources of discomfort even amongst feminist scholars, including those most enthusiastic about celebrating her achievements as a writer. Although Susan Levin has been one of the scholars most responsible for recovering Wordsworth's writing, Levin has also characterised it as 'weirdly idiosyncratic' and has portrayed Wordsworth as 'constantly denigrat[ing] herself and her talent' in a 'process', according to Levin, that 'reflects [her] guilt and torment'.[62] For Patricia Comitini, these are common understandings of Wordsworth: '[w]hether characterising her as a domestic subject, novice writer or helpmate, scholarship has focused primarily on her failure to realise herself, develop her talent, or establish her own home'.[63] Underpinning these treatments of Wordsworth is the unstated assumption that print publication is normative, scribal publication aberrant. Yet, as with early modern women writers who deliberately and rationally chose manuscript circulation over print, Wordsworth's use of manuscript needs to be understood as a choice. As Margaret Ezell has cautioned, rather than asking '"why an author did not use print?"' we should instead ask, '"what is this author attempting to do?"'[64]

If we turn to the physical notebooks in which Wordsworth composed, revised, shared and preserved her writing, we find her inhabiting a thriving manuscript community with neither frustration nor shame but with fulfilment and confidence. Rachel Feder has called for an 'archival reading' of Wordsworth, noting that her writing 'become[s] denatured and dematerialised when removed from the textual corpus that they and their implied readers inhabit'.[65] This chapter undertakes such an approach, re-embedding her writing within physical, generic and social bounds; paying attention to how she writes by hand and in notebooks, using manuscript conventions and genres in addressing herself to family, friends and neighbours. Feder, however, reads Wordsworth as attempting to 'transcend, ironize, and imitate print culture', and in this way amplifies the disjuncture between script and print.[66] By resituating Wordsworth's writing within her manuscript notebooks, an understanding of the writing culture that Wordsworth inhabited emerges that implies less antagonism to and more integration with print. This intermingling of manuscript and print culture is apparent in all aspects of domestic bookmaking within the Wordsworth household, as family labour was pooled in the production of literary texts that moved between social and public realms. Thus within the notebooks we find various readerships imagined, for which the categories of private, social and public are often intermingled.

Wordsworth's notebooks may be roughly divided into four categories, all genres ubiquitous in manuscript culture:

1. journals (Dove Cottage Manuscript [DCMS] 19, 20, 25, 31, 104, 118)
2. travel writing (DCMS 50, 51, 54, 55, 63, 90, 97–99)
3. verse collections (DCMS 51, 120, 121)
4. other prose (DCMS 64, 119, 121).

It should be noted that even these broad generic categories inadequately characterise the materials within the notebooks, for most of the notebooks contain heterogeneous content. My analysis of select notebooks seeks to demonstrate how enmeshed the cultures of script and print were for the Wordsworths; how writing a daily journal, or recording a family tour, were not cordoned off from print, in fact, they were deliberately made available for it. The remainder of the chapter offers examples from each of these genres, to depict paradigmatic aspects of manuscript culture (such as social production, commonplacing, scrapbooking, illustration and extra-illustration) and to describe how they could, on many occasions, be placed in the service of print. The surviving manuscript notebooks document Wordsworth's involvement in a communal project of manuscript production and circulation that was thoroughly permeated by an awareness of – and, at times, an explicit design for – print.

Wordsworth's status as a manuscript author rests on what is widely considered to be her greatest literary achievement, the Grasmere Journals, as they are now known: excerpts from the journals were the first substantial extracts by a woman of the Romantic period to be included in the *Norton Anthology of English Literature* (in the third edition of 1974).[67] The Grasmere Journals comprise a series of four notebooks (DCMS 20, 25, 19 and 31), all of which are intermingled with extraneous material: the first three inexpensive, store-bought, paper-bound notebooks (DCMS 20, 25, 19) were used in Germany during the winter of 1798–9 and include material from this visit, including notes, accounts, fragments of essays and verse by William Wordsworth in his own hand, and other miscellaneous items.[68] As Pamela Woof speculates, Dorothy likely returned to the empty pages in these notebooks when back in Grasmere in

1800.[69] This practice of using a notebook over a number of years and for multiple purposes continues in the fourth notebook, DCMS 31, which includes several drafts of William's poetry. The so-called Rydal Journals (largely unpublished today), dating from 1824 to 1835, are contained within fifteen notebooks and similarly intersperse journal entries with other material. Modern editions of the *Grasmere Journals* such as those by de Selincourt and Woof extract the journal entries without reproducing the other material contained within the notebooks, thus representing the entries as a consecutive set of diary entries. This representation is, of course, a construction, an editorial imposition of order upon a series of entries that are discontinuous.

The journal entries are usually read within edited collections, such as Susan Levin's Longman edition, or the *Norton Anthology*. In these editions, a further imposition is made, as journal entries are selectively chosen to present an unbroken record of Wordsworth's acute observations on her social, familial and natural surroundings. Typically, entries are chosen that emphasise Wordsworth's engagement with the natural world and her relationship with her brother. Through these selections, the Grasmere Journals seem to conform to Marta Werner's descriptions of modern manuscripts, as 'belong[ing] most essentially to the realm of the private'.[70] However, the journals are not drafts: Wordsworth did not intend to and did not revise the material, beyond changes made in the act of writing and a few cancellations. Further, the journals were not private: she anticipated that they would be read and used by others. Her first entry signals her awareness of an audience, as she explains that she writes 'because I shall give William pleasure by it when he comes home again'.[71] Finally, the journal entries were not unpublished in Wordsworth's lifetime, as substantial excerpts appeared in the *Memoirs of William Wordsworth*, written by the poet's nephew in 1851.[72]

In fact, it is the editing of the notebooks that has created the illusion of privacy, of Wordsworth writing for and to herself. Through their selections, anthologists replicate the effects of Wordsworth's first editor, the late-Victorian William Knight, who skilfully excised (as unfit for the public audiences of the day) references, at once colourful and mundane, to illness and bodily functions, to housework such as baking, laundry and gardening, as well to Wordsworth's perspicacious though unseemly observations about drunken priests and battered wives. Modern anthologies often replicate Knight's excisions, literally, by using his edition (as it is out of copyright) as their copy text. It is, however, in large part the descriptions and observations removed by Knight that mark out the territory of the journals as confidential, as these are precisely the details of everyday life that Wordsworth wished to share with her intimate readers.

The notebooks and the journal entries included within their pages were written as much for Wordsworth's pleasure and edification as they were deliberate contributions to her brother's print career. William Knight blushingly observed how '[m]any sentences in the Journal present a curious resemblance to words and phrases which occur in the poems'.[73] This 'curious resemblance' has long been the object of comment and concern; whereas some have charged William with appropriation, alleging that he stifled Dorothy's creativity and prevented her from becoming 'more than half a poet',[74] others, including Lucy Newlyn, understand these borrowings to reflect the communal nature of their shared literary pursuits.[75] To return to the question of intentionality, it is certainly the case that, at the time of writing, Wordsworth could have had no notion that her entries would be published in unadulterated form. But she wrote her journal entries knowing that her brother would read them, and if she did not know at the outset she would have quickly discovered that he would use them as sources of poetic inspiration, sometimes directly lifting words and phrases, scenes and recollections for poems intended for public dissemination. Thus Wordsworth's journal entries were an attempt to participate in her brother's poetic career, which was of vital importance to her and the family as a whole. Within the Wordsworth household, literary and domestic economies were intertwined, and Dorothy was integral to both.

Table 1.1 provides a list of journal entries, with the corresponding poems composed by William, providing powerful proof of the use of her journals as a source of descriptions and recollections to be refashioned for print. This table also establishes that this use of the notebooks was enduring; whereas some poems, like 'The Thorn' and 'Michael', are written in response to recently penned journal entries, others could be delayed by years, even a decade or more. Because the inspiration they provided could be belated, these notebooks, like most of their working manuscripts, were carefully preserved.[76]

Table 1.1 Entries in Dorothy Wordsworth's *Grasmere Journals* with corresponding poems by William Wordsworth

DW's Journals (Manuscript sources: folio)	DW's Journal (references to *Journals*, ed. de Selincourt)	WW's poems (with date of composition; publication)
Alfoxden Journal; now lost	25 January 1798 (I: 4)	'A Night Piece' (1815)
Alfoxden Journal; now lost	20 April 1798 (I: 16)	'The Thorn' (1798)
4 June 1800 (DCMS 20: 17)	4 June 1800 (I: 37)	'Green Linnet' (1803; 1807)
10 June 1800 (DCMS 20: 20–22) 12 March 1802 (DCMS 19: 80–82; 80) 13 March 1802 (DCMS 19: 82–84; 83)	10 June 1800 (I: 38–40); DW re-reads this entry to WW on 13 March 1802 (I: 47, 122)	'Beggars' (13 March 1802) 'Sequel to the Foregoing' (composed in 1817; sixth stanza added in 1827) 'To a Butterfly' (March 1802)
3 October 1800 (DCMS 20: 45–47; 46–47)	3 October 1800 (I: 50–51; I: 63)	'Resolution and Independence' (4 May 1802–4 July 1802, written; DW copying May 8–9, 1802; 1807)
11 October 1800 (DCMS 20: 51–52)	11 October 1800 (I: 53)	'Michael' [October–November, 1800; finished 9 December; 1800]
16 February 1802 (DCMS 19: 53–55; 54–55)	16 February 1802 (I: 93; 112; 115)	'Alice Fell' (12–13 March 1802)
15 April 1802 (DCMS 19: 109–13; 110–12) 16 April 1802 (DCMS 19: 113–20; 118–19) 21 April 1802 (DCMS 19: 124–25)	15, 16, 21 April 1802 (I: 104–11)	'To the Lesser Celandine' (April 30, 1802)
15 April 1802 (DCMS 19: 109–13; 110–12)	15 April 1802 (I: 105–7)	'I wandered lonely as a cloud'

Dorothy's writing from the journals inhabited William's mind and, on at least one occasion, inhibited it: on 13 March 1802, she reread to him her narrative (from two years prior, in an entry dated 10 June 1800) about a family of beggars she had encountered, after which he complained to her that 'he could not escape from those very words, and so he could not write the poem'.[77] This evidence of a kind of linguistic haunting is apparent in William's continual reworking of the theme: in a second poem, 'To a Butterfly', loosely based on her description of the beggar boys chasing a butterfly; in a sequel in 1817; and in the addition of a new stanza to the original poem in 1827. Dorothy's manuscript observations are raw material for William, but he also catches, and cannot entirely abandon, the poetry in her words. Likewise, Dorothy's own journals are replete with the reverberations of her brother's poetry. She frequently quotes short passages from his published poetry, demonstrating her knowledge of and sympathy with it, before trailing off with ellipses signifying her internal recitation of the lines.[78] It is a symbiotic and also a fraught relationship, with the reciprocal exchange of (printed) poetry and (handwritten) journal pointing to the porous boundaries between the two media.

The journals also offer a detailed account of William's practices of poetic composition and revision, and of the communal copying, reading and revising done by brother and sister. Wordsworth could be in no doubt that her manuscript journals were serving her brother's poetic career in print, and she fulfilled the same role by reading to him aloud and copying his verse. At the same time that we find evidence of print culture within Dorothy's manuscripts, however, we also find evidence of more intimate experiences, detailed in the accounts of illness (excised by her first editors), William's affair with Annette Vallon, and Dorothy's reaction to his marriage to Mary Hutchinson, passages which were never meant to be shared beyond the inhabitants of Dove Cottage. Further, the journals were opportunities for Dorothy to explore her own powers of observation and composition; in an entry for 18 March 1802, she declares how a scene she encounters while walking 'made me more than half a poet'.[79] She also kept meticulous records of her near daily walks: almost in the spirit of a contemporary fitness journal, Wordsworth took pride in her walking prowess, and she may have wished to keep a running account of her walks both for herself and for her brother. In other words, like the mixed nature of the notebooks themselves, the journal entries satisfy multiple purposes and were written for different audiences: they offer records of meaningful encounters and descriptions, helpful to William in his poetic composition; accounts of private episodes within the family; and summaries of the everyday activities and labours (physical, domestic and literary) of the household. Thus the notion of intentionality regarding publication of the journals is manifestly complex.

This examination of Dorothy Wordsworth's journals has situated them within a domestic writing economy that belongs to the worlds of both script and print. Her tour notebooks, which constitute the bulk of her written output, further demonstrate the intermix of script and print but also the wider audience her manuscript writing imagined and in fact reached. According to de Selincourt, it is Wordsworth's *Recollections of a Tour in Scotland*, based upon a six-week, 663-mile journey through the Scottish Lowlands and Highlands undertaken from August to September 1803, that holds '[t]he supreme place . . . among Wordsworth's writing', a position reflected 'by the existence of no less than five [complete] manuscripts'.[80] Each textual witness (DCMS 50, 55i, 55ii, 54 and 97) provides evidence for how the copies were used and valued by Wordsworth and her readers. Over a period of roughly two decades, Wordsworth recopied, illustrated, extra-illustrated, annotated and revised the narrative, bringing others into the process; and her last two copies appear to be reworked with a view to publication. The tour notebooks thus provide a fully realised example of the sociability inherent in her bookmaking, as well as her shifting but ultimately unknowable plans for the narrative.

The first three copies of the *Recollections* were clearly intended for her social readers. DCMS 50 is a transcript (based on an original that does not survive) made by her close friend, Catherine Clarkson. Catherine's husband, the abolitionist Thomas Clarkson (1760–1846), drew the half-titles, and George Hutchinson, Mary Wordsworth's brother, embellished the title page. Sarah Hutchinson transcribed an additional copy (DCMS 55i), as did Wordsworth herself (DCMS 55ii), and both are illustrated with elaborate titles and half-titles by Thomas Hutchinson (see Plates 2 and 3 for the title pages of DCMS 55.i and 55.ii).[81] The use of calligraphic flourishes suggests the attention lavished on these manuscripts, but does not necessarily mark them as separate from print, as similarly engraved title pages were used in print. Nor does the use of decorative black letter for her name, as that font was often used on title pages of the period (albeit usually for titles or genre designations). DCMS 55.i's inscription by Coleridge demonstrates that the book was copied for, and gifted to, him, but this feature too does not separate the manuscript from the printed book, as obviously printed books were subject to handwritten inscriptions. What did signal the book's place within manuscript was the designation of a social audience: Wordsworth explicitly notes on the title page that the book is 'addressed to her friends, and she explains that it was written for 'a few . . . who, it seemed, ought to have been with us'.[82] The use of blank notebooks to create beautiful handcrafted books that rival what was possible in letterpress and engraving further destabilises the distinction between the copying technologies, demonstrating how the entire communication circuit could be, as it were, domesticated.

Over the next two decades, Wordsworth continued to revise the *Recollections*, producing two additional copies (DCMS 54 and 97). DCMS 54 began as a fair copy taken from Clarkson's copy, with the inclusion of a table of contents and hand-drawn maps.[83] Wordsworth's maps introduce a visual element that has both a practical purpose (to orient the readers of her narrative) and an aesthetic one (to interrupt blocks of text). Handwriting enables her to unite word and image within the same medium: the same hand both draws and writes (a phenomenon Blake will attempt to recreate in his illuminated books). Sometime in 1822, Wordsworth returned to DCMS 54, transforming the fair copy into a draft through revision, seemingly in anticipation for publication. Later that year or possibly in 1823, she used the revised text of DCMS 54 to prepare a new version, DCMS 97, which differs significantly from the other manuscripts.

Table 1.2 reproduces the opening entry for the three most distinctive versions of the *Recollections* (DCMS 50, 54, 97) – DCMS 55i and ii largely follow DCMS 50 and therefore are not included. The changes between DCMS 50 and 54 are modest: aside from some minor changes, Wordsworth makes two additions. The first sentence, beginning 'Passed the foot of Grisdale', offers a more specific account of their travels and some landscape description. The second phrase, beginning 'caves and caldrons which have been', provides more local colour, explaining how the residents have given 'fairy names' to the spot. But it is in the significant expansion of the entry between DCMS 54 and 97 (which more than doubles in length) that the full effect of Wordsworth's attempt to write for an imagined public becomes apparent. Her lengthy addition (with tendentious descriptions of the landscape and its history, and quotations, presumably added to elevate her prose) provides detail and historical context for the travellers but it does so at a cost, dampening her expression of a direct and vital connection to the environment. Her description of the caves at Caldbeck Falls as 'a delicious spot' becomes the far less emotive 'pleasing spot'. Succumbing to the impulse to regularise her writing and universalise its appeal did not suit Wordsworth's talents as a writer, and this late version of the tour lacks much of the intimacy and perceptiveness of earlier ones.

Table 1.2 Comparison of opening entries in Dorothy Wordsworth's *Recollections of a Tour in Scotland* (DCMS 50, 54, 97)

DCMS 50	DCMS 54	DCMS 97
William & I parted from Mary on Sunday afternoon August the 14th 1803, & William, Coleridge & I left Keswick on Monday Morning the 15th at 20 minutes after eleven o'clock. The day was very hot—we walked up the hills & along all the rough road which made our walking half the days journey—travelled under the foot of Carroch, a mountain entirely covered with stones on the lower part: above, it is very rocky but sheep pasture there; we saw several where there seemed to be no grass to tempt them. At Grisdale our horse backed upon a very steep bank where the road was not fenced, just above a pretty Mill at the foot of the valley & we had a second threatening of disaster in crossing a narrow bridge between the two dales, but this was not the fault of either man or horse. Slept at Mr. Younghusbands public house, Hesket Newmarket. In the Evening walked to Caldbeck Fall – a delicious spot in which to breathe out a summers day.—limestone rocks & caves, hanging trees, pools & waterbreaks.	William & I parted from Mary on Sunday afternoon August 14th 1803, & Wm, Coleridge & I left Keswick on Monday morning, the 15th at 20 minutes after eleven o'clock. The day was very hot; we walked up the hills and along all the rough road, which made our walking half the day's journey. Travelled under the foot of Carroch, a mountain covered with stones on the lower part: above, it is very rocky, but sheep pasture there: we saw several where there seemed to be no grass to tempt them. Passed the foot of Grisdale and Moredale, both pastoral vallies, narrow & soon terminating in the mountains—green with scattered trees and houses, and each a beautiful stream. At Grisdale our horse backed upon a very steep bank where the road was not fenced, just above a pretty Mill at the foot of the valley; and we had a second threatening of disaster in crossing a narrow bridge between the two dales, but this was not the fault of either man or horse. Slept at Mr. Younghusbands public house, Hesket Newmarket. In the evening walked to Caldbeck Fall – a delicious spot in which to breathe out a summers day.—limestone rocks, hanging trees, pools and waterbreaks—caves and caldrons which have been honoured with fairy names, and no doubt continue in the fancy of the neighbourhood to resound with fairy revels.	On Monday the 15th of August 1803, I left Keswick with two companions –our vehicle a jaunting car, of the kind which is jestingly called an Irish vis-à-vis, the Parties sitting back to back. We chose it for the conveyance of alighting at will in the rough and mountainous regions through we were about to wander. On quitting the Vale of Kewsick, passed on our right hand, the well-known druidical circle, and, soon after, the village of Threlkfeld, where formerly stood one of the Mansions of Sir Launcelot Threlkeld. A domain which he was proud of for being so well stocked his Son-in-law, Lord Gifford, when the Youth was obliged to hide himself in Shepherd's Garb to avoid the power of the revengeful Yorkists. Crossed, in travelling under Saddleback (formerly called Blencathara) several ravines almost choked up in places with rubbish brought down by the waters from the mountain-side and spread upon the road and adjoining fields. These formidable inundations are principally caused by the bursting of thunder-clouds; and Blencathara (allow me to give the mountain its ancient appellation) shews in a remarkable degree with what perseverance the fountains of the sky are wearing away the bodies of these giants of earth. At no very great elevation from the road, though entirely hidden from it, on the side of this mountain, lies a pool or small Tarn of singularly melancholy appearance. It is enclosed by circular rocks very steep and one side rising to a great height, and you might fancy that the pool had filled up the crater of a volcano, a notion one is disposed to encourage as Blencathara has more the appearance of having undergone the action of fire than any of her brethren. Beyond the 5th mile-stone, turned off from the Penrith Road. Passed the foot of Grisdeale and Mosedale, both pastoral vallies, narrow and soon terminating in the mountains – green – with scattered trees and houses, and each a clear brook. Travelled at the base of Carrock Fell, covered with loose stones to a considerable height, and very rocky above. The aspect of the whole recalled that characteristic and laboriously moving verse of Dyer *Huge Bredan's stony summit once I climbed.* Had time allowed, we should have been inclined to ascend this mountain, to visit some vestiges of antiquity of which writers give but a confused account, agreeing, however, that the work must have been of a very remote age. Heaps of stones (some of the stones being of enormous size) are said to be scattered over a large area upon the summit. In what form the architecture had arranged these stones cannot be even conjectured; but the country people believe in the tradition that some of those heaps are the remains of a church without troubling themselves with a question what sort of a building such masses would compose or with a doubt whether the worship was different from that of their own days. Reached Hesket Newmarked and in the evening walked to Caldbeck Falls, a pleasing spot in which to breath out a summer's day—lime-stone rocks—hanging trees—pools and water breaks—caves and caldrons, which have been honoured with fairy names, and no doubt continue, in the fancy of the neighbourhood, to resound with fairy revels.

Wordsworth also made cancellations in DCMS 54 (carried forward in DCMS 97) that indicate her anticipation of a wider audience. For example, in the 17 August 1803 entry, she removes passages that reference shared memories with her brother:

> the trees were stunted~~, but, growing irregularly, they reminded me of the Hartz forest near Goslar and I was pleased; besides Wm. Had spoken to me two years before of the pleasure he had received from the hether plant in that very spot~~.

It is in DCMS 97, however, that Wordsworth effects a complete eradication of personal references; Coleridge and William, for example, become merely 'companions'. She depersonalises the manuscript not only by removing names but also by excising descriptions of the hardships they encountered while travelling – walking up steep hills and on rough roads, and two near disasters that they experienced on their first day of travel. This loss of biographical detail seems self-defeating, as being the most likely to attract readers to the narrative. Wordsworth, however, appears to have anticipated that these descriptions could prove objectionable. Although her journals are replete with descriptions of the pedestrian lifestyle she shared with her brother (walking dozens of miles in a day, in all weathers), these pursuits were by no means an acceptable female activity (recall how Elizabeth Bennet's much shorter walk through fields to visit her ill sister is greeted by the Bingley women in *Pride and Prejudice*). Wordsworth was an unmarried woman of a more indeterminate class than many other women of the late eighteenth century who printed their journals, and her participation in these jaunts was socially precarious. Although the two poets' reputations had changed from 1798, when Coleridge declared that '[William] Wordsworth's name is nothing – to a large number of persons mine stinks',[84] Dorothy may not have been mistaken to assume that many readers would be uninterested in, or even hostile to, reading about the antics of the two rambling poets. Nevertheless, in de Selincourt's considered view, Wordsworth subjected her last version of *Recollections* to 'too drastic a revision', and it is readily apparent, even in the one extended example provided above, that her writing, grounded as it is in human community, suffers from her alterations.[85] As Wordsworth formalises her grammar and language, her style becomes stiffer ('We chose it for the convenience of alighting at will'; 'ancient appellation'; 'with what perseverance the fountains of the sky') and hence less engaging. DCMS 97 thus provides one example of Wordsworth's failure to bridge script and print.

Dorothy Wordsworth's poetry moved more harmoniously between the two realms. Although her poetry was written in the first instance for her domestic circle, from 1815 onward William included several of her poems in various editions of his poems: in 1815, 'An address to a child in high wind', 'The Mother's Return' and 'The Cottager to her Infant', all by a 'Female Friend of the Author'; in 1836, he added 'Loving and Liking. Irregular Verses Addressed to a Child' by a 'Female Friend of the Author'; and in 1842, 'The Floating Island at Hawkshead', finally, 'by D. W.' All subsequent collected lifetime collections of William's poetry reprinted these five poems. Dorothy never printed a separate collection of her poems, and they were not published under her own initials until 1842, but her verse appeared in print alongside her brother's for over three decades of her life.[86]

Following a pattern repeated with Anna Barbauld (discussed in Chapter 3), Wordsworth preserved and disseminated copies of her unpublished verse, which might have otherwise perished. Most of these poems are collected in DCMS 120, a repository of her manuscript verse that includes transcriptions of twenty-two separate poems (only one of which, 'Loving and Liking', had been printed). The notebook is both and archive and a workbook; of the twenty-two poems, seven have multiple copies, 'Grasmere – a Fragment' is recopied and reworked four times, and one other poem ('Lines written (rather say begun) on the Morning of Sunday April 6th') appears, in various incarnations, no less than seven times. Within individual copies of poems, as well, Wordsworth includes variants, queries to herself, and even emotional responses to her own verse. In 'A Winter's Ramble in Grasmere Vale' (see Plate 4), a version of 'Grasmere – A Fragment', she includes marginal and interlinear pencilled revisions that are at variance with each other, without deciding upon any particular reading. The two line choices – 'And lodged in many a sheltered chink' and 'There, too, in many a sheltered chink' – hover spectrally around the poem, quite literally, in Lamb's terms, 'fluctuating, successive, indifferent'. Similar examples abound throughout the notebook. By permitting different versions of her poems to rest side by side, Wordsworth reproduces what Sharon Cameron, in discussing Emily Dickinson's fascicles, has termed 'choosing not choosing', as both poets resist any final decision, embracing the capacity of manuscript to support variety and uncertainty.[87]

An instance of Wordsworth's affective response to her own poetry may be seen in one of the copies of 'Irregular Stanzas: Holiday at Gwerndovennant' (see Plate 5). In it, she recopies, twice, the expression 'Trust me' from the first line of the stanza, emphatically repeating to her younger readers and herself that they should trust her about the importance of their youthful present, now Wordsworth's past. Cameron observes that many of Dickinson's variants appear to place her both within and 'outside the ostensible boundaries of the poem',[88] and Dorothy's notations seem to have the same effect, as she circles back on a younger self, in a poem that itself thematises ageing and the passage of time.

Wordsworth's poetry appears in multiple copies – in DCMS 120 and other notebooks and also on separate sheets – suggestive of the demand for copies of her verse.[89] Unlike Smith's, then, Wordsworth's poems were preserved in manuscript copies, signalling, I believe, not only their lifetime circulation but also an awareness of the possibility of posthumous publication, a futurity she explicitly acknowledged in relation to her other writing.[90] The care she took to revise, preserve, and recopy her poems demonstrates both her dedication to them and the pride that she and other members of her circle took in them. We observe her returning to her poems years later, rereading, revising and recopying them. DCMS 120 reveals the sociable bookmaking practices inherent in the Wordsworths' writing lives, as Dorothy transcribed the writing of others, invited others to transcribe her writing, and used the codex form of the notebook to bring them together. Attention to the complexity and range of handwritten forms within a single notebook undermines the attempt to separate draft from fair copy and to distinguish an intimate scene of writing from a sociable one, as both creation, revision and dissemination for Wordsworth were individual and collective. As a manuscript notebook, used primarily to collect unpublished material, it belongs, with her travel writing and journal notebooks, to a domestic literary economy that was never separate from print. In the descriptions she entered into her notebook for use by her brother in his printed poetry, in the manuscripts she revised and preserved with print in mind, even after her death, and in the writing of hers that actually entered print, as poems, travel narratives and journal entries, Wordsworth's manuscript writing reveals the impossibility of decisively separating manuscripts into those that were intended for print and those that were not.

Conclusion

Wordsworth's manuscript notebooks and Smith's printed sonnets are structured by paradoxes. They address private, social, and public audiences, often at once; they are highly personal, yet they are not private. Many of Wordsworth's manuscript texts are unsettled, but we should not, like Lamb, overstate the fixity of print. The nine editions of Smith's *Elegiac Sonnets* reveal the instability of printed textuality, as collections were rearranged, enlarged and reframed through different paratextual elements, a phenomenon we will see repeated in Byron's early verse collections, discussed in Chapter 4. Examining literary manuscripts can unsettle our notions of print by reminding us that print, particularly in the age of moving type, was itself a fluid and dynamic medium, as we see evidenced again and again in William Wordsworth's printed poetry. As a final example, it is worthwhile to point out that Lamb, when he collected 'Oxford in the Vacation' into book form in his *Essays of Elia* (1823), removed his rant against 'Lycidas', thus disproving his own claim about the settling effect of print.

Smith and Wordsworth, notwithstanding their apparent differences, exemplify how writers of the day necessarily operated within the overlapping spheres of manuscript and print culture, and demonstrate how the conceptions of the former as private and the latter as public wither under close analysis. Even though Smith left behind virtually no literary manuscripts, and printed, out of financial necessity, nearly every literary work she penned, we cannot simply classify her as a print author. This is because she began writing her sonnets within a sociable context and, more importantly, attempted to situate her poetry within the non-commercial realm of social manuscript circulation. Similarly, although Wordsworth wrote many literary manuscripts that she did not publish, her writing practices and life were never autonomous from the world of print, and indeed she lived to see some of her writing in print. Her manuscripts were always audience-oriented, though the anticipated size and shape of that audience could be various and shifting. This chapter has demonstrated that assigning intention to any given manuscript is a fraught enterprise, and one that rests on the problematic assumption that there are distinct and dichotomous spheres of script and print culture. As we will continue to see in the chapters to come, it is often impossible to make a stable determination about the intention to publish for a number of reasons: because intention was rarely fixed and stable, because script and print operated interdependently, and because boundaries between the two were being contested. It is this struggle over the very identity and nature of print and script, as it is played out in the periodicals of the day, that is taken up in the next chapter.

Notes

1. For a general overview of the meanings ascribed to and found within literary manuscripts, see Gioia, 'The Magical Value of Manuscripts'.
2. 'To the Great Variety of Readers', n.p.
3. Isaac Disraeli, 'Autographs', II: 210.
4. John Keats, *The Texts of Keats's Poems*, p. 243.
5. Florence Gaillet-De Chezelles, 'Wordsworth, a Wandering Poet', p. 18.
6. Henry Austen, 'Biographical Notice of the Author', p. xvi.
7. Charles Lamb, 'Oxford in the Vacation', p. 367n.
8. These are also internally consistent with Lamb's views stated elsewhere: with his attack on 'Mrs. Barbauld's stuff', that is, her children's writing, which he believed had 'banished . . . that beautiful interest in wild tales, which made the child a man' (Charles Lamb to Samuel Taylor Coleridge, 23 October 1802, *Letters of Charles Lamb*, I: 235–6); and with his claim, in 'On Garrick, and Acting; and the Plays of Shakspeare, considered with reference to their fitness for Stage Representation', that Shakespeare's plays were by and large better read than seen, for when performed 'the imagination is no longer the ruling faculty' and 'we are left to our poor unassisted senses': p. 309.
9. William Wordsworth, 'Preface to *Lyrical Ballads*, 1800', in *Lyrical Ballads and Other Poems* (Cornell University Press, 1992), p. 744; letter from John Keats to John Taylor, 27 February 1818, *Selected Letters of John Keats*, p. 97. For a fuller examination of the Romantic ideology of the solitary author, see Jack Stillinger, *Multiple Authorship and the Myth of Solitary Genius* and Levy, *Family Authorship*.

10. Lamb, 'Oxford in the Vacation', p. 367. Lamb also promises never to go to the 'work-shop of any great artist again, nor desire a sight of his picture, till it is fairly off its easel'.
11. Lamb, 'Oxford in the Vacation', p. 365.
12. Marta L. Werner, '"Reportless Places"', p. 63; Anna Chen, 'In One's Own Hand', para. 3.
13. Ibid. p. 63.
14. Ibid. pp. 63, 64.
15. Ibid. pp. 61–2. Here Werner cites Jean-François Lyotard.
16. W. K. Wimsatt Jr and Monroe C. Beardsley, 'The Intentional Fallacy', p. 3.
17. Love, *Culture and Commerce of Texts*, p. 36.
18. Love and Marotti, 'Manuscript Transmission and Circulation', p. 58.
19. Ibid. p. 60.
20. Werner, '"Reportless Places"', p. 62.
21. Percy Shelley, *The Complete Poetry of Percy Bysshe Shelley*, I: xxxi.
22. Donald Reiman, *The Study of Modern Manuscripts*, p. 65.
23. Bland, *Guide to Early Printed Books*, p. 107.
24. Ezell, *Social Authorship*, p. 38.
25. William Wordsworth to George Beaumont, 3 June 1805, *The Early Letters of William and Dorothy Wordsworth*, p. 497.
26. For a detailed account of Wordsworth's posthumous publications, see Stephen Gill, 'Copyright and the Publishing of Wordsworth', pp. 74–92.
27. Stillinger, *Coleridge and Textual Instability*, p. 79.
28. Ezell, *Social Authorship*, p. 39.
29. Charlotte Smith, *The Poems of Charlotte Smith*, p. 3.
30. Percy Shelley, *The Poems of Percy Shelley*, II: 475.
31. C. Smith, *Poems*, p. 3.
32. Ibid. p. xxvii.
33. Ibid. p. 323. These two poems were published posthumously in *Beachy Head: with other Poems* (1807).
34. Bland, *Guide to Early Printed Books*, p. 106.
35. Editions were published in 1784 (1st and 2nd), 1786 (3rd and 4th), 1789 (5th), 1792 (6th), 1795 (7th), 1797 (8th, including the first edition of the second volume) and 1800 (9th, including the second edition of the second volume).
36. Smith considered subscription a kind of beggary – she wrote to her publisher Thomas Cadell that 'in cases of subscription an Author is always consider'd as a kind of literary beggar'. Letter from Charlotte Smith to Thomas Cadell, 14 May 1799, *Collected Letters of Charlotte Smith*, p. 323. For a thorough discussion of Smith's use of subscription and her relation with Cadell and then Cadell and Davies, see Michael Gamer, *Romanticism, Self-Canonization, and the Business of Poetry*, Chapter 2.

37. Love and Marotti, 'Manuscript Transmission and Circulation', p. 59.
38. Samuel Johnson, *The celebrated letter from Samuel Johnson.*
39. C. Smith, *Poems*, p. 13.
40. William Wordsworth, *Lyrical Ballads, and Other Poems, 1797–1800*, p. 751.
41. John Keats, *The Poems of John Keats*, p. 369, line 1.
42. Percy Shelley, *Shelley's Poetry and Prose*, pp. 135–6, lines 19–20.
43. C. Smith, *Poems*, p. xxv.
44. Ibid. p. xix.
45. Anna Barbauld, *The Poems of Anna Letitia Barbauld*, pp. 81–4, line 54.
46. Reggie Allen, 'The Sonnets of William Hayley and Gift Exchange', pp. 383–92.
47. C. Smith, *Poems*, p. 3.
48. Ibid. p. 5.
49. Ibid. p. 5.
50. Ibid. p. 6.
51. Jane Austen, *Later Manuscripts*, p. 176.
52. C. Smith, *Poems*, p. 5.
53. Ibid. p. 11.
54. Ibid. p. 8.
55. Ibid. p. xiv.
56. Jacqueline Labbe, *Charlotte Smith: Romanticism, Poetry and the Culture of Gender*, p. 31.
57. Antje Blank, 'Charlotte Smith After 200 Years', p. 3.
58. Sarah M. Zimmerman, 'Smith, Charlotte (1749–1806)'.
59. Jared Curtis, 'The Cornell Wordsworth', p. 7.
60. D. Wordsworth, *Journals*, ed. de Selincourt, I: v.
61. *Norton Anthology of English Literature*, 9th edn, II: 383.
62. Susan M. Levin, *Dorothy Wordsworth and Romanticism*, pp. 4–6.
63. Patricia Comitini, '"More Than Half a Poet"', p. 307.
64. Ezell, *Social Authorship*, p. 23.
65. Rachel Feder, 'The Experimental Dorothy Wordsworth', p. 543.
66. Ibid. p. 542.
67. *Norton Anthology of English Literature*, 3rd edn, II: 263–83. The first and second editions (published in 1962 and 1968), include only a single page from a sole female author – from Ann Radcliffe's *Mysteries of Udolpho*. For more details on the Norton's inclusion of female authors, see Michelle Levy and Mark Perry, 'Distantly Reading the Romantic Canon'.
68. These notebooks contain entries for the period 4 May 1800 – 16 January 1803, with a gap, between DCMS 20 and 25, from 23 December 1800 to 9 October 1801.

69. Pamela Woof, 'The Uses of Notebooks', p. 10.
70. Werner, '"Reportless Places"', p. 62.
71. D. Wordsworth, *Journals*, ed. de Selincourt, I: 37.
72. Christopher Wordsworth, *Memoirs of William Wordsworth* (1851). As Mary Ellen Bellanca has shown in her essay 'After-Life-Writing: Dorothy Wordsworth's Journals in the Memoirs of William Wordsworth', these extracts were sufficient to establish a considerable *public* reputation for Dorothy during the second half of the nineteenth century.
73. Dorothy Wordsworth, *Journals of Dorothy Wordsworth*, ed. William Knight, pp. xviii–xix.
74. This strand of argument can be found in the following monographs: Margaret Homans, *Women Writers and Poetic Identity* (1980); Meena Alexander, *Women in Romanticism: Mary Wollstonecraft, Dorothy Wordsworth, and Mary Shelley* (1989); Susan Levin, *Dorothy Wordsworth and Romanticism* (1987; revised 2009); Elizabeth Fay, *Becoming Wordsworthian* (1995).
75. Lucy Newlyn, *William and Dorothy Wordsworth*.
76. It was Knight who apparently lost the Alfoxden Journal notebooks (a notebook that he likely heavily edited, as he did with the Grasmere journals).
77. D. Wordsworth, *Journals*, ed. de Selincourt, I: 223.
78. For example, on both 26 May 1800 and 24 October 1802, Dorothy quotes a short passage from her brother's 'Lines Written in Early Spring' (first published in 1798).
79. D. Wordsworth, *Journals*, ed. de Selincourt, I: 127.
80. D. Wordsworth, *Journals*, ed. de Selincourt, I: viii.
81. Hutchinson also prepared the ornamental title pages for DCMS 53, a fair copy of the thirteen-book *Prelude* prepared by Mary Wordsworth for Samuel Taylor Coleridge.
82. D. Wordsworth, *Journals*, ed. de Selincourt, I: vii.
83. This copy also bears an inscription: 'Dora Wordsworth, from her aff[ectiona]te Father J Wordsworth. Nov 1 1866', an intergenerational example of re-gifting, as the book was passed down from the poet's eldest son (John) to his daughter, more than sixty years after it was first composed.
84. Coleridge, *Collected Letters*, I: 142.
85. D. Wordsworth, *Journals*, ed. de Selincourt, I: xii.
86. In his *Guide to the Lakes* (1822), William included without acknowledgement substantially revised versions of her narratives, *Excursion on the Banks of Ullswater* (1805) and *Excursion up Scafell Pike* (1818): see *The Prose Works of William Wordsworth* (1974) II: 3.
87. Sharon Cameron, *Choosing not Choosing*, pp. 21–4, 6, 14.

88. Ibid. p. 24.
89. See Levin, *Dorothy Wordsworth*, pp. 177–220, where she provides an inventory of some of the manuscript sources for Wordsworth's poems.
90. Dorothy contemplated posthumous publication of her *Narrative of the Life of George and Sarah Green* (1808), which had circulated in manuscript (there are three extant authorial copies, DCMS 64, DCMS 167 and another copy in the British Library, Add MS 41267 A). She acknowledged the possibility of future publication, saying '[t]hirty or forty years hence when the Characters of the children are formed and they can be no longer objects of curiosity, if it should be thought that any service would be done, it is my present wish that it should be then published whether I am alive or dead'(letter from Dorothy Wordsworth to Catherine Clarkson, 9 December 1810, *Letters of William and Dorothy Wordsworth*, II: 454). For a more detailed account of the *Narrative*, see Michelle Levy, 'The Wordsworths, the Greens and the Limits of Sympathy'.

Chapter 2

Literary Reviews and the Reception of Manuscript Culture

The previous chapter has described how many literary manuscripts produced in the Romantic period occupied a middle ground, serving as instruments of sociability and as potentially commercially objects, often both at once. As we have seen from the examples of Charlotte Smith and Dorothy Wordsworth, no one involved in writing and exchanging handwritten documents, even in private forms like letters and journals, could be unaware of their possible passage into print. Undoubtedly, given the expanding print marketplace, increasing numbers of literary works were written directly for print. Likewise, many literary manuscripts were produced without any explicit thought of print. But between these two extremes was a broad continuum that consisted of literary works for which, as the previous chapter has shown, intentionality regarding publication was uncertain or changeable. This chapter shifts attention more directly to the print marketplace, surveying the reception of printed literary works with ostensible social origins as a means of investigating the range of attitudes towards the rapid migration of literature from sociable manuscript to public print. This chapter turns to the literary reviews, influential institutions that reveal the contested nature of print, as some professional readers challenged the publication of certain writing deemed unsuitable for print. As we have seen in the Introduction, the *Monthly Review* derided Coleridge for collecting some of his poems in *Sibylline Leaves*, claiming that they were 'more adapted to the silence and the privacy of domestic enjoyment, than to glaring and repulsive publication'.[1] Similarly, in his review of Byron's first commercially published volume, *Hours of Idleness*, Henry Brougham, writing in the *Edinburgh Review*, speaking about the translations and other school exercises Byron had included, asked, 'Only, why print them after they had their day and served their turn?'[2] The literary reviews became the battlegrounds that debated 'the very identity of print', to use Adrian Johns's phrase, and with it, prevailing concepts of manuscript writing and its proper bounds.[3]

We find evidence for the disputed nature of print in the many explanations authors furnished for why they were printing their writing, a particularly common feature of works that originated in domestic and social circles. Charlotte Smith, as we have seen, claimed that she had to publish her sonnets to prevent 'mutilated copies' being printed by others. Anna Barbauld and John Aikin, in the introduction to their six-volume miscellany *Evenings at Home; or, The Juvenile Budget Opened* (1792–6), describe a more organic, less antagonistic process of textual migration from private audiences to social ones, and finally, to the public at large. They explain how a variety of short pieces were composed for the entertainment and instruction of the family's own children. These pieces were placed inside and selected from a 'budget' (a leather pouch), to be read aloud as the evening's entertainment. Through this means of oral and written transmission, the participants in these readings gradually expanded: additional contributions were made by visitors to the household, 'the intimate friends or relations' of the family, and eventually, 'other children were admitted to these readings' such that the work 'became somewhat celebrated in the neighborhood'.[4] '[I]ts proprietors were at length urged to lay it open to the public', such that the work was ultimately published.[5] Social approbation and encouragement, as well as circulation both within and beyond the control of the original creators, were the forces that drove publication in this and many other cases.

Some twenty-five years later, Mary and Percy Shelley offer another account of the migration of their travel writing from script to print in *History of a Six Weeks' Tour* (1817). In their description, however, the Shelleys manifest an awareness of how commonplace and how controversial the publication of such materials had become. Their preface reads:

> Nothing can be more unpresuming than this little volume. It contains the account of some desultory visits by a party of young people to scenes which are now so familiar to our countrymen, that few facts relating to them can be expected to have escaped the many more experienced and exact observers, who have sent their journals to the press. In fact, they have done little else than arrange the few materials which an imperfect journal, and two or three letters to their friends in England afforded.

> They regret, since their little History is to be offered to the public, that these materials were not more copious and complete. This is a just topic of censure to those who are less inclined to be amused than to condemn.[6]

The authors are apologetic about transforming handwritten materials – 'an imperfect journal', letters to friends in England and a poem composed while abroad (Percy Shelley's 'Mont Blanc') – into a published book, in part because their volume cannot compete with those of 'the many more experienced and exact observers'. A defensiveness permeates the preface. They use the third person plural to refer to themselves in an act of distancing, and voice 'regret' at the *Tour*'s shortcomings. The claim that the book is 'unpresuming' signals their understanding that reviewers had issued many sharp disapprovals of similar tours, which their authors had also claimed were not written for the press.

To trace the diversity of attitudes towards an expanding print culture, this chapter adopts a comparative methodology, contrasting the first decade of literary reviews published in the well-known *Edinburgh Review*, with those that appeared in the little-known *Annual Review*, both of which were launched in 1802. The two reviews have been selected because they had much in common: both were liberal in politics and addressed a Whig middle-class readership; both advertised their use of professional reviewers and marketed themselves as offering something entirely new to readers. They even shared the same London publisher, Longman (though the *Edinburgh* was printed in that city by Archibald Constable). These two reviews, though sharing many similarities, diverge markedly in terms of their design, format and editorial policy, reflecting the different personal associations, literary values and ethical motivations of their editors and reviewers. The *Edinburgh Review* was a quarterly, the *Annual*, an annual; the former sought to cultivate a reputation for extreme selectivity, the latter pledged to be comprehensive in its reviews of *all* new books. Neither, of course, initiated an entirely new phase in reviewing – the *Monthly Review* had been issuing reviews of literary works for over half a century (it was founded in 1749). Nevertheless, the reviews employed disparate strategies to organise and regulate the proliferation of print.

By comparing their statements of editorial policy, reviewing practices, and select reviews of literary works, it is possible to trace the emergent discourses surrounding script and print, and ultimately of authorship and literary value. The *Annual* and the *Edinburgh* both responded to the quantitative rise in the output of the press, but in markedly different ways. The particularly wide divide between the *Annual* and the *Edinburgh* affords a clear glimpse into debates about who should be authors and what was suitable for print. It was a battle, in essence, about whether the print marketplace should be confined to highly talented authors, writing for a broad readership and indeed for posterity, or whether print could support a broader constituency of writers, addressing themselves to smaller communities, on matters of current but not necessarily longstanding interest – a struggle, in other words, about the inclusivity and diversity of print. The divergent fates of the two reviews also warrants our attention. The *Edinburgh* rose to prominence to become the most influential British magazine of the early nineteenth century, not ceasing publication until 1929; the *Annual* survived for less than a decade (it appeared in seven volumes between 1802 and 1808).[7] The *Edinburgh* has been extensively discussed by scholarship; the *Annual* has gone unstudied and remains largely unknown.[8]

The Contested Identity of Print

The reviews developed distinct editorial identities, with the design of the two journals immediately signalling their opposing attitudes towards literary culture.[9] The *Annual*, in its prospectus, promised that 'each volume will be scrupulously devoted to the review of the works of the preceding year, so no book published in the United Kingdom will be intentionally omitted'.[10] Its opening number reiterated that 'it is an essential part of our plan to give an account of all the productions of British literature that have been published during the past year', and in addition to individual reviews one of its strategies was to offer summaries for each of its generically organised chapters.[11] By examining large quantities of books of a particular genre, the *Annual* was able to provide a general commentary on the year's developments, enabling a synoptic analysis of literary trends for the year. In its promise of inclusivity, the *Annual* acknowledged that all publications were worthy of some consideration, all authors deserving of some notice. The advertisement for the second volume markets this feature explicitly, perhaps hoping to appeal to those authors whose works were not (or not likely to be) reviewed elsewhere:

> out of about FIVE HUNDRED Articles, which form the Contents of this Volume, it appears, from a very accurate examination, that about ONE HUNDRED only (and those by no means the most important) have yet been noticed by any Literary Review published in this country.[12]

The enormous output of reviews demanded by the *Annual*'s editorial strategy required its editor, Arthur Aikin, to solicit contributions – all unsigned – from members of his immediate family, including his aunt, Anna Barbauld, and his sister, Lucy Aikin. Another major though antagonistic contributor to the review was Robert Southey, who lamented the low rate of pay and the nature of the work generally (apparently not being of the view that all works were entitled to notice).

The *Annual* addressed itself at least in part to those 'residing at a distance from the Metropolis, for exportation to foreign parts, and for the Library'; thus it sought to review a large number of print works not noticed by other reviews and to reach those without direct access to the range of printed matter available in London or other large towns. It also optimistically endorsed the view that the output of the press could be contained and mastered, and that this regulation did not have to come at the expense of neglecting (or abusing) some publications. The *Annual* also, as we will see, defined literary success in terms that radically differed from the *Edinburgh*, refusing to demand exacting standards of literary value, espousing no definite expectation that books would survive beyond the present moment, and finding merit even in works appealing to small readerships.

The *Edinburgh*, by contrast, sought from the outset to distinguish itself for rigorous selectivity and critical severity: in its first issue it refers to itself as a kind of literary police.[13] Begun by Sydney Smith (1771–1845), who edited the first three numbers, after which the editorship was taken over by Francis Jeffrey (1773–1850), with contributions by Francis Horner (1778–1817) and Henry Brougham (1778–1868), '[w]hat made the *Edinburgh* such a success was largely the vigour of its discourse and a signature style that managed to be at once authoritative and entertaining'.[14] Its editors announce in the advertisement to the first issue that they repudiate any attempt at universal coverage: 'it forms no part of their object, to take notice of every production that issues from the Press'.[15] Indeed, the editors express their 'wish [that] their Journal [should] be distinguished, rather for the selection, than for the number, of its articles', and 'propose to carry this principle of selection a good deal farther' than its competitors by 'declin[ing] any attempt at exhibiting a complete view of modern literature'.[16] Thus the *Edinburgh* marketed itself in terms precisely opposite to the *Annual* (though it took no direct notice of it): the value it offered was the capacity to discriminate between the deserving and the undeserving. The editors explain that they have deliberately 'confined their notice, in a great degree, to works that either have attained, or deserve, a certain portion of celebrity'.[17] The *Edinburgh* sought to identify only newsworthy books, to establish itself as a gatekeeper and tastemaker, assuming a position of cultural authority that it quickly achieved.

A quantitative comparison bears witness to the *Annual*'s inclusivity compared to the *Edinburgh*'s exclusivity. Although the *Annual*'s notice of novels was not complete, it reviewed far more novels than the *Edinburgh*. The *Annual* reviewed a minimum of six novels per year (in 1806) reaching a maximum of nineteen (in 1808), and averaging around thirteen per year; the *Edinburgh*, from its inception in 1802 to the end of the 1820s, reviewed just over thirty novels, a number almost surpassed by the *Annual* in its first two years in existence.[18] The *Annual*'s reviews of poetry also greatly exceeded those of the *Edinburgh*. Ranging from a low of twenty-six books of poetry (in 1806) to a high of forty-nine (in 1805 and 1809), and averaging forty volumes per year, the *Annual*'s engagement with verse publication was extensive. The *Edinburgh* had a comparatively low output of poetic reviews: ten in 1805, nine in 1806, only four in 1810, and an average of eight per year during the period 1802–9, less than a quarter of the number reviewed by the *Annual*. The *Edinburgh* made only one concession to inclusivity and breadth by beginning, in 1803, to list all books published during the quarter.[19]

The *Annual*'s strategy for achieving its objective of reviewing all books published in the preceding year involved categorising books into different disciplines or genres and collecting reviews of each category within separate chapters. An advertisement in its third issue describes this organisation as one of the *Annual*'s advantages: 'By reviewing together the Works of a Year, the Publications are sufficiently numerous to render each Chapter important and interesting, and the Reader may select for Perusal those Chapters which may suit his Taste or his Pursuits.'[20] This organisational strategy was designed to allow readers to navigate more easily the hundreds of titles it reviewed in each volume. (It did have to refine its generic categories on occasion, as the market rapidly expanded even within the short lifespan of the journal.[21]) Given that the *Edinburgh* reviewed far fewer books (an average of seventy-one per year over its first decade), no such elaborate organisational structure was required.[22] The *Annual*'s attempt to render itself serviceable to the consumer resonates with the generous attitude it adopts towards both its readers and the authors it reviewed.

In *History of a Six Weeks' Tour*, the Shelleys compare the more receptive readers, those who were 'inclined to be amused', to the more critical ones, those who were disposed to 'censure', precisely describing the distinction that came to characterise the editorial stances of the *Annual* and the *Edinburgh*. Through their editorial policies and reviews, the *Edinburgh* and the *Annual* articulate different conceptions of what is worthy of being printed in the first place, as well as what is worthy of being noticed in a review. In their first 'advertisement', the editors of the *Edinburgh* voice their contempt for the vast number of books being printed:

> Of the books that are daily presented to the world, a very large proportion is evidently destined to obscurity, by the insignificance of their subjects, or the defects of their execution; and it seems unreasonable to expect that the Public should be interested by any account of performances, which have never attracted any share of its attention. A review of such productions, like the biography of private individuals, could afford gratification only to the partiality of friends, or the malignity of enemies.[23]

At the start, therefore, the *Edinburgh* asserts that it need not concern itself with 'a very large proportion' of works which are 'evidently destined to obscurity'. They conceive of their audience, and the audience for print generally, as 'the Public', a broad, educated readership who wished to cultivate a discriminating literary taste. According to the *Edinburgh*, a vast quantity of current publications, such as most 'biograph[ies] of private individuals', will rarely be worthy of print, and thus will fall beneath its notice.

The *Edinburgh* also espoused fixed standards of literary value, and thus committed itself to rooting out all books with 'defects of their execution'.[24] It opened its first literary review, of Southey's *Thalaba*, by unequivocally pronouncing its conservatism on matters of poetic taste: 'Poetry has this much, at least, in common with religion, that its standards were fixed long ago, by certain inspired writers, whose authority it is no longer lawful to call in question.'[25] This famous inaugural review – which also launched the *Edinburgh*'s harangue against 'a *sect* of poets', the Lake Poets – was to be relentlessly applied to all new modes of poetic expression, particularly those cultivated by Wordsworth and those associated with him.[26] Specifically, the *Edinburgh* claimed that this 'new school of poetry' 'constitutes, at present, the most formidable conspiracy that has lately been formed against sound judgment in matters poetical'.[27]

The *Edinburgh*'s promise to avoid notice of books 'destined to obscurity' was, however, on occasion tested by works that had achieved some success, even though the review thought they were unworthy of it. In its review of Wordsworth's *Poems in Two Volumes* in 1807, Jeffrey could not prevent himself from dismissively mentioning Barbauld's 'Washing Day', published a decade before, along with other poems that '[a]ll the world laughs at' but which, clearly, were not forgotten and could not be entirely ignored.[28] Samuel Jackson Pratt's *Bread, or, the Poor: A Poem*, first published in 1801, was a work that the reviewer also ridiculed, contemptuously imagining that it

> would be entirely forgotten before the First Number of this publication could issue from the press. As we profess to confine our criticisms to works which are likely to engage some portion of public attention, we did not feel ourselves called upon to quote metaphors which seemed doomed to quiet repose in a snuff-shop, or comment on similes which would be known only to the pastrycook.[29]

The reviewer admits, however, to being confounded by the interest taken in the poem by the reading public: the book had reached a third edition, with additions, by 1803. The *Edinburgh*, however, stood its ground, refusing to acknowledge any error in judgement. Instead, the review proceeds to quote mockingly from the work, and to dismiss those readers who had enjoyed it:

> Such are Mr Pratt's verses, which have been so fortunate as to find admirers; to whom we resign them, without farther commentary. Readers of Poetry, of equal discernment, we are informed, were to be found in former times: they therefore reflect no particular discredit upon the present age.
> 'Qui Bavium non odit, amet tua carmina Mævi,
> Atque idem jungat vulpes et mulgeat hircos'.[30]

The Latin quotation that closes the review provides a further gesture of derision and exclusion, and likely alludes to William Gifford's *The Baviad* (1791) and *The Maeviad* (1795), conservative satires against the poetry and drama of the day.[31]

Throughout these early numbers, the *Edinburgh* repeatedly evaluated titles based on their conjectured longevity. Its review of 'The Works of Lady M. W. Montagu' provides one example. Bestowing high praise on her letters, which 'have so long engaged the admiration of the public', the reviewer castigates her poetry, which 'is already consigned to that oblivion in which mediocrity is destined, by an irrevocable sentence, to slumber till the end of the world'.[32] Works originating in the private sphere, such as Lady Mary's poems and letters, are subject to particular scrutiny: her letters are worthy of print because of their vivacity and wit, whereas her poems, lacking the 'patient labour and application' required in the production of fine poetry, are not. By contrast, the *Annual*, in its review, lavishes praise on her poems, finding that Lady Mary's poetry 'partakes much of the character of her prose'.[33]

Demanding 'the genius of a Burns, or the originality of a Cowper'

Throughout its existence, the *Annual* asked not whether a work would endure but whether a reader found it 'agreeable', 'pleasing', 'amusing', 'delightful' or 'entertaining'. There is no talk in the *Annual*'s pages of an author 'address[ing] himself to more than one generation', as was a constant strain in the *Edinburgh*. From the publication of its first volume, the *Annual* set a modest standard for poets:

> Of the poetical productions [of the past year], none are first rate, and but a few can fairly lay claim to a reputation of longer duration than an almanack. If their composition has not entrenched on the more serious occupations of the authors, if they have remunerated the bookseller for his risk and expence, if the perusal of them has agreeably filled up a few leisure hours that might have been worse employed, they have been crowned with all of the success to which they could reasonably aspire.[34]

The *Annual*'s disagreement with the *Edinburgh* is not about whether many of the volumes they reviewed would survive beyond the season; they agreed that most would not. But for the *Annual*, this fact is not decisive. Rather, they offer a different definition of success: that poetry pleases, that it does not draw authors away from more serious pursuits and that it compensates the bookseller. The *Annual* thus supported the printing of a great deal of sociable verse (such as Montagu's), whereas the *Edinburgh* insisted that a different set of standards be met for print publication.

This contrast is apparent in a collection of poems with discernible sociable origins, Mrs Anne Hunter's (1741–1821) *Poems* of 1802. Hunter was the wife of a prominent Edinburgh physician and anatomist and an active participant in Bluestocking salon culture.[35] Prior to 1802, her poems and songs circulated primarily in manuscript, though she had published a handful of poems in periodicals as well as several well-received collections of songs and airs prior to the release of *Poems*.[36] Hunter had also provided composer Franz Joseph Haydn (1732–1809) with lyrics to a series of *Canzonettas* printed in 1794 and 1795, all of which were published anonymously or 'by a lady'.[37] Hunter's publication of a selection of her manuscript verse and songs in 1802 exemplifies the migration of sociable poetry into print at the beginning of the century. Dedicated to her son, an army captain recently returned from Gibraltar, *Poems* includes lyric poems 'consisting chiefly of Odes, Ballads, and Songs', with many occasional poems addressed to friends and her children.[38] In her dedication to her son, she describes the domestic nature of the verse and its circulation, writing, 'you are already acquainted with part of its contents; but there are some things in it which you have never seen', presumably because of his time spent abroad.[39]

Notwithstanding her popularity as a songwriter and her position in Edinburgh society, the *Edinburgh*, in a review written by Francis Jeffrey, dismisses her poems as forgettable:

> Upon the whole, we are of [the] opinion that this volume will scarcely carry down the name of its author to a very distant generation . . . Her verses are such as we might expect from half of our well-educated ladies, if poetry were to be taught, like music or painting, in the ordinary course of female instruction, and odes and elegies exacted at the boarding school with as much rigour as concertos and pieces in crayons.[40]

In this review, it is the female amateur whose foray into print is questioned, though, as we will see below, a similar position is taken with respect to Lord Byron's first publication, in which he is sternly counselled to confine his efforts to manuscript. The *Edinburgh* had no patience with the dilettante.

The *Annual*'s review of the same volume two months later reads almost as a direct rebuke to the *Edinburgh*, admonishing those who form unrealistically high expectations:

> They who are so unreasonable as to demand the genius of a Burns, or the originality of a Cowper, from every poet or poetess, who offers to the public the gifts of the muse, will be disappointed in ninety-nine cases out of a hundred, and in this among the rest. They who are satisfied with correct and pleasing sentiments, expressed in flowing and agreeable numbers; with pretty verse rather than fine poetry, – will thank Mrs Hunter for an hour's innocent amusement; and allow her book a deserved place on the dressing room table, or parlour window.[41]

For this reviewer, it is unreasonable to expect genius from 'from every poet or poetess, who offers to the public the gifts of the muse'. What matters is that poetry offers 'innocent amusement'. This review may have been written by Anna Barbauld, who, according to Mary Waters, wrote for the 'Belles Lettres' section, from which this review originates, in the early years of the *Annual* (this review was issued in the first volume).[42] This attribution is suggested because it echoes, in language and sentiment, Barbauld's 1810 introductory essay to *British Novelists*: '[Novelists] are condemned by the grave, and despised by the fastidious; but their leaves are seldom found unopened, and they occupy the parlour and the dressing-room while productions of higher name are often gathering dust upon the shelf.'[43]

The reviewer of Mrs Hunter's poems in *The Annual* (like Barbauld in *British Novelists*) praises writing that is actually enjoyed and read, as evidenced by the presence of these books in living spaces; they are not shut up on library shelves 'gathering dust'. The reviewer respects the choices made by the common reader and does not demand that a book please for decades or even years, or that it please scores of readers. The *Annual* expresses this view even more strongly in its review (possibly also by Barbauld) of W. Holloway's 'The Peasant's Fate' in the same inaugural volume, recommending the work only '[t]o that class of gentle readers who are capable of receiving entertainment from natural descriptions of common objects and characters, in easy flowing verse', and suggesting that readers 'who deem that unworthy of being read, which will instantly be forgotten' should look elsewhere.⁴⁴ That a book which could be instantly forgotten could still worthy of being read challenges the standards being articulated by the *Edinburgh*.

The *Edinburgh*'s obsession with assessing the likely endurance of a literary work is evident in its review of Walter Scott's epic poem *Marmion* in 1808. Here a poem written directly for print establishes a standard that is applied to the reception of all poetry. In his review of *Marmion*, Francis Jeffrey repeatedly chides the poet for his topical allusions and faddish settings, and implores him to address himself to future generations:

> His genius, seconded by the omnipotence of fashion, has brought chivalry again into temporary favour; but he ought to know, that this is a taste too evidently unnatural to be long prevalent in the modern world. Fine ladies and gentlemen now talk, indeed of donjons, keeps, tabards, scutcheons, tressures, caps of maintenance, portcullises, wimples, and we know not what besides; just as they did, in the days of Dr. Darwin's popularity, of gnomes, sylphs, oxygen, gossamer, polygynia, and polyandria. That fashion, however, passed rapidly away; and if it be now evident to all the world, that Dr Darwin obstructed the extension of his fame, and hastened the extinction of his brilliant reputation, by the pedantry and ostentatious learning of his poems, Mr Scott should take care that a different sort of pedantry does not produce the same effects. The world will never be long pleased with what it does not readily understand; and the poetry which is destined for immortality, should treat only of feelings and events which can be conceived and entered into by readers of all descriptions.⁴⁵

Jeffrey's central complaint is that Scott fails to address himself to 'immortality', as Jeffrey regards 'these allusions to objects of temporary interest, chiefly as instances of bad taste, and additional proofs that the author does not always recollect, that a poet should address himself to more than one generation'.⁴⁶ For Jeffrey, the key to seeking immortality is to address a future readership; Jeffrey also regrets the speed with which Scott turned out his tales, advising that '[h]e who writes for immortality should not be sparing of time'.⁴⁷ Finally, Jeffrey bemoans the 'epistolary effusions' that preface each of the cantos, for revealing the 'private feelings and affairs of the author' and expressing 'the most trite common places of politics and poetry'.⁴⁸

The *Annual*'s review of *Marmion*, although not entirely positive, demonstrates the very different set of literary values it endorsed. Overall, the periodical declares the poem to be 'an original, spirited, and entertaining poem' and notes that the space allotted in its review – eleven pages in a journal in which many reviews ran only a few lines – 'may serve in part to show our sense of its merits and importance'.[49] The review's chief objection to the poem is the carelessness of its versification, which is attributed (in a manner echoing the *Edinburgh*) to a rush towards publication:

> of its imperfections we have spoke with less reserve, because they appear to us rather the avoidable faults of haste and negligence at which the public has a right to be offended, than the pitiable failures of overtasked abilities, or the venial errors of an ill formed taste.[50]

The *Annual* also disliked *Marmion*'s introductory epistles, but for reasons entirely different than the *Edinburgh*. Whereas the *Edinburgh* objected to the personal nature of the poems, the *Annual* observed that the form was simply not Scott's métier:

> This kind of writing, would have been delightful in the hands of Cowper, but it will never answer with Mr. Scott. Sentiment must be the life of it, and he is not a poet of sentiment, but of action and manners.[51]

The *Annual*'s chief objection, therefore, is that Scott's poems were not executed with proper feeling. Such poetry can be 'delightful in the hands of' another, but Scott's genius occupies another realm:

> Carry him to the camp or the court, place before his eyes a battle, a festival, a hunting match, and he will know how to reflect back the busy scene upon the mind of his reader, with the truth, the spirit, the fine touches of life itself.[52]

The *Edinburgh*, as we have seen, explicitly concerned itself with the question of whether a particular poem is worthy of publication by asking if it had been addressed to a sufficiently large audience and indeed to posterity. It mounted attacks on occasional poetry as literary productions which, while in some cases worthy of being written, were rarely worthy of print. In this way, the *Edinburgh* assigned itself the task of evaluating whether a manuscript should pass from script into print. Repeatedly, the *Edinburgh* interrogates the decision to publish. Its review of the Revd J. Mant's *Poems* (1807) exemplifies its approach:

> though the poems evince (what is no small or vulgar praise) considerable powers both of describing and enjoying the pleasures of an elegant and virtuous retirement, yet we cannot help hint to Mr Mant, that we think he had more merit in composing than in publishing them. To write smooth verses is a very innocent amusement for a man of leisure and education, – and to read them in manuscript to his family or intimate associates, is also a very venial and amiable indulgence to vanity; – but to push them out into the wide world, is not altogether so safe or laudable a speculation; and, though we are happy to tell him, that we think his talents respectable, yet we feel it a duty to announce to him, that we have not been able to discern in his works any of the tokens of immortality; and to caution him not to put himself in the way of more unmerciful critics.[53]

As with Mrs Hunter's poetry, the mere fact that the poems are respectably executed and enjoyed by the poet's domestic circle does not alone justify them being 'push[ed] . . . into the wide world', a description characterising the act of printing as an act of physical aggression. For the *Edinburgh*, when a work is 'pushed' into the world, it subjects the author and his writing to scrutiny. 'Addresses to private friends, and the occurrences of private families', like Mant's and Hunter's poems, 'require', pronounces the *Edinburgh*, 'a very nervous lyre indeed to preserve them from the ridicule of a world, to whom their persons are uninteresting, and their characters probably unknown'.[54] Poems lacking a nervous (meaning 'vigorous, powerful, forcible; free from insipidity and diffuseness', *OED*) style are acceptable for scribal but not print dissemination. Thus the *Edinburgh* constructs print as a public and durable medium, confined to works that display 'tokens of immortality'.

One of the *Edinburgh*'s most notorious excoriations of manuscript poetry may be found in its 1809 review of Byron's first commercial print publication, *Hours of Idleness*. In his provocatively titled debut, Byron styled himself as a gentlemanly amateur, a mere dabbler (albeit one of noble birth) who expected neither profit nor praise from his writing. In addition, in what is surely one of the most outrageous broken promises in literary history, Byron swore that he would never again write for print.⁵⁵ His posturing proved too tantalising for the *Edinburgh*'s professional editors, who could boast for themselves very few unencumbered hours and who could not resist the urge to implore the young lord to abide by his promise. Writing anonymously, Henry Brougham eviscerates Byron, not necessarily for writing the poems, but for publishing them:

> that very poor verses were written by a youth from his leaving school to his leaving college, inclusive, this we will believe to be the most common of all occurrences; that it happens in the life of nine men in ten who are educated in England; and that the tenth man writes better verse than Lord Byron.⁵⁶

Echoing the dismissal of Mrs Mant's poems ('Her verses are such as we might expect from half of our well-educated ladies, if poetry were to be taught [to ladies]'), the *Edinburgh* accepts that men and women will compose and circulate verse in manuscript; it is the act of printing these poems that is questioned, even mocked. A review of James Montgomery's *The Wanderer of Switzerland* made a similarly derisive pronouncement, intoning that 'there is no mistake more gross or more palpable, than [in believing] that it requires any extraordinary talents to write tolerable verses upon ordinary subjects'.⁵⁷ Writing 'tolerable verses' is so easy and common, according to the *Edinburgh*, that publication can never be justified on these grounds alone. Indeed, the *Edinburgh* made routine 'protests, as we have always done, against the multiplication of needless quartos, and the publication of ordinary epistles'.⁵⁸

The *Annual* did not display the same hostility towards 'tolerable verses upon ordinary subjects', as we have seen in the review of Mrs Hunter's *Poems*. Similar sentiments to those found in the review of Hunter's *Poems* are expressed in Lucy Aikin's review of *Hours of Idleness*. Aikin warmly greets Byron's maiden publication: she reverses the judgement of the *Edinburgh*, asserting that 'the poems before us give proof of very promising talents'.⁵⁹ She praises the original compositions in particular, 'especially those which may be supposed to express the real sentiments of the writer'.⁶⁰ Overall, the review expresses tolerance for and encouragement of new writers:

> whenever a young nobleman shows himself disposed to employ his 'Hours of Idleness' in paying his humble devoirs to any of the Nine,

whether with or without success, we shall certainly be disposed to yield him all praise and honour.[61]

The key phrase, 'whether with or *without* success', demonstrates the willingness of the *Annual* to dispense with traditional markers of achievement. According to Aikin, most writers deserve respect and praise because 'the amateur, even the feeblest, of literature' promotes advantages 'both to himself and to society at large'.[62]

Aikin's belief that a social good arose from the writing *and* publication of even feeble literature permeates the reviews that appeared in the *Annual*. For example, although one reviewer spoke dismissively of the poems included in *The Poetical Register, and Repository of Fugitive Poetry for 1804*, she or he nevertheless concluded that 'if the world is content to pay for such wares, let the market by all means be abundantly supplied'.[63] This is not to say that the *Annual* never expressed concern about publication. In its assessment of George Hay Drummond's *Verses, social and domestic* (1802), for example, the reviewer takes the unusual step of suggesting that it may have been better not to have printed the poems:

> in the domestic and social circle, where every relative connexion of the author's was known, and every incidental allusion understood, we doubt not that they have given pleasure; but it would have been better, perhaps, for the credit of the author, if to that circle they had been confined.[64]

The reviewer also notes their highly conventional titles ('*To Laura, with a breast pin of hair; the grateful Robin; on a root house; acrostic, &c*'), the carelessness of the Latin translations, and the execrable nature of the French. The reviewer acknowledges unreservedly that the poems would have given pleasure in the circle in which they originated but questions of the act publication, though she does so in the mildest terms. Here we find that although both journals could scrutinise whether a given work should remain in manuscript, they engaged in these questions with varying degrees of frequency and intensity. In general, as we have seen, the *Annual* understood print as a medium that could serve small readerships as well as large, the present moment as much as some imagined future.

The *Annual's* embrace of new and middling writers was not without its challenges: 'there exists a class of writers', says one reviewer, 'who occasion no small trouble and perplexity to us periodical critics'. These are poets who subsist 'below the rank of *great poets*':

> To apportion to each of these his due share of applause and censure, encouragement and reproof; to discriminate between the rude vigour of untutored genius, and the cold extravagance of labouring mediocrity; between lively ignorance which seeks to learn, and dull conceit that never can be taught – is certainly no easy task.[65]

One solution devised by the *Annual* was to repudiate absolute judgements and defer to readers, for ultimately it was up to '[e]ach individual reader [to] determine for himself what qualities he most requires in verse, or best can do without'.[66] Here the reviewer establishes ethical limits on criticism to shape public opinion, offering a counterpoint to the more authoritarian style of the *Edinburgh*. The *Annual*'s deference to the reader becomes evident in their struggle to evaluate verse collections; their strategy again is to leave it up to the reader: 'Poetical selections are so romantic a matter of individual taste, accidental association, and often mere whim, that there is no arguing the matter.'[67] In this review of *The Chaplet*, the critic explains that while she might have made a different selection of poems, this did not entitle her 'to call it a bad one . . . all the blame which we can lay on the anonymous collector is that of having gathered daisies and crowfoot and hawthorn, when with nearly the same trouble he might have culled roses and hyacinths and myrtle'.[68] The mildness of this metaphor intimates the *Annual*'s resistance to casting harsh judgements, so unlike the bold dismissals found in the pages of the *Edinburgh*.

The *Edinburgh*'s review of another verse collection, Southey's *Specimens of the Later English Poets* (1807), provides another instance of the two publications' sharp disagreements. Southey had adduced another botanical metaphor to explain his selection process: 'My business', he explained, 'was to collect specimens as for a *hortus siccus* [herbarium, or collection of preserved plant specimens], not to cull flowers as for an anthology'.[69] To the *Edinburgh*, this was an unsatisfying method: 'The nominal English poets have been extended in number beyond all toleration, by the ignorance, the bad taste, or the avarice of those who have edited their works for profit.'[70] The review objected that, 'if every writer, good, bad, and indifferent, was to be haled into his system of dry gardening, we wonder that the list was so narrow'.⁷¹ The reviewer also could not help pointing out Southey's apparent disdain for the very specimens he had selected, which he

> seems to produce ... with no satisfaction to himself. The prefatory notices are generally, though not undeservedly, expressive of contempt for the miserable bard of whom he tosses us a morsel. Nor is this all: the former and the future reader seem to be sneered at, from the implied conjecture, that, as this has pleased so many fools foregoing, it may probably impose on as many admirers in the time to come.⁷²

The contradiction the reviewer observes – that Southey adopts an undiscriminating method for selecting poems but is unable to stop himself from criticising the very poems he has chosen – rehearses in many ways the problem Southey himself faced in reviewing for the *Annual*, a point to which I will return.

On rare occasions, the *Edinburgh* could summon praise for occasional poetry, but it was only after careful scrutiny of the author's motivations in printing his verse. It found the second edition of James Mercer's posthumous *Lyric Poems* acceptable, first, because Mercer was honourably employed in the defence of his country for much of his life and therefore did not pursue poetry as a profession, and second, because he himself did not have a hand in its printing:

> Though the far greater part of his time had been dedicated to the acquisition of knowledge, yet his native modesty appears to have repressed the ambition of communicating to the world the fruits of his studies; and though the correctness of his taste enabled him to contribute very valuable aid to the literary undertakings of others, it does not appear that he ever seriously employed himself in writing for the public eye. The little collection of poems which has appeared under his name, cannot be regarded as an exception. They are obviously the effusions of a man of sensibility and cultivated mind, rather than the anxious efforts of a poet, ambitious of extended or permanent fame: they seem to have been originally destined to float within the circle of private friendship; and their publication appears rather to have been permitted than sanctioned by the ingenious author.⁷³

The *Edinburgh* scrutinises the role Mercer played in bringing about the publication, and he is absolved for having merely acquiesced to it. The *Annual* speaks highly of the volume too, but tellingly makes no mention of the circumstances of the volume's publication or of its author's career.[74] It is easy to see how judgements like the *Edinburgh*'s may have prompted authors to dissemble when describing, in their prefatory materials, the circumstances leading to the publication of their work.

A final contrast emerges in their respective analyses of the nation's poetry. Throughout its volumes, the *Annual* delivers enthusiastic encomiums to literary progress. In its review of Joanna Baillie's *A Series of Plays*, notice is frequently taken of the improvements in 'most departments of polite literature': 'good writing upon every subject', declares one reviewer, 'is more frequently to be met with, than it was some centuries ago'.[75] Poetry in particular is singled out. The *Annual*'s 1805 summation in the headnote to its chapter on poetry reviews expounds that 'comparing our modern verse-writers with those who lived a century ago, it is impossible not to be struck with the vast superiority of the former over the latter in all that relates to the mechanical and musical part of poetical composition'. 'In our opinion', the article continues, 'no age of British literature has been so favourable to the production of excellent poetry as the present is: the degree of encouragement is greater than at any former period'.[76] For the *Annual*, the increased number of poets and of poetry has been a boon, bringing advantages, in Lucy Aikin's words, 'both to [the poet] himself and to society at large'.[77]

The *Edinburgh* disavows this narrative of improvement. The reviewers constantly chastise poets for failing to live up to their potential, and they relish bidding poets farewell or washing their hands of them. We have seen how in 1808 it warned Scott to 'take care that a different sort of pedantry [in his poetry] does not produce the same effect' it had on Erasmus Darwin's. Although the *Edinburgh* later reversed itself with respect to Byron, in 1809 it declared itself fortunate that his poems are 'the last we shall ever have from him'.[78] Of Southey, in 1810, it stated that 'none has ever "made these rich gifts poor"' to the same extent, by failing to exercise the talents he had been given.[79] Similar complaints were lodged against Coleridge, who was 'always promising great things . . . and performs nothing',[80] and Wordsworth, about whom the *Edinburgh* declared in 1814: 'The case of Mr. Wordsworth is, now we perceive, manifestly hopeless; and we give him up now as altogether incurable, and beyond the power of criticism.'[81] With so many poets failing to achieve what was expected of them, and with so many poems unworthy of publication being printed, the *Edinburgh* reached the inevitable conclusion that literature was in a dangerous state of decline.

Private Memoirists and 'Book-Making Ramblers'

In two other genres – memoirs and travel writing – the *Edinburgh*'s characteristic severity and the *Annual*'s usual leniency prevail. Here the reviews continue to probe the nature and circumstances of publication, though once again with different force and emphasis. In addition to questioning the print-worthiness of the 'ordinary epistles' being published in abundance, the *Edinburgh* early on signalled its distaste for memoirs, with its opening 'Advertisement' declaring itself opposed, in principle, to the publication of 'the biography of private individuals'.[82] Objecting both to memoirs penned by relations, who were thought invariably to be partial to their subjects, and to autobiography, especially if published during the author's lifetime, it left a very small opening for biographies of public figures.[83] The *Edinburgh* allowed these biographies because they addressed 'the Public', and not merely a small group of readers, the friends (or enemies) of the author (in the case of autobiography) and subject (in the case of a biography). In its review of Dugald Stewart's *Account of the Life and Writings of William Robertson* (1803), the reviewer declares that 'the public is wholly unconcerned' in the lives of 'an individual, who is known only to the private circle of his friends'.[84] The *Edinburgh*'s critics condemn what they believe to be the too frequent instances when 'the feelings of friends, we mean their silly and preposterous vanity, induce them to print (they perhaps cannot so easily publish) a narrative of the deceased's life'.[85] Here the *Edinburgh* invokes the distinction between printing, paid for by the author, and publishing, financially underwritten by the publisher, as a means of insulting the author who self-publishes. In making this distinction, however, the *Edinburgh* suggests that finding a commercial publisher willing to take on a work provides some measure of the work's merit.

The *Annual*, as we have seen, took a different attitude to publication, accepting that many works were 'printed by the author', and that in most cases no harm and even some good was done. The *Annual*, furthermore, seemed to understand that although bookselling was a commercial activity, it was worthwhile for books to be published even if their sale only 'remunerated the bookseller for his risk and expence'. When the *Annual* intervened to question a decision about publication, it usually did so on narrower grounds. For example, it objected to *The Memoirs of the Life of Mrs. Elizabeth Carter* (1807) having been printed in quarto: 'It is certainly desirable that memoirs of eminent and exemplary persons should be written, but ... those of Mrs Carter, whose life was singularly barren of incident, might have been comprised in a moderate octavo.'[86] An expensive quarto format clearly implied importance and endurance beyond what her *Memoirs* could justify. The *Annual* also advised authors to be cautious about printing a second edition, acknowledging that, for many works, one edition would be sufficient to meet demand. One *Annual* critic praised James Woodhouse's *Love Letters to my Wife* as 'do[ing] credit to the feelings, as well as the wife to whom they are addressed, as of the author himself', but advised the author not to print a second edition until he was certain the demand would warrant it.[87] For the *Edinburgh*, the failure of a work to reach a second edition might itself be indicative of failure.

Travel writing was another genre that was subject to heavy scrutiny by the literary reviews. The *Edinburgh* reviewed a great number of travel narratives; as Massimiliano Demata notes, this is likely because the genre allowed for reflections on global trade and politics. As a result, the review regularly 'attacked the superficiality of those who published accounts lacking scientific data or indeed any practical utility'.[88] Sir John Carr, a prolific author of travel accounts, was ridiculed for his inclusion of a 'variety of particulars so little interesting to the generality of mankind'.[89] At the same time that the *Edinburgh* objected to printed books financed by the author, it also expressed its vexation at writing driven by profit. Its review of Kotzebue's 1806 *Travels to Italy* disparaged the author as being

> true to the character of the literary German, [who] only lives to print. We doubt if either any thing has of late years happened to him in life, or any idea has entered his mind, without a corresponding movement of his pen. Nothing flops by the way; nothing is treasured up for reflection or correction; and, that anything should be written down without coming to the press, is a case not to be supposed.[90]

In its review of Kotzebue's *Travels to Paris*, which came out the year before, the *Edinburgh* meted out similar condemnation, railing against '[t]he rapid communication of ideas which results from the art of printing', which allowed a book to be written, printed, translated, circulated and reviewed within months of the completion of his travels. The overall complaint was against the book as 'a commodity so quickly raised' and 'calculated only for immediate consumption'.[91] This was a common strain of invective running throughout the pages of the *Edinburgh*, one that it also directed against booksellers, 'who will sell whatever can be wire-wove and hot-pressed', and who are reproached for transforming slight texts into multi-volume tomes in order to make money.[92] It is this species of criticism that the Shelleys anticipate in pre-emptively defending the publication of their tour.

The *Annual* applied a very different standard to its assessment of travel writing. They find Kotzebue's travel narrative of Paris 'amusing and lively', even whilst acknowledging that it was written rapidly and for the press. In speaking of his quick passage from Berlin to Switzerland, the review speaks of how 'Kotzebue popped his head out of the carriage every now and then, and if any thing chanced to strike his fancy, it went into his pocket-book, and was, in all likelihood, transferred verbatim to his proof-sheets.'[93] Yet for this reviewer, the haste with which the book was written and the palpable commercial aims of Kotzebue's travels do not preclude it from being of interest. However, even the *Annual* could have its patience tested: in reviewing Kotzebue's Italian tour of the following year, he is finally denounced as a trifler, as pert and arrogant. Still, the reviewer acknowledges that the writer is 'a man of genius', and though '[i]t would cost us no trouble to select other [examples from the work that are] equally silly, but it is an ungrateful task to censure – we take no delight in it'.[94] The *Annual* again gestures towards an ethical position in its reviewing work, seeking out what is 'curious and interesting' and refraining from outright attack.

In its treatment of memoirs and travel writing (as well as poetry and other genres, as we have seen), the *Edinburgh* insisted that printed writing address and appeal to 'the Public'. Somewhat ironically, it singled out for particular mockery many works that appeared to be written directly for a public readership, describing them as crass and mercenary. The line of attack had appeared in its first issue, in the *Edinburgh*'s review of Southey's *Thalaba*: 'It is impossible', claims the reviewer, 'to peruse this poem, with the notes, without feeling that it is the fruit of much reading, undertaken for the express purpose of fabricating some such performance.'[95] Echoing its accusations against Kotzebue and Carr, the review condemns the poet's single-minded pursuit of print: 'When [Southey] had filled his common-place book, he began to write, and his poem is little else than his common-place book versified.'[96] Here the allegation is that manuscript culture has been perverted: common-placing, a tradition central to manuscript culture for the purposes of improving the compiler, now serves no other purpose than as copy for the press. In these ways, the *Edinburgh* sought to establish standards both for print and for print authorship – rejecting both the amateur and the hack. The *Annual* accepted as natural and conducive to the public good the transition of social manuscripts into print, and it also raised no alarm at books being written manifestly for the press. It accepted writers seeking to print (or publish) their works, encouraged amateurs and professionals alike and, in contrast to the *Edinburgh*, refused to investigate the careers of its authors and their motivations for publication.

Furnishing Useful Hints to the Writer

The *Annual* understood that literary pursuits in many if not most cases would not constitute the career of the writer. It asked only that 'composition has not entrenched on the more serious occupations of the authors'.[97] To the extent that the *Annual* took a more personal interest in its authors, reviewers adopted the role of mentors. 'Our critical duty', one reviewer explains, 'in general has two distinct objects: – to afford useful information to the public, respecting the actual merit of a work, and to furnish useful hints to the writer, for the future improvement of his literary manufacture.'[98] The *Annual* thus showed sensitivity to the feelings of authors, taking its ethical responsibilities to them seriously, commenting directly on the duties of reviewers, perhaps as a direct reprimand to the scorched-earth reviewing style of the *Edinburgh*. Reviewers frequently remind readers that since criticism operates upon 'those productions of human intellect which peculiarly distinguish highly cultivated societies', and exerts a 'powerful influence . . . on the public taste', reviewers were under certain obligations: to be impartial and honourable, to defend judgements with evidence drawn from the text in question, and, presumably, not from the private character of the author, and to refrain from abuse.⁹⁹ Thus one reviewer, as we have seen, felt it 'an ungrateful task to censure – we take no delight in it'.

The *Annual* even went so far, on one occasion, to apologise for any 'blamable impatience of temper' that may have appeared in some of its earlier numbers.¹⁰⁰ It is almost certain that the author of these intemperate reviews, of which there are a few and which stand apart from the others for their harshness, was Robert Southey. Southey had been a regular contributor in the first few years of the *Annual*, but he and the Aikins were often at odds about reviewing protocols (and the pay offered by the *Annual*), and this bitterness carried forward even decades later. When Southey's *Life and Correspondence* appeared in 1850, it included several derisive comments about the *Annual* and its editor, Arthur Aikin: that the *Annual* paid too little, and that '*King Arthur* [an allusion to Aikin's supposed imperiousness as editor] cut out what was displeasing to the booksellers'.¹⁰¹ Lucy Aikin's indignation at these remarks prompted her to publish a rebuttal in the *Gentleman's Magazine*, which had repeated Southey's allegations in its review of Southey's *Life* in June 1850. In a letter to the editor, Aikin points out, first, that the *Annual* was owned by Longmans, and that they alone set the terms of remuneration, and second, that Southey's reviews were edited to bring them into conformity with the principles and style of the *Annual*, which emphasised courteousness and forbearance:

> The 'many editorial tricks' imputed by Mr. Southey to Mr. Arthur Aikin consisted merely in the exercise of the just authority of his office to cut short digressions, and occasionally to strike out remarks made by Mr. Southey in that spirit for the display of which so much scope was afterwards allowed in other quarters [here, she implicitly references Southey's contributions to the *Quarterly Review*, a journal founded in 1809 that emulated the assaultive style of the *Edinburgh*]. His own interference never went further with respect to articles sent him; he allowed of *none* on the part of the proprietors.¹⁰²

That Southey appears to have misapprehended Aikin's editorial interventions, believing them to be motivated by a wish to please the booksellers as opposed to a desire to implement a more humane reviewing policy, may speak to how exceptional the *Annual's* reviewing principles had already become.

One of the procedures the *Edinburgh* used to evaluate the merit of a publication was to ask whether the author could be said to have used his or her time wisely in its creation. As William Christie has noted, the *Edinburgh* often engaged in 'animated speculation ... about the conditions and motivations for authorship', particularly on the part of authors whom they believed could have been better occupied.[103] Its review of John Thelwall's 1801 collection *Poems Written Chiefly in Retirement* provides a singular example:

> Literature opens so obvious and so pleasant a way to distinction, to those who are without the advantages of birth or fortune, that we need not wonder if more are drawn into it, than are qualified to reach the place of their destination. The task of ministering to the higher wants and more refined pleasures of the species, being both more dignified and agreeable than that of supplying their vulgar necessities, multitudes are induced to undertake it without any great preparation; and the substantial business of life is defrauded of much valuable labour, while the elegant arts are injured by a crowd of injudicious pretenders. The gradations by which increasing luxury accomplishes these seductions are sufficiently distinguishable. Ploughboys and carpenters are first drawn into the shops of mercers and perfumers, and into the services of esquires, baronets, and peers; the runaway apprentice next goes upon the stage; hair-dressers and valets write amatory verses; coffeehouse waiters publish political pamphlets; and shoemakers and tailors astonish the world with plans for reforming the constitution, and with *effusions of relative social feeling*.[104]

This passage expresses fear of the 'multitudes' entering print, and condemns their lack of 'preparation' (i.e., education), offering a distinct (and possibly intentional) allusion to Burke's infamous 'swinish multitude' passage from *Reflections on the Revolution in France*.[105] These sentiments are similarly applied in a review of Kotzebue's *Travels in Italy*, where the reviewer laments 'the multitude of strong men, who are withdrawn from the more useful and lucrative employments of common industry, to share the miserable pittance of the literary labourer'.[106] Clearly, the contributors to the *Edinburgh* felt a need to regulate entry into print, restricting it to an intellectual and professional elite.

According to Michael Scrivener, Francis Jeffrey was 'attacking self-taught writers in general by attacking Thelwall', in passages such as the following:

> Our author probably is not the first who has spoiled a good tradesman, by an unlucky ambition of literary or political glory; but he is the only

one we recollect who has left a minute and authentic record of the steps of his transformation . . . In every page of this extraordinary Memoir, we discover traces of that impatience of honest industry, that presumptuous vanity, and precarious principle, that have thrown so many adventurers upon the world . . . [107]

For the *Edinburgh*, these men should not abandon their proper station in life to seek laurels that are beyond their reach; rather, they should continue to provide the 'vulgar necessities' for their betters:

> After selling two thousand copies of his book, and lecturing on politics to crowded and intelligent audiences, we are afraid there is no great probability of Mr Thelwall submitting to cut out cassimeres, or stich in buckram; we are persuaded that he was infinitely more useful and respectable in his old occupation, than those to which lately he has betaken himself.[108]

Thelwall (1764–1834) was a particular target not only because of his humble beginnings but also because of his radical beliefs, having been charged and imprisoned for – but ultimately acquitted of – treason, for allegedly conspiring against the government in his lectures for the London Corresponding Society. After he was cleared of these charges in 1794, Thelwall emerged as a radical hero. Moreover, his associations with Wordsworth and Coleridge would not have ingratiated him to the *Edinburgh*. So outraged was Thelwall by Jeffrey's review that he launched a pamphlet war, printing, in 1804, a 131-page attack on his abusers. And he would not be the last to do so: Byron responded to the attack he suffered in the pages of the *Edinburgh* in 1809, with *English Bards and Scotch Reviewers*.[109]

One of Thelwall's counter-attacks was to point out that *Poems Written Chiefly in Retirement*, though printed, was not a work of 'general publication', raising the distinction that the *Edinburgh* had made between works printed and published, but in his own defence.[110] Quoting from the review's opening advertisement, Thelwall wonders why a periodical committed to 'the principle of selection' would bother to take notice of 'a work that has never been regularly announced in the London papers; and which, in its present form, it was not the intention of the author ever to have so announced'. He explains that the poems were printed 'in compliance with the solicitations of some friends' and that 'all the publicity that was given to the book, was an occasional notice at the bottom of the advertisements of my lectures, in the provincial towns that I visited'.[111] Thelwall thus contends that *Poems Written Chiefly in Retirement*, as a work not addressed to 'the Public', should not have been subject to the review's attentions.[112] The *Edinburgh*, however, insisted that print alone, however financed and whatever audience was imagined, inevitably 'put [authors] in the way of more unmerciful critics'.[113] According to Michael Scrivener, the result of the battle was a draw: Thelwall was successful enough to renew his elocution business; and Jeffrey succeeded in diminishing Thelwall's literary prospects.[114] The one unequivocal success for the *Edinburgh* was the rejection of Thelwall's claim for a realm of sociable print, shielded from the scrutiny of reviews. At the very least, Thelwall believed that reviews could acknowledge the range of potential audiences that print enabled, the very understanding that the *Annual* cultivated. The *Edinburgh*, however, would have none it; for them, print was essentially and inevitably a public medium; although never stated explicitly in this review, the *Edinburgh* had one solution for authors who wished to protect themselves from the reviews, which was not to print their writing.

Conclusion

Even though in nearly every respect the reviewing practices of the *Annual* stood in stark opposition to those of the *Edinburgh*, there is one area in which they found common cause: the novel. Their shared response is not to be found in the quantity of reviews – the *Edinburgh*, as we have seen, was greatly outstripped by the *Annual* in the number of novel reviews it published. However, in its first issue the *Annual* made an immediate exception to its promise to review everything, specifically excluding 'the innumerable volumes of novels and romances that are continually issuing from the press', on the grounds that many of them 'furnish[ed] no proper subjects of criticism'.[115] As a result, the two reviews converge in their frustrations over the proliferation of novels.

Both the *Annual* and the *Edinburgh* frequently adopted a scornful attitude towards fiction, much like the reviewers Austen refers to in *Northanger Abbey*, who 'abuse such effusions of fancy at their leisure, and over every new novel . . . talk in threadbare strains of the trash with which he press now groans'.[116] It complained that many novels tend 'to debilitate the minds, and loosen the morals, of our youth of both sexes'.[117] While most novels were dismissed as so many 'loads of trash', or as containing 'much sickening absurdity',[118] the *Annual* was quick to acknowledge that there were many

> able writers [who] have had recourse to the composition of novels of an opposite tendency, and we are happy to find have displayed equal skill, and excited equal interest, in the defence, as others have in the violation of the laws of morality, and the dictates of sound sense.[119]

It stood ready to praise worthy novelists such as Walter Scott (1771–1832), Amelia Opie (1769–1853), and Maria Edgeworth (1768–1849). Once again the *Annual* placed its faith in readers, for

> [a] bad novel was never known to retain its popularity long: . . . it is read and thrown upon the shelf, neglected, forgotten, or despised. We think highly of the public feeling and the public taste: many of our old novels which illustrate the manners of the times, which awake the sensibilities of the reader, which excite to heroic deeds, or lead to the cultivation of gentler and more peaceful virtues, are still read by the rising generation with interest and delight.[120]

When the *Edinburgh* meted out praise for a work like Amelia Opie's *Simple Tales*, it did so by admiring her stories for *seeming* not to have been written for the press:

> There is something delightfully feminine in all Mrs. Opie's writing; an apparent artlessness in the composition of her narrative, and something which looks like want of skill or practice in writing for the public, that gives a powerful effect to the occasional beauties and successes of her genius.[121]

The paradoxical nature of the *Edinburgh*'s position becomes apparent: writing commercial fiction is generally impermissible, unless the composition appears 'artless'. In other words, 'writing for the public', perhaps especially by women, is acceptable only when it appears not to have been; Charlotte Smith's authorial presentation in the *Elegiac Sonnets* seems to perfectly anticipate this strain of criticism.

As has been shown throughout this chapter, the *Annual* refused to prescribe how literary works should be circulated, accepting that author-financed publications, small print runs, diverse publication formats, selective distribution outlets and complex systems of referral and recommendation allowed printed books to be disseminated to those who wished to read them. By refusing to neglect or denigrate authors who achieved neither commercial nor critical success, the *Annual* supported the literary marketplace that in fact prevailed in the period, one in which print publication need not be financed by a publisher nor supported by a large readership. Further, the *Annual* did not seek to draw rigid boundaries between what was suitable for print and what was better confined to manuscript circulation; in fact, it celebrated a print marketplace that seamlessly absorbed writing originating in sociable exchange, and embraced literary works that were always destined for print. The *Annual* thus acknowledged and promoted what cultural economists refer to as a 'long tail': a market for cultural commodities that does not attract large audiences or sales but nevertheless serves the interests of various and diverse communities of writers and readers.

In our current technological moment, the long tail in cultural commodities has enjoyed a resurgence, enabled by online marketplaces and digital technology. This market thrives not by the sale of blockbusters, but by satisfying demand for less popular cultural goods: the so-called 'tail' of the market, where many cultural products exist but are consumed by the few.[122] Paul Duguid has termed this process one of 'demassification', by which 'socially complex technologies can be made not just for broad masses of people, but for small groups and individuals'.[123] In the Romantic period, print was becoming a mass medium. In fact, the *Edinburgh* was an early example of print's massification, with the review achieving an unprecedented degree of market penetration: by 1805, it was printing 5,000 copies of each issue, and this rose to 7,000 in 1807, 9,000 in 1809 and 13,000 by 1815.[124] A market dominated by the 'head', by popular items selling in larger quantities, like the books the *Edinburgh* promoted and like the *Edinburgh* itself, represents a very different cultural economy than a long tail. There was no reason that the print marketplace could not be both, and indeed, during this period the book trade supported the production of both extremely popular and relatively unpopular works. But the *Edinburgh*, through its aggressively selective and hostile reviewing style, sought to construct literary print as properly residing in the head, not the tail.

In the final volume of the *Annual*, the editor celebrates the abundance of literary print as evidence of progress. The editor observes that '[t]he history of literature is the history of the human mind', and declares that '[t]he works to the review of which the present volume has been devoted, yield us the satisfactory assurance that our national literary career is progressive'. Moreover, notwithstanding that

> the whole continent of Europe has been convulsed by political occurrences ... the love and the pursuit of knowledge have continued undiminished, and to extend its sphere of operation and of enjoyment, have been unremitting, and to an almost unprecedented degree successful and triumphant.[125]

For the *Annual*, the proliferation of print augured the spread of knowledge and pleasure, whereas for the *Edinburgh*, it signalled the degeneration of culture. Whether or not the *Edinburgh*'s dim view of literary progress prevailed, their conception of print as a public medium did. But this conception of print, however influential it became, was strongly opposed and far from inevitable.

The next three chapters present author-based case studies as a means of investigating these ongoing debates about script and print. The chapters examine how three very different authors – Anna Barbauld, Lord Byron and Jane Austen – confronted these shifting attitudes towards what was believed to be requisite for print. Their encounters are manifest in a variety of ways; in the reluctance to print, an element of Anna Barbauld's poetic career; in the challenges faced when transforming sociable manuscript writing for print, a feature apparent in Byron's and Austen's manuscripts; and in the desire to maintain social audiences through manuscript circulation, an aspect that persists in the careers of all three authors, even after they were established print authors.

Notes

1. 'Review of *Sibylline Leaves*', *Monthly Review*, p. 33.
2. 'Review of *Hours of Idleness*', *Edinburgh Review*, p. 287.
3. Johns, *Nature of the Book*, p. 2.
4. Anna Barbauld and John Aikin, *Evenings at Home*, I: 1.
5. Ibid. I: 3.

6. Mary Shelley and Percy Shelley, *History of a Six Weeks' Tour*, pp. iii–iv.
7. The termination date of the *Annual* is critical in another respect, marking the entrance of the *Quarterly Review*, founded to compete directly with the *Edinburgh* by providing a Tory alternative to the established journal, initiating a rivalry that shaped the *Edinburgh* as it moved into its second decade.
8. In the new waves of scholarly work on Romantic-era periodicals in the past decade, virtually no mention can be found of the *Annual*. The *Annual* is not mentioned in book-length studies of the period's reviews by David Higgins, *Romantic Genius and the Literary Magazine* (2005); Mark Parker, *Literary Magazines and British Romanticism* (2000); and Mark Schoenfield, *British Periodicals and Romantic Identity* (2009).
9. I am adopting Mark Parker's claim that periodicals developed distinct personalities and that 'there is a dynamic relation among contributions that informs and creates meaning' (*Literary Magazines*, p. 3).
10. 'Prospectus of a New Work, the first Volume of which will be published in early 1803 to be entitled "The Annual Review, or Register of Literature"', p. 3. Bound with *Annual Review* (British Library shelf mark 250.k.1).
11. 'Novels and Romances', *Annual Review* 1 (1803): 717.
12. The advertisement is bound with the second volume: *Annual Review* 2 (1804), British Library shelf mark 250.k.3.
13. 'Review of *Public Characters of 1801–1802*', *Edinburgh Review*, p. 122.
14. Ina Ferris, 'The Debut of *The Edinburgh Review*, 1802', n.p.
15. 'Advertisement', *Edinburgh Review* 1, no. 1 (October 1802): n.p.
16. Ibid.
17. Ibid.
18. Peter Garside, 'The English Novel in the Romantic Era', II: 16–17.
19. 'Advertisement', *Edinburgh Review* 3, no. 5 (October 1803): n.p. The editors indicated that they 'have in contemplation to enlarge it, in some of the succeeding Numbers, by the addition of very brief characters of such of the new works as have been perused, and are not thought to require a more extensive discussion', but no such enlargement was forthcoming.
20. [Advertisement,] *Annual Review* 3 (1804): [957]–[958].
21. Some of the chapters with which the *Annual* began (such as 'belles lettres') had to be divided and then subdivided again into various new categories (for example, philology, poetry and drama).
22. The *Edinburgh* had a grand total of 496 reviews for the entire period of the *Annual*'s existence. The annual breakdown of reviews reveals this pattern: in 1802, the *Edinburgh* published only one volume, premiering in October, with twenty-nine reviews; in 1803, ninety reviews; in 1804, only seventy-two reviews; in 1805, the downward spiral continued with only sixty-nine reviews; in 1806, sixty-six reviews; in 1807, fifty-seven

reviews; in 1808, fifty-six reviews; and finally, in 1809, it held steady at fifty-six reviews.
23. 'Advertisement', *Edinburgh Review* 1, no. 1.
24. Ibid.
25. 'Review of Robert Southey, *Thalaba, the Destroyer*', *Edinburgh Review*, p. 63. This sentiment is echoed in its later review of Wordsworth's *Poems in Two Volumes*, in which the collection is accused of being in 'open violation of the established laws of poetry': 'Review of *Poems in Two Volumes*. By William Wordsworth', *Edinburgh Review*, p. 231.
26. 'Review of Robert Southey, *Thalaba, the Destroyer*', *Edinburgh Review*, p. 63.
27. Ibid. pp. 83, 64.
28. 'Review of *Poems in Two Volumes*', *Edinburgh Review*, 218. 'Washing Day' was first published in the *Monthly Magazine* 4 (December 1797): 452.
29. 'Review of Mr Pratt, *Bread; or, the Poor. A Poem*', *Edinburgh Review*, p. 109.
30. Ibid. p. 112.
31. The lines may be translated as follows: 'Who hates not Bavius's Verse, may he love thine, O Maevius: And the same Fool may join Foxes in the Yoke, and milk He-goats.' *The Works of Virgil*, p. 16.
32. 'Review of *The Works of the Right Honourable Lady M. W. Montagu*', *Edinburgh Review*, pp. 512, 521.
33. 'Review of *The Works of the Right Honourable Lady Mary Wortley Montagu*', *Annual Review*, p. 507.
34. 'Belles Lettres and Miscellanies', *Annual Review* 1 (1802): 629.
35. Daniel F. Floyd, 'Anne Hunter's Poetry in Manuscript', pp. 411–13.
36. Her practices of manuscript circulation have been documented by her biographer and editor, Caroline Grigson, who has recently published approximately sixty-five poems for the first time (a number greater than the sixty poems Hunter printed in 1802): see *The Life and Poems of Anne Hunter* (2009).
37. G. T. Bettany, 'Hunter, Anne (1742/3–1821)'. See also Grigson, *Life and Poems*, p. 84.
38. Mrs John Hunter, *Poems*, p. v.
39. Ibid. pp. iii–iv.
40. 'Review of Mrs John Hunter, *Poems*', *Edinburgh Review*, p. 426. For the attribution to Jeffrey, see Elisabeth Schneider, Irwin Griggs and John D. Kern, 'Brougham's Early Contributions to the Edinburgh Review', p. 160. For an account of the *Edinburgh*'s reception of women writers more generally, see Stuart Curran, 'Women and the *Edinburgh Review*', pp. 195–209.

41. 'Review of *Poems*. By Mrs. John Hunter', *Annual Review*, p. 650.
42. On Barbauld's contributions to the *Annual*, see Mary Waters, '"Slovenly Monthly Catalogues"', p. 63.
43. Anna Barbauld, 'Essay on the Origins and Progress of Novel Writing', I: 1.
44. 'Review of *The Peasant's Fate: a Rural Poem* by W. Holloway', *Annual Review*, p. 652.
45. 'Review of *Marmion: a Tale of Flodden Field*. By Walter Scott', *Edinburgh Review*, p. 32.
46. Ibid. p. 32.
47. Ibid. p. 34.
48. Ibid. p. 35.
49. 'Review of *Marmion: a Tale of Flodden Field*. By Walter Scott', *Annual Review*, p. 472.
50. Ibid. p. 472.
51. Ibid. p. 472.
52. Ibid. p. 472.
53. 'Review of *Poems*. By the Rev. J. Mant', *Edinburgh Review*, pp. 170–1.
54. Ibid. p. 170.
55. George Gordon (Lord Byron), *Hours of Idleness*, pp. vii–ix.
56. 'Review of *Hours of Idleness*. By Lord Byron', *Edinburgh Review*, p. 285.
57. 'Review of *The Wanderer of Switzerland* by James Montgomery', *Edinburgh Review* 9, no. 18 (January 1807): 347–54.
58. 'Review of *An Account of the Life and Writings of James Beattie*. By Sir W. Forbes', *Edinburgh Review* 10, no. 19 (April 1807): 172.
59. 'Review of *Hours of Idleness* by Lord Byron', *Annual Review*, p. 530.
60. Ibid. pp. 529–30.
61. Ibid. p. 529.
62. Ibid. p. 529.
63. 'Review of *The Poetical Register for 1804*', *Annual Review*, p. 532.
64. 'Review of *Verses, social and domestic*. By George Hay Drummond', *Annual Review*, p. 670.
65. 'Review of *The Battle of Largs: a Gothic Poem*', *Annual Review*, p. 566.
66. Ibid. p. 566.
67. 'Review of *The Chaplet, a Collection of Poems*', *Annual Review*, p. 621.
68. Ibid. p. 621.
69. 'Review of *Specimens of the Later English Poets*', *Edinburgh Review*, p. 31.
70. Ibid. p. 36.
71. Ibid. p. 36.
72. Ibid. p. 31.
73. 'Review of *Lyric Poems*. By James Mercer, Esq.', *Edinburgh Review*, p. 473.

74. 'Review of *Lyric Poems* by James Mercer', *Annual Review*, p. 563.
75. 'Review of *A Series of Plays* by Joanna Baillie', *Annual Review*, p. 680.
76. 'Poetry', *Annual Review*, p. 535.
77. 'Review of *Hours of Idleness*', *Annual Review*, p. 529.
78. 'Review of *Hours of Idleness*', *Edinburgh Review*, p. 288.
79. 'Review of Robert Southey, *The Curse of Kehama*', *Edinburgh Review*, p. 429.
80. 'Review of S. T. Coleridge's *The Statesman's Manual*', *Edinburgh Review*, p. 446.
81. 'Review of Wordsworth's *The Excursion*', *Edinburgh Review*, p. 2.
82. 'Advertisement', *Edinburgh Review* 1, no. 1.
83. See 'Review of *The Works of Lady M. W. Montagu*', p. 507; 'Review of *Memoirs of Richard Cumberland: Written by Himself*', *Edinburgh Review*, p. 108. See also 'Review of *The Life and Posthumous Writings of William Cowper*', *Edinburgh Review*, which also rejects both 'the egotism of *confessions*, and the questionable narrative of a surviving friend, who must be partial, and may be mistaken' (pp. 64–5). It objects to the telling of his life through his letters, on the grounds that it 'requires so much room for its execution, and consequently so much money and so much leisure in those who wish to be masters of it, that it ought to be reserved, we conceive, for those great and eminent characters that are likely to excite an interest among all orders and generations of mankind' (p. 65).
84. 'Review of Dugald Stewart's *Account of the Life and Writings of William Robertson*', *Edinburgh Review*, p. 236. In 'Review of *The Works of Richard Owen Cambridge*', *Edinburgh Review*, it was argued that men like Owen 'generally receive their whole portion of fame in their life, and but seldom obtain any reversion of posthumous celebrity. Few are so fortunate as to have their scattered pieces collected into a handsome quarto' (p. 57).
85. 'Review of Dugald Stewart's *Account of the Life*', p. 236.
86. 'Review of *Memoirs of the Life of Mrs. Elizabeth Carter*', *Annual Review*. The *Annual* admonished Edward Jerningham (1737–1812) in slightly stronger terms, suggesting that had he 'contented himself with circulating in manuscript a few vers de societe, contributing occasionally to the vase at Bath Easton, and giving to the world his poems ... through the medium of the Gentleman's Magazine, he certainly might have escaped all criticism', but in printing so much he 'cannot expect to come off so easily': 'Review of *Poems and Plays* by Mr. Jerningham', *Annual Review*, p. 529.
87. 'Review of *Love Letters to my Wife*. By James Woodhouse', *Annual Review*, p. 596.

88. Massimiliano Demata, 'Prejudiced Knowledge: Travel Literature in the *Edinburgh Review*', p. 90.
89. Ibid. p. 91. Byron takes up this point explicitly in a deleted stanza in *Childe Harold's Pilgrimage*; see Chapter 4.
90. 'Review of Augustus Von Kotzebue, *Travels through Italy*', *Edinburgh Review*, pp. 456–7.
91. 'Review of Kotzebue's *Travels to Paris*', *Edinburgh Review*, p. 78.
92. 'Review of *An Account of the Life of Samuel Johnson*', *Edinburgh Review*, p. 436, in which the bookseller is accused of printing a manuscript (apparently snatched from the flames by Johnson's servant, contrary to his wishes) that should never have been made public. He is also accused of going beyond the usual stratagems to extend the length of a work, by 'eking out art, types, vignettes, and margins' to produce a volume from a very small number of manuscript scraps. Many other reviewers in the *Edinburgh* also complained of additions or prolixity as a way of puffing up works that should have been kept shorter.
93. 'Review of *Travels from Berlin, through Switzerland, to Paris, in the year 1804*', *Annual Review*, pp. 88, 83.
94. Review of *Travels Through Italy in the years 1804 and 1805*', *Annual Review*, p. 44.
95. 'Review of Robert Southey, *Thalaba*', p. 77.
96. Ibid. p. 78.
97. 'Belles Lettres and Miscellanies', *Annual Review* 1 (1803): 629.
98. 'Review of *Poems and Tales* by Miss Trefusis', *Annual Review*, p. 524. In her essay on Barbauld's contributions to the catalogue section of the *Monthly Review*, Mary Waters notes how she took her task seriously and often took 'the occasion of the review as an opportunity to educate the writer, and to offer suggestions or guidance' ('"Slovenly Monthly Catalogues"', p. 74).
99. 'Preface', *Annual Review* 3 (1804): iii.
100. Ibid.
101. 'Review of *Life and Correspondence of Robert Southey*', *The Gentleman's Magazine*, p. 611.
102. Lucy Aikin, 'Southey and "The Aikins": His Injustice Towards Mrs. Barbauld', *Gentleman's Magazine*, p. 26. The letter Aikin wrote to John Hunter, asking for his assistance with the insertion of the letter in the *Gentleman's*, is in the British Library: Add Ms 24864, ff. 14, 16.
103. William Christie, *The Edinburgh Review in the Literary Culture of Romantic Britain*, p. 22.
104. 'Review of John Thelwall, *Poems written chiefly in Retirement*', *Edinburgh Review*, p. 197.

105. This is Burke's exact quotation: 'Learning will be cast into the mire, and trodden down under the hoofs of a swinish multitude', *The Writings and Speeches of Edmund Burke*, VIII: 130.
106. 'Review of Augustus Von Kotzebue, *Travels through Italy*', p. 457.
107. 'Review of John Thelwall', p. 200; Michael Scrivener, *Seditious Allegories*, p. 280.
108. 'Review of John Thelwall', pp. 201–2. Thelwall had attempted several occupations prior to writing and lecturing, but the *Edinburgh* in this statement alludes to his abandoned apprenticeship as a tailor.
109. Byron, in *English Bards*, mistook Jeffrey as his attacker.
110. John Thelwall, *A Letter to Francis Jeffray*, p. vii. An anonymous defence was published as *Observations on Mr. Thelwall's Letter to the Editor of the Edinburgh Review* (1804), by either Jeffrey himself or a close friend, and Thelwall responded with *Mr Thelwall's Reply to Observations on Mr. Thelwall's Letter to the Editor of the Edinburgh Review* (1804). For a detailed analysis, see Scrivener, *Seditious Allegories*, pp. 277–82.
111. Thelwall, *A Letter to Francis Jeffray*, p. vii.
112. Thelwall also attacks Jeffrey's class politics and the personal insults levelled against him, pointing out that Jeffrey himself was the son of Scottish barbers.
113. 'Review of *Poems*. By the Rev. J. Mant', pp. 170–1.
114. Michael Scrivener, *Seditious Allegories*, p. 280.
115. 'Novels and Romances', *Annual Review* 1 (1803): 717.
116. Austen, *Northanger Abbey*, p. 30.
117. 'Novels and Romances', *Annual Review* 1 (1803): 717.
118. 'Novels and Romances', *Annual Review* 3 (1804): 542; 'Novels', *Annual Review* 7 (1809): xiii.
119. 'Novels and Romances', *Annual Review* 1 (1803): 717.
120. 'Review of *The Cottagers of Glenburnie* by Elizabeth Hamilton', *Annual Review*, p. 608.
121. 'Review of *Simple Tales*. By Mrs Opie', *Edinburgh Review*, p. 467. See Curran, 'Women and the *Edinburgh Review*', pp. 195–6, for his reading of the 'strained paternal kindness' that this review exhibited towards Opie.
122. Chris Anderson, populariser of the long tail, has provided multiple contemporary examples that establish the profitability of this business model today. For example, Amazon's online sales demonstrate that unpopular books, when combined, sell far more copies than bestsellers. See Chris Anderson, *The Long Tail: Why the Future of Business Is Selling Less of More* (New York: Hyperion, 2006). Preliminary findings suggest that booksellers of 200 years ago likewise sought profitability in

'the tail'. Richard Sher's analysis of 360 Scottish Enlightenment books, for instance, finds that a large majority, some 65 per cent of all titles, were neither popular nor enduring – with 28 per cent being 'modest sellers', selling two to three editions, and the largest group, some 37 per cent, being 'poor sellers', selling only one edition: *The Enlightenment and the Book*, p. 701.
123. Paul Duguid, 'Material Matters: Aspects of the Past and the Futurology of the Book', p. 84.
124. Lee Erickson, *The Economy of Literary Form*, p. 77; Massimiliano Demata and Duncan Wu, 'Introduction', in *British Romanticism and the Edinburgh Review*, p. 3.
125. 'Introduction', *Annual Review* 7 (1808): xiv.

Chapter 3

Anna Barbauld's Poetic Career in Script and Print

Anna Barbauld's status as a canonical poet is now beginning to approximate the success she enjoyed in her own lifetime. In the most comprehensive collection of women's poetry for the period, Paula Backscheider and Catherine Ingrassia's *British Women Poets of the Long Eighteenth Century* (2009), more lines of verse by Barbauld are included than of any of the other eighty female poets represented.[1] Barbauld's poems were highly regarded in her own day: one reviewer pronounced her *Poems* (1773) to be 'inferior only to the works of Milton and Shakespeare';[2] and, after her death, she was declared to be 'the first of English female authors; and we should find it difficult to name more than two or three modern authors of the other sex who can stand a comparison with her in both verse and prose'.[3] Her commercial success was also nearly unprecedented, with *Poems* reaching five editions by 1777 and a corrected sixth edition in 1792, more published editions than any of her female predecessors, aside from Mary Chandler (1687–1745).[4] Barbauld's poetic eminence was commemorated by a Wedgwood cameo in 1777 and by her inclusion in Richard Samuel's epic painting 'The Nine Living Muses of Great Britain', exhibited at the Royal Academy in 1779.[5] Yet Barbauld's astonishing rise to poetic fame followed the print publication of a slim volume of fewer than three dozen poems, first published in 1773, at the urging of her brother, with a nearly identical final edition appearing in 1792, more than three decades before her death.[6] Although she continued to write poems for the rest of her life, she could not be prevailed upon to print more than a handful of these, about sixteen, most of them in magazines and many of them without attribution. Overall, Barbauld elected to print just over a third, that is, fifty-three of her total output of 161 known poems.[7]

This chapter paraphrases Margaret Ezell: instead of asking, 'Why didn't Barbauld use print' for so many of her poems, it asks, 'What is she attempting to do?'[8]

Barbauld's career before the appearance of the 1773 *Poems* follows a conventional trajectory: her verse circulates in manuscript within widening circles, gaining appreciation, and then is collected and printed in a single-authored volume. What is unusual is what follows after the success of *Poems*, as may be seen graphically, in Plate 6, which categorises all of Barbauld's poems according to when and how they were printed; it discriminates between those poems that appeared in her book publications, those that appeared in magazines and collections, and, if in magazines or collections, whether with or without her consent. By noting when poems were printed, it establishes the quantity of poems printed during her lifetime and after. The orange bars include all poems printed by her in single-authored, signed volumes (namely those that appeared in *Poems* in the 1770s; *An Epistle to William Wilberforce* in the 1790s; *Eighteen Hundred and Eleven* in the 1810s; and authorised editions published by her nice, Lucy Aikin, after her death in the 1820s); the green bars represent poems she authorised for print in magazines and collections;[9] the red bars represent poems printed without her authorisation;[10] and the blue bars represent poems that were unprinted (the blue bars are slotted into the decades when the poems were first printed). Significantly, the blue bars, representing unprinted poems, are quantitatively much greater than all the other categories combined, comprising nearly two-thirds of her total known output of 161 poems. Most of the unprinted poems were published in the 1820s, in Lucy Aikin's *The Works of Anna Laetitia Barbauld* (1825) and *Legacy for Young Ladies* (1826); and then again in the 1990s, when William McCarthy and Elizabeth Kraft's *The Poems of Anna Letitia Barbauld* published twenty-three poems for the first time.

What this chart does not provide is information about composition history, though as best we can tell Barbauld wrote poetry in fairly measured quantities after her initial burst of poetic activity in the 1760s and 1770s. Further, because this graphic represents when a poem was published, it fails to quantify her prodigious use of manuscript circulation. Many of the poems printed in 1773 had previously circulated in manuscript, and the same is almost certainly true of many of the poems that were printed in periodicals (whether with or without her authorisation). From the surviving manuscript record, the nature of the poems themselves, and other external evidence, we can be confident that nearly all of the unprinted poems circulated in manuscript. The remainder of this chapter will offer several strategies for reading Barbauld's poetry not simply textually, but bibliographically. This chapter offers a variety of methods to establish the dissemination, sometimes extensive, of her poems within manuscript; it analyses the poems themselves to understand Barbauld's rationale for electing to print some of her poems and not others; and it explores Barbauld's attitude towards the unauthorised publication of her poetry.

Manuscript Culture and Barbauld's Poetry

Manuscript culture, a term developed by scholars of the sixteenth and seventeenth centuries, describes a method of textual reproduction and dissemination that occurs through the composition and circulation of copies. Certain material features of handwritten documents are indicative of manuscript culture: for example, fair or presentation copies, written in a neat hand with even lines and margins, with few corrections and alterations, are legible and hence easily read and copied by others. Further, they reflect a state of finality compatible with their being shared for the purposes of written or oral transmission. *Perdita Manuscripts, 1500–1700*, a digital collection of more than 230 manuscripts by women, with detailed descriptions of each, has created a rich set of genre designations that 'recogniz[e] the heterogeneity of most manuscripts'. Importantly, the editors distinguish between descriptions of the physical manuscripts themselves and the many unique genres that describe their contents: 'The editors [have] devised sixty-six manuscript type categories (such as account book and devotional book) and sixty-seven separate item-level genres, ranging from "Culinary writing" to "Vision".'[11] Many of the manuscript types and literary genres the editors identify disclose their social origins and functions.

Margaret Ezell, one of the leading scholars in the field of seventeenth-century manuscript studies, has advanced a model of social authorship in which literary production is embedded in a particular community, with writers and readers regularly exchanging roles in the creation and dissemination of handwritten texts.[12] Ezell (amongst other scholars) has noted the importance of manuscript circulation for women writers in particular – and not simply because print was feared, discouraged or otherwise unavailable to them. Rather, Ezell's archival work demonstrates that for many women, manuscript was the medium they purposefully chose, as best serving their particular needs and purposes. Barbauld provides a strong example of the persistence of manuscript culture through the end of the eighteenth century and into the early nineteenth century. Handwriting remained an important copying technology for some of Barbauld's major poetic forms: social and occasional verse, and satiric poetry. There is little evidence, contrary to Harold Love's assertion, that what was unprinted after 1800 lacked the quality requisite for publication. Consider just three of the poems that Barbauld did *not* print in her lifetime: 'To a little invisible Being who is expected soon to become visible' (100), 'Life' (126) and 'The Caterpillar' (133) – all three are amongst the most celebrated of her poems, as suggested by their frequent reprinting in modern anthologies of her work.[13]

To demonstrate Barbauld's engagement with manuscript culture, we must look beyond the manuscript record alone, which is, unfortunately, scant.[14] Of the 161 total known poems, there are manuscripts of forty-seven poems, only twenty-three of which are holographs. All surviving manuscripts, even autographs, are essentially fair copies. With no drafts, and with very few poems for which more than one copy exists (and with minor variants in these cases), a collative methodology (in which literary manuscripts of a single text may be compared) is not tenable for Barbauld, as it is with investigations of Byron and Austen, for whom there are manuscripts of a single text in multiple stages (Byron has many extant examples of his process, while Austen has only one). There is at least one example of Barbauld sharing her working drafts with others, but how common a practice this was, we do not know. The surviving manuscript record, a very small portion of what must have existed at one time, suggests that Barbauld may have only shared her poems when they were in a more finished, fair-copy state, but it is impossible to know for certain. There is, however, ample evidence that her poems, once in a more final state, circulated, sometimes very widely. Once her poems were in circulation, whether in script or print, she seems to have made only minor revisions. Her practices thus appear very different from those of a poet like Dorothy Wordsworth, who continued to tinker with poems long after their first composition.

Many of the poems that first appeared in print in *The Works of Anna Letitia Barbauld*, the 1825 collection edited by her niece, Lucy Aikin, have no surviving lifetime manuscripts (only six manuscripts from the poems first printed in *Works* survive).[15] The lack of an autograph copy of a poem first published in 1825 such as 'To a Little Invisible Being' does not, however, mean that it was written merely for Barbauld's own private amusement or edification. From the fact of its non-publication during her lifetime we can infer that Barbauld did not view the poem as suitable for a public readership, though it was obviously meant for the expectant mother and it may have circulated to others concerned with the unborn child. For Aikin to have published the poem, she, obviously, must have had a copy of it. What happened to this copy cannot be known. It is possible, as was common at the time, that the copy (and any transcript Aikin may have made) was destroyed upon publication; it may have been the case that Aikin preserved the manuscript, and passed it down, only for it to have been destroyed with the rest of Barbauld's papers during the Blitz. What we do know is that even the most private poems were written to be shared with others. The first two poems she wrote to her husband – 'To Mr. Barbauld, with a Map of the Land of Matrimony' (63) and 'To Mr. Barbauld, November 14, 1778' (66) – were addressed to and meant to be read by him (and she had the map itself, though not the poem, printed by Johnson in 1772). Of the two poems she wrote about her husband after his death ('Dirge' [116] and 'Dejection' [117]), she allowed her brother to read 'Dirge', evidently to show him how she felt about her husband.[16] That these poems were included by Lucy Aikin in the posthumous edition of Barbauld's *Works* further suggests that, though personal, they were not deemed (by those to whom Barbauld was closest) to have been too intimate or revealing for a public audience after the death of the subjects involved.

We might expect the four poems she wrote to and about her brother – 'To Dr. Aikin on his Complaining that she neglected him, October 20th 1768' (7), '[John Aikin]' (49), and the 'Verses Inscribed on a Pair of Screens' ('To Dr. A[ikin]' [104] and 'To Mrs. A[ikin]' [105]) – to have been meant for his (and the later his wife's) eyes only.

She published none of these poems, and Aikin included only the last three. The first poem, however, was not written for her brother alone, as it enjoyed wider circulation during her lifetime, presumably with her approval. The poem survives in two separate manuscript copies taken by friends of the family, evidence that Barbauld (or her brother, presumably with Barbauld's explicit or implied consent) showed the poem to others and allowed copies to be taken.[17] Likewise, 'Verses Inscribed on a Pair of Screens', given to John and Martha Aikin upon their departure from London for Stoke Newington in 1798, may, as household items, have been on display for visitors, the inscription of the poems on the screens being a form of publication itself. As housewarming gifts, the poems reflect upon and reinforce the domestic comforts provided by the screens themselves, securing comfort, peace, and health for the family in their new dwelling. For Barbauld, poetry was an instrument of sociability.

Once we move beyond Barbauld's immediate family – her husband and brother, the two individuals with whom she was most intimate – we find that most of her poems were oriented to an audience. Many of her poems were, like 'Verses Inscribed on a Pair of Screens', gifts or accompanied gifts ('To Mrs. P[riestley], with some Drawings of Birds and Insects' [3]; 'To a Lady, with some painted Flowers' [55]; 'To Mr. Barbauld, with a Map' [63]; 'Lines with a Wedding Present' [144]). She inscribed, or imagined inscribing, poems on various domestic items: on a new pocketbook presented to a pupil ('Verses written in the Leaves of an ivory Pocket-Book, presented to Master T[urner]' [11]); on the back of Joseph Priestley's coat of arms ('Verses written on the Back of an old Visitation Copy of the Arms of Dr. Priestley's Family, with Proposals for a new Escutcheon' [13]); in a lady's album ('Lines written in a young Lady's Album of different- coloured Paper' [150]); and on a marble used in a children's game of taw ('Written on a Marble' [78]). She wrote verse to be placed over a Chimney-Piece ('Lines placed over a Chimney-Piece' [72]) and on the entrance to an Ice-House ('Inscription for an Ice-House' [95]). She wrote poems in reply to requests for copies of other poems ('To Miss F. B. on her asking for Mrs. B[arbauld]'s "Love and Time"' [69] and 'To the Miss Websters, with Dr. Aikin's "Wish," which they expressed a Desire to have a Copy of' [86]). She wrote poems for, or about, her pupils ('Petition of a Schoolboy to his Father' [67]; 'Lines to be spoken by Thomas Denman, on the

Christmas before his Birthday, when he was four Years old' [74]; 'A School Eclogue' [79]; and for amateur theatrical performances ('Prologue to "The Man of Pleasure" by John Aikin' [29]; 'Prologue to the Play of Henry the Eighth. Spoken by a Warrington Student in his morning Gown' [30]; 'Epithalamium' [31]). Her hymns (Hymns I–V [33–7]) were likewise meant to be performed in a communal setting.

Although many of the poems described can be classified as occasional verse it is important to observe how many different kinds of occasions she wrote for; she was prompted to compose and present her poems to commemorate births (6, 100), birthdays (97), and weddings (31, 65) and to eulogise the dead (76, 103, 107); to introduce amateur theatricals (29, 30, 149); and to accompany the presentation of gifts (3, 84, 104, 105, 144). As the foregoing tally suggests, it is the rare poem that does not have an explicit or implied addressee (it is telling that the titles of well over thirty poems include the formulation 'To . . .' or 'Lines to . . .') or an occasion that marks it. Barbauld also wrote poems extempore and for fun, including riddles and 'bouts rimés'.[18] Such poems, capturing the sociable nature of Barbauld's verse, are almost by definition acts of what Ezell calls 'social authorship' and, but for the fact that we lack many of the original manuscripts, seem to belong to Donald Reiman's category of 'confidential manuscripts'. While we often lack direct evidence about how the manuscripts circulated, it seems that only an accident could have prevented a poem entitled 'To the Miss Websters, with Dr. Aikin's "Wish," which they expressed a Desire to have a Copy of' (86) from circulating as intended. This is one of a handful of Barbauld's poems, the title of which describes the activities of manuscript culture. Barbauld's use of inscription also grounds her poems within a domestic economy, as verse ornaments to household spaces (the ice house, the hearth) and household items (fireplace screens, children's marbles). Evidence as to the method of delivery of some of the poems, such as 'The Mouse's Petition' [19], which she cheekily left pinned to the bars of the mouse's cage; or 'On Mrs. P[riestley]'s Leaving Warrington' [1], which she, with both petulance and sorrow, tossed into their departing carriage, reminds us again that these poems were written for, and presented to, others – often in playfully dramatic ways. Barbauld used script as an intimate medium of sociability, ideally suited to communicate with her community of friends and family: at once personal and flexible, handwritten documents were capable of being produced and circulated with rapidity and ease amongst social networks.

It is difficult to find a poem that does not mark Barbauld as a profoundly social and occasional poet, a fact acknowledged by Lucy Aikin, who observed that her aunt 'could seldom excite herself to the labour of composition, except on the spur of occasion'.[19] Although a handful of surviving poems are genuinely fragmentary or incomplete, and a small number may have been deemed too trivial for publication, the vast majority of the nearly one hundred poems that were unprinted in her lifetime were not unworthy of print publication; indeed, many of them are her most celebrated poems today. By examining the poems she elected to print in 1773, and those she had written by that time but did not publish, we begin to understand what Barbauld was 'attempting to do' by circulating her poems in manuscript.

Poems up to 1773

Prior to 1773, Barbauld had written about sixty-two poems that we know of and can date to this period. At the end of 1772, she published thirty-three of these,[20] and of those only two autograph copies survive that could have predated the print version (they are holographs for two of her 'Characters', and the survival of these manuscripts is likely due to them forming part of a series). Yet, despite manuscripts of only two of the poems surviving, it is believed that many, if not all, of the verses that appeared in *Poems* circulated in manuscript between the students and tutors at Warrington Academy and beyond before they were published.[21] How can we establish the circulation of these printed poems in the absence of a manuscript record?

In part, as I have suggested above, we can deduce their circulation from the nature of the poems themselves, many of which were written for family members and friends and delineate a social circle. Barbauld made little effort to disguise and no attempt to eradicate these sociable traces when she printed a handful of these poems in 1773, a period, it should be noted, nearly thirty years before the *Edinburgh Review*, and its hostile attitude towards the publication of social verse, emerged. Nevertheless, even in the early 1770s,

Barbauld took a cautious approach to publication. In addition to six songs and five hymns that had been previously published,[22] Barbauld published twenty-two poems for the first time, seven of which explicitly name or address specific individuals associated with the Warrington community. Although Barbauld retains the names of public figures such as Elizabeth Singer Rowe (57) and Joseph Priestley (who is named in 'The Mouse's Petition'), she does elide or abbreviate other proper names to protect the identity of living individuals, using an apparently random mix of asterisks and dashes: 'The Invitation, To Miss B*****' (4); 'To Mrs P--------, with some Drawings of Birds and Insects' (3); 'To Miss R----, On her Attendance on her Mother at Buxton' (8). The dashes substituted for Mrs. P[riestley] and Miss R[igby] are precisely numbered, allowing for identification amongst a knowing audience (Miss B[elsham] is, however, one asterisk short). The volume is also geographically sited in the north-west of England through the dedication to the local peer, Lady Mary West, and the references to 'Warrington' in many of the poems. Finally, several poems specifically address the Dissenting milieu of Warrington Academy: 'The Invitation', for example, laments that 'Mersey's gentle current' has been 'too long / By fame neglected, and unknown to song' (lines 85–6), whereas 'The Groans of the Tankard' (38) pokes gentle fun at the abstemiousness of Dissenting culture.

Prior to their publication, the poems circulated and were read beyond Warrington. When William Woodfall reviewed *Poems* for the *Monthly Review* in 1773, he wrote, 'Before these elegant poems appeared in print, we were not wholly unacquainted with this Lady's extraordinary merit', noting that the Warrington community had 'celebrated her genius, and diffused her praises far and wide', with 'some of her compositions having been read and admired by persons of the first taste and judgment in the republic of Letters'.[23] McCarthy and Kraft speculate about the avenues that brought the poems to the attention of Woodfall, a London-based journalist, but how direct or indirect their path to Woodfall remains a mystery, given the dearth of extant manuscripts of the poems printed in 1773.

One explanation for the lack of surviving handwritten copies of poems printed in 1773 may be the widespread availability of *Poems* itself – which reached five fairly inexpensive editions by 1777.[24] This was a period in which readers, authors and printers generally treated print as replacing script. Hence, most printers discarded the manuscripts from which they worked to set type, and many authors did not retain copies of their drafts or fair copies of works that were printed.[25] It is entirely possible – indeed likely – that many holders of manuscripts of poems that were printed in *Poems* simply discarded them once they had a print copy in hand. This destruction was common with non-autograph copies, which held no sentimental value. Not surprisingly, then, the largest extant collections of verse manuscripts by Barbauld – the Nicholson papers (held at the Liverpool Record Office) and those formerly held by Lady Rodgers (who wrote an early biography of Barbauld and her family) – contain a high proportion of unpublished poems. Unfortunately, the loss of Barbauld's archive, without any record of what it contained, makes it impossible to know whether she (or her first editor, Lucy Aikin) saw print as replacing her autographs.

Manuscript copies survive for most of the poems written before 1773 but not printed in *Poems*, evidence that these texts circulated during Barbauld's lifetime. However, the number of surviving copies (usually just one per poem) does not necessarily reflect the breadth of their actual circulation. In the first place, in many instances Barbauld's poems could have circulated without additional physical copies having been made. In his review of *Poems*, Woodfall demonstrated his personal familiarity with her manuscript poems by noticing the absence in print of several poems that he had 'seen in manuscript' (he mentions '*Fragment* of an Epic Poem, written by a young Lady, who had lost a Game of *Chess*, by being sleepy' and 'an Epistle to her Brother', as well as 'one or two other pieces'), questioning why these had not been included.[26] In *Works*, Lucy Aikin cites another similar example when she reports the comments of 'a friend who had expressed his surprise at not finding inserted in her volume a poem which he had *admired* in manuscript'.[27] These examples demonstrate that manuscripts were often shown, as opposed to copied: Woodfall appears not to have possessed a copy of the poems he mentions, stating that he had 'seen' them in manuscript. Thus, a single handwritten document could be the basis of multiple acts of reading. Further, as discussed in the first chapter, there are many well-known examples of individuals who were able to recall long passages of texts after many years, even after a single reading or recitation, making oral transmission of these poems a possibility.[28]

Another example of a set of poems that may have been 'seen' in manuscript but not copied is Barbauld's 'Characters' (14, 20; 40–9): fourteen brief poetical sketches of individuals in her milieu, a collection of poems that define and cultivate a social community.[29] Only two of these poems (40–1) were published, but the fair copy manuscripts themselves suggest they were shared. All but one of the poems are accompanied by a silhouette portrait, made by Barbauld, which is centred at the top recto of each page, with later annotations identifying the subject of each on the verso.[30] The cutting of silhouettes, or 'profiles' as they were called, began in the mid-eighteenth century and quickly became a popular pastime – a rapid, low-cost method of taking a likeness that did not require special materials or skills to execute. As intimate portraits of members of her social circle, the manuscript pages were likely kept together, possibly in a folder (which might explain their fine state of preservation, as well as their retention as a group – to the present day – in the hands of one of Lady Rodgers's heirs).[31] While we do not know precisely how this collection would have been kept and shown to others, the absence of names or addressees in the poems themselves suggests the possibility that it was presented to visitors as a set of enigmas – requiring them to decode the textual and visual descriptions of the unnamed subject. According to McCarthy, who has viewed the manuscripts, the later addition of the names by Barbauld suggests that, with the passing of time, it became necessary to identify the subjects for her readers – and possibly for herself.[32] The collection is clearly oriented towards an audience, insofar as it reconstructs and commemorates a community. Their presentation may be another example of circulation in the form of individual acts of reading that left no paper trail. This form of household circulation was common with bound books – commonplace books, albums, miscellanies and notebooks – which were often prepared for, and kept within, a specific household. *Evenings at Home*, the six-volume miscellany Barbauld compiled with her brother, describes in its frame narrative how even loose sheets could be used for this mode of household sharing, as short pieces, written by various members of the household, were collected in and drawn from a 'budget'.

Evidence of copying, however, does exist, even for some of the seemingly more private poems such as 'To Dr. Aikin on his Complaining': two copies survive, one in the hand of a member of the

Meadows Taylor family, on paper watermarked 1811; and the other in the Nicholson family papers (both the Taylors and the Nicholsons were family friends of Barbauld). Specific details as to how these copies came to be made remain elusive: all we can say, given the friendship between the Aikins and the Nicholsons and Taylors, is that these copies were likely authorised.[33] But we do not know whether it was Aikin or Barbauld (or both) who showed the poem to others, nor how the copies came to be made, nor to whom these copies were shown, nor whether any additional copies were made that have not survived (though there is evidence to suggest that the poem circulated even more widely than these two copies might suggest: Woodfall refers to having seen this poem in manuscript). The difficulties in dating these manuscripts underscore the impossibility of reconstructing lines of transmission with any degree of certainty: the Nicholson copy may be from the early nineteenth century, though the intimacy with the family appears to have occurred in the 1770s or even the 1760s, whereas the Taylor copy must postdate 1811. Therefore, at least one of these copies was made more than four decades *after* the poem was written, evincing the ongoing interest in collecting copies of Barbauld's unpublished poems. Indeed, some twenty-three manuscript copies survive of the twenty-nine or so poems that Barbauld did not print in 1773.

A careful comparison of the poems Barbauld printed with those she did not elucidates her rationale for withholding some poems from the press. 'To Dr Aikin on his Complaining', for instance, was not only unpublished by Barbauld; it was also unpublished by her niece, who held back very few poems from print in 1825 (it was first printed in 1994 by McCarthy and Kraft). The poem's explicit challenge to the ideology of the separate spheres may explain why Barbauld (and later, Aikin) deemed the poem acceptable for a coterie but not for the public. Although in the poem Barbauld attempts to reconcile herself to her fate – as a woman she is unable to participate in her brother's intellectual and professional path – she does so grudgingly, and much of the poem expresses her indignation at the unfairness of a social system that separates brother from sister, siblings who had been raised together and share an equal thirst for knowledge:

> Those hours are now no more which smiling flew
> And the same studies saw us both pursue;
> Our path divides – to thee fair fate assign'd

> The nobler labours of a manly mind:
> While mine, more humble works, and lower cares,
> Less shining toils, and meaner praises shares.
> Yet sure in different moulds they were not cast
> Nor stampt with separate sentiments and taste.
> But hush my heart! nor strive to soar too high,
> Nor for the tree of knowledge vainly sigh;
> Check the fond love of science and of fame,
> A bright, but ah! a too devouring flame.
> Content remain within thy bounded sphere,
> For fancy blooms, the virtues flourish there. (lines 48–61)

The turn from the first- to the third-person plural in line 54 – 'Yet sure in different moulds *they* were not cast' (emphasis added) – cannot disguise Barbauld's resentment, nor does she seem satisfied with the promise of finding fancy and virtue within woman's 'bounded sphere' (line 60). Indeed, within the poem she insistently challenges gender roles, which she asserts are indefensible by any recourse to essential sexual difference: the siblings have not been 'stampt with separate sentiments and taste' (line 55) that could justify the divergence in their educational opportunities. Barbauld critiques a social order that unjustly parts sister from brother ('Our path divides'), women from men. Though Barbauld does not explicitly demand equal access to professional education, it should be recalled that even the most famous radical feminist of the period, who wrote nearly twenty-five years *later*, did not *publicly* question the separate spheres, arguing instead that women should aspire to be 'affectionate wives and rational mothers'.[34] But even if Barbauld's direct challenge to educational and professional restrictions based on gender were considered unprintable by her and, over fifty years later, by her niece, these views appear to have been deemed eminently worthy of dissemination in manuscript to those within her social circle, who took and preserved copies of the poem, and disseminated it to like-minded readers (like Woodfall).

The eight poems she wrote to the Priestleys provide fertile ground for Barbauld's preference for manuscript circulation, for she published only two of these poems, and many of them directly address her discomfort with publication. Barbauld's first known poem, 'On Mrs. P[riestley]'s Leaving Warrington', was written to quell her grief at the Priestleys' departure. It was given as a parting gift to Mary Priestley, tossed into the carriage of the unsuspecting couple, who did not know, till that moment, that their friend had been writing verse. As McCarthy observes, the act is one of deflection, similar to the mediation involved in sharing her feelings indirectly through the page.[35] There is playfulness but also inhibition in conveying her poem to the Priestleys in this way, and it evinces reservations that she had about the circulation of her verse which would persist for the rest of her life. We know that 'On Mrs. P[riestley]'s Leaving Warrington' circulated; Barbauld herself gave a copy to the Priestleys, a copy survives in the Nicholson papers, and William Turner, writing in 1813, had a copy and spoke about the opinions of 'those who have seen it' in manuscript, implying a wider audience still.[36] Unlike 'On Mrs. P[riestley]'s Leaving Warrington', which remained unprinted until McCarthy and Kraft's edition of 1994, Barbauld did publish 'To Mrs. P[riestley], with some Drawings of Birds and Insects' in *Poems*. No manuscript copies of this poem are known today, though it seems likely that it also circulated in manuscript prior to publication; the difference in surviving manuscripts may again be the availability of print versions of this poem. While both poems share many similarities – they were written to the same woman within the same short period of time, in celebration of their friendship – the latter poem stages several moments of demurral from literary ambition, whereas the unpublished poem does not reflect on the act of composing poetry.

Indeed, it may be that Barbauld's willingness to publish 'To Mrs. P[riestley], with some Drawings' arose from its explicit disavowal of any desire for poetic eminence. Throughout the poem, Barbauld insists that she is motivated solely by friendship:

> Amanda bids; at her command again
> I seize the pencil, or resume the pen;
> No other call my willing hand requires,
> And friendship, better than a Muse inspires. (lines 1–4)

This is the first of three similar gestures within the poem. In the second, Barbauld retreats from her evaluation of the respective merits of the 'kindred arts' (line 6) of painting and poetry (lines 5–18), claiming that 'humbler themes my artless hand requires' (line 19), thus denigrating both her chosen subject matter and her poetic ability. At the poem's close, she again renounces any aspiration to poetic achievement: 'I envy not, nor emulate the fame / Or of the painter's, or the poet's name' (lines 125–6), insisting that friendship is 'far, far dearer' (line 128) than the acclaim of genius. Although the speaker's breathless pursuit of birds and insects pushes against the constraint the poem seeks to impose, ultimately the speaker demurely yields (a pattern familiar from 'To Dr Aikin on his Complaining'). A similar structure – a flight of fancy followed by reluctant submission – characterises another poem she deemed suitable for print, the 1773 volume's concluding poem, 'A Summer Evening's Meditation' (58).

Between the late 1760s and early 1770s, Barbauld addressed three poems to Joseph Priestley (12, 13, 19), she wrote one more poem to him in the 1790s (94), and she describes his character in a further two poems (20, 21). Of these six poems, she printed only one, 'The Mouse's Petition' (19), in 1773. These poems to Joseph Priestley bear comparison to the poem to her brother insofar as they also register rebukes of various sorts; in fact, most of her Priestley poems mock him to various degrees and for various foibles. In 'A Fragment of an Epic Poem' (12), she light-heartedly blames Priestley for causing the drowsiness that results in her loss at chess, and then more teasingly accuses him of being in league with Morpheus, referring to those occasions in which he preached his congregation to sleep. In 'Verses written on the Back of an old Visitation Copy' (13), her chastisement of Priestley intensifies, shifting from gentle ribbing to charges of hypocrisy in seeking a new coat of arms: 'Armorial ensigns crested conquerors use / Ill-suit the sons of science, and the Muse' (lines 3–4). The fourth poem (20), his 'Character', though generally very laudatory, also reveals how she both 'admired and criticized him'.[37] In 'An Inventory of the Furniture in Dr. Priestley's Study' (21), it is possible to read Barbauld's description of his study's disarray as a reflection of his chaotic mind, and the 'Forgotten rimes, and college themes, / Worm-eaten plans, and embryo schemes' that clutter his private space as emblematic of unrealised promise (much as she will read a lady's handwriting as reflective of her character, in 'On a Lady's Writing', a poem discussed in Chapter 6).[38] It is difficult to imagine Barbauld publishing these poems to Priestley, in which she, however gently, satirises an older, married man.

Her one published address to Priestley, 'The Mouse's Petition', is arguably different from all the rest, for here the upbraiding is more tender, appealing as it does to Priestley's mercy, and less satiric, as the plea seems to issue from the mouse itself (as is suggested by the manner in which she delivered the poem). The prisoner's diminutive status thus comically defuses the threat that is uttered – 'Beware, lest in the worm you crush / A brother's soul you find; / And tremble lest thy luckless hand / Dislodge a kindred mind.'[39] Nevertheless, even this mild reproach resulted in unwelcome public criticism of Priestley. Woodfall, for example, expressed his hope that the poem 'will be of service to that gentleman as well as other *experimental* philosophers, who are not remarkable for their humanity to the poor harmless animals, that are so ill-fated to fall in their way'.[40] In the third edition of *Poems*, Barbauld felt compelled to defend Priestley, adding the following note:

> The Author is concerned to find, that what was intended as the petition of mercy against justice, has been construed as the plea of humanity against cruelty. She is certain that cruelty could never be apprehended from the Gentleman to whom this is addressed; and the poor animal would have suffered more as the victim of domestic economy, than of philosophical curiosity.[41]

From this episode, Barbauld would have understood that printing even light-hearted rebukes to friends could have adverse consequences.

One of Barbauld's chief difficulties in reconciling her poetry to print was that, like Byron and Austen, she was at home working in a satirical vein. The foibles and moral weaknesses of friends and enemies alike were a stimulant to poetic composition, and she was convinced of poetry's emancipatory powers. One of her earliest poems, 'To Mrs. P[riestley], with some Drawings', muses upon the affective capacity of poetry, which, 'with deeper art' than that of painting, 'Can pierce the close recesses of the heart; / By well set syllables, and potent sound, / Can rouse, can chill the breast, can sooth, can wound' (lines 11–14). A later unprinted poem is more explicit still: the purpose of literary art is 'To wake new feelings in the callous mind, / With skill to set distorted judgments right, / To purge the taste, and clear the mental sight.'[42] As William McCarthy has compellingly argued, Barbauld believed that poetry could 'incite moral action', but such an end often demanded the use of print.[43] The years before 1773 reveal how Barbauld attempted to reconcile her own reluctance to share her poetry beyond her social circle with her desire to use print as a vehicle for moral suasion, a conflict that would intensify with the series of political crises that arose after 1773.

Poems after 1773

During the more than five decades that followed the publication of her poetry in 1773, Barbauld wrote another one hundred or so poems.[44] Leaving aside the *Epistle to William Wilberforce* (and the two Hymns published with it) and *Eighteen-Hundred and Eleven*, an additional twenty-five poems appeared in print in her lifetime: sixteen which she authorised, nine which she did not.[45] In all, then, Barbauld authorised the printing of a very small number of poems after 1773. Not only did Barbauld's poetic productivity decrease after 1773, so too did her willingness to commit her poetry to print, with her authorised publication rate falling from 50 per cent to approximately 17 per cent of known works.

At the same time, much stayed the same for Barbauld. If we look at some of her latest known poems, dating from the 1820s – 'To Mrs. –, on Returning a fine Hyacinth Plant' (141), 'To Mr. Bowring, on his poetical Translations from various Languages' (143), 'Lines with a Wedding Present' (144) – we find occasional verse addressed to specific individuals, replicating her poetic habits of the 1760s and 1770s. As with so much of her earlier verse, we have no manuscript record for any of these compositions, but at the same time we can safely deduce, from the nature of these poems, that they were intended for and (in the absence of some accident) circulated to their recipients as handwritten notes or inscriptions. The same is true of most of the poems she wrote but did not print from the 1780s to the 1810s. And as with her early poems to Priestley, Barbauld continued to rely on manuscript for chiding her male friends, as in '[Lines to Samuel Rogers in Wales on the Eve of Bastille Day, 1791]' (89), in which she rebukes the poet for 'Hid[ing] in shades … Far from Freedom's jubilee' (lines 22–4) on the second anniversary of the storming of the Bastille. The poem survives in a letter Barbauld sent to Rogers (1763–1855), undoubtedly a common mode of circulating her poems, although few of the original letters have survived. A personal letter was an appropriate mode of transmission for such a poem; she would not have wished to embarrass Rogers publicly, though she did wish to communicate her views to him, to 'set distorted judgments right'.

There were, however, many poems that could have been safely published, without embarrassment to herself or others. Why then did Barbauld not follow the more usual path, taken by so many of her contemporaries, of allowing more of her poems to be printed after they had shown their worth through the circulation of handwritten copies? Lucy Aikin emphasises her aunt's cautiousness about publication for the general public: 'She offered to the public none but the happiest inspirations of her Muse, and not even these till they had received all the polish of which she judged them susceptible.'[46] In providing this explanation, Aikin quotes Barbauld: 'I had rather it should be asked of twenty pieces why they were not here, than of one why it is.'[47] As we have seen, many did ask 'why they were not here', suggesting that Barbauld achieved her stated desire. However, the ratio of unprinted to printed poems that Barbauld gives (of twenty to one) may imply that some of her manuscript poems have been lost altogether. Only Barbauld's scrupulousness about print, evidenced in the many poems she held back from 1773, and carrying forward into the 1800s, can explain why, near the end of her life, she believed she had so few poems worthy of a print collection. In early 1822, Barbauld expressed her reluctance to provide a poem for her friend Joanna Baillie's charitable anthology, 'because I have not entirely relinquished the intention of publishing them myself, & I have so very few that I hardly know how to spare one'.[48] Barbauld had also, in 1805, refused to grant Richard Phillips's request to republish her poetry from the *Monthly Magazine*, likely for the same reason.[49] These comments suggest that Barbauld had been contemplating, apparently for many years, a new collection of her poetry. By the 1820s, she would have had nearly one hundred unprinted poems at her disposal; however, she still felt she had 'so very few', likely because she felt many of these to be unworthy or unsuited for print. Her demurral must be a consequence of the extremely high standards she set for what qualified as publishable.

Barbauld's use of manuscript circulation continued after 1773, but the political crises that arose beginning in the 1790s altered both the content of her poems and the ways in which she allowed her handwritten poems to be disseminated. Increasingly, it became difficult to prevent politically inflected poems that circulated in manuscript from being printed, a fact that Barbauld must have quickly learned. Although the poem she penned about the repressive measures that followed the Birmingham riots, her final poem to Joseph Priestley, 'To Dr. Priestley. Dec. 29, 1792' (94), was not intended for print, Barbauld found that ministers who had resisted signing loyalty oaths 'got hold of & would print' the poem to support their cause.[50] Its 1792 unauthorised private printing was followed by its appearance, unsigned, in the *Morning Chronicle*, on 8 January 1793, an example of a manuscript poem being subject to much wider dissemination than the author intended. Its circulation, however, may not have been unwelcome to Barbauld, who may have been pleased by the political use to which the poem was put. Another similar example dating from this period is 'To a Great Nation' (93), in which she urges France to 'Obey the laws thyself hast made, / And rise – the model of the world!' (lines 35–6). This poem must have circulated fairly widely, for it was printed, without Barbauld's authority but again possibly with her tacit approval, in *The Cambridge Intelligencer* on 2 November 1793. A similar fate befell 'The Apology of the Bishops, in Answer to "Bonner's Ghost"' (88), a poem she wrote in response to 'Bishop Bonner's Ghost', sent to her by its author, Hannah More (1745–1833). More's poem is written from the perspective of Queen Mary I's Catholic bishop, Edmund Bonner (c. 1500–69), who was notorious for his persecution of heretics, and whose ghost laments the reforms to the modern church. In her counter-poem, Barbauld writes satirically from the perspective of the modern bishops, indicating that their restraint is '[t]he fault of the nation' (line 13). According to Anna Le Breton, 'copies of the poem must have circulated', as lines 31–2 'were quoted in a Church debate in the House of Commons'.[51] The poem was not, however, printed until 1869, by Henry Crabb Robinson. The counter-poem, never sent to More herself and possibly never seen by her, demonstrates the darker side of manuscript culture, as manuscript circulation leads to a breakdown rather than a continuation or enhancement of social exchange. As with other poems written around the same time, Barbauld used manuscript to voice her objections to other writers. To do so, she deployed a range of strategies: she sent poems in letters with mild reprimands to friends, such as those to Priestley and Rogers; she anonymously published other similar poems, such as 'To Mr. S. T. Coleridge'; and she composed but did not share her reply to More, to Mary Wollstonecraft in 'The Rights of Woman' and 'To Lord Byron' (131). Manuscript thus could serve as a vehicle of dissent rather than consensus and could be withheld from the objects of complaint rather than shared with them.

The differing methods of transmission for many of these poems suggests that Barbauld made deliberate calculations about whether and how to share and publish. The printing of her two most politically incendiary poems as pamphlets, *An Epistle to William Wilberforce* (1791) and *Eighteen Hundred and Eleven, A Poem* (1812), must be regarded as measured interventions into the public sphere; that they are extremely rare publication events for Barbauld supports this view.[52] When the latter poem appeared in print, she had not printed a poem as a separate publication for more than twenty years (*An Epistle to William Wilberforce*), yet she decisively overcame her reluctance to print. There are obvious substantive resonances between *An Epistle to William Wilberforce* and *Eighteen Hundred and Eleven*: both adopt a Juvenalian tone, expressing intense scorn for the nation's failings, and both prognosticate a permanent decline for Britain as a global power. What has been less remarked upon, however, is that both poems share the same mode of publication as relatively inexpensive, and hence ephemeral, pamphlets: the *Epistle*, at fourteen pages, was sold for 1 shilling, and *Eighteen Hundred and Eleven*, a twenty-five-page pamphlet in quarto, was sold for 2 shillings and sixpence. Barbauld opted for this mode of publication to ensure that her poems were published quickly and dispersed widely.[53] She also signed both pamphlets and printed them under the imprint of Joseph Johnson, a publisher with strong Dissenting and radical connections: a deliberate positioning of herself and these poems within a revolutionary milieu. His sarcasm aside, Croker's description of Barbauld as acting from 'an irresistible impulse of public duty' in the hope of 'saving a sinking state' is, in fact, a reasonably accurate description of her motivations.[54]

The two poems also share a similar compositional history. Unlike most of her poems, these were composed directly for print; like most of her poems, they were written in response to events. The *Epistle* was a reaction to the parliamentary debates held on Wilberforce's bill on 18–19 April 1791, and was published on 17 June, less than two months later. We know that she read *Eighteen Hundred and Eleven* to Martha and John Aikin on 1 December 1811 and discussed her intention of 'publishing it immediately'.[55] Indeed, it was printed just over two months later, on 5 February 1812. Unlike the poems she printed in 1773, it would appear that neither of these works circulated extensively in manuscript, with *Eighteen Hundred and Eleven* being presented to the public possibly after having been seen only by her brother, sister-in-law and publisher. This lack of preprint circulation may explain in part why some of the negative reactions to the poem, even amongst those most sympathetic to her views, came as a surprise.

Barbauld's more common method of publishing her poems, after 1773, was in print magazines: in this medium she chose to disseminate eleven poems, mostly during the politically incendiary decades of the 1790s and the 1810s. Her use of magazine publication is suggestive of her habitual restraint. Six of these poems appeared in two journals edited by her brother (five in the *Monthly Magazine*, between the years 1797 and 1800, and one in the *Annual Register* in 1819): most likely, her brother again urged her into print, as he had done decades before. The six remaining poems appeared in the *Monthly Repository* between 1807 and 1823; both journals were Dissenting publications edited by and addressed to that community, thus ensuring Barbauld as receptive an audience as possible. Further, in magazine publication, anonymity was readily available: eight of the eleven poems were published unsigned. And finally, even signed magazine poetry could offer a more discreet, less provocative method of publication for the conveyance of radical views than a single-authored pamphlet or volume. While Barbauld herself would have had little control over the arrangement of her poems within the journal, this venue allowed for a politically stirring poem such as 'Hymn: "Ye are the salt of the earth"' (96; published in the *Monthly Magazine*, July 1797) in praise of those who 'lift on high the warning voice, / When public ills prevail' (lines 33–4) and whose speech 'turns the tyrant pale' (line 35), to be followed by more innocuous poems, written by others, such as the 'Ode to Contemplation' and the sonnet 'To Loch-Lomond'. Similarly, 'On the King's Illness' (122), printed in the *Monthly Repository* just months before *Eighteen Hundred and Eleven*, is followed by a poem on the Great Comet of 1811. This context may have served to defuse the controversial ideas expressed in that poem: while sympathetic to the ailing monarch, Barbauld reminds her readers that, in death, 'The peasant and the king repose together' (line 4); adverts to the king's 'erring judgment' (line 26); and exclaims, 'Oh, that thou hadst closed the wounds of war! / That had been praise to suit a higher strain' (lines 27–8). Barbauld herself knew that the poem was not 'quite calculated to please a courtly ear'.[56]

Even after the nearly unanimous outcry against *Eighteen Hundred and Eleven*, Barbauld continued to circulate politically charged poems in manuscript and print, and sometimes both. In her 'Memoir' of her aunt's life, Lucy Aikin initiated the narrative of Barbauld's painful retreat from print publication following the vituperative reviews of *Eighteen Hundred and Eleven*. 'This was the last', Aikin writes, 'of Mrs Barbauld's separate publications', which she explains as an act of self-preservation, necessary to secure Barbauld from 'the scorns of the unmanly, the malignant, and the base'.[57] Aikin proceeds to enumerate the other consequences of these attacks: her aunt, though continuing to compose verse, 'for the most part confined to a few friends all participation in the strains which they inspired'; and '[s]he even laid aside the intention which she had entertained of preparing a new edition of her Poems, long out of print and often inquired for in vain'.[58] To conclude this portrait of withdrawal, and to further suggest that the public reception of *Eighteen Hundred and Eleven* marked the beginning of a long decline, Aikin writes:

> No incident worthy of mention henceforth occurred to break the uniformity of her existence. She gave up all distant journeys; and confined at home to a narrow circle of connexions and acquaintance, she suffered life to slide away, as it were at its own pace . . . [59]

According to her niece, Barbauld was so overcome by the negative reception of the poem that she abandoned her plan to reissue her printed poems and retreated into the realm of manuscript circulation.[60] However, the activities that Aikin describes her aunt adopting after 1812 are in no way discernibly different from those she participated in during the previous six decades of her writing life: she had always shared most of her poems with those friends who had inspired her to write.

When Aikin presented this story in 1825, the narrative of the misunderstood and even persecuted poet had become proverbial: it had been prevalent at least since Thomas Chatterton's suicide in 1770, had been reasserted by William Wordsworth in his 'Essay Supplementary to the Preface' in 1815 (in which he declared that 'every author, as far as he is great and at the same time *original*, has had the task of *creating* the taste by which he is to be enjoyed').[61] It had been resurrected in the wake of John Keats's death in 1821 with Percy Shelley's *Adonais* (1821), and repeated, in Byron's comic rehash, in Canto XI of *Don Juan*, which contends that Keats was 'killed off by one critique'.[62] But these accounts – of career and even life-ending critiques – were mythological.[63]

An analysis of two poems, both dating from 1817, five years after the publication of *Eighteen Hundred and Eleven* – 'To Miss Kinder, on Receiving a Note dated February 30th' (134) and 'On the Death of Princess Charlotte' (135) – work to disrupt this lingering narrative. Both poems circulated in manuscript and were also printed. The first was published in a provincial newspaper, apparently without Barbauld's consent, and the second was printed with her consent, in the *Annual Register . . . for the Year 1818* (1819). It seems that her brother prevailed on her (as he had done before) to print 'On the Death of Princess Charlotte'; she describes the poem has having been printed 'in one of my Brother's Annual Registers'.[64] Both poems challenge Aikin's narrative by pointing to Barbauld's continued use of both script and print to forward her political ideals. They further document the necessity and interconnectedness, for Barbauld, of using both media as means of social commentary and political activism: 'To Miss Kinder', an ostensibly confidential and occasional poem, nevertheless critically reflects on the ongoing struggle to bring about a better future; and 'On the Death of Princess Charlotte', a public poem about the death of the heir to the throne, which circulated privately both before and after publication, acquired enhanced political significance through its placement in a publication openly hostile to the policies of the government and Prince Regent. Both poems, through their social and public circulation, became instruments of political commentary, though this commentary is often achieved indirectly.

'To Miss Kinder' was suggested to Barbauld by the dating of a note she had received from her cousin-in-law, Hannah Kinder, of 'February 30th' – precisely the sort of trivial error that her imagination seized upon. The result was an eighteen-line poem in heroic couplets, possibly sent to Ms Kinder in a letter, though no letter survives. The only surviving autograph, which is undated, is now held in the archives of the Massachusetts Historical Society. Possibly this is a copy that was brought to America by the Priestleys, but whether this is the same copy that was sent to Kinder, or another fair copy, cannot be ascertained. Two other copies, possibly contemporaneous, exist, one taken by Elizabeth Rayner Priestley (1797–1877), Joseph Priestley's granddaughter, and the other by Mary Anne Nicholson. A fourth manuscript copy, probably in the hand of Lucy Reid Sharpe, dates from the 1830s. The poem appears to have been first printed in the *Derby Mercury* on 17 December 1817 under the heading 'Verses of Mrs. Barbauld'. The printed version differs in a few respects from the holograph. Lines 15–16 in the holograph are transposed to lines 11–12 in the *Mercury* copy. In this respect, it is like the Nicholson copy. In addition, the *Mercury* provides the year in the title, a detail shared only in the Nicholson and Sharpe copies. Thus it seems likely that the *Mercury* copy derived from the Nicholson copy. The three transcripts of the poems that survive suggest that it was admired within her social circle; although we do not know how the poem came to be printed, the extent of manuscript copies that survive may explain its fairly rapid appearance in print.

Although the poem was written for the amusement of her friend, as a work imagining an alternate reality – the events that will unfold on 30 February 1817 – it offers an opportunity to satirise the dystopic elements of her own day, and to reflect on her own practice of futurological thinking. The mistaken date launches Barbauld into conceiving of 'a day of more wonders than soon can be told' (line 3), one that appears, at least at first, to be utopian, in contrast to the degraded and doomed nation she represents in her epic. On this day, human character is reformed: the bigot will leave off frowning, the sceptic cease from sneering (line 14); 'the Miser, content with his store, / Shall no longer be craving and thirsting for more' (lines 7–8); and, in lines of more potential relevance to *Eighteen Hundred and Eleven*, the statesman will possess 'no interest, the Patriot no spleen' (line 6). The eradication of bigots and misers, and the reformation of politicians and splenetic patriots, such as those who had attacked Barbauld for challenging their governance of the country, suggests an improved world.

But there are some sinister hints about the imagined wondrous day. While undesirable forms of human greed and selfishness are eliminated, the topsy-turvy universe that Barbauld imagines is also one in which 'the young are all prudent, all charming the old' (line 4), perhaps a less pleasing inversion of human behaviour. Announcing that on this day 'all creeds shall be like, and all the mysteries clear' (line 11), Barbauld presents a world she herself would find unwelcome. She would not wish to see differences in belief eradicated or even lessened – she strongly advocates for toleration in 'Difference and Agreement; or, Sunday Morning', a piece from *Evenings at Home* – any more than she would wish for the mysteries of life, which she yearns to uncover in 'A Summer Evening's Meditation', to be fully known. Such a world, the poem hints, is not only unattainable but undesirable. The poem sketches a series of scientific discoveries that will be ushered in on this day – some that are clearly beneficial (measuring longitude and calculating the depths of the ocean), but others that are theoretically impossible (squaring the circle) (lines 15–16). We are also told that on the 30th of February 'the lamb and the lion together shall play' (line 9), an event as alien to nature as its paired couplet, in which 'green Erin [Ireland] weave garlands to crown Castlereigh' (line 10). Here Barbauld sardonically paints a world not merely unnatural but also grotesque, as Ireland crowns its oppressor. The naming of Lord Castlereagh (1769–1822) is unusual and contributes to the mixed tone of the poem.[65] Unlike Byron and Shelley, poets active in this decade, Barbauld rarely singled out and named her enemies: it should be recalled that Castlereagh would appear two years later, personified as 'Murder' in Shelley's unpublished (and unpublishable) 'Masque of Anarchy', and Byron scandalously references him as an 'intellectual eunuch' in the suppressed dedication to *Don Juan*. His mention in Barbauld's 1817 poem signals to her knowing readers that she had not forgotten Castlereagh's past offences against the Irish – and that they should not be forgotten, in any future with moral integrity. It also serves as a reminder, again to her sympathetic readers, that the old tyrants were still alive and well: as leader of the House of Commons under Lord Liverpool, Castlereagh was responsible for the government's introduction in 1817 of repressive 'Gagging Acts' (*The Treason Act* and *Seditious Meetings Act*) to curtail freedom of speech and association.

The poem's final lines support the reading that Barbauld sets up an ideal only to undermine it by casting the ambitions that she and many others cherished into absurdity:

> From the Pole to the Line, and from Spain to Cathay,
> The good and the wise on the throne shall bear sway.
> To the depths of the Ocean the plummet shall sound
> And the circle be squared and the longitude found;
> All wars, in all climes, on this day too shall cease,
> And it just coincides with the *Calends of Greece*. (lines 13–18)

The promise of the first three lines is seductive, but it quickly unravels in the fourth line, with the promised solution to the theoretical impossibility of circling the square, and comes apart in the final four words – 'the Calends of Greece' – which humorously reference a time that will never come to be, as the Calends were specific days of the Roman calendar, not of the Greek. The phrase is thus proverbial for what can never be, precisely what is evoked by the date of 30 February.

In 'To Miss Kinder', therefore, Barbauld at once sympathises with and parodies herself, as she is simultaneously sincere, comical and bitter in her efforts to imagine a better world. The longing for an improved world is earnestly expressed, but at the same time its manifest impossibility focuses satirical attention on the dreamer herself. As she had done in her unpublished prose work 'Dialogue in the Shades', written in 1813, Barbauld satirises herself as Clio, the muse of history; declaring herself heartily 'sick of mankind', she affects a comical-tragic stance. But she does so within a confidential framework – writing for a known audience, to whom she can divulge her fears in a more comic, self-doubting fashion.[66] 'To Miss Kinder' might also be read as a response to the critics of *Eighteen Hundred and Eleven*, pointing out, with humour, her awareness of the limits of her idealism, an ironical understanding that is present but often overlooked in readings of that poem. In *Eighteen Hundred and Eleven* Barbauld expresses a sense of futility in warning Britain about its current misdeeds; the term 'in vain' is repeated six times in the first thirty lines (a term that also recurs in *Epistle to William Wilberforce*). She emphasises the inescapability of Britain's decline ('The worm is in thy core', line 314); and figures this sense of inevitability in 'The Genius', who 'now forsakes the favoured shore / And hates, capricious, what he loved before' (lines 241–2). Her prophetic voice, even in this most austere of poems, intermixes with deflating irony: after all, it is 'Arts' as well as 'arms and wealth' that 'destroy the fruits they bring' (line 315). And finally, when Barbauld disdains the 'tutored voices [who] swell the artful note' (line 292) as emblems of London's decadence, she appears to be pointing at herself, as one who had spent much of her life tutoring young women, both personally and through works like *The Female Speaker*, published in 1811, just one year prior to *Eighteen Hundred and Eleven*. Barbauld's use of irony – apparent in the early, unpublished poem 'The Rights of Women', where her attitude towards Wollstonecraft is complex and shifting, and later in 'To Miss Kinder' – indicates that even within the sociable realm, Barbauld could chose to express herself obliquely.

'On the Death of Princess Charlotte', a poem written on the death of the princess on 6 November 1817, presents another example of the blurring of the lines between the private and the public, as the princess's death became the occasion for national mourning. The poem begins by calling attention to the universality of suffering for the princess:

> Yes Britain mourns, as with electric shock
> For youth, for love, for happiness destroyed.
> Her universal population wells
> In grief spontaneous; and hard hearts are moved,
> And rough unpolished natures learn to feel
> For those they envied . . . (lines 1–6)

Here, Barbauld alludes to the terrible suffering of Prince Leopold, who feels the 'anguish of a husband's heart'; she contrasts the prince's agony with the obliviousness of the ageing king, urging her readers to 'set apart one sigh, / From the full tide of sorrow spare one tear / For him who does not weep' (lines 33–5). As with 'On the King's Illness', the death of Princess Charlotte offers an occasion for musing on the levelling effects of death, as a member of the royal family had been 'humbled in the dust / By fate's impartial hand' (lines 6–7).

The poem thus exemplifies the merging of private ethics and public morals that is the hallmark of many of Barbauld's political poems and prose works. Its circulation likewise suggests this mixture of the private and the public, as it first circulated within a coterie before being brought forward publicly, and it appears to have circulated in script even after its first appearance in print. Barbauld sent a fair copy to William Roscoe on 20 March 1818, before its printing in the *Annual Register*, and she sent two other autograph fair copies to friends, one to Joanna Baillie and another to Sarah Carr. Although these copies cannot be precisely dated, it appears that Baillie's copy agrees with the 1819 printing (which has a few minor changes from the Roscoe copy). According to McCarthy, Carr's copy includes another minor change that he believes represents her 'second thoughts on revision and the latest state of the text'.[67] In this reading, it is likely that both the Baillie and Carr copies postdate the first printing in the *Annual Register*. The three autograph copies – more than exist for any other poem by Barbauld – suggest how widely Barbauld's poems may have circulated with her direct participation, and also how circulation could both pre- and post-date print.

The poem's political significance became even more explicit when it was printed in the *Annual Register . . . for the Year 1818* (1819), appearing under the title 'Elegy' and signed 'Mrs B – d'.[68] Within the pages of the *Annual Register*, the poem forms part of a larger series of attacks on the character and policies of the Prince Regent. The *Annual Register* is explicitly hostile to the prince for his support of the government's response to the supposed 'acts of insurrection and treason' directed against him, which included the 'Gagging Acts', rushed through Parliament in January 1817 after a missile had been flung into the prince's coach on his way to Parliament. The *Annual Register* fiercely condemns the government's hasty passage of these measures. Read in this context, Barbauld's request for sympathy towards the impotent king (lines 33–4), with no mention of the princess's father, could be interpreted as an implicit rejection of the Throne Speech delivered on behalf of the prince on 27 January 1818. In that speech, parliamentarians were begged to 'deeply participate in the affliction with which his royal highness has been visited, by the calamitous and untimely death of his beloved and only child the Princess Charlotte'.[69] The placement of Barbauld's poem within this larger debate allows the poem to be read as part of a general rebuttal of any claim for leniency towards the prince. It also participates in castigating the unprecedented suspension of civil liberties undertaken in his name – measures that, as Lord Holland pointed out in the parliamentary debates reported in the *Annual Register*, were not felt to be warranted even at the height of the Civil Wars. By allowing her poem to be published within this context, Barbauld joins forces with a larger opposition movement that voices explicit hostility towards the government.

Conclusion

This chapter has made several claims about Barbauld's poetic career in script and print. It began with the assertion that Barbauld was primarily a manuscript poet who disseminated handwritten copies of her poems to members of her social circle. It is a mark of the approbation that these poems enjoyed from readers, as well as of the ongoing vitality of manuscript culture, that they often circulated far beyond their intended audiences. For the majority of her poems,

Barbauld wrote when prompted by an occasion or event, and seemed to prefer circulating her poetry in manuscript form, leaving it to her readers to determine the worth of a poem by their decision to copy or otherwise share it. Rarely did Barbauld write directly for print, and when she did it was usually in response to an immediately pressing political event or issue, such as the defeat of Wilberforce's Bill to abolish the slave trade. On these few occasions, Barbauld was willing to use print to intervene directly in public debates, much as she did with her prose pamphlets, particularly in the 1790s. With her poetry, Barbauld preferred more indirect means of both expressing and disseminating her political opinions – and this observation holds true both before and after the publication of *Eighteen Hundred and Eleven*. Many of her satirical poems as well as her later political poems, such as 'On the Death of Princess Charlotte', circulated in both manuscript and print, both before and after they were published. By choosing, after 1773, to publish only a small handful of new poems, very infrequently, usually unsigned, in Dissenting periodicals, and by allowing handwritten copies of other poems to be taken with imperfect knowledge about whether and how they might be further disseminated, Barbauld displayed her life-long preference for more mediated, socially oriented forms of publication. Barbauld did, however, use manuscript circulation strategically, as a means of 'publishing' her verse to members of her radical, Dissenting culture, who could use it to advance their ends, but without the notoriety and intentionality implied by print. Nevertheless, often her intentions respecting publication are impossible to discern with certainty. Throughout this chapter, attention has been focused on the messy and unpredictable journeys by which her poems actually moved through the world.

The final example this chapter offers is that of the extensive circulation of Barbauld's 'A Thought on Death' (129). Four manuscript copies of the poem are known, none in Barbauld's hand, and only one, which was written on paper watermarked 1830, can be dated. There are three distinct versions of the poem within these four manuscripts: a twenty-line version with the 'faith' stanza placed the last of five stanzas (the Pierpont Morgan copy); a twenty-line version with the 'boon to die' stanza coming last (and the 'faith' stanza second to last) (the Manchester College Notebook, held at the Manchester College Library, Oxford, and the Stewart Scrapbook Copy 2, held at the Edinburgh University Library); and a sixteen-line version with the 'faith' stanza omitted altogether (Stewart Scrapbook, Copy 1, held at the Edinburgh University Library).[70] The poem itself was printed at least five times in Barbauld's lifetime, three times in the United States and twice in England.[71]

The poem's printing history demonstrates how manuscripts could travel far beyond what was intended or expected by an author. It was first printed in the *New-York Literary Journal, and Belles-Lettres Repository* in June 1820, and then in Boston in the *Christian Disciple* in November–December 1821, the New York printing likely descending from the Manchester College Notebook copy, the Boston printing from the Pierpont Morgan copy. The circuitous route it took to New York is suggested by the following editorial explanation: 'We were favoured with a copy by a lady, who received them from a friend to whom they were presented by Mrs. Barbauld.'[72] The poem was then reprinted in an English periodical, the *Monthly Repository*, in October 1822, which cited its American printing in the *Christian Disciple*. Upon finding her poem printed in the *Monthly Repository* via Boston, Barbauld expressed astonishment at its migration across the Atlantic: 'how it got there', she wrote, 'I know not'.[73] It appears, however, to have travelled through transatlantic Unitarian networks, as the *New-York Literary Journal* explains. Similarly to Charlotte Smith, who objected in 1784 that her poems 'found their way into the prints of the day in a mutilated state', Barbauld expressed displeasure that the poem had been 'very inaccurately given', and sent a corrected version, which appeared in the *Monthly Repository* for November 1822. Unlike Smith, however, Barbauld did not object to the poem being published; almost certainly she realised, having experienced her poems having 'found their way into' print without her participation many times before, that this transition was inevitable.

A slightly different version of the poem was also reprinted in the *Christian Disciple* in September–October 1822, without reference to the previous printing. This reprinted poem, included in an essay seeking to refute the charge that Unitarians were not Christians, is almost identical to the previous version but has a different subtitle, 'Written in her ninetieth year', instead of 'Written in her eightieth year'. The editor of this second *Christian Disciple* printing thought it is more likely that Barbauld was in fact in her eightieth year but claims 'no exact knowledge of the fact'.[74] (Barbauld was in fact seventy-nine years old in 1822; the poem was written when she was seventy-one.) The editor's inability to verify her date of birth suggests how far the manuscript had travelled from its source, such that the poem was published by those without even the most tenuous personal connection to or knowledge of the author. Though Barbauld's poems almost always began within a sociable exchange, transatlantic correspondence and migration were one of the means by which her intended audience was expanded.

A final indication of the wide and unpredictable dissemination of this poem can be found in a letter from Thomas Jefferson to John Adams, dated 1 June 1822, in which Jefferson copies two stanzas of the poem, though without attribution to Barbauld.[75] The copy follows the ordering of the stanzas in the *Christian Disciple* printings, but there are four substantive differences within the eight lines that are copied, none of which match any other known manuscript.[76] It is possible that Jefferson viewed another (unknown) manuscript; that he miscopied it from the *Christian Disciple* or some other unknown printed source; that he misremembered the poem (if he had no copy); or that he deliberately changed it. Jefferson's letter demonstrates the multiple paths through which verse was transmitted in the period, and it is of interest in another regard, for within it we find him complaining of the very act that he had, perhaps unwittingly, been guilty of: that of reproducing, as it were, a confidential utterance without the consent of the author. Jefferson expresses his trepidation of putting pen to paper in writing the letter to Adams, and even considers abandoning writing altogether, 'because of the treacherous practice some people have of publishing one's letters without leave'.[77] He approvingly cites a 1769 decision of the English courts, *Millar* v. *Taylor*, which had ruled that publishing private papers without consent was 'a breach of trust, punishable at law, with Jefferson adding his own belief that 'it should be a penitentiary felony'.[78] Adams's reply exhibits the ubiquitous desire to print manuscript texts, even that of a letter itself condemning the practice: he states that he found Jefferson's letter 'so excellent that I am almost under an invincible temptation to commit a breach of trust by lending it to a printer', and shares his son's calculation that 'it would be worth five hundred dollars to any newspaper in Boston, but I dare not betray your confidence'.[79]

Manuscript copies of texts like Barbauld's 'A Thought on Death' and Jefferson's letters circulated rapidly and extensively and often presented an 'invincible temptation' to print by those whose hands they passed through. It is often impossible to reconstruct the precise lines of transmission: we do not know how William Woodfall, a London-based journalist with no personal ties to Barbauld or to Warrington, came to see her poems in manuscript prior to their publication in *Poems,* nor do we know precisely how, some fifty years later, Barbauld's 'A Thought on Death' migrated across the Atlantic. But even though we cannot retrace the exact lines of transmission, we can reconstruct more generally the pervasive spread and influence of manuscript culture in the early nineteenth century, within and beyond Britain's borders. Barbauld's 'A Thought on Death', a poem that she did not print, held considerable significance for both American presidents, whose shared appreciation of Barbauld's poem in their final years finds a fitting echo in their shared death date of 4 July 1826, the fiftieth anniversary of American independence.

Like Barbauld, Lord Byron – the most famous poet of the early nineteenth century and the subject of the next chapter – circulated his poems in script and print for the duration of his career, resolving not to publish many of them and choosing instead to circulate many of them in manuscript amongst his various coteries of friends, family members and literary advisers. But unlike Barbauld, whose early poems glided easily from script to print, Byron's youthful verse enjoyed no such easy transition: his attempts to print his poems as he first wrote them, almost always with a coterie readership in mind, encountered resistance from his publishers and advisers, readers and reviewers. Indeed, getting his poems into print as he wished was a battle he would fight for the duration of his life.

Notes

1. At just over 1,123 lines, she just surpasses Anne Finch (1,049 lines), her closest rival. Most other female poets, from Aphra Behn (208) to Elizabeth Rowe (441), enjoy fewer than half the number of lines devoted to Barbauld: Paula Backscheider and Catherine Ingrassia (eds), *British Women Poets of the Long Eighteenth Century: An Anthology* (2009). Roger Lonsdale's anthology, *Eighteenth-Century Women Poets: An Oxford Anthology*, was the first to bring Barbauld to the attention of modern readers.

2. [William Woodfall], 'Review of *Poems*, by Miss Aikin', *Monthly Review* 48 (January 1773): 54.
3. 'Review of the *Works of Anna Laetitia Barbauld*', *Monthly Repository* 20 (1825): 562.
4. Three editions were published in 1773 (February and early May, both quarto; September, octavo), a fourth edition in June 1774, and a fifth edition in 1777. A new and corrected edition in 1792 added the *Epistle to William Wilberforce* (published on its own in two editions in 1791). According to William McCarthy, Chandler was the only one of her twenty-six predecessors (included in Lonsdale's anthology) to have a volume go into six editions in her lifetime. See William McCarthy, *Anna Letitia Barbauld: Voice of the Enlightenment* (2008), p. 586, n. 75 (hereafter *ALBVE*); and *The Poems of Anna Letitia Barbauld* (1994), pp. 357–8 (hereafter *PALB*). Both works provide detailed bibliographic information confirming that these were all separate editions.
5. In Wedgwood's catalogue, she was, according to McCarthy, 'the only middle-class woman and the only woman writer in his 1777 cohort' (*ALBVE*, p. 116).
6. *Poems* (1773) includes thirty-three poems; *An Epistle to William Wilberforce* was added in 1792.
7. The fifty-three poems that were printed by Barbauld are found in the following publications: thirty-three poems appeared in *Poems*; *An Epistle to William Wilberforce* (87), published with two Hymns (91, 92); *Eighteen Hundred and Eleven* (1812); and sixteen authorised poems in magazines or collections. See note 9, below, for the authorised poems.
8. Ezell, *Social Authorship*, p. 23.
9. Whether a poem was published with Barbauld's consent is not always entirely certain, but generally speaking, poems are considered to have been printed with her authorisation only if they were included in a magazine or book edited by her brother or by an individual with whom she was closely affiliated, or if other evidence exists that she authorised it. The sixteen poems that she authorised for publication in a magazine (11) or collection (5) are: 75 ('Animals') [published in *Evenings at Home*, a children's miscellany edited by her brother]; 79 ('A School Ecologue'), 96 ('Hymn: "Ye are the salt of the earth"'), 101 ('To Mr. S. T. Coleridge'), 102 ('Washing-Day'), 106 ('Peace and Shepherd') [all published in the *Monthly Magazine*, during the period when her brother John Aikin was editor]; 109–11, Three Hymns [IX–XI published in an 1802 collection on social worship and may be presumed to have been included with her tacit if not explicit consent; 114 ('The Pilgrim'), 118 ('The Unknown God'), 122 ('On the King's Illness'), 139 ('Lines written at the Close of the Year') and 140 ("To the New Year, 1823')

[all appeared in the *Monthly Repository*; in the 'Obituary of Mrs. Anna Laetitia Barbauld', *Monthly Repository* 20 [1825]: 186, the editor notes that these poems 'were communicated by Mrs Barbauld to this magazine'; see also *PALB*, pp. 326–7]. Also, 'Elegy' ('On the Death of Princess Charlotte' [135]) appeared in the *Annual Register for 1818*, which her brother edited at the time. 'To Mrs. —, on Returning a fine Hyacinth Plant after the Bloom was over') appeared in Joanna Baillie's charitable collection *A Collection of Poems: Chiefly in Manuscript, and from Living Authors* (1823), along with a reprinting of 'On the King's Illness'.

10. By my calculations, a total of nine poems were published without Barbauld's authorisation: 12 'A Fragment of an Epic Poem', 61 '[A Character of John Mort]', and 73 'A Portrait' in the 1780s; 30 'Prologue to the Play of Henry the Eighth', 93 'To a Great Nation' and 94 'To Dr. Priestley Dec. 29, 1792', in the 1790s; 134 'To Miss Kinder' in the 1810s, and 107 'On the Death of Mrs Martineau' and 129 'A Thought on Death' in the 1820s.

11. Laura Estill and Michelle Levy, 'Evaluating digital remediations of women's manuscripts', n.p.

12. Ezell, *Social Authorship*, pp. 21–44.

13. Numbers in parentheses refer to the numbering of the poems used in *PALB*. Most modern anthologies print a roughly equal combination of her printed and unprinted poems. Four of the eight poems in the most recent edition of the *Norton Anthology of English Literature* were unprinted in Barbauld's lifetime: the unprinted poems are 'An Inventory of the Furniture in Dr. Priestley's Study', 'The Rights of Woman', 'To a little invisible Being' and 'The Caterpillar' (*Norton Anthology*, 9th edn, vol. 2). Four out of the ten poems in the fifth edition of the *Longman Anthology of British Literature* were unprinted: 'Inscription for an Ice-House', 'To a little invisible Being', 'To the Poor' and 'The First Fire' (*Longman Anthology of British Literature*, 5th edn, 2012, vol. 2a). And, in the *Broadview Anthology of British Literature: The Age of Romanticism*, 2nd edn, 2010, vol. 4, seven of the twelve poems were unprinted: 'To the Poor', 'To a Little Invisible Being', 'Life', 'The Rights of Woman', 'The Baby-house', 'The First Fire' and 'The Caterpillar'.

14. Most of Barbauld's manuscripts, in the possession of her descendants, were destroyed during the bombing of London in the Second World War.

15. *The Works of Anna Laetitia Barbauld*, 2 vols (1825).

16. See William McCarthy, 'Introduction: Anna Letitia Barbauld Today', p. 5.

17. See *PALB*, pp. 228–9. The surviving manuscripts are discussed later in this chapter.

18. Examples include 'Bouts Rimés in Praise of old Maids' (16), '[Extempore on being shown the Shoe Buckles worn by David Garrick in his

last Performance]' (64) and 'Lines to Mr. W[ynch] on his forty-fifth Birthday' (97). These poems – all unpublished by Barbauld and Aikin – caused some anger or embarrassment when they appeared in print after Barbauld's death. Lucy Aikin complained in a letter to the *Monthly Repository* when the latter two poems were printed in the *Amulet* in 1827. Aikin accused the holder of the manuscript of 'the very gross impropriety of giving them up for publication', and the editor of the *Amulet* for 'receiving them'. The editor of the *Monthly Repository* agreed, expressing 'our regret that any pieces of that lady's should find their way to the public, which we were sure she would not herself have printed under the sanction of her name': 'Mrs Barbaulds MSS. To the Editor', *Monthly Repository and Review*, n.s., II (January–December 1828): 55.

19. Barbauld, *Works*. The first volume was prefaced by Lucy Aikin's 'Memoir', p. xxxvii.
20. In Plate 6, the thirty-three poems in the bar for the 1770s are divided into the twenty-six poems (2–4, 8–9, 17–19, 32–41, 51–8) that first appeared in *Poems* (in orange), and the six songs (22–7) and 'The Origin of Song-Writing' (28) that had previously appeared in John Aikin's *Essays on Song-Writing* (1771) (in green).
21. *PALB*, p. xxix.
22. All of the songs had been previously published in John Aikin's *Essays on Song-Writing* (1772), and five of the hymns had appeared in William Enfield's *Hymns for Public Worship* (1772).
23. [Woodfall], 'Review of *Poems*, by Miss Aikin', p. 55.
24. For the first edition, a 'sewn copy' was available for 6 shillings and an 'elegantly bound' copy for 10 shillings, both in quarto. The third edition, published in September 1773, was made available in octavo for 3 shillings.
25. A comparison with the surviving archive of another female author, Jane Austen, presents a similar pattern. With Austen, the manuscripts that survive are precisely those that were *not* printed. No manuscript of any printed work of Austen's survives, with the exception of the two cancelled manuscript chapters of *Persuasion*, which likely survive because they were not published, with Austen sending the substituted chapters to the press. Practices were changing, however, especially for poets, though this often had a great deal to do with poetic reputation and with family members who were willing and able to collect and preserve manuscripts. The preservation of literary manuscripts is discussed in Chapter 6.
26. [Woodfall], 'Review of *Poems*, by Miss Aikin', p. 135.
27. L. Aikin, 'Memoir', p. lx, emphasis added.

28. We know that oral recitation was a common feature of the social gatherings described in *Evenings at Home*. There is evidence that Barbauld recited her poems to others: for example, Henry Crabb Robinson noted that Barbauld read 'On the King's Illness' (122) to him in August 1811. According to Martha Aikin, her sister-in-law, she read *Eighteen Hundred and Eleven* (124) to her and her brother in advance of its publication, in December of that year: *PALB*, pp. 307, 309.
29. Lucy Aikin labelled two poems that she printed in *Works*, poems 14 and 20, 'Characters'. These two poems also survive as part of a set of ten holographs.
30. Three of the profiles are reproduced in *ALBVE*, Figures 17–19.
31. I am grateful to William McCarthy for this description of the manuscript pages. He describes the pages as being uniform and in a good state of preservation, without any indication that they were bound together. The holographs are still retained as a single collection, currently in the possession of Sir Piers Rodgers.
32. *ALBVE*, p. 572, n. 20.
33. As McCarthy points out, the relationship is 'poorly documented', but the known connection is sufficient to conclude that the copies were probably taken with Barbauld's approval: *ALBVE*, p. 572, n. 21.
34. Mary Wollstonecraft, *Vindication of the Rights of Woman*, p. 79.
35. *ALBVE*, p. 74.
36. *PALB*, pp. 219–20.
37. McCarthy and Kraft quote a letter she wrote to the *Norwich Iris* defending Priestley that very much echoes the language of the poem (*PALB*, p. 246).
38. *PALB*, p. 38–9, lines 37–8.
39. *PALB*, p. 36–7, lines 32–5.
40. [Woodfall], 'Review of *Poems*, by Miss Aikin', p. 58.
41. Reprinted in the editions 4 and 5, deleted in 1792 (*PALB*, p. 245).
42. 'Prologue to "The Man of Pleasure" by John Aikin' (29), lines 24–6.
43. *ALBVE*, p. 299.
44. The imprecision arises because a handful of poems cannot be dated.
45. See notes 9 and 10, above.
46. Aikin, 'Memoir', p. lx.
47. Ibid. p. lx.
48. Betsy Rodgers, *Georgian Chronicle: Mrs. Barbauld and Her Family* (1958), p. 242.
49. In a letter to Richard Phillips, founder of the *Monthly Magazine*, dated 8 May 1805, Lucy Aikin discusses her preparation of an edition of a selection of poetry from that periodical. She explains that she has about 8,000 lines of verse, 'having taken all that was good,

except Mrs. Barbauld's pieces, which are omitted by her particular desire'. The most significant contributors are Robert Southey and William Taylor, and she states: 'I think it would be proper to ask their permission before their pieces are printed; but this is entirely your affair' (British Library, Add. MS 60,484, f.8). Perhaps Phillips did, and consent was not granted; their refusal might explain why no edition was forthcoming.

50. *PALB*, p. 293. Barbauld may have written another poem to/about Priestley and the riots, 'Ode, addressed to the Rev. Doctor Priestley' (159.1). This poem is known in only a single printed sheet, which is endorsed by an unknown hand with Barbauld's name. For a discussion of the possibility of its being Barbauld's, see *PALB*, p. 345. If the poem is in fact hers, the private printing suggests both that the poem circulated in manuscript and that caution was thought necessary to protect both the author and the printer, whose names do not appear on the sheet.
51. *PALB*, p. 287. The editors note that they were unable to find any reference to the poem in parliamentary debates. The provocative nature of this last poem is evidenced by Lucy Aikin's decision, over three decades later, to omit it from *Works*.
52. Emma Clery provides the fullest and most persuasive articulation of the calculated risk Barbauld took in publishing the poem: see *Eighteen hundred and eleven: poetry, protest and economic crisis* (2017).
53. She did the same with other publications as well. *An Address to the Opposers of the Repeal of the Corporations and Tests Act* (1790), a forty-four-page octavo pamphlet, sold for 1 shilling, and *Civic Sermons to the People* (Number 1) (1792), a twenty-page octavo pamphlet, sold for sixpence. Although these prices seem consistent with other pamphlets, Barbauld could have produced a more expensive edition, had she decided to collect her prose works.
54. See note 28, above; [John Wilson Croker], 'Mrs. Barbauld's *Eighteen Hundred and Eleven*', *Quarterly Review* 7 (June 1812): 309.
55. *PALB*, p. 309.
56. Quoting a letter from Barbauld to Lucy Aikin, dated 12 December 1811, *PALB*, p. 307.
57. L. Aikin, *Memoir*, p. lii.
58. Ibid. pp. lii–liii.
59. Ibid. p. liii.
60. This account has been repeated by modern scholars. In an otherwise superb essay, William Keach repeats Aikin's narrative: 'A Regency Prophecy and the End of Anna Barbauld's Career'.
61. William Wordsworth, 'Essay, Supplementary to the Preface', I: 368.

62. Lord Byron, *Don Juan*, V: 483, canto XI, stanza 60, lines 473, 480. It was fuelled as well by Shelley's death – though the most important articulation of the poet's suffering and death being the result of the scorn he was subject to while he was alive is to be found in Mary Shelley's *Poetical Works of Percy Bysshe Shelley* (1839).
63. Keats, of course, died of tuberculosis. Chatterton's suicide has been recently called into question by Nick Groom, who believes that 'he died simply from unwisely mixing his venereal medicine (arsenic) with his recreational (opium)': see 'Chatterton, Thomas'. Wordsworth's claim that poetic genius was never recognised in the poet's lifetime has been widely viewed as self-serving.
64. *PALB*, p. 324.
65. Robert Stewart, Viscount Castlereagh (1769–1822), known as Lord Castlereagh, was a British/Irish statesman. He played a critical role in suppressing the Irish rebellion of 1798, and he was responsible for shepherding the Act of Union with Ireland through Parliament in 1800. Barbauld, like others, held Castlereagh in contempt for breaking the promise to Irish Catholics that they would be allowed to sit in Parliament after the Union.
66. See, for example, this speech by Clio from 'Dialogue in the Shades': 'For above these three thousand years have I been warning them and reading lessons to them, and they will not mend: Robespierre was as cruel as Sylla, and Napoleon has no more moderation than Pyrrhus. The human frame, of curious texture, delicately formed, feeling, and irritable by the least annoyance, with face erect and animated with Promethean fire, they wound, they lacerate, they mutilate with most perverted ingenuity. – I will go and record the actions of the tigers of Africa; in them such fierceness is natural – Nay, the human race will be exterminated if this work of destruction goes on much longer': William McCarthy and Elizabeth Kraft (eds), *Anna Letitia Barbauld: Selected Poetry and Prose* (2002), p. 472.
67. *PALB*, p. 324.
68. *PALB*, p. 323; John Aikin, *Annual Register, or a View of the History, Politics and Literature, for the Year 1818* (London: Baldwin, Cradock and Joy, 1819). Barbauld gave her permission to Joanna Baillie to republish this poem for *A Collection of Poems* (1823); instead, Baillie included 'On the King's Illness' and 'To Mrs. – , on Returning a fine Hyacinth Plant'.
69. J. Aikin, *Annual Register*, pp. 2, 1.
70. McCarthy provides this analysis in *PALB*, p. 320.
71. The poem appeared in the following periodicals: *New-York Literary Journal, and Belles-Lettres Repository* 3, no. 2 (15 June 1820): 158;

Christian Disciple [Boston], n.s. 3 (November–December 1821): 440; *Christian Disciple*, n.s. 4 (September–October 1822): 322–3; *Monthly Repository* 17 (October 1822): 636; *Monthly Repository* 17 (November 1822): 679.
72. *New-York Literary Journal*, p. 158.
73. *Monthly Repository* (November 1822), p. 679.
74. *Christian Disciple* (1822), p. 322.
75. *PALB*, p. xxxvii; letter from Thomas Jefferson to John Adams, 1 June 1822, in *The Writings of Thomas Jefferson*, III: 244.
76. Line 9, 'those' is 'our'; line 12 'Ah!' is 'Oh!' and 'easy 'tis' is 'sweet it is'; line 20 'Previous' is 'kindest'.
77. *Writings of Thomas Jefferson*, III: 244.
78. Ibid. III: 244
79. Letter from John Adams to Thomas Jefferson, 11 June 1822, in *The Portable John Adams*, p. 523.

Chapter 4

Lord Byron, Manuscript Poet

Jerome McGann, Byron's leading editor and scholar, has challenged 'the text-centered procedures of twentieth-century criticism', which, he asserts, 'have never been able to read Byron's work in interesting ways'.[1] Implementing his own theory of the socialisation of texts, McGann contends that a Byron poem can never be regarded 'simply as an event in "language"'.[2] Rather, McGann promotes the concept of a publication event, asking that contemporary readers take into account Byron's 'actual practice of installing the poetical experience as a social and historical event'.[3] '[T]hroughout his career', McGann explains, 'Byron's books cultivate direct communication with the people who are reading them . . . [h]is work assumes the presence of an audience that talks and listens.'[4] As in the previous chapter's exploration of Barbauld's use of manuscript to transmit her poetry, which sought to reunite her poems with the material forms in which they were circulated and read, this chapter seeks to understand how and what Byron, for much of his career the most celebrated poet of the day, was 'attempting to do' by circulating his poetry in script. The assumption that Byron was primarily a print poet has meant that his extensive use of manuscript has never been systematically studied; nor has its impact on our understanding of his poetry and career. This chapter reconstructs the complex processes by which Byron's poems were composed and mediated in his lifetime, as he regularly chose manuscript for his confidential and satirical poems.[5] By scrutinising Byron's practices of literary production and circulation in print and script, we heed McGann's call for new strategies of reading Byron's poetry.

This chapter founds its claims about Byron's use of manuscript circulation in part by adapting techniques from the 'quantitative humanities', what Franco Moretti has more broadly termed 'distant reading'.[6] To date, no effort has been made to quantify and analyse Byron's poetic output. For example, we do not know how many poems Byron printed in his lifetime in comparison with how many were left unprinted; nor do we know how many of his poems circulated in manuscript, how often he used private print, and the consequences, or how many of his manuscript poems were printed without his authorisation. With these questions in mind, this chapter experiments with different forms of quantitative analysis to chart Byron's poetic career over time. The chapter begins with a survey of Byron's publication history to identify basic patterns in the production and dissemination of his poetry. Because Byron wrote and published more poetry than Barbaud, and because far more of his poetry survives in manuscript form, the analysis is more complex than the previous chapter's exploration of Barbauld's poetic career in print and script. Drawing upon Jerome McGann's seven-volume *Complete Poetical Works* (*CPW*), and his extensive editorial commentaries that outline the publication histories of each poem, we find that of the total 410 known poems, 208 (or 51 per cent) were unpublished in his lifetime.[7] A line graph (Plate 7) charts the number of poems composed by year. Byron's production of poems peaked in 1806, though the sharpness of this peak is somewhat overstated here (and in Plate 8) as a result of McGann's assignment of many early poems to the year 1806, even though some were likely written earlier. The number of poems also spiked significantly in 1812, during his initial rise to fame, and in 1815–16, at the height of the separation controversy. Charting the production of individual poems provides a very crude measure of poetic output. Counting the length of these poems (as measured by the number of pages in McGann's uniform edition), offers a more nuanced metric to analyse his output. Byron's output measured in terms of pages is marked by the orange line in Plate 7, and this visualisation presents a very different picture, one of increasing rather than decreasing productivity.[8] When viewed side by side, we find that his number of poems (the blue line) declines, whereas the length of his poems (the orange line) increases, this inverse relationship telling us that as Byron's career advanced, he wrote fewer but longer poems.

An even more granular mapping is possible by dividing Byron's poems into two categories – that of long and short – the line being drawn at ten pages (as printed in *CPW*). This metric proves useful, as what counts as a long poem (according to this definition) includes all of the long separately published poems, with the one exception of 'The Lament of Tasso' (316), which, though only nine pages, was published on its own.[9] Plate 8 makes visible the relative stability in the poet's production of long poems beginning in 1809, when *English Bards and Scotch Reviewers* (129) first appeared. His production of long poems peaks in 1816 and 1821, years in which he wrote five and seven long poems, respectively. His production of short poems, meanwhile, is shown to have sharply declined after 1806, with accelerated production only in certain years (1811–12 and 1815–16), both periods of considerable biographical significance. Adding a further variable, that of publication status, to Plate 9, we find that only one of Byron's long poems remained unprinted during his lifetime, as may be seen in the barely visible sliver of orange representing *Hints from Horace* (*Hints* 150). However, the left-hand column, representing his output of *short* poems, suggests a more mixed picture: of the 378 short poems that Byron produced, 171 were printed and 207 were unprinted. Of the 171 short printed poems, sixty-seven, or nearly 40 per cent, were published between 1806 and 1809, the largest number of lyric poems printed by Byron at any one time.

Plate 10 combines these variables to present a complete picture of Byron's poetic output. The single long, unprinted poem, *Hints*, exists as a nearly invisible purple dot in 1811. The rest of Byron's long poems (represented by the blue line) were printed, in consistently low single-digit numbers from 1811 to the year preceding his death. The red line, which denotes his short unprinted poems, is characterised by peaks and valleys, but the overall picture reveals that Byron consistently wrote around a dozen short poems that were unpublished per year. The short printed poems (represented by the green line) display the most volatility, erupting in 1806, falling precipitously thereafter, recovering slightly in 1815–16, and then falling off considerably again: Byron wrote seventy-nine short poems from 1817 to his death in 1824, but he printed only eleven of them.

This chapter examines publication events belonging to three critical epochs in Byron's writing life. It begins by scrutinising the 1806 peak in printed short poems, as Byron's poetry rapidly transitioned from manuscript, to private print, to commercial print with the publication of his first four collections of poetry printed verse. It considers how Byron used his coterie readers as a means of testing and shaping his verse to suit expanding audiences. This early phase demonstrates Byron's early desire for 'an audience that talks and listens', a need that would persist throughout his life. During the early period, we witness Byron's early struggles to conform his poetry to the expectations and demands of various audiences.

The second phase of Byron's career that this chapter examines is the transition from *Bards* to the publication of the first two cantos of *Childe Harold's Pilgrimage* (*CHP*), as we encounter Byron struggling to address a public audience in the composition of longer, satiric poems. Through a careful analysis of the revisions to the two surviving manuscripts of *CHP* I and II, its status as a confidential and public manuscript becomes apparent, as Byron uses commentaries, notes and revisions to address his coterie readers at the same time as he undertakes the process of readying his poem for a wider public. These revisions are, in some ways, reminiscent of those made by Dorothy Wordsworth in her *Recollections of a Tour in Scotland*, and the final authorial persona that Byron projects bears resemblance to that of Charlotte Smith, in *Elegiac Sonnets*. Throughout the revision process, moreover, we see Byron's advisers suggesting revisions that align with the conceptions of print being advanced by the *Edinburgh Review*. This chapter concludes by examining instances of Byron's later use of manuscript to circulate his intimate, confidential and satirical poems. This examination focuses on his use of literary associates, above all his publisher John Murray, to channel his literary manuscripts to readers who would admire and enjoy them, and to keep them from those that would not. These three phases illuminate Byron's negotiations with print and his material practices of manuscript circulation, and reveal a productive tension that structured Byron's career as he sought to address himself unhindered to an initiated audience and to seek wider public acclaim.

Byron's Early Verse Collections

Around 1806, the eighteen-year-old Byron enjoyed his first burst of poetic activity, writing over sixty poems (see Plates 7 and 8). Most of these poems were highly conventional: addressed to lovers, family members and school friends, they reflect upon his early experiences and range in style and genre from the mawkish and the hackneyed to the bawdy and the satirical. Byron circulated these poems in manuscript form and also printed four separate verse collections between 1806 and 1808, *Fugitive Pieces* (*Fugitive*), *Poems on Various Occasions* (*Various*), *Hours of Idleness* (*Hours*), and *Poems, Original and Translated* (*Original*). Though these four collections are usually treated as editions of the same work, they in fact should be viewed as separate, as they were prepared for distinct audiences, with substantial differences in the poems included in each and their arrangement.[10]

Table 4.1 presents basic publication information about these four volumes. *Fugitive* and *Various* were 'printed, not published', a distinction Byron and his contemporaries invoked (as did the *Edinburgh Review*, as we have seen, to denigrate certain publications for which, it assumed, a commercial publisher was not available). The third and fourth printings, of *Hours* and *Original*, were, in contrast, commercially printed and thus intended for a public readership.[11] Byron made some alterations to individual poems, but by far the most significant changes he made were to the selections of poems included in each of the four collections. Table 4.1 records the number of poems removed and added from each of the four collections, using the previous collection as the base. As may be seen, each new volume differed significantly from the previous one, though, quantitatively, most changes occurred between the privately printed *Various* and the publicly printed *Hours*. In total, sixty-seven poems were shuffled between the four volumes (their ordering changes as well, sometimes dramatically), with each collection containing between thirty-eight and forty-eight poems.

The first collection, *Fugitive*, was printed privately by Samuel and John Ridge over a five-month period, as Byron added and revised poems incrementally in a process that is not dissimilar from how a

Table 4.1 Poems removed from and added to Byron's four early verse collections

Title of collection	Fugitive Pieces	Poems on Various Occasions	Hours of Idleness	Poems, Original and Translated
Publication date	July–November 1806	Early January 1807	June 1807	March 1808
Number of poems removed	—	2	21	6
Number of poems added	—	12	12	5
Total number of poems	38	48	39	38

manuscript miscellany is created over time. By using a local printer, Byron indulged in an alternative to scribal copying, for it spared him (or, more likely, his female companions) the burden of making copies by hand and would have lent an air of polish and elegance to his verse collections. In fact, the four extant printings of *Fugitive* are more similar to manuscript copies than to printed ones, insofar as each one is substantially different.[12] Andrew Stauffer's examination of the four extant printings demonstrates that 'none of those four surviving texts is the precise bibliographic equivalent of any of the others, so "copies" is probably a misnomer'; in other words, the four surviving texts 'are not the product of a single print run'.[13] Rather, each of the four extant versions of *Fugitive* is unique; not only were they customised, by hand, with different corrections, illustrations and gift inscriptions, but they also vary in their organisation and even in the layout of seemingly identical pages. Further, rather than the fifty to one hundred copies once believed to have been printed, Stauffer believes that at most half a dozen were produced.

The four exemplars of *Fugitive* (as we might call them) share other features in common with manuscript. They appear to have originally ended at page 40, with later sections added incrementally, in stages, such that 'each volume was composed separately at what we might call the user-end', with each exemplar containing different poems, in different arrangements.[14] Here print fails to settle textuality, with the privately printed sheets operating analogously to manuscript presentation copies, in which variation, customisation and enlargement over time are the norm. Although *Fugitive* is a printed volume, Byron's preface announces that 'these POEMS were never intended to meet the public eye' and are 'printed merely for the perusal of a few friends to whom they are dedicated; who will look upon them with indulgence'.[15] This description of the anticipated audience, reminiscent of Dorothy Wordsworth's *Recollections of a Tour in Scotland* and Coleridge's *Sonnets by Various Authors*, demonstrates the coterie nature of manuscript and private print alike. The coterie readership imagined for *Fugitive* is evident in other respects: in the autobiographical nature of the poems, most of which are addressed to friends and relations, and in the conventions of dating and naming the locations in which the poems were written. All of these practices inscribe the volume within Byron's community at Southwell, the Nottinghamshire town where he visited his mother on school vacations.

Byron's faith that private print would allow him the expressive freedom and control associated with manuscript culture was swiftly tested. In *Fugitive*, Byron had included a few sexually risqué poems and others that, as Willis Pratt observes, display 'a humorously mocking quality', written to entertain and titillate members of his social circle.[16] While collecting the poems for *Fugitive*, he realised that there were some poems that would not be appropriate even for the modest circulation he imagined for the privately printed volume. His solution was to have several of these poems 'printed *separate* from my other compositions', explaining to his friend John Pigot on 10 August 1806: 'you will perceive [these poems] to be improper for the perusal of ladies; of course, none of the females of your family must see them'.[17] Byron seems to have assumed that separate printed sheets could be more easily secreted, or possibly these sheets were made for binding up in certain copies, access to which could be more carefully controlled. Whether any of these separates were in fact printed is not known, for none have survived. However, what can be known is that from the outset of his literary career, Byron understood the need for discretion in the circulation of some of his poems, and sought strategies to direct his poems to their intended readers.

Immediately after the printings of *Fugitive* were complete (the last poem bears the date of 16 November), Byron encountered resistance from readers whom he had offended with the inclusion of one erotic poem in particular, 'To Mary' (77). The poem's references to sexual intimacy, in the form of 'circling arms', 'bosom heaves', 'polluted kiss', 'fond caress', 'folds of pleasure' and 'panting, dying' lovers were simply too suggestive, and also hinted at what may have been Byron's actual dalliances with the young women of the neighbourhood. Encountering these complaints, Byron immediately began to prepare a new volume of poems and attempted to have the existing printings of *Fugitive* destroyed.[18] In urging his friends John and Elizabeth Pigot to destroy their copies, Byron conveyed his belief that he retained the right to manage the physical copies of *Fugitive*, even after they had been distributed. If, as Stauffer suggests, only a few copies were actually printed, the survival of four copies (two of which belonged to Elizabeth Pigot, one to John Pigot, and the other to John Becher), suggests that he did not in fact enjoy this control, as his friends did *not* obey his request to return their copies for destruction.[19]

The next collection, *Various*, was privately printed in January 1807 by the same publishers, retaining the identical dedication used in *Fugitive*, in which Byron describes his verses as 'trifles' 'solely intended' for his particular friends. However, as evidenced by his choice to remove the two most objectionable poems, 'To Mary' and a similar poem, 'To Caroline' (73), Byron prepared *Various* for circulation amongst a slightly wider (but still constrained) audience than that anticipated for *Fugitive*. He also made some surgical excisions to a few of the poems that he retained; for example, he excised the sexually charged stanza 8 of 'To the Sighing Strephone' (86); stanzas 5–10 of 'To Miss E. P.' (84), a comical account of the scriptural basis for the sentiment that 'though women are angels, yet wedlock's the devil'; and stanza 5 of 'To Caroline' (79), which included another mockery of marriage.[20] *Various* may be properly described as a transitional collection, one that retains its sociable origin but also shows Byron bending to the demands of a disapproving readership.

Various inches towards a more public mode of print in a number of other respects. Byron adopted the conventions of print in endeavouring to protect the identities of his female subjects, some of whom were rivals for his attention.[21] Thus 'To Julia' becomes 'To Lesbia' (83); 'To A – ' (who was easily recognised as Ann Houson) becomes 'To M.....' (38); and 'To Maria' becomes 'To Emma' (74).[22] Although Byron described *Various* to John Pigot as 'miraculously chaste', he did not capitulate without voicing his resentment towards readers whom he believed had wilfully misunderstood his verse, or had failed to read it fully.[23] In *Various*, Byron adds a note to the poem, 'To a Lady who presented to the author a lock of hair' (81), attacking those (particularly Julia Leacroft's father) who believed (according to Byron, erroneously) that the reference in the poem to Shakespeare's Juliet was, in fact, an allusion to Julia. In two lengthy notes, Byron denies that Julia Leacroft – who is never named, but whose putative identity would have been well known within the Southwell circle – is the subject of the poem, insulting those who make such inferences as illiterate and indecorous.[24]

Although Byron included in *Various* this complaint against his readers, he withheld his most severe attacks from the collection, electing instead to circulate them in manuscript, indicative of his growing adeptness in negotiating between script and print. In 'To a Knot of Ungenerous Critics' (25), written in December 1806, Byron condemns those readers to whom 'the strain was never sent' (line 65): 'Rail on, Rail on, ye heartless crew! / My strains were never meant for you' (lines 1–2). He claims that his poetry 'For feeling Souls alone 'twas meant' (line 66) and rages against the 'portly Female' who had 'seized, unask'd, unbade, / and damn'd, ere yet the whole was read!' (lines 67–8). In *Various*, he adds a tamer poem on the same theme, 'Answer to Some Elegant Verses, Sent by A Friend to the Author, complaining that one of his descriptions was rather too warmly drawn' (97).[25] In this protest against censorship, Byron professes to apologise for the 'sole error, which pervades my strain' (lines 4–5), but asserts that his poetry can not be tamed: 'Precepts of prudence curb, but can't controul, / The fierce emotions of the flowing soul' (lines 9–10). He disparages 'the nerveless, frigid song' of more chaste poets in this poem as well as in 'The First Kiss of Love' (92) and also elucidates his ideal audience:

> For me, I fain would please the chosen few,
> Whose souls, to feeling, and to nature true,
> Will spare the childish verse, and not destroy,
> The light effusions of a heedless boy. (lines 37–9)

Byron thus uses print circulation to critique the constraints of print, though more restrainedly than in his manuscript verse.

By removing from *Various* the sexually charged poems and the names and initials that hinted at improper intimacies, Byron purged the volume of one of its greatest pleasures: the ability, on the part of his intimate readers, to recognise amatory and erotic allusions. At the same time, many of the new poems did little to add intrigue: of the twelve new poems, five are tame love poems, one is an elegy to his ancestral home, one an admiration of the poet James Montgomery, and two are translations.[26] The result was a volume that was 'more sedate and at the same time less distinguishable from any other juvenile collection of sentimental and imitative verse'.[27] The new collection enjoyed greater circulation than *Fugitive*: it is believed that Ridge produced about one hundred copies, of which, according to WorldCat, thirteen copies survive. The result, however, was a compromised volume that failed to satisfy its different constituencies of readers: '[w]hat was liveliest had been skimmed off; what was blandest remained for general circulation'.[28] Three of the newly added poems – 'Answer to some Elegant Verses' (97), 'Childish Recollections' (93) and 'To the Rev. J. T. Becher' (96) – do, however, hint at the Byronic persona that would soon emerge, prefiguring the satirical, disaffected youth Byron would perfect in *CHP*. In 'Childish Recollections', the poet declares himself 'Weary of love, of life, devour'd with spleen, / I rest, a perfect Timon, not nineteen'; 'A wretched, isolated, gloomy thing, / Curst by reflection's deep corroding sting' (*CPW* I: 170). In 'To the Rev. J. T. Becher', he pronounces: 'retirement accords with the tone of my mind, / I will not descend to a world I despise' (3–4). Despite this pledge (the first of many to come), Byron immediately began preparing a new, third volume, this time for a public audience.

The unfortunately titled *Hours of Idleness*, released in June 1807, initiated the most significant changes between the four verse collections, with the removal of twenty-two and the addition of twelve poems. In the twelve new poems, Byron augmented the themes of *Various* and developed several new directions. There are more translations and poems on classical subjects (44, 53, 54, 57), more poems addressing women or romance (45, 62, 42), male friendship (65, 66) and Scottish themes (46, 61, 64), as well as the addition of six epigraphs to retained poems (two Latin, three Greek and one English). It is the removal of twenty-one poems from *Various* – nearly half of the thirty-nine poems included in *Hours* – that marks the radical adjustment Byron believed necessary. Gone are most of the amatory poems that survived into *Various* ('To ---' [72], 'To Caroline' [78], 'Untitled' ['When I hear you express an affection so warm'] [79], 'To Emma' [74], 'To a Lady' [81], 'To Lesbia' [83], 'Lines addressed to a Young Lady' [88]); poems to relations ('On the Death of a Yong Lady, Cousin to the Author' [20]); poems that delineate a Southwell coterie, including poems addressed to the Pigots ('Lines Written' [75], which begins with a quatrain written by Elizabeth Pigot, 'To Miss E. P.' [84], 'Reply to some verses of J. M. B. Pigot' [85], 'To the Sighing Strephon' [86], 'To M. S. G' [90]); poems associated with Harrow, including two translations ('To D. . . .' [71], 'On the Change of Masters' [76], 'Imitation of Tibullus' [89], 'Horace, Ode 3' [91] and 'To The Rev. J. T. Becher' [96]; 'Answer to a beautiful poem, written by Montgomery' [94]); and poems addressed to the Cambridge choirboy John Eddleston ('To E---' [69], 'The Cornelian' [87]).[29]

Byron's explanation for removing 'On a Change of Masters, at a Great Public School' (76), a poem that satirised the incoming headmaster at Harrow, Dr Butler, demonstrates that he had absorbed an understanding of print as a public medium. He explains that he withdrew the poem because it

> alludes to a character printed in a former private edition for the perusal of some friends, which with many other pieces is withheld from the present volume; to draw the attention of the public to insignificance would be deservedly reprobated.[30]

Again, using a discourse that appears to be lifted from the pages of the *Edinburgh Review*, he acknowledges that the praise his poems have received from friends is at once 'partial' and possibly 'injudicious', admitting that 'admiration of a social circle, is not the criterion by which poetical genius is to be estimated'.[31] Byron expressed his indifference to public acclaim in his preface, in which he presents himself as a youthful amateur who declares it 'highly improbable . . . that I should ever obtrude myself a second time on the Public'.[32] In the preface Byron disingenuously claims that he shuns a career as a poet and ostentatiously pronounces himself indifferent to public opinion. Reviewers pounced upon the incoherence of Byron's public stance, of seeming at once to court and dismiss public opinion. They also attacked what they perceived to be his flaunting of aristocratic privilege – the volume is after all provocatively entitled *Hours of Idleness* – and of his minority status, reflected in the collection's many allusions to college and school exercises. Byron mistakenly drew attention to his nobility and minority in an attempt to use them to extenuate any deficiencies in the poetry. Both the paratextual material and the verse itself invited a reviewer like Henry Brougham to use, in Peter Graham's words, 'the adolescent author's own prefatory and poetic words to damn him'.[33] These missteps were, however, at least in part the result of Byron's own uncertainty about why he was publicly printing his poems. On the one hand, he repeatedly claimed that he sought only those readers to whom he could write freely and from whom he could expect admiration; on the other hand, he moved swiftly to print, seeking an audience who could 'estimate' his 'genius'.

Another method for assessing how Byron understood the demands of print involves identifying poems that appear across multiple volumes. Only sixteen of the total sixty-seven poems appear in all four volumes; of these, six are classical translations or school exercises, and another three allude to his public school and college days ('Thoughts suggested by a College Education' [58], 'Granta: A Medley' [60] and 'On a distant view of the Village and School, of Harrow' [80]).[34] Of the remaining seven, three ('On Leaving Newstead Abbey' [31], 'Untitled' [33], and 'An Occasional Prologue' [35]) allude directly to his aristocratic heritage. The remaining four poems meditate on general topics, such as women ('To Women' [39]), love ('The Tear' [40]), friendship ('Epitaph on a Friend' [32]) and politics ('On the Death of Mr. Fox' [36]). Further evidence of the status of *Hours* as a safe harbour for seemingly unobjectionable poems is supported by the fact that it includes no unique poems, unlike the three other volumes: *Fugitive* has two unique poems, *Various* has four and *Original* has five. Poems survive into *Hours* (and are carried forward into the fourth collection, *Original*) chiefly because they are perceived to be harmless. The first two collections (*Fugitive* and *Various*) are more similar to each other than the later two (*Hours* and *Original*): eighteen poems appear only in *Fugitive* and *Various*; twelve in *Hours* and *Original*; only four are shared between *Various* and *Hours*; and none are common to both the first and final collections, *Fugitive* and *Original*, demonstrating the complete overhaul that has taken place between them. The clear demarcation between the first two private collections and the final two public ones, and the thorough distinctness between the first and last, reinforce the claim that Byron saw certain categories of poems as suitable largely or exclusively for coterie circulation, others for public consumption.

When Brougham's review of *Hours* appeared in the *Edinburgh Review* in February 1808, Byron reacted with high drama, writing to John Hobhouse: 'As an Author, I am cut to Atoms by the E Review; it is just out, and has completely demolished my little fabric of fame.'[35] According to Andrew Rutherford, there is reason to believe that Byron was not exaggerating, as Hobhouse noted privately that the poet 'was very near destroying himself' on this occasion.[36] Peter Graham notes that 'Brougham's review taught [Byron] to distinguish private poems, the occasional verses he sent to friends or circulated in a coterie, from candidates for publication.'[37] While it is certainly true that Byron would never again release a collection of lyric poems on similar topics, the foregoing analysis has sought to demonstrate that Byron had in fact spent much of the previous eighteen months attempting to discriminate between poems according to their imagined audiences. The immediate consequence of Brougham's review was that Byron sought to have the second edition of his commercially printed poems, *Original*, suppressed and made available only to friends. In this he failed, as he would in future attempts to control the circulation of his printed poetry.[38]

The *Edinburgh Review* arguably had an effect of longer duration, rendering Byron averse to publishing collections of his lyric poems, as he came to understand the *Edinburgh*'s intolerance for lyric poetry, particularly of the milquetoast variety included in *Hours*.[39] With the one exception of *Poems* (1816) – a collection initiated by Murray and not embraced by Byron – the poet never again collected and printed his lyrics in a stand-alone volume. He also wrote fewer short poems, immediately experimenting with the composition of longer works. It is possible that his shifting practices were the outcome not only of the *Edinburgh*'s reception of his own work, but of other lyric collections, particularly Wordsworth's *Poems in Two Volumes*. Wordsworth's *Poems in Two Volumes* was reviewed by Byron himself in the *Monthly Literary Recreations* for 13 July 1807. While generally favourable, Byron did not restrain himself from describing Wordsworth's poetry as 'puerile', 'namby-pamby' and 'trifling'.[40] These views were echoed and intensified in the *Edinburgh*'s review, published in October 1807, just three months before its review of *Hours* in January 1808. Francis Jeffrey's review of Wordsworth's collection issued a staggering rebuke to Wordsworth's publication. Since it had appeared, *Poems in Two Volumes* had been the target of a 'firestorm of scathing ridicule', but it was Jeffrey's review that dealt the final blow, denigrating the poems as 'the theme of an unpractised schoolboy', demonstrating 'babyish absurdity, a very paragon of silliness and affectation' and a 'mass of childishness, and insipidity'.[41] These terms of derision were echoed in the *Edinburgh*'s castigation of Byron as 'an infant bard' and 'noble minor'.[42] Jeffrey's review of Wordsworth's *Poems* had gone even further, insinuating that the lyric form itself was feeble. The association drawn between lyric poetry and poetic immaturity, to say nothing of triviality and triteness, seems to have had a powerful and lasting effect on Byron, shaping both his poetic practices and the public presentation of his poems.

Revising *CHP* I and II for Print

Between 1809 and 1812, Byron wrote four long poems: *Bards* (129), begun in October 1807 and printed in early 1809; cantos I and II of *Childe* (174), begun on 31 October 1809, finished on 28 March 1810, and printed in early 1812; *Hints* (150), written in March 1811; and *Curse of Minerva* (151), written between March and November 1811. His intentions regarding the dissemination of these poems was shifting and uncertain, as they circulated in various forms and existed in a suspended state during which time Byron pondered their future. Ultimately, he made very different decisions for each of these four poems:

1. *English Bards* – Byron elected to print the poem with James Cawthorne in March 1809, and printed three further, substantially enlarged editions between 1809 and 1810. In 1812, Byron attempted, without success, to suppress the fifth edition.
2. *Childe I* and *II* – Byron wavered while revising the poem about whether it was suitable for print. After undertaking extensive revisions, in stages, he published it on 10 March 1812. After its publication, Byron exclaimed: 'I awoke one morning and found myself famous.'[43]
3. *Hints* – Byron's plans for the publication of this poem were far advanced at two different periods: in 1811–12, when he planned to publish it with the fifth edition of *Bards* and *Curse*, and in 1820–2. Ultimately, however, the poem was not printed in his lifetime.
4. *Curse* – Byron claimed that this poem was never intended for public dissemination. In May 1812 he privately printed eight copies, which were promptly pirated and more widely distributed.

The disparate publication histories of these four poems reveal the diffidence with which Byron approached print in the aftermath of Brougham's review of *Hours* and the diverse paths by which his longer poems of this period circulated. These histories also remind us the challenges faced by attempts to determine intentionality with respect to publication.

Byron's preface to *Bards* demonstrates how self-conscious he was about the satire's publication. In just over 500 words, the preface references the 'public' three times, 'publish' four times, 'author' five times and 'publication' once.[44] Although his stance is one of studied indifference – 'I'll publish, right or wrong: / Fools are my theme, let Satire be my Song' (lines 5–6) – the preface betrays his preoccupation with questions of propriety and publicity. In his refusal to abide by the advice of his friends, who 'have urged me not to publish this Satire with my name', Byron stakes a claim to gentlemanly honour (refusing 'to be terrified by abuse, or bullied by reviewers, with or without arms') and professionalism ('An Author's works are public property: he who purchases may judge, and publish his opinion if he pleases').[45] By removing fourteen lines inserted by 'an ingenious friend of mine', Byron explains he is motivated by 'a determination not to publish with my name any production which was not entirely and exclusively my own composition'. He thereby disavows social authorship, as he had done previously, in removing from *Hours* all traces of poems written by members of his coterie.[46]

Byron enjoyed the rapid sales of *Bards*, but he regarded its success as transient: 'My Satire it seems is in a fourth edition, a success rather above the middling run, but not much for a production which, from its topics, must be temporary, and of course be successful at first, or not at all.'[47] Byron sought to suppress the poem, as it caused him considerable embarrassment upon his return to England in July 1811. In *Bards*, he had lashed out against several literary men with whom he had since become acquainted, prompting a flow of retractions, apologies and even favours to those whom he had lampooned.[48] Byron's tendency to compose, dispatch and sometimes print his poems in haste, deploying an uncompromising satirical method, presented an ongoing personal challenge for a poet whose allegiances rapidly shifted. Although Byron told Walter Scott in a letter dated 6 July 1812 that the poem was 'suppressed *voluntarily*', he could not prevent his new printer, Cawthorne, from issuing a fifth edition in 1816; nor could he prevent a flood of piracies.[49] As with his early verse collections, Byron was no more successful in having *Bards* suppressed than he had been in having copies of *Fugitive* destroyed and *Original* suppressed. Nevertheless, the work became so 'exceedingly scarce' that, according to T. J. Hogg, 'some curious persons even took the trouble to transcribe it'.[50] As late as October 1815, when Byron gifted his only copy of the poem to Leigh Hunt, he observed that its 'greatest value is its present rarity'.[51]

As he had done previously first in *Various*, then in *Hours* and again in *Bards*, Byron made another false promise, vowing that 'should I back return, no tempting press / Shall drag my Journal from the desk's recess: / Let coxcombs printing as they come from far, / Snatch his own wreath of Ridicule from Carr' (lines 1023–6). However, almost as soon as *Bards* was issued in England, Byron began a new travel narrative. The first draft of what became *CHP* was written between 31 October 1809 and 20 March 1810. Only a small fragment of this original draft survives (Manuscript T), but it was recopied, and almost certainly expanded and revised in the process, in early 1811.[52] This draft, known as Manuscript M, survives, and presents the poem in two states, the original copy (made from the draft) and the original copy as transformed by revisions.[53] This early version of the poem was shared by Byron with his coterie: Byron added an annotation to the cover page in 1812, stating that the 'marginal remarks penciled occasionally were ~~written~~ made by two friends [John Hobhouse and R. C. Dallas] who saw the thing in M.S. some time prior to publication'. Dallas made a fair copy from Manuscript M, in late July and early August of 1811, and this copy, known as Manuscript D, also survives and shows the poem in two states, as Byron made further revisions to Dallas's fair copy over the next few months. Manuscript D ultimately served as printer's copy. With these two manuscripts showing the text in four states, we are able to trace how Byron and his advisers worked to anticipate the demands of print. Unlike the movement of poems across the four collections, in which Byron tended to suppress rather than revise his poems, with Cantos I and II of *Childe* the revisions can be tracked within a single poem.[54] By examining the changes within and between Manuscript M and Manuscript D, it is possible to observe those aspects of the poem Byron and his advisers immediately objected to as unviable for a public readership, and those that were more gradually pared away as the poem transitioned from a confidential to a public audience.

Manuscript M was shown to and written with Byron's friends in mind. His address to these intimate readers becomes apparent both in the poem itself and in the accompanying notes, many of which offer caustic or uncouth commentaries that were clearly directed towards his confidential readers. For example, to stanza 32 [29] about Maria I of Portugal, 'Lussian's crazy Queen' in Manuscript M,

Byron added the following note: 'Her insane majesty was religiously mad, & Dr Willis who so dexterously cudgeled kingly pericraniums [he treated King George III] could make not a thing of hers.'[55] Byron added annotations about the precise locations in which stanzas had been written, personal anecdotes, and other local knowledge, enhancing the confidential tone by providing intimate details, most of which were removed when the poem was presented to a public audience.[56] This manuscript provides a valuable example of the difficulty of pinning down a single intention in the manuscript, for as he wrote Byron was simultaneously addressing his confidential readers and contemplating future publication.

The earliest set of changes to Manuscript M are those Byron made when he was copying or drafting the manuscript in the first instance. He begins by calling his hero 'Burun' in stanzas 2 [3], 3 [4], 5 [6], 7 [8], 9 [10], and 33 [30] (and the poem is titled 'Childe Burun's Pilgrimage'), and then, part way through Canto I, in stanza 47 [45], he is renamed Harold, the first apparent shift away from this explicit autobiographical referent.[57] At some point, Byron went back and cancelled the references from earlier stanzas, substituting 'Harold' for 'Burun'. It is likely that the first whole stanzas to be removed were those with homoerotic references. Table 4.2 provides two versions of stanza 7 [8], describing Byron's relationship with John Eddleston. At first, Byron attempted to obscure the homoerotic nature of the relationship with Eddleston, deleting 'guilty' and 'loved'. Soon, however, he appears to have realised that the stanza could not be satisfactorily reworked, so he substituted, by pasting over the original, a less explicitly autobiographical stanza in which Harold suffers from some unnamed trauma.[58] Additionally, Byron excises entirely the next stanza, 8 [9], which had also referred to

Table 4.2 Comparison of manuscript and print versions of Canto I, stanza 87, *Childe Harold's Pilgrimage*

Manuscript M, stanza 7 [Erdman 20–21]	Manuscript M, pasted over stanza 7 [Erdman, 22–23]
Of all his train there was a ~~guilty~~ henchman-lively page	Yet oft-times in his maddest mirthful mood,
A ~~dark-eyed~~ peasant boy who ~~loved~~ served his master well	Strange pangs would flash along Childe Harold's brow,
And often would his pranksome prate engage	As if the memory of some deadly feud,
~~Ch~~ Childe ~~Burun's~~ Harold's ear, when his proud heart did swell-	Or disappointed passion lurked below,
With sable thoughts that he disdained to tell	But this none knew, or haply cared to know;
Then would he smile on him, &/ ~~Robin~~_{Alwin} as Alwin Rupert smiled	For his was not that open artless soul,
When aught that from his young lips archly fell	That feels relief by bidding Sorrow flow,
The gloomy film in ~~Burun's~~ from Harold's eye beguiled	Nor sought a friend to counsel or ~~se~~ condole,
~~And pleased the Childe appeared, nor eer the boy reviled.~~	Whateer this grief mote be, which he could not control.

Eddleston, pasting over it a stanza that presents a more generalised context for the hero's melancholy and isolation, beginning, 'And none did love him'.[59]

A related set of revisions pertain to stanza 22 [unpublished], apostrophising William Beckford (1759–1844; author of the novel *Vathek*), and alluding sympathetically to his homosexuality:

> Unhappy Vathek! In an evil hour
> ~~By one fair form~~ ^{Gainst Nature's voice} seduced to deed accurst,
> Once Fortune's minion, now thou feel'st her power!
> Wrath's vials on thy lofty head have burst,
> In ~~mind, in science,~~ ^{wit in ~~talents~~ genius} as in wealth the first.
> How wonderous bright thy blooming Morn arose
> But thou wert smitten with unhallowed thirst
> Of nameless crime, and ~~round thee twining~~ ^{thy sad days must} close
> ~~Scorn, Exile,~~ ^{In scorn, and} Solitude unsought – the worst of woes.[60]

These lines, referencing Beckford's affair with the younger William Courtenay ('one fair form'), could be included only when Byron was sure of a private audience. Byron attempted, at first, to revise the stanza, though these revisions do little to alter its meaning. Arguably, the addition of 'Gainst Nature's voice' augments the positioning of Beckford's homosexuality as a crime, albeit one for which he is unfairly persecuted. Immediately under this stanza is a pencilled notation, by Hobhouse, 'I would not have this about Beckford', and then Byron's response: 'If ever published I shall have this stanza omitted. Byron February 1st, 1811.'[61] With this note, Byron made it explicit that the text in its manuscript form was intended for a limited audience whom he could expect to identify, and possibly to share his feelings about Beckford's 'nameless crime'. At the same time, the pledge to omit the stanza gesture equivocally to the possibility of publication. At some point, perhaps after reading Hobhouse's remark, Byron cancelled the stanza with several fine vertical and diagonal lines. In doing so, he left the original perfectly legible, allowing his privileged readers access to material that he knew could not be printed. In this way, the manuscript imagines two separate audiences simultaneously.

Additional purges worked to depersonalise Manuscript M. After disambiguating his name from his protagonist, Byron removed several references to his family. He crossed out stanza 6 [unpublished] (which references a mother who 'much misliketh me / She saith my riot bringeth shame / On all my ancestry' and a sister whose 'fair face I have not seen / For three long years & more'). And he excised what was originally to be stanza 10 of *Childe Harold's Goodnight*:

> Methinks it would my bosom glad
> To change my proud estate
> And be again a laughing lad
> With one beloved playmate
> Since youth I scarce have passed an hour,
> Without disgust or pain,
> Except sometimes in Lady's bower
> Or when the bowl I drain.[62]

These deletions remove references that would have identified Byron with Harold: about his sister, whom he has not seen in years; his riotous youth, of which his mother complains; and his inheritance of a 'proud estate', which came to Byron in 1798 at the age of ten. Byron's drafting and revising of Canto I in Manuscript M plainly demonstrate that he was thinking of the poem as potentially publishable. After changing the name of his protagonist and deleting some of the early stanzas, including the *Vathek* stanza, 22 [unpublished], there are no more stanzas deleted whole, and there are no deleted stanzas whatsoever in Canto II of Manuscript M, suggesting that, through the process of copying and expanding the manuscript from the earlier draft, self-censorship was at work.[63]

In early August 1811, Dallas presented Byron with Manuscript D, a fair-copy transcription Dallas had made from Manuscript M. Byron revised this fair copy, which ultimately served as the printer's copy for the first edition of the poem. Within Manuscript D, a new round of eliminations of whole stanzas and indeed groups of stanzas takes place, with Byron transitioning from removing the obviously objectionable to the comical and satirical. Though scholars have noted that the printed poem is less comical and bitter than the manuscript version, it is important to note the staging of Byron's cuts, and how late they take place in the poem's march towards print.[64] Most of the excisions in Manuscript D seem to have been prompted by Byron's new publisher, John Murray. On 4 September 1811, Murray, provided a forceful, if diplomatic, objection to stanzas in which Byron voiced both his critique of the Peninsular War and a certain religious 'skepticism', drawing attention to passages that do not harmonize with the general feeling, [and] would so greatly interfere with the popularity which the poem is, in other respects, so certainly calculated to excite, that, in compassion to your publisher, who does not presume to reason upon the subject, otherwise than as a mere matter of business, I hope your Lordship's goodness will induce you to obviate them.[65]

Byron's reaction to Murray expression of self-interest, in being deprived of custom, was a blustery, if respectful, demurral: 'With regard to the political and metaphysical parts, I am afraid I can alter nothing.'[66] Byron did, however, make concessions to pacify his readers, as he had done to his early verse collections. He removed four of those stanzas from Canto I (24–7 [unpublished]) that had critiqued, albeit in comic terms, the Convention of Cintra, a treaty that was despised in Britain for being too lenient with the defeated French army.[67] Although the Convention had been widely condemned, Byron's mocking tone, and his insistence upon naming the miscreants – as may be seen in the following sample – likely prompted the removal of the offending stanzas:

> Dull victors! baffled by a vanquished foe
> Wheedled by conynge tongues of laurels due,
> Stand – worthy of each other in a row –
> Sirs Arthur, Harry, and the Dizzard Hew,
> Dalrymple, seely wight, sore dupe of th'other tew. (24 [unpublished])

Also in deference to Murray's wishes, Byron removed the 'skeptical' stanza 8 from Canto II, a disdainful commentary on the 'phantasy' of a 'churlish Priest' who believes in an afterlife, replacing it with the innocuous lines, 'as holiest men have deem'd, there be / A land of souls beyond that sable shore'.[68]

In his letter to Byron seeking revisions, Murray called upon his new poet to consider his reputation. In terms that again rehearse those found in the *Edinburgh*, Murray advises Byron, 'you are raising a Monument that will outlive your present feelings, and it should therefore be so constructed as to excite no other associations than those of respect and admiration for your Lordship's Character and Genius'.[69] Murray's characterisation of Byron's poem as 'a Monument' presents the poet with a different conception of his poetry than *Bards*, whose popularity Byron always regarded as 'temporary'. Exploiting Byron's recent embarrassment over that poem, Murray attempted to prevail upon the poet to consider posterity. The composition history of *CHP* demonstrates Murray's success in this endeavour as within Manuscript D, Byron made further changes. He revised, in three distinct stages, stanza 87 [88] of canto I, one of four comical stanzas in the satirical flavour of *Bards*. Table 4.3 tracks these changes, transcribing the stanza in three states: (1) the original stanza, as it appears in Manuscript M; (2) the first set of revisions in Byron's hand, in Manuscript D; and (3) a substituted, final version of the stanza, recopied in Byron's hand into Manuscript D. In his first attempt at revising, in Manuscript D, Byron deletes lines 2–5, featuring the mock-heroic interleaving of tourism and war, the allusion to the bookselling area of Paternoster Row, and the ribbing of Sir John Carr, the prolific travel writer and 'man of ink' who had also received drubbings in the *Edinburgh*, as we have seen. He substitutes four new lines that make no reference to London booksellers and authors. He retains the final four lines, with only the slight revision (one perhaps meant explicitly for Murray's benefit): instead of 'borrow, steal (don't buy)' the lines are revised to 'borrow, steal (or buy)'. Without the reference to 'the Boke of Carr', however, these lines make little sense, and thus in the final version Byron revises the entire stanza, eliminating the final four lines and doing away entirely with the satire on the contemporary book trade. The result is a graver, less ironic account of the nature of war without the levity (and personal attack) present in earlier drafts. Shorn of its local and temporal specificity and pointed satire, the stanza's concerns are universalised, with the revisions to this stanza exemplifying the nature of the changes Byron brought into effect throughout the first two Cantos.

Table 4.3 Comparison of manuscript and print versions of Canto I, stanza 87, *Childe Harold's Pilgrimage*

Manuscript M, f. 81, stanza 88; Erdman, 78, 85	Manuscript D, f. 29v; Erdman, 84–85	Manuscript D, substituted stanza (in Byron's hand), f. 30r; Erdman, 84
Ye! who would more of Spain and Spaniards know	Ye! who would more of Spain and Spaniards know	Ye, who would more of Spain and Spainards know,
Sights, Saints, Antiques, Arts, Anecdotes, and War,	~~Sights, Saints, Antiques, Arts, Anecdotes, and War,~~ Go read whate'er is writ of bloodiest strife	Go, read whate'er is writ of bloodiest strife,
Go! hie ye hence to Paternoster Row,	~~Go! hie ye hence to Paternoster Row,~~ Whate'er keen Vengeance roused gainst Foreign foe	Whate'er keen Vengeance urg'd on foreign foe
Are they not written in the Boke of Carr,	~~Are they not written in the boke of Carr,~~ Can act, is acting there upon Man's life	Can act, is acting there against man's life.
Green Erin's Knight! and Europe's wandering Star!	~~Green Erin's Knight! and Europe's wandering Star!~~	War mouldeth there each weapon to his need:
Then listen, readers, to the man of ink,	Then listen, readers, to the man of ink,	So may he guard the sister & the wife,
Hear what he did, and sought, & wrote afar	Hear what he did, and sought, & wrote afar	So may he make each curst oppressor bleed,
All these are cooped within one Quarto's brink	All these are cooped within one Quarto's brink	So may such foes deserve the most remorseless deed!
This borrow, steal (don't buy) and tell us what you <u>think</u>!	This borrow, steal (~~dont~~ or buy) and tell us what you think.	

By obscuring the personal circumstances of the author, Byron's revisions in many ways echo those Dorothy Wordsworth made to her *Recollections of a Tour in Scotland*. In place of what was lost, however, Byron intensified his portrayal of his melancholic hero, emphasising his world-weariness and linking it directly to events unfolding on the world stage. In this regard, Byron's strategy in 1811 mirrors that of Charlotte Smith, who, over a quarter century before, had sought to present her personal woes in a generalised form to the public. Both Byron and Smith succeed by crafting enigmatic personas, whose suffering is not named directly (at least, by Smith, it is unnamed in the early editions of *Elegiac Sonnets*). In the interpolated 'Song to Inez', Byron allows Harold to speak directly, albeit coyly, voicing a question the reader might put to the poem: 'And dost thou ask, what secret woe / I bear, corroding joy and youth?', but without indulging the reader. Smith likewise succeeded with the public so long as she masked the nature of her 'secret woe', failing when she began to offer more specific revelations about her private sufferings in 1797.[70]

Byron deleted three further stanzas, which had continued to address Spanish topics by carrying forward the mockery of what one might read in 'the Boke of Carr'. These stanzas almost certainly did not meet with Murray's approval, as they satirise the excessive and mundane detail provided in many published travel narratives, a genre in which Murray specialised. Two of the excised stanzas begin 'There may you read' and proceed to enumerate the minutiae reported in these accounts:

> How many buildings are in such a place,
> How many leagues from this to yonder plain,
> How many relicks each Cathedral grace
> And where Giralda stands on her gigantic base.[71]

The stanzas also move into political territory with commentary on the Peninsular War. Described by David Erdman as a 'Don Juan-esque extravaganza', the three deleted stanzas mock 'the Wellesleys [who] did embark for Spain' and lampoon 'Vulpes', Lord Holland.[72] Two further vituperative stanzas from Canto II, describing Sir William Hamilton, Lord Elgin and Thomas Hope, all collectors of antiquities, as 'classic thieves of each degree', also fall prey to the demands of print.[73] Three further stanzas (69–71) are cancelled in Manuscript D, possibly at Byron's initiative. Described by Byron to Dallas as the 'stanzas of a buffooning cast (on London's Sunday)', Byron added that they 'are as well left out'.[74] Nevertheless, perhaps because these stanzas ridicule activities like bear-baiting on the Sabbath (and thus voice religious scruples that would appeal to the '*Orthodox*'), they were in fact retained. Byron's humorous tour through London's 'sundry suburbs' of 'Hampstead, Brentford, Harrow' seems, however, out of place in the published version of the poem, with the many similar stanzas that had originally accompanied them having been removed.[75]

When Byron began his revisions to Manuscript D, on 25 September 1811, he boasted to Frances Hodgson:

> I have attacked De Pauw, Thornton, Lord Elgin, Spain, Portugal, the *Edinburgh Review*, travellers, Painters, Antiquarians, and others, so you see what a dish of Sour Crout Controversy I shall prepare for myself. It would not answer for me to give way, now; as I was forced into bitterness at the beginning, I will go through to the last.[76]

But almost all of these attacks were excised in the revisions to Manuscript D. With these removals, and the addition of inoffensive stanzas, the poem became less humorous, the bitterness diffused into a generalised melancholic detachment, a pattern that was already evident in his early verse collections, with Byron removing, or regretting and seeking to suppress, his satires. Although Byron's success empowered him to take great risks in print (and to implore Murray to support him in doing so), Byron continued to use script as a primary vehicle for circulating his short verse, much of it unpublishable because of its satiric or personal content. With the assiduous John Murray as his main dissemination channel, Byron could express himself without restraint and without the significant risks that accompanied print in the later phase of his career.

The Haven of Manuscript Circulation

Throughout his career Byron composed short poems. Plate 8 charts the numbers short poems Byron wrote from 1812 onward: twenty-nine in 1812, forty-one in 1815, twenty-five in 1816, and eighteen in 1820. The publication history of these poems may be seen in the red (published) and green (unpublished) lines in Plate 10, with the green line demonstrating the precipitous dropping off of the number of short poems that were printed after 1815. In other words, Byron

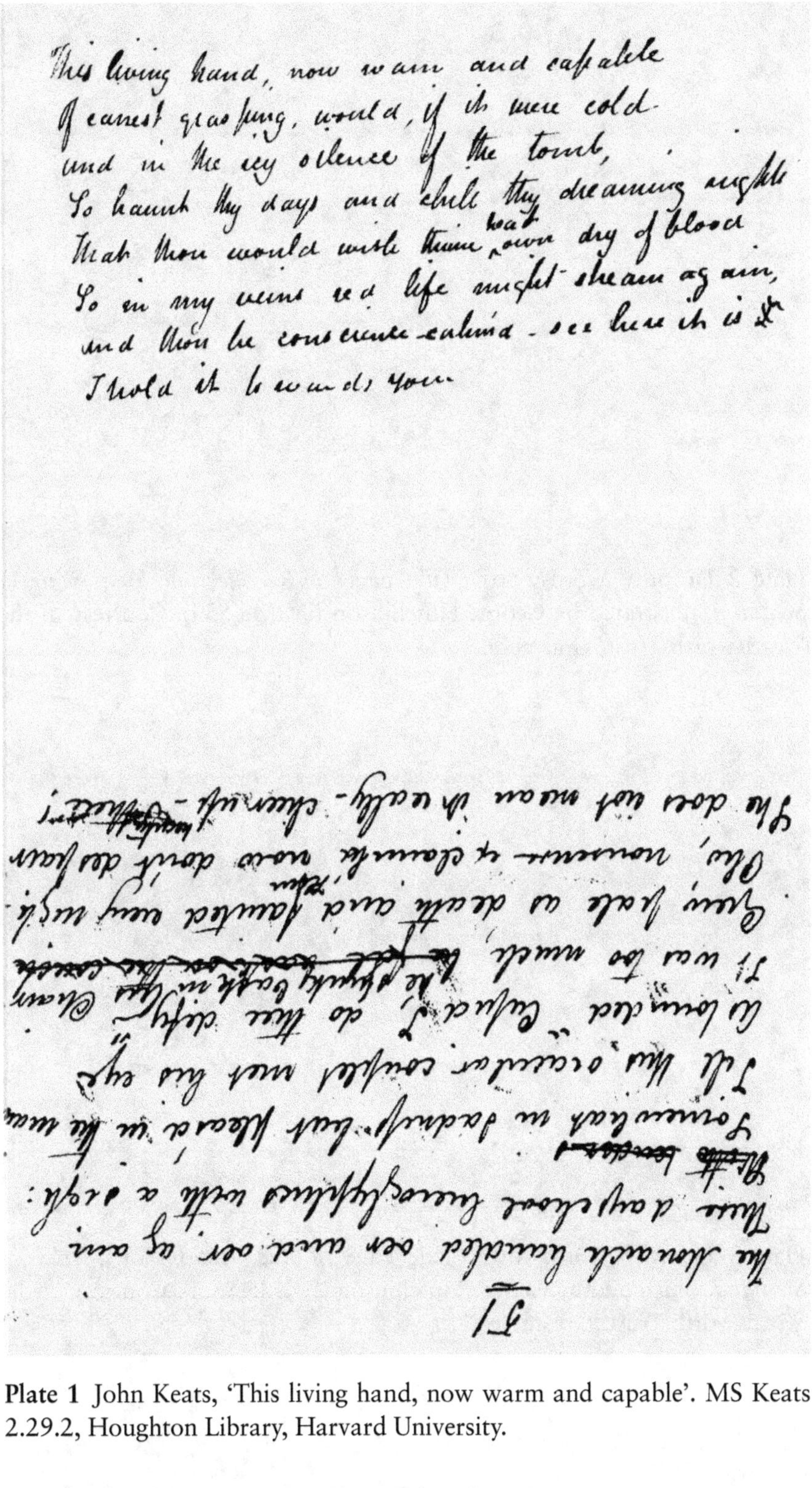

This living hand, now warm and capable
Of earnest grasping, would, if it were cold
And in the icy silence of the tomb,
So haunt thy days and chill thy dreaming nights
That thou would wish thine own heart dry of blood
So in my veins red life might stream again,
And thou be conscience-calm'd — see here it is —
I hold it towards you.

Plate 1 John Keats, 'This living hand, now warm and capable'. MS Keats 2.29.2, Houghton Library, Harvard University.

Plate 2 Dorothy Wordsworth, Title page of *Recollections of a Tour in Scotland*, illustrated by George Hutchinson (DCMS 55.i). Courtesy of the Wordsworth Trust, Grasmere.

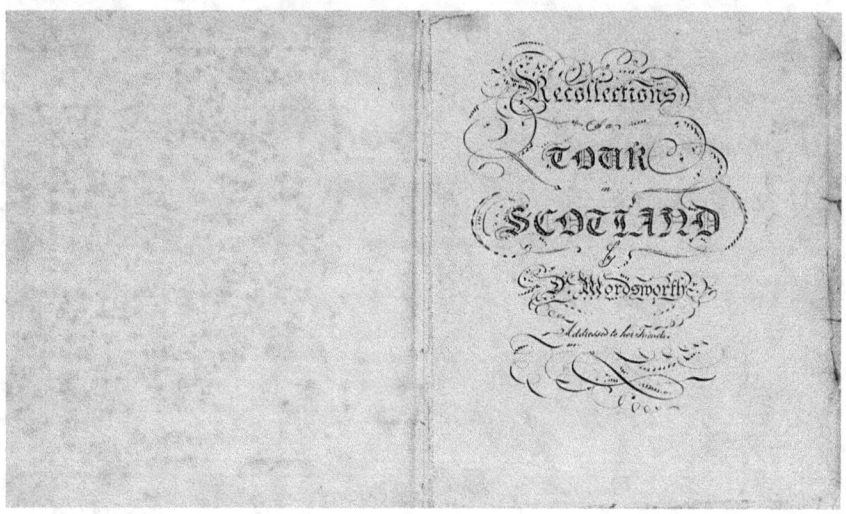

Plate 3 Dorothy Wordsworth, Title Page of *Recollections of a Tour in Scotland*, illustrated by George Hutchinson (DCMS 55.ii). Courtesy of the Wordsworth Trust, Grasmere.

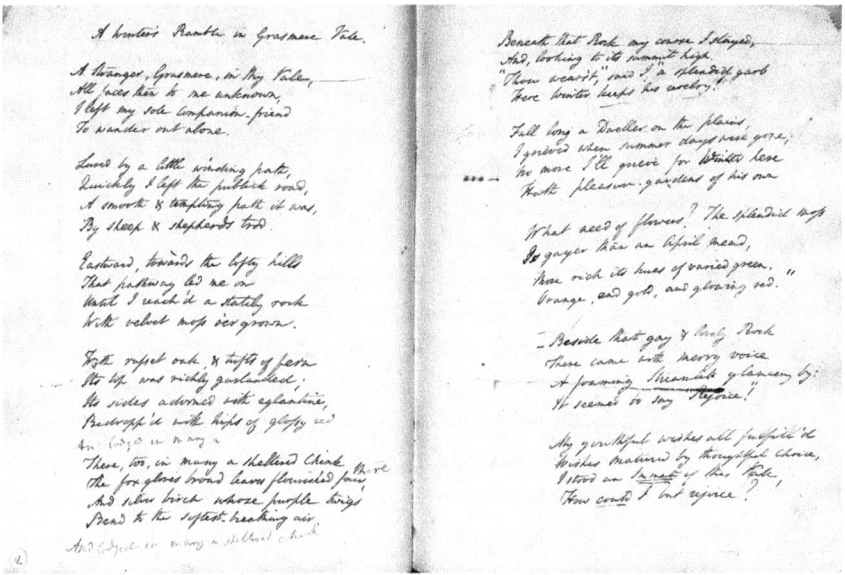

Plate 4 Dorothy Wordsworth, first page of 'A Winter's Ramble in Grasmere Vale' (DCMS 120). Courtesy of the Wordsworth Trust, Grasmere.

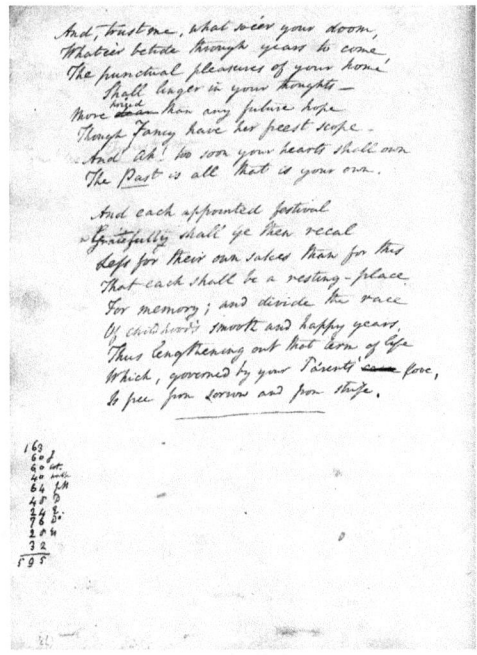

Plate 5 Dorothy Wordsworth, last page of 'Irregular Stanzas: Holiday at Gwerndovennant' (DCMS 120). Courtesy of the Wordsworth Trust, Grasmere.

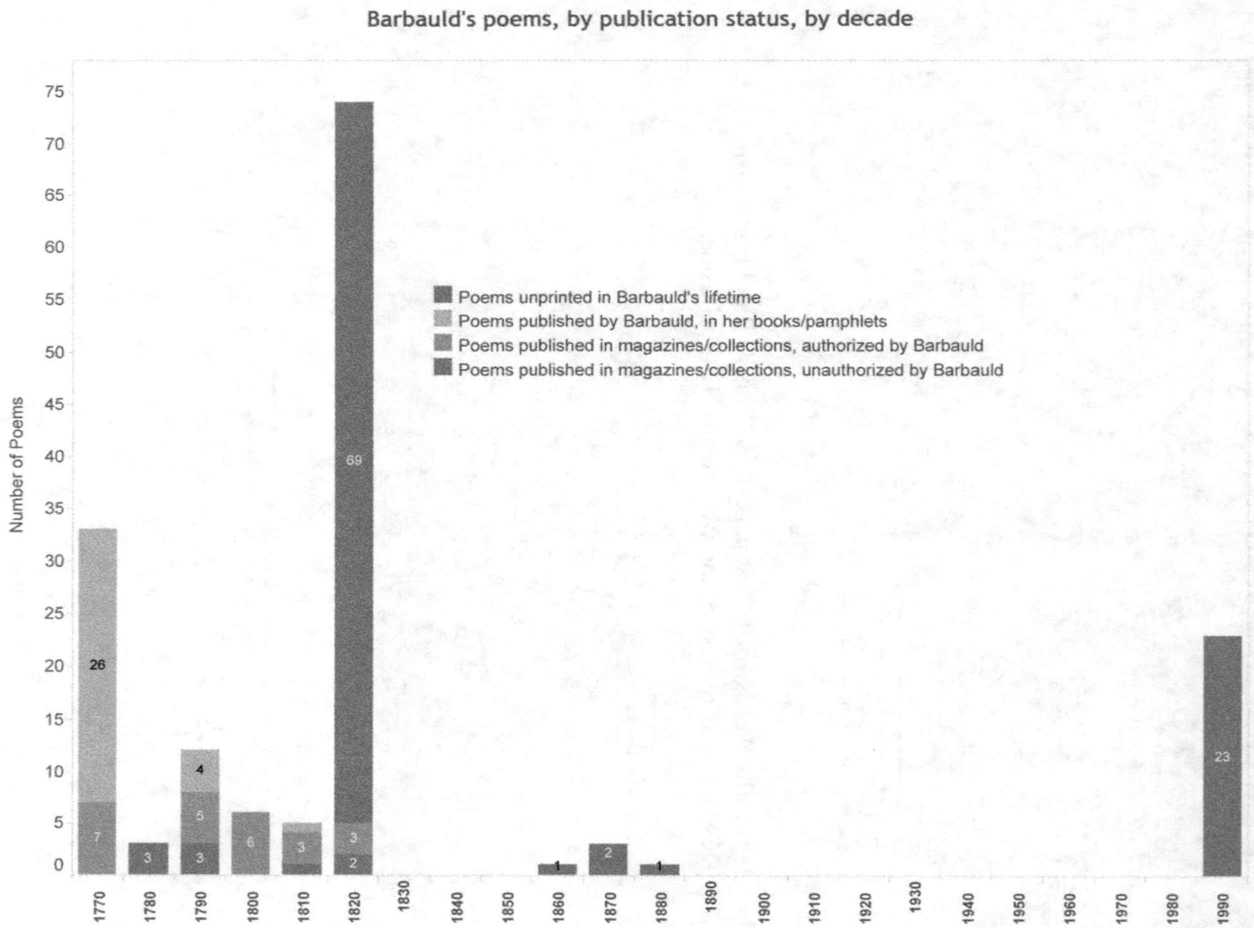

Barbauld's poems, by publication status, by decade

Plate 6 Barbauld's Poetry, by publication status, by decade.

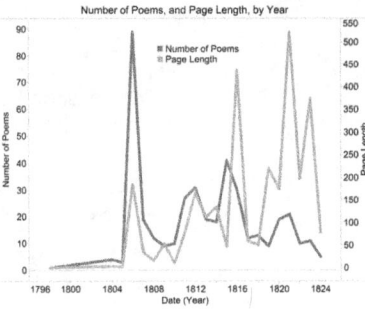

Plate 7 Byron's poetic output, by poem and page length, by year.

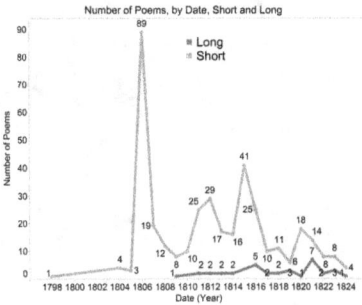

Plate 8 Byron's poetic output, short and long poems, by date.

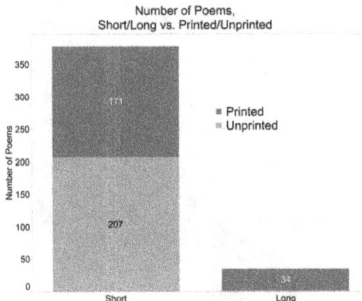

Plate 9 Byron's poems, long/short, unprinted/printed.

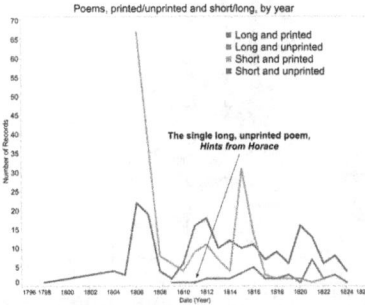

Plate 10 Byron's poems, printed/unprinted, short/long, by year.

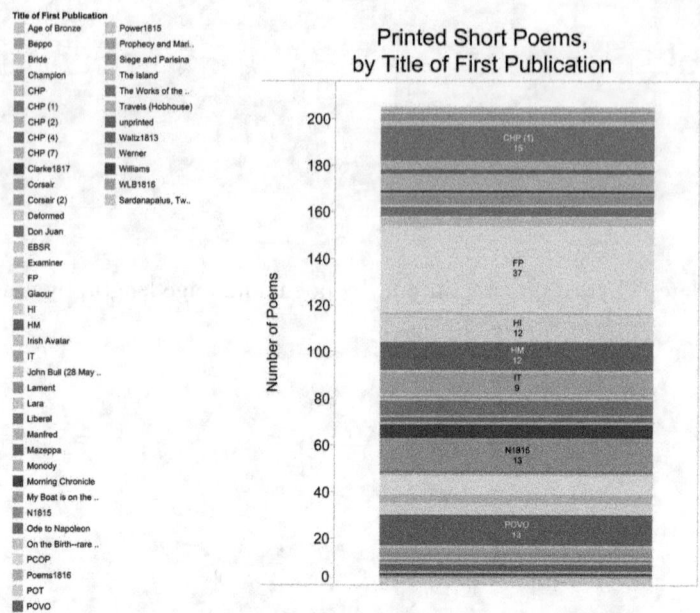

Plate 11 Byron's short poems, printed/unprinted, by title of first publication.

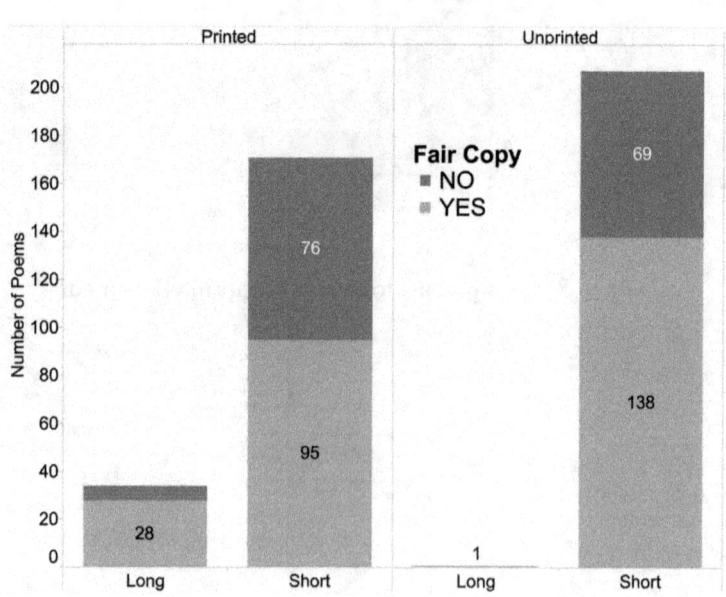

Plate 12 Fair copies of Byron's printed/unprinted and short/long poems.

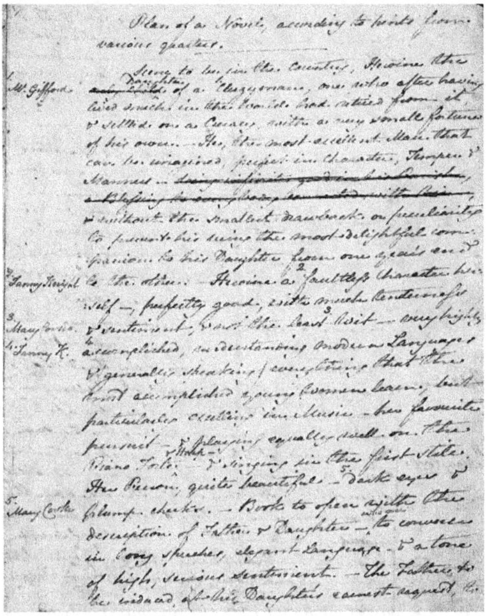

Plate 13 Jane Austen, 'Plan of a novel, according to hints from various quarters'. The Morgan Library & Museum. MA 1034.1. Purchased by J.P. Morgan, Jr. 1925. Photographic credit: The Morgan Library & Museum, New York.

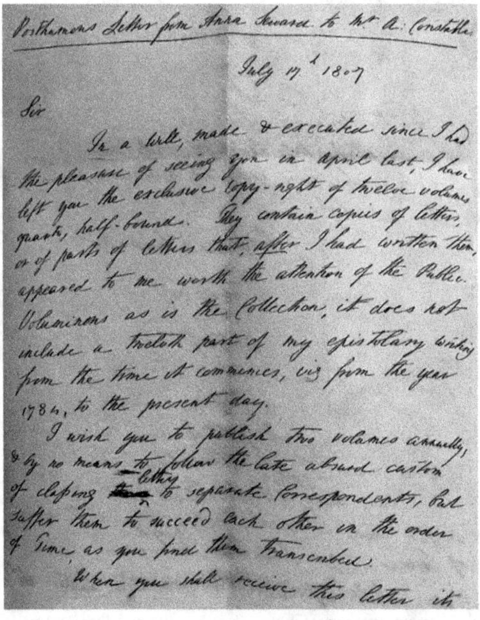

Plate 14 Engraved letter from Anna Seward to Archibald Constable, tipped into volume 1 of *The Letters of Anna Seward. Written between the years 1784 and 1807* (1811). Houghton Library, Harvard University. 2003J-EC372.

Plate 15 Frontispiece, *The Works of Anna Laetitia Barbauld. With a Memoir by Lucy Aikin.* Volume I. London: Printed for Longman, Hurst, Rees, Orme, Brown, and Green, 1825. Provided by Special Collections, University of Otago Library, Dunedin, New Zealand.

Plate 16 William Blake, 'The Little Boy Lost', *Songs of Innocence and Songs of Experience*, British Museum, copy T, object 13. © The Trustees of the British Museum. All rights reserved.
http://www.blakearchive.org/copy/songsie.t?descId=songsie.t.illbk.13

Plate 17 William Blake, 'Infant Joy', *Songs of Innocence and Songs of Experience*, British Museum, copy T, object 25. © The Trustees of the British Museum. All rights reserved.
http://www.blakearchive.org/copy/songsie.t?descId=songsie.t.illbk.25

continued to write short poems after 1812, but after 1815 he printed fewer of them. Why? Although in *Bards* Byron suggested that manuscript poems would remain private – 'no tempting press / Shall drag my Journal from the desk's recess' – in fact, most of Byron's unprinted lyrics were circulated by him in manuscript. Of Byron's 378 short poems, 207, or 55 per cent, were unprinted in his lifetime; 171, or 45 per cent, were printed (Plate 9). Of the 171 printed short poems, the majority, 102, were first published in one of six volumes: *Fugitive* (thirty-seven poems), *Childe* (fifteen), *Various* (thirteen), *Hours* (twelve), and two collections compiled by Isaac Nathan, *A Selection of Hebrew Melodies* (thirteen) and *Hebrew Melodies* (twelve). All of these publications appeared before 1816, a sign of Byron's lingering distaste for lyric collections after *Hours*. The only separate collection of short lyrics that was published by Byron after 1807 was *Poems* (1816), a volume that Murray essentially compelled. The 'Advertisement', unusually written by Murray (or an editor on his behalf), explains that the poems were 'not intended for general circulation', but since they had 'been already dispersed through the medium of the public press', their collection and publication had become necessary to the bookseller.[77] Of the eleven poems included in the slim volume, in fact only five had been previously printed in newspapers.[78] Even though Byron had allowed many of these poems to circulate in Whig newspapers, he viewed the collection with distaste and took no direct part in it. In the 'Advertisement', the publisher remarks that the poems' previous circulation in print 'must take away the regret which, under other circumstances, the reader might perhaps experience in finding them included amongst the acknowledged publications of the Noble Author'.[79]

Plate 11 depicts the diverse venues in which Byron published his short poems, with the many thin horizontal stripes reflecting the appearance of his short poems in dozens of diverse publications during his lifetime. Although he printed 45 per cent of his short poems, Byron exerted little control over these poems: most were appended to the publication of his longer poems by Murray, printed in sympathetic (and occasionally unsympathetic) magazines and periodicals, and collected in publications initiated, edited, and published by others.[80] This pattern of publication was described by Coleridge in his introduction to *Sibylline Leaves* (1817), a collection that he had prepared in order to gather together '[p]oems published at very different periods, in various obscure or perishable journals, &c. some with, some without the writer's consent; many imperfect, all incorrect'.[81] But unlike Coleridge, Byron was largely indifferent to the scattering of his leaves; like Barbauld, he seemed content that they be disseminated in 'various obscure or perishable journals' and made no effort to collect them.[82]

How were the unprinted short poems, some 55 per cent of the total, disseminated? The rich archive of extant manuscripts of Byron's verse establishes that most of these poems circulated, and that may were read, copied and shared by others. Of Byron's total output of 410 poems, at least 312 have at least one extant manuscript witness, and many of these are autographs, an extremely high survival rate that provides important clues as to how they were used during his lifetime.[83] Many of the extant manuscripts are fair copies made by Byron or others, on separate sheets, or inserted in letters or albums. Such manuscripts demonstrate prima facie evidence that these poems were shared and read by others, as the act of fair copying implies reading by at least the copyist and often denotes an intention that the copy be shared and read by others.[84] Plate 12 quantifies the number of extant fair copies for Byron's poems, divided into the categories of unprinted/printed and short/long. Of the 207 unprinted short poems, fair copies – often multiple copies – survive for 138, or 67 per cent of the total. This astonishing proportion of surviving fair copies almost certainly underestimates the total in existence during Byron's lifetime and likely even today.[85] Fair copies were produced in almost every year of Byron's career, with the early years of 1806 and 1807 being numerically significant. In 1811, 1812, 1819 and 1820, Byron also produced many fair copies that survive.

Many of the unprinted poems are trifles, very short poems of four lines or less, written quickly or extempore, without any thought of publication, yet many of these were still meant to be shown to and read by others. A large proportion of the poems Byron circulated in manuscript were either socially or politically oriented, or, as was often the case, both. By 1812, Byron had become savvy not only about which poems could safely be printed, but also about how to control the manuscript circulation of those that could not. For example, with one of his society poems, 'To one who promised on a lock of hair' (230), about Lady Caroline Lamb, he encouraged a wide dissemination. Sending a copy of the poem in letter to Lady Melbourne on 25 April 1814, he noted: 'I don't often bore you with rhyme – but as the wrapper to this note – I send you some upon a *brunette* – which I have shewn to no one else – if you think them not much beneath the common places – you may give them to any of your "Album" acquaintances.'[86] Here Byron encourages an indiscriminate showing and copying of the poem which was, in fact, copied into other albums: in 1844 it, along with 'To Lady Caroline Lamb' (189), was published from George Brummell's album book of verses.[87]

Byron turned to John Murray to circulate poems that he did not think were suitable for publication, but which he did want to share. Many of Byron's short poems passed through Murray's hands, with his publisher acting as the conduit for a large class of poems intended for circulation amongst members of Byron's inner literary circle. As Graham observes, Murray 'was the designated recipient of many of the most brilliant, detail-packed, verse-enriched letters because Byron was certain that the publisher would selectively circulate them'.[88] Murray was sent both intimate and satirical poems, and he handled them all with the utmost sensitivity, one of the ways in which the publisher's propriety served Byron well. Less than two weeks before he left England for good, Byron sent Murray 'Stanzas to [Augusta]' (299), written on 12 April 1816. Byron carefully instructed Murray not to circulate it 'at present', and he asked that his sister's consent be obtained before printing either 'Stanzas to [Augusta]' or '[Epistle to Augusta]' (300).[89] At first, Augusta refused publication for both, but she subsequently relented and allowed the first to be published: 'Stanzas to [Augusta]' appeared in *The Prisoner of Chillon and other Poems* in December 1816. This decision shows Augusta's (and Murray's) discrimination between the two poems: whereas '[Epistle to Augusta]' directly alludes to 'My Sister', with reminisces about their past life together, 'Stanzas to [Augusta]' presents a more generalised address to his beloved, referred to only as '*thee*'.[90] But even though '[Epistle to Augusta]' was deemed unsuitable for print (and was not published until 1830), Byron felt at liberty to circulate the poem to his friends, sending a copy of both poems to Madame de Staël on 27 July 1816.[91] Byron also kept an Alpine Journal for his sister while abroad, which he also sent, in three letters, to Murray, with the following instructions: 'It is not at all for perusal; but if you like to hear about the romantic part, she will, I dare say, show you what touches upon the rocks, etc. but it has not – nor can have anything to do with publication.'[92]

Another example of Murray's discretion is apparent with 'To the Po. June 2nd 1819' (333), a poem addressed to Teresa Guiccioli that survives in multiple fair copies but was not published in Byron's lifetime. Here we encounter Byron's uncertainty about whether the poem should be copied and published.[93] Andrew Stauffer has found that Byron delayed circulating the poem for a year, before allowing the poem to circulate in manuscript: permitting Mary Shelley to make copies in her journal, in June 1819; making a copy for Douglas Kinnaird in April 1820, and allowing Kinnaird to make a copy for Murray in June of the same year, and then another copy for Medwin in 1821–2. Stauffer describes how Byron wavered about whether to publish the poem, first instructing Murray in April 1820 not to print it, as it was 'written upon private feelings and passions'. Later he changed his mind, allowing Murray to print but then changed his mind again after a two-year delay.[94] With 'To the Po.', we find a supremely accomplished and celebrated poet wavering about whether to transition his lyric from private to social to public audiences.

Byron also relied on Murray to confine the circulation of his most outrageous lampoons. 'An Extract from a Parish Register' (287), an attack on Byron's father-in-law that portrays him as a bastard, was sent to Murray with explicit instructions: 'I trust you have given no copies as it was never intended for publication at all.'[95] Byron understood the dangers of allowing copies to be made, though he does not prohibit Murray from showing the poems to others. Murray must have followed these instructions, as the poem was not printed in Byron's lifetime. The only manuscript copy that survives is an autograph fair copy, and the poem was published for the first time by McGann. Murray also served as an outlet for many of Byron's satirical poems aimed at his literary adversaries. Some of these poems he aimed at the usual targets – Southey, Wordsworth and Coleridge – though there were others as well.[96] The limited social circulation of these poems is evident in the 'devastatingly vitriolic lampoon' of Samuel Rogers ('Question and Answer' [323]) that Byron sent to Murray on 28 September 1820, a poem which had been written nearly three years prior.[97] Byron again gave explicit instructions to Murray 'to *give no copies* – to permit *no publication*', but allowed him to '*show* it – to Gifford – Hobhouse – D. Kinnaird and any two or three of your own Admiralty favourites'.[98] The effect of these 'showings' is recorded in a letter from Murray to Byron, dated 24 October 1820, describing the hysteric delight that Byron's verse could evoke, and the extreme caution Murray exercised in circulating the poem:

> As to the Satire it is one of the most superlative things that ever was written – I hastened with it the next morning to Mr Gifford I put it into his hand without saying a word – and I thought he would have died with extacy – he thinks that if it do not surpass it at least equals anything that you have written & that there is nothing more perfect of its kind in the language – he knew the Portrait as readily as if the Person had been before him . . . I will give no one a Copy of this upon any account not [sic] allow it to go out of my sight – once or twice since when I have been alone with Gifford I have taken it out & it operates like a cordial – Today I met Mr Kinnaird & brought him home to read it & he was much astonished & delighted as we had been – I conjured him not to speak of it – to Hobhouse I will shew it--& to one more – *Ward* – but he shall call to read it in his chaise as he goes to the Continent – for I will not trust him with such a marketable commodity otherwise – in a word it is exquisite – the Person is behaving very well just now & I am under obligations for his allowing me the honour of being his publisher & I trust therefore you will not allow another Copy to escape – for in all his conversations with me of late he speaks with unfeigned honour of you – .[99]

By showing the poem only to select men whom Byron had approved, by not allowing the poem out of his sight (and thereby ensuring no copies were taken), by demanding that the men 'not speak of it', and by enjoining Byron himself to 'not allow another Copy to escape', Murray ensured the poem would not circulate beyond its intended readers, and importantly, would never be seen by Rogers himself. The need for prudence on Murray's part was paramount: as both Byron's and Rogers's publisher, Murray was playing a dangerous double game.[100]

All of these examples suggest that Byron treated Murray as a conduit, asking him to share his poems with suitable readers only. They also demonstrate how, with Murray, manuscript circulation was a relatively safe haven for Byron, as throughout his career he managed to avoid major scrapes with his manuscript poems. In large part, this is because Byron's publisher and literary advisers protected him, taking precautions to avoid unfettered circulation.[101] Although many of Byron's works were pirated from *authorised* print publications, only a small number of poems, collected in Table 4.4, were printed during his lifetime without authorisation from privately printed or manuscript

Table 4.4 Unauthorised poems published during Byron's lifetime, published from manuscript or private print sources

Poem	McGann, *CPW*	First publication	Source
The Curse of Minerva	151	*New Monthly Magazine* III (1815) ['The Malediction of Minerva; or, The Athenian Marble Merchant']	Private printing, eight copies, May 1812
'[Windsor Poetics]'	209	*English Bards and Scotch Reviewers . . . etc. Suppressed Poems* (Paris: Galignani, 1818)	Various manuscript sources, though none a precise antecedent (a copy by James Northcote has some of its features: *CPW* III: 425)
'[Condolatory Address to Sarah, Countess of Jersey]'	234	*Champion*, 31 July 1814	Letter from Byron to Lady Jersey, 29 May 1814 (*BLJ*, IV: 120)
'Fare Thee Well!'	285	*Champion*, 14 April 1816	Private printing, fifty copies, 8 April 1816
'A Sketch from Private Life'	286	*Champion*, 14 April 1816	Private printing, fifty copies, 8 April 1816
'New Song ('How came you in Hob's pound to cool')'	349	*Morning Post*, 15 April 1820	Letter from Byron to Murray, 23 March 1820 (*BLJ*, VII: 59)
'[Lines Addressed by Lord Byron to Mr. Hobhouse]'	350	*The Works of Lord Byron. Including Several Poems Now First Collected*. (Philadelphia: Moses Thomas, 1820)	Copies derived from letters sent from Byron to Murray on 9 April 1820 (*BLJ*, VII: 73–74) and Douglas Kinnaird on 14 April 1820 (*BLJ*, VII: 75)
'To Penelope, January 2, 1821'	356	*John Bull*, 28 May 1821	Manuscript letter from Byron to Murray, 26 February 1821 (*BLJ*, VIII: 86)
'When I left thy shores O Naxos'	C2 [406]	Sheet music 'Published and for sale by A. R. Poole . . . Philadelphia' (n.d.)	No MS
'On the Regency'	C4 [408]	*The Works of Lord Byron. Including Several Poems Now First Collected*. (Philadelphia: Moses Thomas, 1816)	No MS

sources.[102] Three of these poems, *Curse of Minerva* (151), 'Fare Thee Well!' (285) and 'A Sketch from Private Life' (286), were taken from private printings, which, as Byron knew (or ought to have known) from his very first verse collection, *Fugitive*, were very difficult to control. One of the poems was first printed in Paris, two in Philadelphia, indicative of the global demand for Byron's poems. The remaining poems for which a source can be traced were taken from private letters. Three of the unauthorised poems (349, 350, 356) published may be traced to their inclusion in letters to John Murray, a very small number given the extent of risky material that passed through Murray's hands. 'Condolatory Address' (234) was printed from a letter to Lady Jersey on the subject of the Prince Regent's political treachery. According to Byron, the poem 'was transmitted in a single copy to Lady Jersey'. Byron wondered how it made its way into the press, first in *The Champion* on 31 July 1814, and then in the *Morning Chronicle* the following day.[103] Lady Jersey told Byron that her copy had gone missing.[104] Byron melodramatically lamented in a later letter to Lady Jersey that it must be his 'fate not to be left quiet, even when disposed to remain so'.[105] Nevertheless, Byron's considerable efforts to control access to his manuscript poems were for the most part effective.

Byron also used manuscript to circulate his more dangerous political lyrics.[106] Although the consequences of committing a public libel were far less severe than they had been in previous centuries – Gary Dyer has not found a single example of a prosecution for public libel for manuscript circulation during the period – Byron nevertheless was prudent in the dissemination of poems that were libellous, or potentially so.[107] As with his 'Condolatory Address', 'Lines to a Lady Weeping' (182) targeted the Prince Regent. The poem was written less than two weeks after a dinner at the regent's residence at Carlton House, at which the prince was rumoured to have publicly abused the Whigs, whom he had previously vowed to support. The lady weeping was the young Princess Charlotte, who had become overwhelmed by her father's betrayal. Byron, though not present at the dinner, heard about it and used the incident to shame the prince. Byron sent the poem to the Whig *Morning Chronicle*, which published it as 'Sympathetic Address to a Young Lady', 7 March 1812. The publication was anonymous, as Byron would have insisted. An autograph fair copy, dated 22 September 1812, suggests that Byron continued to promote the poem via scribal copying even after its appearance in print. The prince's support for the Tories was so firmly established, by 1814, that Byron wished the poem to have 'all possible circulation' and to own publicly his authorship of it.[108] He instructed Murray in January 1814: 'the lines "to a Lady weeping" must go with the Corsair – I care nothing for consequences on this point – my politics are to me like a young mistress to an old man the worse they grow the fonder I become of them'.[109] Murray acceded, and the poem appeared in the second edition of *The Corsair*, on 1 February 1814, under Byron's own name. According to Jonathan Gross, Byron's publication of 'To a Lady Weeping' 'became notorious, in part, because Byron [had been] so prophetic' about the prince's political about-face.[110] The furore that resulted from Byron's publication of the poem was so great that Murray removed it, without Byron's consent, from the third edition of *The Corsair*, only to reinstate it, at Byron's insistence, in all subsequent editions.

Byron was even more constrained with another poem, written in early 1813, titled 'The Vault' and later more commonly known as 'Windsor Poetics' (209). Written upon the prince's ordering of the opening of the shared tombs of Charles I and Henry VIII on 1 April 1813, the darkly comic image of the prince standing between a 'headless Charles' and a 'heartless Henry' proved irresistible to Byron: 'Charles to his People, Henry to his Wife / – In him the double Tyrant starts to Life' (Version A, lines 5–6). Byron delighted in equating the three despotic monarchs: 'Each Royal Vampyre wakes to life again' (line 8). He allowed the poem to circulate in manuscript, but never published it himself. He first sent a copy of the poem in a letter to Lady Melbourne on 7 April 1813, encouraging her to disseminate the poem: 'Will you give Ld. Holland (or anybody you like or dislike) a copy of this – but I suppose you will be tender or afraid – you need not mind any harm it will do me.'[111] Although he observed to Moore, a year later, that '[t]he Vault reflection is downright actionable, and to print it would be a peril to the publisher', and claimed to be unable to 'conceive how the vault has got about, but so it is', he had himself encouraged Lady Melbourne to circulate it extensively.[112] Indeed, Moore, who was in Derbyshire, reported that the poem was 'circulated with wonderful avidity – even Clods in this neighbourhood have had a copy sent by some "Young Ladies in Town"'.[113] The large quantity of extant, contemporaneous manuscripts suggests that the poem had indeed 'got about'.[114] Interestingly, even with this widespread dissemination of the poem in manuscript, the first appearance of the poem in print was in Galignani's pirated Paris edition of *Bards* in 1818.[115] Notwithstanding Galignani's claim to be publisher of Byron's 'Suppressed Poems', it appears that 'Windsor Poetics' was the only one of these so-called suppressed poems that was printed from manuscript.

Conclusion

From his earliest burst of poetic production, Byron used manuscript circulation as a means of expressing himself to members of his social circle. In his early commonplace book (NLS MS 43340), with entries made between autumn 1807 and late 1808, we witness Byron copying, revising and collecting his early poems and some prose, as well as taking extracts from other authors. His sister Augusta copied several of his poems; in acts of shared labour, he supplied the titles and signatures in his own hand for some poems, and she copied the content of the poems themselves fair, presumably from another copy. Several of the pieces Byron copied and his two longer reflections on his reading, 'List of the different poets, Dramatic or otherwise, who have distinguished their respective languages by their productions', and 'List of Historical Writers whose Works I have perused in different languages', reveal Byron's use of manuscript as a ground for collection, experimentation and sociability.[116] These practices situate Byron within a community, one that he constructs with various groups throughout his career. This chapter has focused on his early Southwell coterie and his later engagement with Murray and his circle, but there were others, including, briefly, his wife, and later the Shelleys and Teresa Guiccioli, all of whom assisted Byron, in a variety of ways, in the production, copying, circulation and preservation of his verse.

To the very end of his life, Byron continued to write for his confidential readers. We find him addressing these readers in his Cephalonia Journal (NLS MS 43353), which he kept from 19 June 1823 to 15 February 1824, two months before his death on 19 April. His entry for 17 October 1823 emblematises the rhythms that characterise his writing life. He speaks about how he discontinued his journal writing but had resumed it that evening, in part because of the beauty of the night:

> the calm though cool serenity of a beautiful and transparent Moonlight – showing the Islands – the Mountains – the Sea – with a distant outline of the Morea traced between the double Azure of the waves and skies – have quieted me enough to be able to write – from which (however difficult it may seem for one who has written so much publicly – to refrain) is and always has been to me – a task and a painful one – I could summon testimonies were it necessary – but my handwriting is sufficient – it is that of one who thinks much, rapidly, – perhaps deeply – but rarely with pleasure. -- -- -- But – 'En Avant!'

Byron playfully but seriously addresses those who might doubt that writing for him has been 'a task and a painful one', offering to furnish evidence in support but relying chiefly on the exhibit immediately before his interpolated reader, his handwriting, which he suggests offers proof of his painfully wrought words. In imagining readers of his journal, possibly even a public readership who would question the difficulty he professes in writing, Byron demonstrates his abiding attention to audience and perhaps even his premonition that his manuscripts would be viewed by others. Byron's writing was never intended for 'the desk's recess', always for 'feeling Souls'.

Byron's extensive use of manuscript culture existed alongside of, and sometimes in strategic coordination with it, his rise as a celebrity author in print. The portrait of the author that emerges from this chapter is that of a poet devoted to writing for a range of audiences, experimenting and manipulating his use of the media of script and print to channel his poems to the appropriate readers. This elucidation of Byron's career frustrates the conventional narrative of a writer moving from more private or social audiences in script to more public audience in print – a narrative that also erroneously describes the career of Anna Barbauld, as we have seen, and Jane Austen, as the next chapter will demonstrate. The following chapter presents another instance of how attention to an author's literary manuscripts can reframe our understanding of her career, demonstrating the ongoing vitality of script as a means of addressing confidential readers. In addition to establishing Austen's persistent use of manuscript culture, this next chapter examines the difficulties that she shared with Barbauld and Byron in seeking wider audiences for her writing. As such, it urges a more fluid and holistic consideration of her writing career, one that embraces her simultaneous and entwined use of scribal and print publication.

Notes

1. Jerome McGann, 'Byron and "The Truth in Masquerade"', pp. 194–5.
2. Ibid. p. 195.
3. Ibid. Many skilled readers of Byron's poetry, including Gary Dyer, Tom Mole and Andy Stauffer, have taken up McGann's exhortation by examining Byron's manipulation of *both* poetic conventions and bibliographical codes. See Gary Dyer, *British Satire and the Politics of Style, 1789–1832* (1997) and 'The Circulation of Satirical Poetry in the Regency'; Tom Mole, *Byron's Romantic Celebrity* (2007); Andrew Stauffer, 'The Career of Byron's "To the Po."'; 'New Light on Byron's Regency in America'; and 'Sorting Byron's "Windsor Poetics"'.
4. Jerome McGann, 'Private Poetry, Public Deception', p. 120.

5. Dyer observes that when we recognise the multiple means by which satirical poetry of the day circulated, including via manuscript, 'we not only place literary texts in broader contexts, but also recognise a kind of poetic production in which text and context resist being differentiated': 'The Circulation of Satirical Poetry in the Regency', p. 73.
6. Franco Moretti, *Distant Reading* (2013).
7. George Gordon (Lord Byron), *Complete Poetical Works*, 7 vols, ed. Jerome McGann (Oxford: Clarendon Press, 1986). In collecting data from McGann, I have borne in mind his view that 'any database represents an initial critical analysis of the content materials': 'Database, Interface, and Archival Fever', p. 1588), and accordingly I have had to interpret McGann's accounts of the publication history of various poems.
8. Overall the counting of pages provides a good measure of the relative length of the poems, as the pages are uniform throughout the volumes of *CPW*, although this measure is somewhat crude, particularly for short poems, since many are only a few lines long. All such fractional poems are assigned a value of one page. The most accurate method would be to count words. The page numbers for serially published poems have been assigned to the year in which the first instalment appeared.
9. All references to poems in this chapter are given McGann's titles and the numbers he assigns them in *CPW*, denoted after the titles in parentheses.
10. Typically, one version is given precedence; for example, McGann treats *Hours of Idleness* as his base text in *CPW*.
11. Letters in which Byron mentions the differences between publication and printing include the following: letter from Byron to William Harness, 8 December 1811, *Byron's Letters and Journals*, hereafter *BLJ*, II: 142; letter from Byron to Francis Hodgson, 2 December 1811, *BLJ*, II: 140; letter from Byron to John Murray, 2 September 1814, *BLJ*, IV: 163. See also *CPW*, III: 448, where Byron refers to the lines he borrows for the opening fifty-four lines of Canto III of *The Corsair* as having been taken from the 'unpublished (though printed) poem', *The Curse of Minerva*.
12. The four extant printings are currently held at the Morgan Library (Elizabeth Pigot's copy), the British Library (Elizabeth Pigot's), the University of Texas (Byron's), and Newstead Abbey (John Pigot's). I rely on Stauffer's examination of individual printings; see the following note.
13. Andrew Stauffer, 'Lord Byron's *Fugitive Pieces*', unpublished essay, pp. 2–3, 6.
14. Ibid. pp. 4–5.
15. *CPW*, I: 363. Byron wrote and published the poems for his friends: 'I never looked beyond the moment of composition, and published merely at the request of my friends': letter from Byron to William Bankes, 6 March 1807 *BLJ*, I: 111–12.

16. Willis W. Pratt, *Byron at Southwell* (1973), p. 44.
17. Letter from Byron to John M. B. Pigot, 10 August 1816, *BLJ*, I: 97.
18. In August, Byron begged John Pigot to return all copies and asks him 'not even [to] reserve a copy for yourself and sister' (letter from Byron to John M. B. Pigot, 18 August 1806, *BLJ*, I: 98–9). Also discussed in letters from Byron to Pigot on 26 August 1806, I: 99; and 13 January 1807, pp. 103–4.
19. *CPW*, I: 361.
20. See *CPW*, I: 150, lines 43–8; I: 145, lines 17–40; I: 137, lines 17–18.
21. See Pratt, *Byron at Southwell*, p. 44.
22. Even in *Fugitive*, Byron had begun to adopt the convention of using initials and dashes and pseudonyms to disguise the identities of his addressees. Many poems carried forward from *Fugitive* to *Various* without change already had identities obscured: for example, 'To E---' (69), 'To D.---' (71), 'To ---' (72), to name just a few. In *Fugitive*, Byron also used syncopation in a feeble attempt to obscure meaning, as may seen in a title like 'On leaving N-st-d Abbey' (31). The missing letters are restored in *Various*, where the poem is titled 'On leaving Newstead Abbey' perhaps an acknowledgement of the silliness of the practice. Even in manuscript, Byron uses the censuring dash, however half-heartedly. A poem to Anne Houson is titled 'To A – ' (105), although the poem begins 'Oh, Anne! . . .' and she is referred to again by name in the closing lines of the poem. See Peter Cochran, *Byron's Early Poems of Nottinghamshire and London*, p. 44.
23. Letter from Byron to John M. B. Pigot, 13 January 1807, *BLJ*, I: 103.
24. For Byron's note, see *CPW*, I: 379, notes to poem 81.
25. Other poems on the same subject were unpublished. These poems are more vituperative than the one discussed above, and include 'Soliloquy of a Bard in the Country' (27), 'Egotism: A Letter to J. T. Beecher' (109) and 'To those Ladies who have so kindly defended the author, from the attacks of unprovoked malignity' (24). The last poem lashes out at the 'Matrons of the prudish school', whom he accuses of 'pin[ing] for envied Bliss' (*CPW*, I: 17–19, lines 15, 26).
26. These new poems are: 'To M. S. G.' (90), 'To M. S. G.' (40), 'The First Kiss of Love' (92), 'Love's Last Adieu' (95), 'Stanzas to a Lady, with the Poems of Camoens' (37), 'Elegy on Newstead Abbey' (63); 'Horace, Ode 3 lib. 3' (91), 'Fragment of a Translation from the 9th Book of Virgil's Aeneid' (56); 'Answer to a beautiful poem, written by Montgomery' (94), 'Answer to some Elegant Verses' (97), 'Childish Recollections' (93), 'To the Rev. J. T. Becher' (96).
27. Leslie Marchand, *Byron: A Biography* (1957), I: 122–3.
28. Peter Graham, 'Byron and the Business of Publishing', p. 28.

29. The poem 'Lines Written' (75) is counted twice by Byron, as he treats the reply as a separate poem. McGann does not, treating it as a single poem – hence the list of excluded poems adds up to twenty-one. The one poem that is somewhat mysteriously removed from *Various* is 'Answer to a beautiful poem, written by Montgomery' (94). Three other new poems are also removed (90, 91 and 96).
30. Found in a note added to 'Childish Recollections' (93) in *Hours* (1807), 154; *CPW*, I: 383, note for poem 83, line 120. Byron had also attempted to suppress 'Childish Recollections' but was discouraged from doing so by Ridge, likely because of its length (in *Hours* it is 412 lines). In this poem, he had attacked Butler, with whom he had recently reconciled: 'I cannot allow my satire to appear against him, nor can I alter that part relating to him without spoiling the whole' (Letter from Byron to John Ridge, 11 February 1808, *BLJ*, I: 155). Byron, however, relented in the face of Ridge's objections, removing the offending parts for *Hours* and thus allowing the revised poem to be printed. Throughout his career, Byron would likewise be forced by changing circumstances, or other external pressures, to remove the names of those he sought to ridicule from his public verse.
31. *Hours of Idleness* (Ridge, 1807), p. vi.
32. Ibid. p. ix.
33. Graham, 'Byron and the Business of Publishing', p. 29.
34. The latter survives only into *Hours*.
35. Letter from Byron to John Hobhouse, 27 February 1808, Marchand, *Byron*, I: 148.
36. Andrew Rutherford (ed.), *Lord Byron: The Critical Heritage* (1995), p. 4.
37. Graham, 'Byron and the Business of Publishing', p. 29.
38. Byron's publisher now had a saleable commodity on his hands – largely due to the notorious review in the *Edinburgh* – and so he refused to comply with his request, publishing *Original* a month later, in March 1808: letter from Byron to the Reverend John Becher, 28 March 1808, *BLJ*, I: 162–3.
39. *Hours* was more favourably reviewed elsewhere: 'I have been reviewed in twenty different publications, in several very favourably indeed, in others harshly': letter from Byron to Edward Noel Long, 23 November 1807, *BLJ*, I: 139.
40. 'Review of *Poems, in Two Volumes*', *Monthly Literary Recreations* (13 July 1807): 66. The review of his own collection, in the same issue, was more favourable: see 'Review of Hours of Idleness. By Lord Byron', *Monthly Literary Recreations* (13 July 1807): 67–71.
41. James A. Butler, 'Poetry 1798–1807', p. 52; 'Review of *Poems, in Two Volumes*. By William Wordsworth', *Edinburgh Review* 11, no. 22 (October 1807): 218, 220, 221, 231.

42. 'Review of *Hours of Idleness*. By Lord Byron', *Edinburgh Review* 11, no. 22 (January 1808): 288, 289.
43. Thomas Moore, *Life of Lord Byron* (1854), II: 138.
44. This was printed from the second issue of the first edition onward (Byron intended to remove it for the suppressed fifth edition): *CPW*, I: 227–9.
45. *CPW*, I: 228.
46. Ibid., referring to lines by Hobhouse that were removed from *Bards*. The gesture echoes a similar manoeuvre by Wordsworth, in the removal of Coleridge's poems, in 1815: see my discussion in *Family Authorship*, p. 63.
47. Letter from Byron to Robert Charles Dallas, 28 June 1811, *BLJ*, II: 53. In the draft preface to *Hints*, Byron similarly wrote that '[a] Satire if not very bad indeed will generally meet with temporary success because it administers to the malignant . . . propensities of our Nature': *CPW*, I: 428.
48. Letter from Byron to Walter Scott, 6 July 1812, *BLJ*, II: 182; letter from Byron to Thomas Moore, 29 January 1812, *BLJ*, II: 160; letter from Byron to Coleridge, 31 March 1815, *BLJ*, IV: 285–86.
49. Robert Charles Dallas, *Recollections of the Life of Lord Byron* (1824), p. 243. Byron had Murray's solicitor sue Cawthorne, successfully, for an injunction, but he continued to print 'third' and 'fourth' editions as late as 1819.
50. Thomas Jefferson Hogg, *The Life of Percy Bysshe Shelley* (1858), I: 300. Several of these transcripts are held in the Pforzheimer Collection of the New York Public Library, and there is one in the Houghton Library, MS Eng 1484.
51. Letter from Byron to Leigh Hunt, 18 October 1815, *BLJ*, IV: 318.
52. See *CPW*, II: 265–9.
53. Manuscript M is held by John Murray, 50 Albemarle Street, London; Manuscript D is held by the British Library, Egerton MS 2027. In what follows, when citing the manuscript, I provide the stanza number in the original manuscript first, with the final, published stanza number in *CPW* in square brackets. I also provide citations to David V. Erdman and David Worrall (eds), *Childe Harold's Pilgrimage* (1991), hereafter Erdman.
54. One exception is 'Childish Recollections', see note 30, above.
55. Manuscript M, f. 17; *CPW*, II: 277, n. 334.
56. With the exception of the lengthy note highly critical of Lord Elgin, which is retained in both manuscripts and in print, most of the confidential and satirical notes are removed. For example, a note about the vengefulness of the Spanish is transferred from Manuscript M to D but ultimately eliminated from Manuscript D (f. 28v). Another, about Thomas Hope as one who 'publishes quartos on furniture & fashion', is also deleted (f. 41v).

57. Byron does name the song inserted after stanza 12 'Childe Harold's Good Night', but this occurs on an inserted separate sheet, likely made when his revisions were further along: Manuscript D, f. 6B.
58. From the wax deposits, it is clear that this (and the following stanza) had the substituted stanzas pasted on top. In the bound copy of the manuscript, they have been removed and attached to a new sheet, bound in with the original.
59. Manuscript M, f. 6; Erdman, 24–5. The cancelled stanza reads as follows (I have used Erdman's reading for the last line, which I cannot make out):

> Him & one yeoman only did he take
> To travel Eastward to a far countree,
> And though the boy was grieved to leave the lake
> On whose firm banks he grew from Infancy,
> Eftsoons his little heart beat merrily
> With hope of foreign nations to behold,
> And many things right marvellous to see,
> Of which our vaunting voyagers oft have told,
> In many a tome as true as Mandeville's of old.

The final lines seem to offer a satire on the 'vaunting' travellers, and their use of scribes and print to circulate their lies.
60. *CPW*, II: 18, stanza 22var, lines 270–8; Erdman, pp. 36–7.
61. Manuscript M, f. 12, stanza 22 and below. *CPW*, I: 276, note to lines 270–9var.; Erdman, pp. 36–7.
62. Manuscript M, f. 6D and 6E. *CWP*, II: 14, 159–65var., 164–5; II: 15, 174–81var., 175, 178; Erdman, pp. 28–9.
63. In writing about the composition of *Don Juan*, Graham observes a similar pattern whereby Byron wrote the final cantos 'rapidly, with little of the revising and expanding that had characterised the earlier cantos': 'Byron and the Business of Publishing', p. 41. Graham attributes this in part to his ability 'to shed any remaining ambivalence about the subversive nature of the poem', but Byron in fact became more conservative about the content of the poem; according to William St Clair, 'Byron wanted to keep his intellectual property rights, and he was willing to make textual changes to ensure that the remainder of the poem was not "injurious."' As a result, there was nothing illegal in the later cantos: St Clair, *Reading Nation*, pp. 18–19. A similar pattern is evident in *Childe*: taking into account both Manuscript M and Manuscript D, only three stanzas were cancelled from Canto II, compared to the nine removed from Canto I. In other words, as Byron composed his long poems, he became more confident as to what could be said within an individual poem.

64. See *CPW*, II: 271; Jerome McGann, *Fiery Dust* (1968), p. 104. According to Pratt, this narrative playfulness does not reappear until *Beppo* in 1818 (and of course thereafter in *Don Juan*); however, it seems possible that Pratt was not familiar with the original manuscript version: *Byron at Southwell*, p. 44.
65. Letter from John Murray to Byron, 4 September 1811, in Nicholson, *Letters of John Murray*, p. 3. Graham notes that, during this early phase of their partnership, 'Murray went on to shape Byron's choice of subjects through discreet suggestion', moving him towards the popular Eastern tales and away from the more potentially alienating, and dangerous, satire: 'Byron and the Business of Publishing', p. 33.
66. Letter from Byron to John Murray, 5 September 1811, *BLJ*, II: 90.
67. On the Convention of Cintra: BL Egerton MS 2027, Canto I, stanzas 24–7, which are crossed through in pencil, with handwritten annotation of 'omitted' beside each; *CPW*, I: 24var a, b, c, d; Erdman, stanzas 25–8, pp. 38–41.
68. BL Egerton MS 2027, Canto II, stanza 8, f. 37r and 38r; Erdman, pp. 102–3.
69. Letter from John Murray to Byron, 4 September 1811, *Letters of John Murray to Lord Byron*, p. 3.
70. Zimmerman, 'Smith, Charlotte (1749–1806)'.
71. BL Egerton 2027, f. 29v.; I: 87var b, c, d in *CPW*; 88(b), 89(c) and 89(d), in Erdman.
72. Erdman, pp. 83, 86–7, 90–1.
73. BL Egerton MS 2027, f. 40r and 41v, Canto II, stanzas 15 and 16; Erdman, 14(a) and 15(b), pp. 108–9.
74. BL Egerton MS 2027, 69–71 are cancelled with a diagonal ink line through them. Letter from Byron to R. C. Dallas, 21 August 1811, *BLJ*, II: 75.
75. *CPW*, I: 68–70; Erdman, pp. 70–2.
76. Letter from Byron to Francis Hodgson, 25 September 1811, *BLJ*, II: 106.
77. See 'Advertisement', *Poems* (1816), n.p.
78. The poems, and their original publication venues, are as follows: 'Bright be the place of my soul' [273], 'On the Star of "the legion of honour"' [277], 'Napoleon's Farewell' [274], all in the *Examiner*; 'Fare thee Well' [285] in *The Champion*; and 'Ode' [283] in the *Morning Chronicle*; two had been previously published as songs, with the poet's consent ('When we two parted' [279]; 'Stanzas for Music' [245]); and four were new poems, not previously published ('To ---[Augusta]' [288]; 'Stanzas for Music' [284]; 'From the French' [276]; 'To Samuel Rogers' [186]).
79. See Byron, 'Advertisement'.
80. See Plate 11.
81. *Sibylline Leaves* (1817), p. ii.

82. In 1815, John Murray began to issue multi-volume editions of Byron's works that collected some of his lyric verse for other publications: see vol. IV of *The Works of the Right Honourable Lord Byron*, 4 vols (1815).
83. According to the *Index of Literary Manuscripts*: 'Autograph MSS of most Byron poems are extant. Of the longer poems, only *The Blues* and *Heaven and Earth* are not represented by a complete MS. The MSS used by the printer for poems published by John Hunt, with the exception of *The Vision of Judgment* (ByL 751), have also remained untraced and may have been destroyed.' The editors note the significant role John Murray played in preserving Byron's manuscripts, particularly his press copies, which in most cases were routinely destroyed after printing was complete. In some cases, Murray must have sought their return from the printers.
84. Byron also shared his drafts. One example of a draft that may have circulated is 'Epilogue. [A Parody of Wordsworth's *Peter Bell*]' (348). The draft, written into the first page of Wordsworth's prologue, is tipped into the first volume of Murray's *New Edition of the Poetical Works of Lord Byron*: see *BLJ*, IV: 517.
85. Undoubtedly many non-autograph copies have not survived.
86. Letter from Byron to Lady Melbourne, 25 April 1814, *BLJ*, IV: 105.
87. *CPW*, III: 458.
88. Graham, 'Byron and the Business of Publishing', p. 35.
89. Letter from Byron to John Murray, 15 April 1816, *BLJ*, V: 67–8; letter from Byron to John Murray, 28 August 1816, *BLJ*, V: 90–1.
90. *CPW*, IV: 33–40.
91. Letter from Byron to de Stael, 27 July 1816, *BLJ*, Supplementary Volume, 45. In this letter, Byron explains that, 'to prevent any mistakes which my readers are sometimes disposed', the smaller poems 'are addressed but to one person now in England – and she a near relation'.
92. Letter from Byron to John Murray, 30 September 1816, *BLJ*, V: 108. The manuscript collection of these letters is in the National Library of Scotland (NLS), MS 43350.
93. Stauffer, 'The Career of Byron's 'To the Po.', p. 119.
94. Ibid. pp. 119–20.
95. Letter from Byron to John Murray, 15 April 1816, *BLJ*, V: 67–8.
96. Examples include: [Verses on W. J. Fitzgerald] (204), [To Thomas Moore] (211), [On Lord Thurlow's Poems] (212), 'To' [Lord Thurlow] (213), 'Fragment of an Epistle to Thomas Moore' (235), [Pretty Miss Jaqueline] (294), [To Thomas Moore] (307), [Versicles] (313), [To Mr. Murray] (314), [No Infant Southeby Whose Dauntless Head] (318), [Epistle from Mr. Murray to Dr. Polidori] (319), [Epistle to Mr. Murray] (321), 'Question and Answer' (323), 'Ballad to the Tune of "Sally in Our Alley"' (324), 'Another Simple Ballat' (325), [To Mr. Murray] (326), [On R. C. Dallas] (346) and [A Volume of Nonsense] (354).

97. Andrew Nicholson (ed.), *The Manuscripts of the Younger Romantics: Lord Byron, Volume XII.* (1998), p. 122.
98. Letter from Byron to John Murray, 28 September 1820, *BLJ*, VII: 181.
99. Letter from John Murray to Byron, 24 October 1820 (Nicholson, *Letters of John Murray to Byron*, p. 350).
100. Ibid. p. 350.
101. Murray's one major error was in circulating the privately printed copies of 'Fare Thee Well', and in particular 'A Sketch of Private Life'. According to *The Champion* no. 172 (21 April 1816), which had printed these poems without authorisation from the private publications, 'the two Poems were sent under cover to Members of Parliament, directly from Mr. Murray. Mr. Murray gave numerous copies of them, in his shop, to applicants; they were read at Parties: we had half a dozen copies sent to our office, from various quarters; and we have scarcely a single acquaintance that had not seen them' (19).
102. Other poems that appeared in certain periodicals and separate publications can be presumed to have been published with his knowledge and consent, implied or explicit, because of his associations with the individuals involved in these publications.
103. A similar example dates to January 1808, when Byron complained that a poem entitled 'Libellus' (no longer extant) had been circulated, even though he had 'never transmitted a single copy till October, when I gave one to a boy, since gone, after repeated importunities': letter from Byron to Henry Drury, 13 January 1808, *BLJ*, I: 145.
104. Letter from Byron to Lady Jersey, 29 May 1814, *BLJ*, IV: 120. In her letter to Byron, explaining that her copy of the poem has gone missing and begging for another copy, she states that the maid had burnt it. See *The Works of Lord Byron: Letters and Journals*, ed. Rowland Edmund Prothero Ernle (1899), III: 85. It was later hypothesised that the maid had in fact stolen the manuscript.
105. Letter from Byron to John Murray, 2 August 1814, *BLJ*, IV: 149. Interestingly, on 14 August 1814, Byron received a request from Murray for a copy of the poem, pledging his 'word to allow no copy to be taken': Nicholson, *Letters of John Murray to Byron*, p. 108.
106. For an account of early modern circulation of political satire, see Harold Love, *English Clandestine Satire, 1660–1702* (2004).
107. Dyer, 'The Circulation of Satirical Poetry in the Regency', p. 71.
108. Letter from Byron to Thomas Moore, 12 March 1814, *BLJ*, IV: 80. As Jonathan Gross explains, whereas '[i]n 1812, one could still construe the Prince Regent's betrayal of his Whig friends as an act of loyalty to an ailing father[,] [b]y 1814, . . . any hope for George III's

mental recovery was over', such there could be no pretence that the prince's support of the Tories was temporary or filially motivated: *Byron: The Erotic Liberal* (2001), p. 23.
109. Letter from Byron to John Murray, 22 January 1814, *BLJ*, IV: 37.
110. Gross, *Byron: The Erotic Liberal*, p. 23.
111. Letter from Byron to Lady Melbourne, 7 April 1813, *BLJ*, III: 38.
112. Letter from Byron to Thomas Moore, 12 March 1814, *BLJ*, IV: 80.
113. Dyer, 'The Circulation of Satirical Poetry in the Regency', p. 68.
114. No complete inventory exists, though McGann notes eleven copies: *CWP*, III: 425, commentary to poem 209.
115. Ironically, when Byron finally wrote a poem in praise of the prince in 1819, 'To The Prince Regent' (337), commending him for granting royal assent to the restoration of the rights of Irish patriot Lord Edward FitzGerald (1763–98), and asked Murray to print it, with his name, the poem languished in manuscript until after Byron's death. It was first printed by Moore: *CWP*, IV: 505, commentary to poem 337.
116. Both annotated lists have been published in Lord Byron, *The Complete Miscellaneous Prose* (1991), pp. 1–7.

Chapter 5

Jane Austen's Fiction in Manuscript

After Thomas Cadell rejected *First Impressions* (an early version of *Pride and Prejudice*) unread, 'declined by Return of Post', in 1797, it took Jane Austen another fourteen years to break into print, with the publication of *Sense and Sensibility* in 1811.[1] This fourteen-year delay was preceded by at least a decade of writing, in which she produced and collected a substantial body of fiction and satire known collectively as the 'juvenilia'. Why did it take Austen, now regarded as one of the greatest of English novelists, nearly a quarter century to produce writing that was publishable? Austen's surviving manuscripts provide a window into her compositional process and thus allow us to better understand, and explicate, her ongoing struggle to enter print, difficulties she shared with other authors of the period, including those examined in the previous two chapters. This chapter presents a final opportunity to return to the manuscript record of a single writer, in this case a highly canonical author, working within one of the most commercial of genres, for what it can tell us about her working methods and perceptions of print.[2] Scrupulous scholarly examination of Austen's working drafts has dispelled the myth, first perpetuated by her brother, that '[e]very thing came finished from her pen'.[3] With new editions of Austen's fiction manuscripts – *The Cambridge Edition of the Works of Jane Austen*, *Jane Austen's Manuscript Works* and *Jane Austen's Fiction Manuscripts: A Digital Edition*, the last of which includes digital photo-facsimiles and diplomatic transcriptions of all Austen's fiction manuscripts – we enjoy unprecedented access to high-quality print and digital copies of her manuscripts that allow us to see what issued from her pen.[4] These editions, when consulted in combination with the rich scholarly readings of her manuscripts we possess, make it possible to precisely study Austen's lifelong practices of domestic manuscript production and their likely impact on the production of her six novels.[5]

Table 5.1 provides an inventory of Austen's surviving fiction manuscripts, which include manuscripts of all kinds, from drafts showing various states of revision to fair copies, from all periods of her writing career.[6] The table simplifies the state of her manuscripts somewhat, insofar as the juvenilia contains corrections and revisions, made both at the time of copying and subsequently; nevertheless, the general distinction holds, as most of the pieces were copied, not drafted, into the three volumes that Austen labelled, with mock pretension, *Volume the First*, *Volume the Second* and *Volume the Third*.[7] These three volumes establish Austen's collaborative practices (with her sister Cassandra's illustrations in 'The History of England', and occasional contributions by other family members) and delineate a circle of readers (all but one of the collected pieces are dedicated to named family members, and some of her characters are named for them).[8] As Kathryn Sutherland has observed:

> All three notebooks embody features of sociable performance, permitting the modern reader valuable glimpses into the workings of coterie writing and its reception within a gentry family at play at the end of the eighteenth century. The 13 dedicatory prefaces to the mini-novels, dramas, and verses of *Volume the First* spin fanciful and provocative connections to an immediate community of readers – family and friends – figured for the occasion as beneficent patrons of the aspiring author. Not least in the continued use of dedications in *Volume the Second* and *Volume the Third*, there persists a sense of the notebooks' contents as designed to be shared, and of their voice as mediated rather than private.[9]

The three volumes further demonstrate her thorough knowledge and imitation of print (through conventions such as tables of contents, dedications, indices, and pagination) and signal her (and her family's) pride in the early writing, which has been carefully copied, illustrated (in the case of 'The History of England') and preserved.[10] Beyond these bibliographical and paratextual elements, the content of the juvenilia assumes shared knowledge and values. Providing oblique allusions to facts or circumstances that only certain intimate readers would recognise, Austen inscribes a confined set of readers within the texts themselves. In these pieces, Austen appears at her most satiric and parodic, demonstrating her comfort in performing

Table 5.1 Inventory of Austen's surviving fiction manuscripts

Date of earliest draft	Working draft	Fair copy
1787–93		'Volume the First'
1790–3		'Volume the Second'
1792		'Volume the Third'
1793–4		Lady Susan (1805–9)
1804	The Watsons	
1816	Persuasion (two cancelled chapters)	
1816		'Plan of a Novel'
1816		'Opinions of *Mansfield Park*'; 'Opinions of *Emma*'
1817	Sanditon	

these modes with her family. This writing thus readily belongs to the class termed by Donald Reiman as 'confidential manuscripts'.[11]

Austen's early fiction does not appear to have circulated outside of the household. According to Peter Sabor, '[d]uring [her] lifetime, the existence of her early writings was unknown outside her immediate circle of family and close friends'.[12] Interestingly, several of her known poems did circulate; like Barbauld's, they were given as gifts or to mark important occasions, and like both Barbauld and Byron, Austen included some poems in letters. We also know that the Austen family engaged in composing, collecting and copying charades, in a book kept by the family.[13] Nevertheless, familial practices of manuscript culture within the Austen household seem to have been more constrained than those described by Aikin and Barbauld in *Evenings at Home*, where neighbouring families and friends were invited to participate in readings. Austen's circulation of her early writing appears to have been confined to reading by, and oral recitation and performance for, members of her household. Evidence that Austen did not copy all of her childhood writing into the three volumes, and deleted some passages, suggests that even within the family, curation, and possibly self-censorship, was necessary, undertaken in the act of revising when fair copying the individual pieces into the three notebooks.[14] It seems likely as well, given the sensitive nature of some of her later confidential fiction manuscripts, that Austen may have curtailed access to particular pieces even beyond the small numbers of readers exposed to the juvenilia. That most of Austen's fiction manuscripts are in her hand alone may also point towards a more autonomous, less communal practice.

As a collection, the juvenilia offers evidence of Austen's maturation as a writer: the pieces grow longer and more intricate, with later stories serving as possible prototypes for print. Sutherland notes that in *Volume the Third* there is 'more evidence of immediate composition', suggesting that Austen may have transitioned within these notebooks from collecting and fair copying to actively composing.[15] The three-volume collection has generally been regarded as reflecting her most serious and prolonged engagement with manuscript culture. The sharp differences that have been apparent to readers between the scribal juvenilia and the printed novels have facilitated this conceptual narrative of separation and development. R. W. Chapman, following Edward Austen-Leigh, was largely dismissive of the juvenilia, regarding it as something of an embarrassment.[16] Both men justified its publication, in stages as the public demanded, primarily as proof of the apprentice-work Austen needed to undertake to achieve the mature vision of the novels. By contrast, some modern editors and scholars of the juvenilia, especially Margaret Doody, regard Austen's entry into print with less exultation. For Doody, Austen's juvenilia reveals an exuberant energy that had to be sacrificed for print.[17] She claims that only through a revolutionary process of accommodation and domestication did Austen become publishable. For Sutherland, Austen's novels reflect how she succumbed to 'a subsequently acquired moral and print conformity'.[18] Whether conceiving of Austen's career in terms of development or confinement, advance or decline, the competing narratives juxtapose the juvenilia with the print novels, dividing her early engagement with manuscript in the juvenilia from her later involvement with print culture. Jan Fergus's *Jane Austen: A Literary Life* (1991), intended as a corrective to the portrait of Austen as an amateurish, gentle 'Aunt Jane', further entrench this separation between Austen's work in script and print by providing an authoritative portrayal of Austen as 'the ambitious professional author'.[19]

This chapter draws upon a central insight of Sutherland's, that Austen never abandoned the kind of writing we find in the juvenilia:

> The evidence suggests that by the 1810s Austen maintained simultaneous yet distinct identities as amateur and professional author – on the one hand participating in and encouraging longstanding habits of family writing, on the other circumscribing its influence on her professional development.[20]

Sutherland's understanding of Austen's ongoing engagement in both commercial print and family writing is supported by an understanding of the novelist's chronology, as there is no precise date when we can say that her scribal, or amateur, period ends. If we look to 1793, the year she finished transcribing her juvenilia, we are left with a wide span of eighteen years before Thomas Egerton printed *Sense and Sensibility* in 1811. We might also notice that Austen's aspirations towards a professional career in print emerged far earlier than 1811 – at least as early as 1797, when George Austen approached Thomas Cadell with 'a Manuscript Novel, comprised in 3 Vols. about the length of Fanny Burney's Evelina'.[21] Even earlier, in 1786, Austen began to collect and thereby preserve her childhood writings, with mock titles and dedications that demonstrate a thorough engagement with and determination for print. As this chapter will explore, even after she completed her juvenile volumes and her novels began to appear in print, Austen continued to use manuscript to circulate short satirical pieces that addressed her confidential readers. She also returned to her juvenile writing: younger family members revised and continued her unfinished stories, almost certainly with her participation and approval, between 1809 and 1811 and again between 1814 and 1816.[22] Temporally, it is impossible to locate a clear moment of transition between Austen's uses of domestic manuscript and public print, for her career provides ample proof of a thorough knowledge of and desire for print arising very early, and demonstrable signs that her engagement with confidential manuscript culture persisted until the end of her life.

In addition to questioning the chronological separation of Austen's writing practices, this chapter seeks to offer a fuller examination of her attraction to confidential writing, asking, as the previous two chapters have done for Barbauld and Byron, what she was attempting to do by writing in manuscript. It does this through a detailed assessment of her later manuscript writing. Austen's later (i.e., post-juvenilia) literary manuscripts may conveniently be divided into two groups:

1. those she wrote immediately following the juvenile period, from the mid-1790s to the mid-1800s, during her so-called fallow decade. The draft of *The Watsons* and the fair copy of *Lady Susan*, both written before she became a published author, are dated to this period; and

2. those she wrote in the final two years of her life, after she had published all four lifetime novels, from 1816 to 1817. These works include 'Plan of a Novel, according to hints from various quarters', the two cancelled *Persuasion* chapters, and *Sanditon*.

By focusing on these two sets of later manuscripts, all written immediately prior to or during her career as a print author, this chapter seeks to describe and evaluate Austen's ongoing use of and need for sociable outlets for her writing and to understand the relationship between Austen's confidential manuscript and her print novels. Sutherland observes that Austen circumscribed the influence of her domestic writing on her professional development, and while it is certainly true that Austen's domestic writing could not be easily assimilated into print, this chapter questions the extent to which Austen was able to separate these two spheres of writing, and protect each from mutual influence.

The domestic publications that Austen wrote before she became a print novelist include *The Watsons* and *Lady Susan*; the former offers important clues as to how and why Austen wished to address her domestic readers; the later offers glimpses into Austen's penchant for biting social criticism, suggesting the challenges she may have faced in writing for a public audience. The domestic publications that Austen wrote after she became a print novelist include several pieces that are not fictional *per se*: the satirical 'Plan of a Novel'; the collections of feedback on her novels, 'Opinions of *Mansfield Park*' and 'Opinions of *Emma*'; a handful of poems; and a series of letters she wrote to her niece reflecting upon her fictional practices.[23] Austen's engagement with domestic manuscript culture thus stretches across her career, from her earliest girlhood writing to her poem, 'When Winchester Races', composed two days before she died. Unlike Frances Burney, who burnt all of her early writing at the tender age of fifteen and held a generally more hostile attitude towards manuscript culture, which she regarded as repressive and anachronistic, Austen's careful preservation and emendation of her unpublished writing further demonstrates its ongoing importance both to herself and to her family.[24]

Austen's working manuscripts, *The Watsons*, as well as the very last fiction manuscripts, the two cancelled *Persuasion* chapters, and

Sanditon, offer important insight into Austen's habits of revision and present the difficulties that seem to have persisted for her in writing for print. The revised cancelled *Persuasion* chapters, in particular, allow us to witness a manuscript text in several stages as it is being transformed for print. Much as we saw with Byron's manuscripts of *Childe Harold's Pilgrimage*, Cantos I and II, for Austen this process of readying her fiction for print was arduous, with many late changes revolving around her satiric depictions of certain characters. In studying this manuscript in particular, we see how the worlds of scribal and print culture intermingle and collide, as elements of her confidential manuscripts persist within a fiction manuscript being prepared for print. Though usually read as an unfinished novel, Austen's intentions regarding *Sanditon* are unknown, and this chapter adopts the 'archival reading' strategy used in earlier chapters, returning the work to its material context as an unfinished draft, and asking what it means to read the work as possibly belonging to her confidential manuscripts. This reading further helps to break down the supposed separation between Austen's career in script and print, as we engage with the manuscript of indeterminate intentionality, and, because unfinished, of unknown futurity.

Austen's Confidential Fiction Manuscripts

Lady Susan, the ten-year-old epistolary novella that Austen revived sometime after 1805 by making a fair copy and possibly adding a direct narrative ending, offers one example of Austen's continued engagement in manuscript culture. At 23,000 words, *Lady Susan*, as Linda Bree and Janet Todd point out, is too short to have been published on its own, though it could have been printed together with a shorter work such as *Northanger Abbey*.[25] Nevertheless, much of the extensive scholarship on the text has approached it as a problem to be solved, noting its dated use of epistolary conventions and its moral anarchism, particularly in its refusal to explicitly condemn Lady Susan.[26] Scholars have observed that such censure would have been supplied by the implicit moral consensus of the Austen family audience, who could be trusted to safely enjoy (without being corrupted by) Austen's depiction of the treacherous and scheming heroine. Their mischievous delight might have been intensified if the original of Lady Susan was Austen's cousin, Eliza de Feuillide, as several scholars have claimed.[27] *Lady Susan* has presented itself as a problem to be solved because of its status as a finished, though unpublishable narrative. But without any evidence that Austen had any intention to share *Lady Susan* beyond her domestic circle, it may be a problem of our own invention, a consequence of our assumption that print must always be the desired outcome for a literary writer of the period. The copying of the story fair, apparently some years after its first composition, possibly with the addition of a conclusion, further suggests that the story continued to be shared, and enjoyed, by her domestic audience, many years after it was originally written.

More than ten years later, in early 1816, after all four of her lifetime novels had been published, Austen drafted 'Plan of a Novel', a short piece that was also designed for modest circulation within her domestic circle. A very short prose parody, it belongs to no obvious print genre but rather to what Harold Love has termed 'clandestine satire'.[28] Like the poems Byron wrote about his father-in-law and Samuel Rogers, which were so potentially dangerous that their circulation had to be carefully controlled, 'Plan of a Novel', a personal attack on J. S. Clarke, the Prince Regent's librarian who had corresponded with Austen over the dedication of *Emma*, could only be seen by those she could trust.[29] In this correspondence, Clarke had proffered unsolicited and self-serving 'hints' for future novels, chiefly modelled on his own life. In writing the mockery of these hints, it was imperative for Austen to keep the lampoon private, for in it, she savages the librarian, quoting verbatim or closely paraphrasing from his letters to her. She borrows many of his specific suggestions as to plot and character, as Table 5.2 demonstrates, to expose how outrageously silly and egotistical they are.

It is apparent from this mimicking of Clarke in 'Plan of a Novel' that Austen had absolute faith in the discretion of her readers and their ability to control its circulation.[30] Because 'Plan' targets more than Clarke alone, with Austen implicating a number of her readers in her critique through her marginal annotations, she may have been especially cautious in showing the manuscript to others. In her marginalia, which may be seen in the manuscript's first page (see Plate 13), Austen annotates phrases and characters to be featured in the planned mock novel with the names of those individuals who had taken the

Table 5.2 Comparison of Austen's letters from J. S. Clarke and her 'Plan of a Novel'

Clarke's Letters	Austen's 'Plan of a Novel'
'And I also dear Madam wished to be allowed to ask you, to delineate in some Future Work the Habits of Life and Character and enthusiasm of a Clergyman . . .—Fond of, & entirely engaged in Literature—no man's enemy but his own.' (*Letters*, L125A, 296–7)	'The Father to be of a very literary turn, an Enthusiast in Literature, nobody's Enemy but his own—' (*LM*, 227)
'—shew dear Madam what good would be done if Tythes were taken away entirely, and describe him burying his own mother—as I did—because the High Priest of the Parish in which she died—did not pay her remains the respect he ought to do. I have never recovered the shock. Carry your Clergyman to Sea as the Friend of some distinguished Naval Character about a Court—you can then bring forward like Le Sage many interesting Scenes of Character & Interest.' (*Letters*, L132A, 307)	'[I]t will comprehend his going to sea as Chaplain to a distinguished Naval Character about the Court, his going afterwards to Court himself, which introduced him to a great variety of Characters & involved him in many interesting situations, concluding with his opinion of the Benefits to result from Tythes being done away, & his having buried his own Mother (Heroine's lamented Grandmother) in consequence of the High Priest of the Parish in which she died, refusing to pay her Remains the respect due to them.' (*LM*, 227)
See passages quoted above	'At last, hunted out of civilized society . . . the poor Father, quite worn down, finding his end approaching . . . expires in a fine burst of Literary Enthusiasm, intermingled with Invectives again[st] Holder's of Tythes.' (*LM*, 228–9)

liberty of offering her their own 'hints'.[31] Overall, she includes fifteen notes referencing seven people (and one to 'many critics'): in fact, five of the annotations are to her cousin, Mary Cooke; four are to her niece Fanny Knight, and only one is to Clarke. The five annotations to Mary Cooke emphasise her hackneyed contrasting descriptions of the heroine ('not the least wit' with 'dark eyes & plump cheeks') and the young woman who seeks the heroine's acquaintance ('light eyes & fair skin, but having a considerable degree of Wit'). The four annotations to Fanny Knight, two of which may be seen on the first page of the manuscript in Plate 13, call upon on Austen to produce a 'Heroine a faultless Character herself – , perfectly good, with much tenderness & sentiment', 'very highly accomplished', 'to be in the most elegant Society & living in high style', and to be wooed by the hero, who is also 'all perfection'. In the 'Opinions of *Mansfield Park*' and 'Opinions of *Emma*', also collected in 1816, Knight had complained of defects in Emma Woodhouse's and Mary Crawford's characters. In 'Opinions of *Emma*', Knight admits that she 'could not bear *Emma* herself' and in 'Opinions of *Mansfield Park*' she objects that she 'could not think it natural that Edm^d. sh^d. be so much attached to a woman without Principle like Mary C. – or promote Fanny's marrying Henry. – '[32] These mocking references to members of her immediate family suggest that 'Plan of a Novel' might have enjoyed greater levels of privacy than others.

One problem we confront in assessing Austen's transition from script to print is the absence of manuscripts of the print novels (with the one exception of the two cancelled *Persuasion* chapters), and the meagre number of extant letters that survive.[33] The next section explores the three extant working manuscripts. These include the one fiction manuscript that we know to have been prepared for a public readership – the cancelled *Persuasion* chapters. These cancelled chapters come at the end of the novel and were revised and ultimately replaced by three new chapters, which survive only in printed form. The status of the other two draft manuscripts – *The Watsons* and *Sanditon* – is more uncertain. Although written over a decade apart, the three working manuscripts reflect continuities in Austen's compositional modes as well as the intermingling of print and script consciousness.

Austen's Working Manuscripts

Austen's three surviving draft manuscripts – *The Watsons* (1804), *Persuasion* (1816) and *Sanditon* (1817) – share many material similarities. *The Watsons* and *Sanditon* are nearly identical (measuring 190 by 120 mm), though *Sanditon* has appreciably more pages, 120 to *The Watsons*'s 85; *Persuasion*'s pages are smaller, at 155 by 90 mm. The drafts are contained in handmade booklets of paper cut, folded and sewn, apparently by Austen herself. *Persuasion* has been taken apart and remounted by conservators, but it began as a handmade booklet of sixteen leaves.[34] Austen used these small booklets, according to Sutherland, 'as they were more easily secreted . . . from prying eyes'.[35] In all three manuscripts, there is no pagination, no clear or regular paragraphing, and no separation of speaking parts from one another. Austen's revision practices also appear consistent. In the absence of margins, the main types of revision are strikethroughs and minuscule interlinear corrections. The working drafts reveal that Austen revised her writing heavily on multiple occasions.[36] Although some revisions were made immediately – for example, where words are cancelled mid-sentence, with the new phrasing continuing on the same line – many if not most of the interlinear revisions involve rephrasing and syntactic modifications that only subtly affect meaning.[37] Where she sought an addition or more robust rewriting, Austen's practice was to add new sections via small slips of paper, either to substitute for cancelled sections or to expand what was already written. These patches are found pinned in *The Watsons* and pasted in *Persuasion*, with none found in *Sanditon*, likely because she did not live to revise it extensively.

The later two manuscripts have chapter divisions and several dates inserted, suggesting modest developments in Austen's compositional practices, which, as Sutherland observes, appear to have 'remained fairly constant over the period 1804–17'.[38] Sutherland also notes that Austen's manuscript booklets are 'already novelistic in physical form',[39] and indeed, they do mimic a codex, with their size and structure mapping onto the printed pages for her novels, which were all published in a small octavo format. In terms of words per line, lines per page and overall words per page, the handmade notebooks constrained Austen to draft pages that roughly approximated print pages. Furthermore, the small booklets enabled modularity, insofar as one booklet could easily be swapped out (or taken apart) if more substantial changes were called for.

Sutherland describes Austen's fiction manuscripts as 'straightforwardly transitional documents that led lives of narrow and thrifty expediency, serving first her expressive needs, then providing copy for the press, before ending up as printing-house wastepaper', that is, as public manuscripts.[40] Certainly, the cancelled *Persuasion* chapters, forming part of a novel that was in fact printed, offer an unambiguous example of a public manuscript. The cancelled manuscript chapters, likely saved because they reflect the dramatic alterations to the novel's denouement, uniquely allow us to observe Austen's revision process at both a late stage in the composition of a novel and a late stage of her career. Scholars have observed some shared features of Austen's revisions within the cancelled chapters. Jocelyn Harris, for example, notes a deliberate minimisation of the satire directed at Lady Russell.[41] Austen strikes through several passages in which Anne might be said to be gloating over Lady Russell's errors in judgement: one at the start of Chapter 10 (in which Anne muses 'upon the fact of her having been right & Lady R wrong, the most discriminating of the two'); and one from the beginning of Chapter 11 ('A young Woman proved to have more discrimination of Character than her elder – to have seen in two Instances more clearly what a Man was').[42] Other instances of Anne's impertinence, however, survive Austen's revisions to the cancelled manuscript chapters, though they are ultimately removed from the substituted print chapters. One example occurs after she has been coerced by Admiral Croft into a meeting with Wentworth, when Anne asks herself whether if she 'did not with a more passive Determination walk quietly out of the room – (as certainly she might have done) may she not be pardoned?'[43] Anne also reflects critically upon the Admiral for mocking his servant. Although this scene is entirely removed, it is nevertheless apparent that even in the heavily revised cancelled chapters, Anne challenges the poor judgement and behaviour of her elders and social betters and acts against them (or at least contemplates doing so, by leaving the room). The survival of her heroine's resistance into the cancelled chapters conforms to Austen's strong compulsion to bestow satirical powers upon her heroines, a feature present in the drafts of *The Watsons* and *Sanditon* as well.

Austen's late revisions evidence an ongoing struggle with the need to temper her representations. As with the amendments to soften the challenge to Lady Russell, a patch added to page 19 of the manuscript moderates the foppishness of Sir Walter. Austen cancels her description of Sir Walter scrutinising his son-in-law's appearance, as he had carefully observed 'his complexion by daylight' and 'his Teeth' 'in conversation'. In the substituted passage, the description of Sir Walter's scrutiny of Wentworth is less vulgar, as there is no longer any mention of complexion and teeth; instead, after Sir Walter 'eyed him well, he was very much struck by his personal appearance'.[44] The overall result, in both small and large revisions, effected on the pages of cancelled chapters, through added sections and through the final substitution of new chapters, is towards minimising her social critique, particularly as it issues from her heroine. The cancelled *Persuasion* chapters provide us with the sole surviving example of how Austen's texts moved towards print, and in them, we find Austen tempering her satire, though the process is a complex one as we witness her attachment to the satirical portrayals of Sir Walter, Admiral Croft and Lady Russell. In the transition from script to print in *Persuasion*, we witness the momentous changes to the narrative ending as a whole. But we may also note subtler shifts that mark Austen's hesitant relenting towards what she perceived to be the demands of print.

Although the status of Austen's two other unfinished drafts, *The Watsons* and *Sanditon*, is more uncertain, they are nevertheless usually characterised as failed, incomplete novels. Such a reading depends, however, on the belief that, for both, print was her aim. *The Watsons*, begun in 1804 and abandoned unfinished by her later that year, was produced at a moment when Austen's prospects in print were not high. *Susan* (a precursor to *Northanger Abbey*) had been sold in 1803 to Benjamin Crosby, but he, for reasons unknown, had failed to publish it. Austen nursed a grudge against Crosby for this inexplicable failure throughout her life; in the posthumously published *Northanger Abbey*, the only novel to which she saw fit to add any prefatory material, she wonders, incredulously, how 'any bookseller would think it worthwhile to purchase what he did not think worth while to publish'.[45] With Austen (in 1804) still seven years away from seeing her first novel into print, *The Watsons* shifts abruptly from the outlandishness and burlesque of the juvenilia, as well as the 'sparkle' of the early novels, to offer a sombre portrayal of female dependency.[46] Claudia Johnson echoes the sentiments of most Austen scholars in finding that it is 'unquestionably Austen's bleakest work'.[47] '[T]he stiffness and the bareness' that Virginia Woolf observed in the fragment are particularly acute in the characterisation of her heroine. Woolf's confident assertion that 'she was one of those writers who lay their facts out rather baldly in the first version and then go back and back and back and cover them with flesh and atmosphere' conveys, in part, the stark differences that are apparent between the working manuscripts and the print novels.[48]

Austen added three patches to the manuscript of *The Watsons*.[49] All three involve a fleshing out of character by reworking and expanding dialogue. The first two additions illustrate how Austen developed Emma Watson, her heroine. In the first, Austen replaces a rather bland dialogue between Emma and Lord Osborne, when he asks why some women do not ride horses. In the substituted passage, Emma's response is much sharper, and includes the famous retort, that 'Female Economy ~~may~~ ^will^ do a great deal ^my^ Lord, but it cannot turn a small income into a large one', a remark that silences Lord Osborne.[50]

According to the narrator, in delivering this remark, Emma's 'manner had been neither Sententious nor sarcastic, but there was a something in ~~what she said~~ its' mild seriousness, as well as in the words themselves which made his Lordship think'. Austen represents Lord Osborne as a man who is not affronted by the remark, but this representation, of a young, poor, and untitled woman unbraiding her social superior, may have provoked some readers. The substituted scene, while heightening the emotional entanglement between Emma and Lord Osborne by evoking sympathy for Emma, also brought with it risk, particularly as the heroine is made the mouthpiece of social critique. That Austen, even in revision, provides her heroine with a speech in which she directly rebukes a nobleman, demonstrates an inability or unwillingness to rein in her satire, a reluctance that appears throughout her manuscript writing.

The second pinned addition to *The Watsons* presents a new scene between Emma and her brother, which also evokes Austen's desire to represent the precarious situation of women of Emma's class. In this exchange, Emma is placed in an impossible situation, forced to defend her uncle's decision to leave all of his money to his wife, even though it has resulted, upon her uncle's recent death and her aunt's recent remarriage, in Emma being dismissed from the only home she has known and returned to her own family. Emma ties herself in knots in attempting to defend her uncle and even her aunt: '"If she [Emma's aunt] has made an imprudent choice [in her second marriage], she will suffer more from it herself, than *I* can possibly do."'[51] Her brother makes his point with brutal simplicity: '"After keeping you at a distance from your family for ~~14 years~~ such a length of time as must do away all natural affection among us & breeding you up (I suppose) in a superior stile, you are returned upon their hands without a sixpence."'[52] But the fault, as Emma's tortured speech makes plain, does not lie only with Emma's uncle or aunt but with an economic and social system that renders women dependent, a point that Emma can hardly make directly. The scene succeeds in emphasising both Emma's economic deprivation and social isolation: her own brother freely admits that, having been separated from her family for many years, they can have no natural feeling for her.

These two added scenes underscore the oppressive nature of Emma's position. The third patch adds a dialogue between Emma and Mr Musgrove, in which his revelation of some tantalising gossip, relating to her, is cut short. Here again, Emma's vulnerability is emphasised.[53] Interestingly, then, the revisions Austen made to *The Watsons* do not attempt to soften the jeopardy of her heroine, but instead intensify it. Austen's additive process, in these two examples, is one of intensified social critique, even though such alterations seem likely to have rendered her work less calculated to attract a publisher, particularly given 'the battering which the novel received at the hands of the reactionary anti-Jacobin movement in the late 1790s'.[54] Perhaps *The Watsons* was simply too bleak and bare, and too unrelenting in its depiction of Emma, for print. Still, although Austen never finished *The Watsons*, she never abandoned it entirely, mining it, as has been shown, for her later novels and retaining the manuscript for the rest of her life.[55]

Sanditon provides a final example of a compositional pattern that demonstrates Austen's continuing resistance to print norms. A 24,000-word narrative, divided into chapters and drafted into three notebooks, it physically resembles the surviving *Persuasion* manuscript, prepared and drafted only the year before. The narrative of *Sanditon*, however, presents a wide divergence from what we find in Austen's print novels – lacking a conventional heroine, plot and even setting; instead, it is replete with satirical figures and experimental elements, features that have left scholars uncertain how to understand its anomalous nature. Some have suggested, explicitly or implicitly, that the manuscript bears the signs of Austen's physical deterioration. This claim, first made by her nephew in 1870, has failed to convince the most careful scholars of the manuscript, including R. W. Chapman and Sutherland. Her nephew and Chapman, did, however, agree that Austen would have made substantial revisions, toning down her satire to prepare it for print. Another suggestion is that *Sanditon* represents a significant and new departure, such that had Austen lived to finish and publish it, it would not resemble the print novels we have. Such a reading is plausible, but there is no compelling explanation for why Austen would make such a change in direction at the height of a successful career. We also encounter D. A. Miller's claim – not that the work would have been revised, or that it reflects something excitingly new – but, perhaps harkening back to the earliest claims about the manuscript revealing Austen's physical and even mental debility, that *Sanditon* represents 'the formal ruination of the Austen Novel, as we have come to know it'.[56] What all of these interpretations have in common is that they pit print against script, with the former setting the standard for the latter, the assumption being that *Sanditon* must have been intended for print. But these attempts to understand *Sanditon* as 'half, or nearly half, a . . . novel', are misguided.[57] If we recollect Austen's longstanding habits of confidential manuscript writing, it may be more reasonable to understand the fragment as belonging to that realm.

Circumstances suggest that print may not have been at the forefront of Austen's mind when drafting the manuscript. When Austen made her first booklet in late January 1817 to begin *Sanditon*, she had in her possession two complete novel manuscripts: *Persuasion*, which she had finished (with the revised ending) the previous summer, and *Northanger Abbey*, which had been revised at some point after it was repurchased from Crosby in early 1816. In submitting neither manuscript novel for print, Austen was breaking with an established pattern. Since 1811, Austen had published a novel almost every year: in 1811, *Sense and Sensibility*; 1813, *Pride and Prejudice*; 1814, *Mansfield Park*; 1815, *Emma*. We have more precise dating of composition and publication for the later two novels. For them, a period of nine to ten months elapsed between their completion and publication (*Mansfield Park* was finished in July 1813, sold in November, and published in May 1814; *Emma* was finished in March 1815 and published in December of that year).[58] With *Persuasion* finished in the late summer of 1816, one would have expected it to appear in print in the late spring of 1817. Yet Austen made no effort to publish either *Persuasion* or *Northanger Abbey* during the last year of her life, though she suggested to her niece that *Persuasion* 'may perhaps appear about a twelvemonth hence'.[59] There are several possible reasons for her delay: Henry's bank failure, in March 1816; her own poor earnings from *Emma*, due to the dismal sales of the second edition of *Mansfield Park*; and her own failing health. Whatever the reason, however, it is important to apprehend the decision to hold on to these two manuscripts as a significant break from her usual pattern. For the last year of her life, Austen was, as it were, on a hiatus from print. In writing *Sanditon*, therefore, she may not have had print directly in mind, perhaps viewing it only as a distant prospect.

Sanditon (like many of the manuscript works) is usually read as a regularised and edited reading text, but this presentation disguises its status as a draft and renders it more readily comparable to the print novels. Reading the work in its manuscript form – that is, as an unfinished draft – establishes some of its material and textual connections to her other confidential manuscripts. If one views *Sanditon* as continuous with works like the juvenilia, *Lady Susan* and 'Plan of a Novel', as well as possibly *The Watsons*, the commonalities and preoccupations in both substance and form become apparent. These connections establish the importance of manuscript as an expressive medium for Austen, one that continued beyond the juvenile period and operated alongside her engagements with print culture. When viewed within the lineage of her manuscript works, *Sanditon* can be read as providing a radical retrospective on her own career in print, a self-assessment of her own capitulation to the norms of early nineteenth-century print fiction, a kind of writing back to herself as the author of six complete, and four printed, novels.

Throughout her career in both script and print, Austen had committed herself to the critical interrogation of social norms and novelistic conventions; this practice begins of course with the early burlesques, which target the excesses of sentimental fiction. But this critique extends into her later confidential writing, particularly 'Plan of a Novel', both of the 'Opinions', and *Sanditon*, where we find its most sustained emergence. In these works, Austen continues to attack sentimentalism, particularly its demand for an ideal heroine, resisted throughout the manuscript drafts of *The Watsons* and *Persuasion*. In 'Plan of a Novel', she had explicitly parodied this particular fictional imperative, strenuously protesting the obligation to furnish such false representations:

> – Heroine a faultless Character herself – , perfectly good, with much tenderness & sentiment, & not the least Wit – very highly accomplished, understanding modern Languages & (generally speaking) everything that the most accomplished young Women learn, but particularly excelling in Music – her favourite pursuit – & playing equally well on the Piano Forte^& Harp – & singing in the first stile. Her Person, quite beautiful – dark eyes & plump cheeks.[60]

In her 'Opinions of *Mansfield Park*' and 'Opinions of *Emma*', she echoes the theme by recording her readers' responses to various heroines, subtly mocking those who disapprove of her characters possessing imperfections. Through her minimalist marginal entries, Austen allows many of her readers to damn themselves in their preference for certain characters and novels. It is *Sanditon*, however, that most fully embodies Austen's defiance: we know that only one week after she put it down, she confided in a letter to her niece about 'ideas of novels and heroines' that '[p]ictures of perfection as you know make me sick & wicked'.[61]

In *Sanditon*, Austen exhibits her aversion to supplying heroines who are 'pictures of perfection'. Although the narrator speaks fondly of Charlotte Heywood as 'my heroine', she 'is self-contained, rational, and happy'.[62] With nothing to overcome, and nothing to be saved from, she adopts moderate and well-informed positions, possesses no love interests and maintains self-control, even checking herself from overspending on trinkets for sale at Mrs Whitby's circulating library. Neither perfect nor imperfect, Charlotte represents a playful repudiation of Austen's previous heroines: unlike the Bennett sisters, Charlotte's parents have been prudent and frugal, even though they have fourteen rather than five children; unlike the Dashwood sisters, Catherine Morland and Fanny Price, Austen's other economically insecure heroines, she need not marry; unlike Emma, she has not had an indulgent upbringing; and, unlike Anne, she has not had her heart broken. The lack of struggle explains, perhaps, the reason why, as George Justice observes, '[t]he narration in *Sanditon* plunges us less into the consciousness of its main character than any of Austen's other post-*Northanger Abbey* novels'.[63]

Much like Catherine Morland, who searches for a Gothic plot to enliven her existence, Charlotte hunts for a heroine, a role she herself fails to occupy. In many ways, Charlotte serves as a substitute for the novelist herself, one who must construct a heroine: if not a picture of perfection, then one in need of rescue. Charlotte's description of Clara Brereton reads, in fact, like 'Plan of a Novel', a hackneyed pastiche of a sentimental heroine:

> – And as for Miss Brereton, her appearance so completely justified M^r. P.'s praise that Charlotte thought she had never beheld a more lovely, or more Interesting young Woman. – Elegantly tall, regularly handsome, with great delicacy of complexion & soft Blue Eyes, a sweetly modesty^& yet naturally Gracefulness of Address, Charlotte could see^in her only the most perfect representation of ~~all the most beautiful & bewitching Heroines~~ ^{whatever} Heroine ^{might} be most beautiful & bewitching, in all the numerous vol:^s they had left behind them ~~in~~ ^{on} M^{rs}. Whitby's shelves. – Perhaps it ~~was from~~ might be partly oweing to her having just issued from a Circulating Library – but she c^d. not separate the idea of a complete

>Heroine from Clara Brereton. Her situation with Lady Denham so very much in favour of it! – She seemed placed with her on purpose to be ill-used. ^ –^Such^ Poverty & Dependance joined to^^such^ Beauty & Merit, seemed to leave no choice in the business. –.[64]

In this passage, Austen critiques Charlotte's quixotic projections, her readerly desire (so similar to that of Austen's own readers) for an imperilled heroine of 'Beauty & Merit'. Through Charlotte, Austen implicates both female readers and writers: the former who demand and the latter who deliver female distress as a means of fuelling the plot. Austen thus appears to be teasing both her readers and herself.

To her readers, she exposes their craving for the spectacle of female poverty, dependency and ill-use. To herself, she challenges her own constructions of female protagonists in her novels, as she had with the outlandish heroines that populate the juvenilia, the outrageously immoral conduct of her anti-heroine Lady Susan, and the mocking sentimentalisation of her heroine in 'Plan of a Novel.' In *Sanditon* Austen attempts another tack, by delivering a heroine (Charlotte) in search of a heroine (Clara) who never emerges. In Charlotte's effort to find a heroine, she proves herself too sensible to allow her imagination to run totally wild:

> while she pleased herself ~~in the~~ ^^first^ 5 minutes with fancying the Persecutions which <u>ought</u> to ~~await~~ ^be the^ Lot ^of^ the interesting Clara, especially in the form of the most barbarous conduct on Lady Denham's side, she found no reluctance to admit from subsequent observation, that they appeared to be on very comfortable Terms.[65]

Without Clara as distressed heroine, Charlotte concocts a romance for her, when she spies Clara and Sir Edward in what she takes to be a 'Tete a Tete'.[66] Here again, Charlotte emerges as a stand-in for the novelist, as one who possesses 'more observant eyes' than her companions, and as one who engages in 'moralising reflecting' while resolving that 'hers was a situation which ~~ought~~ ^must^ not ~~to~~ be judged with severity'.[67] Notwithstanding the secluded spot in which she finds the two, 'a steep bank & Pales never crossed by the foot by Man ~~behind them~~ ^at their back^ – and a great thickness of air, in aid', Charlotte, like the novelist, has privileged access to the scene.[68] Austen appears to be sending up the novelist's omniscience, and slyly mocking the narrator's prurience, which allows her alone to view the 'secret lovers' and to manufacture the 'extreme difficulty' that they 'must have in finding a proper spot for their stolen Interviews'.⁶⁹ As with her treatment of the heroine and romance, Austen's representation of Charlotte-as-novelist is at once an abdication and a critique; Charlotte in fact espies nothing of great interest, her claims to exclusive access yielding little of substance. And Clara, of course, never transforms into the imagined heroine.

The lack of a courtship plot involving either putative heroine is another conspicuous absence from the fragment. As many scholars have observed, in none of Austen's novels do we find the romance between hero and heroine so undeveloped by Chapter 12 (about a quarter of the way into a novel the length of *Persuasion*). This weakened romantic storyline follows directly from the fact that Charlotte, at least, does *not* appear to be in want of a husband. Here again, parallels with the confidential manuscripts emerge: *Lady Susan* ends with the eponymous anti-heroine's supremely *un*romantic marriage, whereas 'Plan of a Novel' delivers a takedown of the excesses of the marriage plot altogether. In that narrative, Austen describes her heroine's romantic travails in the following way:

> – Early in her career, in the progress of her first removals, Heroine must meet with the Hero – all perfection of course – ^& only prevented from paying his addresses to her, by some excess of refinement. – Wherever she goes, somebody falls in love with her, & she receives repeated offers of Marriage – which she always refers wholly to her Father, exceedingly angry that he sh^d. not be first applied to. – Often carried away by the anti-hero, but rescued either by her Father or the Hero——often reduced to support herself & her Father by her Talents, & work for her Bread; – continually cheated & defrauded of her hire, worn down to a Skeleton, & now & then starved to death – . At last, hunted out of civilized Society, denied the poor Shelter of the humblest Cottage, they are compelled to retreat into Kamschatka . . . – Heroine inconsolable for some time – but afterwards crawls back towards her former Country – having at least 20 narrow escapes of falling into the hands of Anti-hero – & at last in the very nick of time, turning a corner to avoid him, runs into the arms of the Hero himself, who having just shaken off the scruples which fetter'd him before, was at the very moment setting off in pursuit of her. – The Tenderest & completest Eclaircissement takes place, & they are happily united. – ⁷⁰

Certainly no Austen novel offers such ludicrous sensationalism; nevertheless, several of her heroines – Elizabeth, Fanny, Emma – receive repeated offers of marriage; and anti-heroes do threaten, in the form of Wickham, Crawford, Elton and Eliot. The novelists' tricks Austen identifies differ in scale, not in kind, from her own.

Sanditon appears deficient, when judged against the standard protocols of the print novels, in at least one other respect. In the fragment, one of the domestic novelist's central tasks – to dispense moral judgement – is withheld. In part this is because the narration is limited, with more character speech than is present in the print novels. Claire Tuite notes that, in *Sanditon*, Austen 'returns to an earlier form of narrative witnessing that occurs through caricatured dialogue', in which Austen's characters expose themselves through their own speech.[71] A thread may be drawn to *The Watsons*, in which over a third of the story is written in direct speech, a much higher proportion than found in the print novels.[72] The dramatic monologues Austen furnishes her characters with in *Sanditon* are not of course entirely absent from the print novels, but they are present in far larger proportion to narration in the fragment: in Tuite's apt description, we find 'a noisy and unruly cast of caricatures who crowd the narrative's field of vision and sound of voice';[73] or, as Tony Tanner memorably put it: 'There is a most uncharacteristic use not so much of dialogue as of actual unrefracted monologue. She lets the endless talkers talk endlessly, without the interposition of her own monitoring, adjudicating voice.'[74] In *Sanditon*, the presumed heroine, Charlotte, also withdraws; with only modest access to her thoughts, and without the usual merging of the narrative voice and the heroine, we are returned to the realm of Austen's earlier first-person narratives, the juvenile epistolary fictions, *Lady Susan*, and perhaps also the narrative void of *Northanger Abbey*.

Offering her readers no heroine, no romance, and no moral centre, *Sanditon* seems an unlikely beginning for a print novel. If written with her domestic readers in mind, however, it appears less strange; Austen would have had confidence that her domestic readers would be able to identify the fragment's defiance of novelistic conventions and to enjoy her penchant for caricature, as they had done since her girlhood. In addition to the satire that had been a mainstay of her domestic writing, her confidential readers may also have welcomed Austen's experimentation in capturing a wider social canvas, with a more diverse representations of physical spaces, social classes and physical objects than she ventures in the novels.[75] As scholars have noted, in *Sanditon* we have a fuller depictions of the working classes, which include coachmen, haymakers, shepherds, gardeners, shoemakers, nursery maids, librarians and shop clerks.[76] Compared to the print novels, *Sanditon* includes more references to things and bodies, to consumer items, to food and its preparation, and to physical bodies generally, to sprained ankles and rubbing ankles, to pulling teeth and applying leeches. It features an unprecedented degree of 'historical immediacy', evident in the extended (and often jargon-laden) disquisitions on medical, literary, and economic matters,[77] and in the more concentrated allusions to contemporary fashion and to books and authors (Robert Burns, Thomas Campbell, James Montgomery, Walter Scott and William Wordsworth are all named in a single paragraph). Austen also playfully engages in stylistic experimentation in *Sanditon*, employing a wider vocabulary ('anti-spasmodic', 'pseudo-philosophy'), and allowing her characters to speak in streams of consciousness, features that are present only in small doses in the print novels. The accumulation of all of these elements aligns *Sanditon* closely with the other domestic manuscript works.

Support for a reading of *Sanditon* as aligned with the confidential manuscript works may also be found in Jocelyn Harris's observations about the similarities between the fragment and a short satirical piece, 'Letter on Watering-places', published unsigned in the *Monthly Magazine* in 1796. Ostensibly written by one 'Henry Homelove', the author was in fact Anna Barbauld.[78] Dragged to a seaside resort from his comfortable country estate in Northamptonshire, Homelove, as first-person narrator, laments having been forced from his home, and complains about, amongst other things, the quackery of the medical establishment, the promise of sea bathing as a cure for invented ailments, the rising prices of provisions due to tourism, and the mixing of classes and intermingling amongst strangers that residence in a seaside resort allows. Homelove, as Harris observes, appears to be channelled into Austen's story in the character of Mr Heywood. In Barbauld's sketch, it is not primarily the speculators but the curmudgeonly Homelove who emerges as a central satirical target. If a source for Austen's narrative, then Mr Heywood himself may recede from the role he is usually thought to occupy within the narrative – as the sturdy, sensible foil to the more eccentric and speculating inhabitants of Sanditon. The result would be an even more destabilising narrative, one that returns us to the moral ambiguity of a piece like *Lady*

Susan. Austen's fragment also shares with 'Letter on Watering-places' a focus on men, with Mr Heywood, Mr Parker and Sir Edward being the chief objects (or victims) of Austen's comic powers. This critical attention to men features, as we have seen, in Barbauld's poetic satires, and seems to have inclined her to circulate those poems in manuscript; similarly, we find Austen disparaging men in particular in confidential works like 'Plan of a Novel' and *Sanditon*.

As an unfinished draft manuscript, *Sanditon* embodies radical contingency, one that requires a different mode of reading. Within the narrative, we have characters who engage in 'the disease ^a spirit^ of ^restless^ activity', with Austen leaving open the possibility that what she depicts is both spirited activity, capable of generating excitement, and diseased restlessness, sowing confusion and disappointment.[79] *Sanditon* elaborates upon the very nature of knowledge itself in the narrative. Mr Heywood is certain that there is no surgeon in 'Willingden, – ^for having^ having lived here^Sir^ ever since I was born, Man & Boy 57 years, without ever hearing of the existence ^and never heard before^ I think I must have known of such a person'. By contrast, Mr Parker insists that such a surgeon in fact exists, relying upon 'advertisements, which I cut out myself from the Morning Post & the Kentish Gazette, ^only yesterday morng. in London^'.[80] In this case Parker is mistaken, lacking the local knowledge to interpret the advertisements correctly. Similarly, we learn that Sir Edward also misreads print: 'Essays, Letters, Tours & Criticisms of the day – & with the same ill-luck which made him derive only false Principles from Lessons of Morality, & incentives to Vice from the History of it's Overthrow, he gathered only hard words & involved sentences from the style of ^the our^ our ^most approved Writers. —'[81] In Austen's world, however, handwritten documents are just as likely to be misinterpreted as printed ones. In *Sanditon*, letters, containing gossip, are conduits of misinformation, as we learn that Miss Diana Parker's imagined two parties seeking lodging are in fact only one. Within the fragment, problems of interpretation are ubiquitous.

In seeking to read *Sanditon* as an unfinished draft manuscript that was not necessarily written with print in mind, my analysis has emphasised its continuities with many elements of the confidential writing, its destabilising energies, its self-deprecating mockeries, its moral ambiguities, its unconstrained caricatures. This analysis is made possible by shifting the ground of comparison, so that a work like *Sanditon* is not evaluated exclusively in relation to the print novels but also interpreted in the context of the domestic writing. This is not to say that Austen's works can be neatly separated into two spheres of writing, any more than scribal and print publication were separable realms. In seems more productive, as I have endeavoured to do, to examine Austen's complex and unstable working manuscripts – *The Watsons*, the cancelled *Persuasion* chapters and *Sanditon* – as existing along a script–print continuum.

Conclusion

Austen's earliest critics did not have access to her domestic manuscripts, nor to any of her surviving working drafts, and so could not have known about the process by which she carefully calibrated her print fiction to be 'received not only as pleasurable, but as', in Clifford Siskin's words '*comfortable*'.[82] As Siskin has shown, Austen's early and continuing success – what she was lauded and remembered for when so many other female authors were forgotten – derives in large part from what Walter Scott articulated in his 'negative appreciation' of *Emma* in the *Quarterly Review* in October 1815. In that review, Scott celebrates Austen for what she leaves out as much if not more than what she left in, such that her 'virtues came to be articulated habitually in terms of what she lacks'.[83] Typically, understandings of Scott's and other contemporaneous reviews of her posthumously published novels, *Persuasion* and *Northanger Abbey* (particularly one in the *British Critic* and another in the *Edinburgh Magazine*), reflect upon the belief that Austen is 'extremely deficient' 'in imagination, of all kinds'; that she appears to be recording and describing the every day, as opposed to inventing it.[84] But these reviews also reflect a coalescence of opinion on Austen's writing and its value in another important respect, in that they understand and praise the novelist specifically for her restraint:

> our authoress never dips her pen in satire; the follies which she holds up to us, are, for the most part, mere follies, or else natural imperfections; and she treats them, as such, with good humoured pleasantry; mimicking them so exactly, that we always laugh at the ridiculous truth of the imitation, but without ever being incited to indulge in feelings, that might tend to render us ill natured, and intolerant in society. This is the

result of that good sense which seems ever to keep complete possession over all the other qualities of the mind of our authoress; she sees every thing just as it is; even her want of imagination (which is the principal defect of her writings) is useful to her in this respect, that it enables her to keep clear of all exaggeration . . .[85]

The reviewer approves Austen's setting of limits, perhaps even detecting a capacity or desire on her part to transgress them. The reviewer of the *Edinburgh Magazine* similarly lauds Austen for the restrictions she has deliberately placed on her art: 'She has confined herself, no doubt, to a narrow walk. She never operates among deep interests, uncommon characters, or vehement passions.'[86]

What is most intriguing about these reviews is that Austen is praised for keeping herself in check, with good sense controlling 'all of the other qualities of mind of our authoress'. Thus the authoress maintains propriety: she does not dip her pen in satire, she demonstrates self-mastery, she steers clear of exaggeration, and she incites us to laugh at others and ourselves but never encourages intolerance. These observations about Austen's art as a process of confinement and control echo Doody's claims about what Austen gave up for print, though Doody reaches this conclusion by studying the juvenile writing, which could not have been known to these reviewers. This chapter's exploration of her later manuscripts, also unknown to contemporary reviewers, allows us to understand how these impulses were never, in fact, entirely abandoned; they were given full rein in her later domestic publications, and as has been argued by myself and others, found some outlet in her print novels as well.[87] Austen of course did not live to read these reviews, but had she done so she would have undoubtedly been amused, for in her social manuscripts, and in *Sanditon* above all, we find precisely what the reviewers find to be laudably absent: the 'deep interests, uncommon characters, [and] vehement passions'.

It was not just the absence of exaggeration, passion and imagination that came to define Austen's reception, as her novels acquired, according to Janine Barchas, a 'long-standing reputation for timelessness and transparency', the view that she 'can never be out of date, because she never was in any particular date'.[88] However, the timelessness apparent in the novels seems also to have been a consequence of her bending to the demands of print, rather than following her natural inclination. In her 'ADVERTISEMENT BY THE AUTHORESS, TO NORTHANGER ABBEY', probably written in 1816, we have one of Austen's few public statements as an author. In it, she directly meditates on the problem that topicality posed for authors. After explaining the thirteen-year delay between the novel's completion and intended publication (in 1803), its projected publication (in 1816), and the even greater lapse of time since it was begun, she remarks upon aspects of the novel that would appear dated, reminding readers: 'during that period, places, manners, books, and opinions have undergone considerable changes'.[89] Austen's peevishness, though ostensibly directed towards the 'extraordinary' conduct of the bookseller who purchased and advertised the novel without publishing it, also registers her awareness that her novel, which had languished in manuscript for nearly two decades, would suffer for its use of stale cultural references. The manuscripts of *Persuasion* and *Sanditon* in particular, however, demonstrate that Austen enjoyed topicality, and never fully abandoned her habits of directly referencing 'places, manners, books, and opinions'. The appearance of timelessness conveyed in the print novels is an achieved effect, the product of strenuous revision, rather than the natural consequence of her unfolding genius.[90] In removing, almost, it seems, under compulsion, many of the topical elements of her fiction before it crossed over into print, she may have been responding to commentaries that regularly appeared in the *Edinburgh Review*. We might recall that journal's attack on Scott's *Marmion*, for its 'allusions to objects of temporary interest, chiefly as instances of bad taste, and additional proofs that the author does not always recollect, that a poet should address himself to more than one generation'. Although they were directed towards poetry, Austen seems to have taken these comments to heart.

    Austen carefully guarded our access to the process by which her drafts, written into small handmade notebooks, were transformed into novels for print. By destroying or failing to retain most of her working drafts, by removing, disguising, or burying most of her lampoons and private jokes in the print novels, and by rarely speaking directly as a public author, she rendered it difficult to discern how she negotiated the transition from confidential to public writing. But she did leave traces of the contact zone between the confidential and the public in both her manuscript works and her print novels, traces that this chapter has sought to excavate. In reading Austen's fiction manuscripts, we encounter a different writer from that of the six printed novels, one who is more playfully metafictional about writing and contemporary literary genres; more caustically embittered, particularly about the status of women and the injustice of the class system; more penetratingly satirical about the world in which she lived; and more willing to touch on both day-to-day life (the extended sequence on the preparation of 'Cocoa & Toast' in *Sanditon* offers one delightful example) and a wider array of social classes.[91] The divergence between the later fiction manuscripts (*The Watsons*, *Lady Susan*, *Persuasion* and *Sanditon*) and the print novels suggests that Austen laboured to adapt her writing to the public realm of print, and continued to resort to confidential manuscripts as a creative space less subject to restriction and scrutiny and more amenable to experimentation. Nevertheless, the confidential realm she explored in her manuscript writing could not be quarantined; it retained its potent influence throughout her career, inevitably seeping into the print novels. For Austen, the media of script and print were never autonomous from one another, one never an exclusive outlet for writing directed at one type of audience. Examining her manuscript and print writing alongside one another, we find an author who finds full expression only by working within and traversing across both media.

Notes

1. Letter from George Austen to Thomas Cadell, 1 November 1797 (St John's College, Oxford University, MS 279). Across the top of the letter, in a different hand (presumably that of Cadell's clerk) is written 'declined by Return of Post'.
2. In *The Appearance of Print in Eighteenth-Century Fiction*, Christopher Flint contends that the novel, as a form that came into maturity in the eighteenth century, 'was written to be published' and exhibited 'a definitional dependence on the print trades': p. 19.
3. Henry Austen, 'Biographical Notice of the Author', in James Edward Austen-Leigh, *A Memoir of Jane Austen*, p. 141.
4. See *The Cambridge Edition of the Works of Jane Austen: Later Manuscripts*, hereafter *LM*; *Jane Austen's Manuscript Works*, hereafter *MW*; *The Cambridge Edition of the Works of Jane Austen: Juvenilia*, hereafter *Juvenilia*; and Kathryn Sutherland (ed.), *Jane Austen's Fiction Manuscripts: A Digital Edition*, hereafter *DE*.

5. The most consequential books are Kathryn Sutherland, *Jane Austen's Textual Lives: from Aeschylus to Bollywood* (2005); Jocelyn Harris, *A Revolution Almost beyond Expression: Jane Austen's Persuasion* (2007); and Brian Southam's two books: *Jane Austen: a Students' Guide to the Later Manuscript Works* (2007), hereafter *Guide*; and *Jane Austen's Literary Manuscripts: A Study of the Novelist's Development through the Surviving Papers*, revised edn (2001), hereafter *Study*. Some important articles on more than one manuscript include: Janet Todd and Linda Bree, 'Jane Austen's Unfinished Business'; Katie Gemmill, 'Jane Austen as Editor: Letters on Fiction and the Cancelled Chapters of Persuasion', and my essay, 'Austen's Manuscripts and the Publicity of Print'.
6. These dates, and those used throughout the chapter, are often educated guesses based upon the available evidence. In particular, I have relied upon information found in *LM* and *DE*.
7. *Juvenilia*, pp. xxxii–xxxiii and Sutherland, 'From Kitty to Catharine: James Edward Austen's hand in *Volume the Third*', pp. 126–7.
8. *Juvenilia*, pp. xxxiv–xxxv.
9. Kathryn Sutherland, 'From Kitty to Catharine', p. 126. See also Robert L. Mack, 'The Austen Family Writing: Gossip, Parody, and Corporate Personality'. Mack demonstrates how 'the Austen family as a whole possessed a tendency to rewrite texts as they read them' (p. 32).
10. See *LM*, p. xliv; *MW*, pp. 12–13; and *Juvenilia*, pp. xxiv, xxxv–xxxvii.
11. Reiman, *The Study of Modern Manuscripts*.
12. *Juvenilia*, p. xxxvi.
13. *LM*, pp. cv–cvi, 741–2.
14. On the texts that were not copied into the three volumes, see *Juvenilia*, pp. xxix–xxxi.
15. Sutherland, 'From Kitty to Catharine', pp. 126–7.
16. Chapman writes in the 'Preface': 'These immature or fragmentary fictions call for hardly any comment': *Jane Austen: Minor Works*, p. v.
17. See Margaret Ann Doody, 'The Early Short Fiction', pp. 12–31. According to Peter Sabor, these readings invert the traditional narrative, for 'rather than [the juvenilia] being pale foreshadowings of the novels, the novels instead are subdued afterwards to the early writings' (*Juvenilia*, p. lvi).
18. Sutherland, *Jane Austen's Textual Lives*, p. 210.
19. See Jan Fergus, *Jane Austen: A Literary Life* and 'The Professional Woman Writer'; and Janet Todd, 'Introduction', *The Cambridge Introduction to Jane Austen*, p. 2.
20. Sutherland, 'From Kitty to Catharine', p. 142.
21. See note 1 above.
22. See Kathryn Sutherland, 'Chronology of Composition and Publication', pp. 12–22, especially p. 14.

23. See Gemmill, 'Jane Austen as Editor', and on her poems, *LM*, pp. cv, 738.
24. On Burney, see *Juvenilia*, p, xxiv; Justice, 'Suppression and Censorship in Late Manuscript Culture', especially pp. 205, 218; and Betty A. Schellenberg, *The Professionalization of Women Writers in Eighteenth-Century Britain*, p. 152.
25. Todd and Bree, 'Jane Austen's Unfinished Business', p. 224.
26. Mary Poovey, *The Proper Lady and the Woman Writer: Ideology as Style in the Works of Mary Wollstonecraft, Mary Shelley, and Jane Austen*, p. 72. Interestingly, one of the earliest reviews of *The Watsons*, by Edith Simcox on 1 August 1871, in the *Academy*, offered a similar explanation for Austen's abandonment of that work, suggesting that 'Austen could not get on comfortably without a leading idea of some sort or a moral to be enforced, and of this there was certainly so far no sign' (quoted in Southam, *Guide*, p. 14). On the datedness of epistolary novels, see James Raven, 'Historical Introduction: The Novel Comes of Age', pp. 15–121, especially pp. 30–1.
27. See Southam, *Study*, pp. 144–9, for a review of the evidence. For a few different reasons, including dating and style, he disagrees with the suggestion that Eliza was the model for Lady Susan.
28. See Love, *English Clandestine Satire*.
29. All letters are quoted from Deirdre Le Faye (ed.), *Jane Austen's Letters*, 3rd edn, hereafter *Letters*. All references include the letter number assigned by Le Faye, followed by the page number.
30. Interestingly, her faith appears at times to have been tested; in 1799, she remarked to Cassandra, perhaps only half-facetiously, that she 'would not let Martha [Lloyd] read First Impressions again upon any account . . . – She is very cunning, but I see through her design; – she means to publish it from Memory, & one more perusal must enable her to do it' (*Letters*, L21, 44). She consistently found her heroines and titles scooped (as with *First Impressions* in 1801 and *Susan* in 1809) and appears to have been fearful, as she wrote to Cassandra in 1811, 'of finding my own story & my own people all forestalled' (*Letters*, L72, 186).
31. According to Janet Todd and Antje Blank, Austen is also ridiculing the peripatetic plot of Frances Burney's *The Wanderer* in the 'Plan' ('Introduction' to *The Cambridge Edition of the Works of Jane Austen: Persuasion*, hereafter, *Persuasion*, p. lxxxi;). Anthony Mandel also sees the 'Plan' as a parody of contemporary novels (*Jane Austen and the Popular Novel: The Determined Author*, p. 181), as does Southam, who points out that two years earlier, in 1814, Austen stated her intention to write a burlesque of Mary Brunton's 1810 novel *Self-Control*. He finds several elements of this novel parodied in the 'Plan' (*Guide*, pp. 99, 110).

32. *LM*, pp. 226, 235, 230. The comments of several other readers, including Mary Cooke, who also supplies four hints, though they cannot be traced directly to the recorded 'Opinions', were likely the result of direct conversations, correspondence, or second-hand reports.
33. Sutherland makes this point as well: *Jane Austen's Textual Lives*, p. 152.
34. 'Headnote to *Persuasion*', in *DE*.
35. Sutherland, *Jane Austen's Textual Lives*, p. 169.
36. Southam, *Study*, 57–9.
37. See, for example, the sentence revised in the middle of the page, where it appears she cancels the sentence as she is writing it: 'The Watsons (2): Diplomatic Display / Oxford Bodleian Library, MS.Eng.e.3764, B7-5', in *DE*; *LM*, pp. lxv–lxvii.
38. Sutherland, *Jane Austen's Textual Lives*, p. 172.
39. Sutherland, *Jane Austen's Textual Lives*, p. 169.
40. Sutherland, *Jane Austen's Textual Lives*, p. 122.
41. See Harris, *A Revolution Almost beyond Expression*, pp. 40, 65–6.
42. 'Two Chapters of *Persuasion*: Diplomatic Display', in *DE*, 1, 21; *Persuasion*, pp. 281, 301.
43. 'Two Chapters', 5; *Persuasion*, p. 285.
44. 'Two Chapters of *Persuasion*: Diplomatic Display', in *DE*, 19.
45. *The Cambridge Edition of the Works of Jane Austen: Northanger Abbey*, hereafter *Northanger Abbey*, p. 1.
46. Austen famously referred to *Pride and Prejudice* as 'rather too light & bright & sparkling' in *Letters*, L80, 203).
47. Claudia Johnson, 'Introduction', in *Northanger Abbey, Lady Susan, The Watsons, Sanditon*, p. xxix.
48. Virginia Woolf, 'Jane Austen', in *The Common Reader, First Series*, ed. Andrew McNeillie (Orlando: Harcourt, 2002), p. 137–8.
49. *LM*, pp. 336–7, 353–5, and 369–70.
50. 'The Watsons (2): Diplomatic Display', *b7-7*; *LM*, pp. 116, 336–7.
51. Ibid. *b9-1*; *LM*, p. 353.
52. Ibid. *b9-2*; *LM*, p. 354.
53. Ibid. *b10-3*.
54. Garside, 'The English Novel in the Romantic Era', II: 40.
55. Todd and Bree, 'Jane Austen's Unfinished Business', pp. 230, 234. Evidence as to its circulation is scant, but we know that Austen confided in Cassandra about how the plot was to develop, and that the manuscript was shown by Cassandra to some of her nieces: Deirdre Le Faye, '*Sanditon*: Jane Austen's Manuscript and her Niece's Continuation', p. 60.
56. D. A. Miller, *Jane Austen, or the Secret of Style* (2003), p. 76.
57. J. St Loe Strachey, 'In "Sanditon," Half of a New Novel by Jane Austen: Modernity of Her Outlook Again Evident in This Unfinished Work', p. 13.
58. See the Chronology in *LM*, pp. xxiv–xxvi.

59. *Persuasion*, p. xli; *Northanger Abbey*, p. xxix. The only mention of these novels is in a letter to her niece written 13 March 1817: 'Miss Catherine is put upon the Shelve for the present, and I do not know that she will ever come out; – but I have a something ready for Publication, which may perhaps appear about a twelvemonth hence. It is short, about the length of Catherine': *Letters*, L153, p. 333.
60. Diplomatic transcription from 'Plan of a Novel: Diplomatic Display', in *DE*, 1; *LM*, p. 226.
61. *Letters*, L155, 335.
62. George Justice, '*Sanditon* and the Book', p. 160.
63. Ibid. p. 160.
64. Diplomatic transcription from '*Sanditon*: Diplomatic Display', b2-21-22; *LM*, pp. 458–9.
65. Ibid. b2-22; *LM*, pp. 459–60.
66. Ibid. b3-38; *LM*, p. 553.
67. Ibid. b3-38-9; *LM*, p. 553.
68. Ibid.
69. Ibid. b3-38; *LM*, p. 553.
70. Diplomatic transcription from 'Plan of a Novel: Diplomatic Display', *DE*, 4; *LM*, pp. 228–9.
71. Clara Tuite (2012) '*Sanditon*: Austen's pre–post Waterloo', p. 621.
72. Sutherland, *Jane Austen's Textual Lives*, p. 145.
73. Tuite, '*Sanditon*', p. 621.
74. Quoted in Southam, *Guide*, p. 20.
75. Arguably this experimentation is evident in the later novels, too: in *Persuasion*, with the naval families as well as Mrs Smith; in *Emma*, with the Bateses; and in *Mansfield Park*, with the Prices. Austen may have been encouraged by the positive reception of the Portsmouth scenes in particular, which were widely lauded in 'Opinions of *Mansfield Park*' (six readers specifically comment on their enjoyment and/or admiration of the Portsmouth scenes: *LM*, pp. 230–4).
76. Southam has observed that in *Sanditon* we are treated to a 'far more extensive' description of society at all levels, in particular of the servant classes, than elsewhere in Austen's writing: *Study*, p. 111. Harris notices in the *Persuasion* manuscript the introduction of three new lower-class characters (a mantuamaker, a servant and a shoemaker): *A Revolution*, p. 58.
77. Southam, *Guide*, pp. 118–19.
78. Austen almost certainly did not know about Barbauld's authorship, as the essay was not published with Barbauld's name until 1825. See 'On Watering-places', first published in *Monthly Magazine* 2 (1796): 605–8, later published in Barbauld's *Works*, II: 295–304; Jocelyn Harris, 'Jane Austen's Unseen Interlocutor', in *Anna Barbauld: New Perspectives*, pp. 237–58.

79. Diplomatic transcription from 'Sanditon: Diplomatic Display', b3-11; *LM*, p. 514.
80. Ibid. b1-6-7; *LM*, pp. 388–9.
81. Ibid. b2-44; *LM*, p. 491.
82. Clifford Siskin, *The Work of Writing: Literature and Social Change in Britain, 1700–1830*, p. 202.
83. Ibid. p. 201.
84. 'Review of Northanger Abbey: and Persuasion' *British Critic* New Series 9 (March 1818): 298.
85. Ibid. p. 299.
86. *Edinburgh Magazine* New Series 2 (May 1818): 454.
87. See Levy, 'Austen's Manuscripts and the Publicity of Print' for an exploration of how Austen strategically smuggles confidential and satirical references into her print novels: pp. 1033–4.
88. Janine Barchas, *Matters of Fact in Austen: History, Location, and Celebrity (2102)*, pp. 1, 7.
89. *Northanger Abbey*, p. 1.
90. Ibid. p. 1. In much the same way that the studied 'elegance and rationality' of the print novels are the result of 'a conscious choice rather than an instinct, a narrowing down of creative options from a much wider span of possibilities', the timelessness apparent in the novels also seems to be a consequence of her bending to the demands of print, rather than following her natural inclination: *MW*, p. 22.
91. The editors of *LM* similarly claim that the reading of the manuscripts can 'come as quite a shock', 'show[ing] Austen pushing the conventional boundaries of fiction in a way quite at odds with the published novels' (12). Sutherland and Elena Pierazzo concur: 'The manuscript evidence therefore represents a different Jane Austen: different in the range of subjects, themes, and narrative experimentation they contain from the novels we know only from print; and different in what they reveal about the workings of her imagination: in particular, what they can tell us of the ebb and flow, the struggle or ease of creation:' 'The Author's Hand: From Page to Screen', p. 191.

Chapter 6

Script's Afterlives

The case studies explored in the previous three chapters have fleshed out the material and social processes that manuscripts witness: practices of composition, revision, sharing, reading, copying, embellishment and preservation. From the moment of their creation, manuscripts almost always pass from hand to hand, as they are written and altered, read and recited, memorised and copied, often by multiple individuals, sometimes over generations. As we have seen, literary manuscripts pass through many hands for a variety of purposes and over time they can acquire new significations. Manuscripts can serve as working papers, subject to revision and correction before being preserved, shared or circulated more widely; when shown to literary advisers and publishers, they can be scrutinised for their literary merit and subject to editorial intervention or commentary; when shared with friends, family and others, they can act as sources of pleasure and entertainment; they can be used as copy for printers to set type; when gifted or inherited, they can serve as mementoes of cherished authors and loved ones; when bought or sold, they can be collected for reasons of profit and prestige by collectors and libraries; when studied by scholars, they can establish the textual history of a work. This chapter focuses on how Romantic literary manuscripts have been conceptualised after their working lives as documents to be shared, revised or printed, is, as it were, over; that is, this chapter turns to the literary manuscript when it has acquired the status of an artefact.

It is appropriate to attempt to discern the cultural understandings of Romantic literary manuscripts, insofar as, according to Dana Gioia, 'the [Romantic] era ... fostered an unprecedented reverence for literary manuscripts. Earlier ages had viewed a poet's holograph in purely functional terms.'¹ For Gioia, '[t]his shift in sensibility could probably only have occurred in the nineteenth century at the height of print culture', as

> [t]he uniformity of machine-printed books slowly imbued the handwritten page with a unique personal aura. As mechanical typography visually standardized written language, the reader was less likely to view an autograph copy of a poem purely as a piece of verbal communication; it now became a unique artifact that invited a different sort of attention . . . The omnipresence of mechanical print made the manuscript's medium its most important message.²

This chapter offers support for Gioia's claims, first by detailing the growing interest in preserving handwritten documents of all kinds, and then by exploring examples of what handwriting and literary manuscripts meant to those living at the time.

This chapter examines the dynamic media landscape within which literary manuscripts began to take on new cultural meanings in the Romantic period. Gioia focuses on the ubiquity of print, and how that brought renewed attention to the handwritten. Increasingly, handwriting was conceived of as a bearer of human affect and a marker of individual character. An interest in writing as a technology of communication and enlightenment may be traced to this period, and with this understanding of the history of writing and its impact arose an imperative to preserve original handwritten documents. Literary manuscripts also came to be invested with value, not necessarily, as we will see, economically, but as possessing cultural and national importance: we might recall how Lamb was 'shown the original written copy' of Milton's poem 'Lycidas' 'in the Library of Trinity, kept like some treasure to be proud of'. Authors like Lamb reflected on the power of the handwritten and the effects of viewing culturally significant objects. This chapter circles back to the authors considered in the previous three chapters to examine the values Barbauld, Byron and Austen attached to handwriting and literary manuscripts. This chapter also investigates the practices, some old and some new, that arose from this new interest in literary manuscripts.

The second half of the chapter shifts perspectives to examine the contemporary use and study of Romantic literary manuscripts, particularly over the last half century. It acknowledges Jerome McGann's nearly thirty-year-old complaint, that '[t]extual and editorial theory has heretofore concerned itself almost exclusively with the linguistic codes', and asks how, when, why and to what end textual scholars have returned to the period's manuscripts.[3] It considers the groundbreaking print scholarly editions of Romantic authors that have appeared over the past five decades, to understand the editors' engagements with and presentations of the period's literary manuscripts. It then considers how digital remediations of the period's manuscripts have not only improved our access to the original documents, but have enhanced our understanding of the period's manuscripts as bearers of meaning beyond the textual. Examining the shift from print to digital representations of Romantic manuscripts, the chapter also asks how this newest medium might assign different values to, and enable different understandings of, the older media of print and script.

Saving Manuscripts

During the second half of the eighteenth century, European encounters with other cultures from across the globe fostered attempts to understand other languages and scripts and focused attention on the diverse history and practices of writing.[4] So too did the print explosion of the later eighteenth century prompt a reconsideration of the material traces and cultural history of writing, much in the same way the digital revolution has initiated a re-examination of the history of print. The first comprehensive account of the history of writing appeared in 1784 with Thomas Astle's *The Origin and Progress of Writing*. Astle observed that the medium of writing 'has been so long known and used, that few men think upon the subject', and sought to amend this intellectual neglect by historicising the processes of writing and the impact of it as a technology, both of which had been rendered invisible by established and extensive use.[5] In the media history that Astle provides, writing serves as an instrument of enlightenment. Demonstrating the impact of exploration, contact and colonisation, Astle creates a now familiar and highly problematic hierarchy, between those with writing technologies and those without: 'The noblest acquisition of mankind is SPEECH, and the most useful art is WRITING. The first, eminently distinguishes MAN from the brute creation; the second, from uncivilized savages.'[6] He continues with a paean to writing as the origin of intellectual enlightenment from which all human progress can be traced:

> By this wonderful invention we are enabled to record and perpetuate our thoughts, for our own benefit, or give them the most extensive communication, for the benefit of others. As without this art, the labours of our ancestors in every branch of knowledge would be lost to us, so must ours to posterity ... From this source, and from ancient paintings, sculptures, and medals, have philosophy, science, and the arts, derived all their successive improvements: succeeding generations have been enabled to add to the stock they received from the past, and to prepare the way for future acquisitions. In the common transactions of life, how limited must have been our intercourse, whether for profit or pleasure, without the assistance of WRITING. Whereas, by this happy mode of communication, distance is as it were annihilated, and the Merchant, the Statesman, the Scholar, becomes present to every purpose of utility, in regions the most remote.[7]

This encomium for writing insists upon on it as a foundational technology, with print serving an important but by no means primary role. Rather, print accelerates the process by which 'knowledge is diffused through most nations, and is attainable by the generality of the people in every free country'.[8]

As an archivist for the British Museum and the State Paper Office, Astle was a public collector of historical manuscripts. Consumed by fear of losing 'the literary treasures of antiquity', Astle laments what had already been lost of the human record: 'Thus it appears, that more of the works of the ancients have perished, than have reached us.'[9] He was one of a chorus of collectors and antiquarians who concerned themselves with the rescue of manuscripts believed to be at risk of imminent destruction. According to John Fenn, writing in 1787, the preservation of the written record is itself critical to civilisation:

> All civilized nations have ever been anxious to preserve every authentic record of their former transactions, both public and private ... since the proof of their very existence, as a notion of consequence ... entirely depends upon such undoubted memorials.[10]

Writing more than a decade before Fenn and Astle, Anna Barbauld, in 'On Monastic Institutions' (1773), offers an expression of gratitude to the monasteries for preserving manuscripts that otherwise would have perished 'in the common wreck', noting that '[m]ost of the classics were recovered by the same means'.[11] Because of 'the books and learning preserved in these repositories, we were not obliged to begin anew, and trace every art by slow and uncertain steps from its first origin'.[12] Barbauld's 'On the Classics', first published after her death in 1825 (though likely written much earlier), returns to the same subject to muse on the endurance of written words:

> It is wonderful that words should live so much longer than marble temples; – words, which at first are only uttered breath; and, when afterwards enshrined and fixed in a visible form by the admirable invention of writing, committed to such frail and perishable materials; yet the light paper bark floats down the stream of time, and lives through the storms which have sunk so many stronger built vessels.[13]

More than two decades later, in an 1807 essay entitled 'Recovery of Manuscripts', Isaac Disraeli would continue the theme: 'Our ancient classics had a very narrow escape from total annihilation.'[14] For Barbauld, Fenn, Astle, Disraeli and many others, writing was the primary historic means of preserving and disseminating knowledge; its recent spread, enabled by print, accounted for Britain's current state of intellectual, social, and economic advancement. It was imperative, therefore, that the modern state serve the role previously held by the monasteries in saving these materials from 'the common wreck.'

Astle and Fenn advocated for both access to and preservation of important manuscripts. Astle provided anecdotes about how manuscripts had been destroyed, burnt for fuel, sold for waste paper, and left to moulder in trunks and attics. In 1787 Fenn regretted that many papers were 'locked up amongst family writings, where they remained unregarded and useless for centuries', and begged 'the ancient nobility and gentry' to

> permit their worm-eaten writings and mouldy papers to be carefully perused by those whose education and pursuits have given them knowledge and taste to do it, it might not even now be too late to discover, and bring to light, many curious and valuable manuscripts.[15]

These requests reveal that what was valued and sought were not only state or historical papers, many of which had already been preserved with the founding of the British Museum a generation earlier, but family papers of the nobility and gentry. Fenn, in his edition of the Paston letters, which he was the first to publish, explains that he holds letters relating to private families 'in equal estimation [to public letters]', for those that relate to 'the private occurrences of these ancient times' improve our understandings of the past, which 'are far from being either clear or satisfactory'.[16] This recognition of the importance of private letters almost certainly impacted the practices of preservation of all kinds of literary documents.

Lamb's humorous contempt for the reverence with which Trinity College, Cambridge kept and exhibited Milton's manuscripts is the same that motivated others to forge documents by Shakespeare, a practice that was soon extended to contemporary authors. Although there have been no systematic studies of the survival rates of literary manuscripts from the period, Donald Reiman's survey does demonstrate a gradual increase in surviving literary manuscripts from the later seventeenth century of British writers, with the late eighteenth and early nineteenth centuries representing a watershed period.[17] The book before you engages with this manuscript evidence and makes claims about it that would not be possible in many earlier periods. The survival of the period's literary manuscripts must be a result of their enhanced status.

Although more literary manuscripts were being retained, whether any individual writer's archive was preserved depended on a range of local factors, including the practices of the author in sharing, copying and retaining her manuscripts; the age of the author and the suddenness of her death; the stability of an author's residence throughout her life; and the reputation of the author at and immediately following her death. William Wordsworth had most of these factors working in his favour: he saved nearly everything, with a lifelong practice of retaining his writing (and that of his family members) in sturdy notebooks; he lived a very long time, within a confined geographical area (and in one home for much of his writing life); and he had rising fame throughout his lifetime, meaning that the value of his manuscripts would have been understood by him and his family. An element of chance also always impacts questions of survival. Thus even though Barbauld lived a long life in a fixed place of residence for much of it, her reputation fell dramatically after her death. As a result, although some of her papers were passed down to surviving family members, they were never put into an archive that might have protected them from the bombs of the Second World War. Jane Austen's manuscripts were preserved by her sister and passed down by Cassandra to her heirs. The reasons for their retention were largely sentimental, as there could have been no thought of their possessing economic value or even that they were potentially publishable. John Murray, for his part, scrupulously kept most of Byron's manuscripts, including press copies, and though he never sold them, he seems to have intuited that they were worth holding on to.

One novelist of the period who retained his fiction manuscripts was Sir Walter Scott. In contrast to what appears to have been the usual practice for most novelists of the day, Scott held onto his authorial manuscripts even after they had gone to press, though he did so because they were not submitted to the press (but copied), as part of an elaborate scheme to protect his identity, and also, as he explains in the 'Introduction' to *Chronicles of the Canongate*, 'with the purpose of supplying the necessary evidence of the truth [of his authorship] when the period of announcing it should arrive'.[18] As a result, he was able to put them up for auction, in 1831, in an effort to clear his debts. However, the manuscripts failed to command a decent price. The Trustees of the Advocates Library had offered £1,000 for them, but Scott's creditors had demanded double that sum, with the result that the original holographs of thirteen of the Waverley novels fetched only £317 at auction.[19] Two of the period's greatest collectors disagreed as to the manuscripts' monetary worth. Dawson Turner, who specialised in historical manuscripts, thought the price received too high, whereas Thomas Frognall Dibdin thought it was catastrophically low.[20] Dibdin melodramatically recounts being 'sorrow-stricken – chop-fallen', at the auction price:

> One would have thought that the original drafts of those master-pieces of human wit, eloquence, and passion – struck-off by the great KNOWN UNKNOWN – would have attracted crowds of competitors within the arena of Mr Evan's auction-room: that scarcely breathing-space, much less standing-room, would have been afforded: and that Scotland herself would have furnished champions to carry off the richer prizes at the point of the claymore![21]

Dibdin also regrets that none of Scott's manuscripts were purchased by major institutions: '"What" (said I to myself,) "Not one specimen for Bodley – for the British – for the London – for the Royal – for the Advocates – for Dublin"'; 'How hesitatingly, and how rarely, are purchases made.'[22] As these widely varying estimates of the value of the collection suggest, the economic value of literary manuscripts, in this case of a living author, was unsettled.

Even though, much to Dibdin's dismay, major public collections did not step forward to purchase Scott's manuscripts, more informal amateur collectors, particularly those seeking autographs (i.e., signatures), did step forward to collect and preserve the literary manuscripts and letters of contemporary authors. As there was little market for literary manuscripts, most activity was driven by amateurs seeking to grow their collections. Many collectors sought specimens for free, by writing to request them of authors, or their correspondents, or by manufacturing ruses to obtain them. Letters and other documents were often mutilated in order to share a sample or preserve the autograph of an author, which was highly esteemed by many collectors.[23] Some collectors were more systematic, gathering enormous quantities of contemporary documents. The most famous of these autograph hunters was William Upcott; autograph hunter is a bit of misnomer, however, for what Upcott in fact collected were entire letters, even collections of letters, as opposed to simply signatures or small samples of handwriting. He described 'the disease . . . that has the strongest hold of my inclinations' as 'the autographic mania', and over three and half decades – between 1810, when he began collecting in earnest, and his death in 1845 – he amassed around 32,000 autograph letters, many penned by important historical figures, both living and dead, which he organised into dozens of thematic collections.[24] Still, like Scott's creditors before him, Upcott was unable to sell his collection, which he had arranged and carefully bound (often in extra-illustrated volumes, with portraits) into 320 volumes, despite multiple attempts to do so between 1833 and 1845. The huge mass of miscellaneous manuscripts was finally sold by auction in June 1846, fetching only £2,421.[25] Many contemporary literary manuscripts were therefore considered worth preserving, by authors, their families, publishers and collectors, but they were not yet recognised as having market value and seem, much to Dibdin's annoyance, to have been rarely purchased by institutions.

Although more and more manuscripts were retained and collected, prices did not begin to appreciate until the last quarter of the nineteenth century, followed by a substantial rise in the inter-war years.[26] Even without an established market, however, the handwritten literary document became a source of attention, even obsession, during the period. Accompanying a broader movement to collect and preserve written documents of historical interest, the *handwritten* nature of literary manuscripts in particular was a powerful source of attraction. The cultural meanings that attached to handwritten documents were regularly commented upon, as a general interest in handwriting spurred specific attention to the handwriting of Romantic authors.

Studying Handwriting

Jeffrey Hamburger has observed that

> One does not necessarily have to be able to read a script in order to respond to it as a highly differentiated and expressive set of marks that provides one of the most immediate, recognisable physical traces of human presence, thought and activity.[27]

The visual components and qualities of handwriting and of handwritten pages were often tied directly to the hand and body that produced them. Chapter 1 explored the commonplace idea, dating back to at least Shakespeare's first folio, that literary manuscripts could be scrutinised for the presence or absence of corrections as a means of discerning the manuscript creator's confusion or clarity of mind. We observed how Lamb reacted to Milton's manuscript, repulsed by the 'fluctuating, successive, indifferent' creative process revealed so startlingly in the draft before him. In addition to the unsettled quality of the draft, with its revisions, corrections and cancels, Lamb also responded, viscerally, to the appearance of handwriting itself, which he confided he found, in all cases, repugnant. The visual components of literary manuscripts are therefore multiple and complex, consisting both in how they reflect the state of the text (whether fragmentary or complete, whether in process or finalised, or as is often the case, on a continuum between the two), as well as the idiosyncratic features of the hand itself. Of course, other elements come into play as well: the spacing and evenness of the lines, the use of margins and other white space, the quality of the paper and ink, the size of the document, and whether it exists within another support (such as a notebook). Many of these elements are present in printed texts as well, though, as we will see, the handwritten page, including those of literary authors, became increasingly the source of attention and scrutiny.

Isaac Disraeli became one of the chief proponents of examining the handwritten manuscripts of literary authors. In 1793, as Aileen Douglas has discussed at length, Disraeli published his third edition of *Curiosities of Literature. Consisting of Anecdotes, Characters, Sketches and Observations, Literary, Critical and Historical*, which included 'A facsimile of Mr. Pope's hand writing', a draft page of his translation of the *Iliad*. Disraeli's rationale for publishing the facsimile is as follows: 'The lover of poetry will not be a little gratified, when he contemplates the variety of epithets, the imperfect idea, the gradual embellishment, and the critical rasures which are discoverable in this *Fac Similie*.'[28] Here, he describes the pleasure in tracing Pope's mind as it unfolds on the page, precisely what Lamb had found so offensive in viewing Milton's draft. Douglas notes that Disraeli's publication of facsimiles was motivated by the desire to make manuscripts 'accessible to the nation ... not preserved like a useless piece of antiquity in the collections of the curious'.[29] In a later essay, from 1824, on 'Autographs', Disraeli repeats the claims made for the importance of studying original literary manuscripts, and drawing the analogy between the physical document and the mind of the creator:

> The elegant and correct mind, which has acquired the fortunate habit of a fixity of attention, will write with scarcely an erasure on the page, as [François] Fenelon, and [Thomas] Gray, and [Edward] Gibbon; while we find in [Alexander] Pope's manuscripts the perpetual struggles of correction, and the eager and rapid interlineations struck off in heat.[30]

As discussed in Chapter 1, Disraeli lavishes special praise on the handwriting of Thomas Moore, who 'appears to be printing down his thoughts, without a solitary erasure'.[31]

Another element that attracted attention itself was handwriting, which was believed to be indicative of character. Dawson Turner, one of the early nineteenth century's greatest manuscript collectors, asserted that both physiognomy and autography were 'indispensible accompaniment[s] to biography ... and both for the same cause, as clues to the deciphering of character'.[32] Another contemporary wrote that, '[n]ext to a portrait ... the autograph of a great man is the most valuable notice of him'.[33] And Isaac Disraeli insisted that 'the hand-writing bears an analogy to the character of the writer'.[34] Many contemporary authors, including all three examined in the previous case study chapters, reflected on handwriting and handwritten documents. In 1773, Anna Barbauld published her short poem, 'On a Lady's Writing'. In this poem she references many visual aspects of handwritten documents and considers their significance for the writing woman. The short poem reads:

> HER even lines her steady temper show;
> Neat as her dress, and polish'd as her brow;
> Strong as her judgment, easy as her air;
> Correct though free, and regular though fair:
> And the same graces o'er her pen preside
> That form her manners and her footsteps guide.[35]

For Barbauld, it is the lady's 'even lines' and her 'correct though free, and regular though fair' handwriting that perfectly conveys her 'steady', '[n]eat', 'polish'd', 'strong' and 'easy' grace. Barbauld equates handwriting with proper female bearing and conduct, as the evenness, steadiness and correctness of the pen, manifest in the characters themselves and the regularity of her lines, reveal the lady's manners and character. Barbauld's poem describes handwriting that is oriented towards others, that serves as an instrument of sociability and hence is celebrated for its legibility and beauty; her poem recognises the need for women to project their character in their outward appearance and bearing as well as in the products of their pen. That is, the poem seems to recognise that women will be judged for their handwriting, much in the same way they are judged for how they dress, talk and otherwise comport themselves. Rather than engage in a futile protest against such superficial assessments, she asserts that women can project competence and power: the hand can embody and reflect the strength of the lady's judgement. Barbauld thus connects the hand that writes to the mind that thinks, drawing attention to the power of women holding the pen, even if for much of history, as Austen notes in *Persuasion*, 'the pen has been in their [men's] hands'.[36]

In *Emma*, Austen takes up, with more humour and greater scepticism than Barbauld, the question of handwriting as a guide to character, in this case, masculine character. Following upon a general discussion of how a style of handwriting may be shared within a family, Emma provokingly comments on Frank Churchill's hand, prompting disavowals from Mr Knightley:

> 'Mr. Frank Churchill writes one of the best gentleman's hands I ever saw.'
>
> 'I do not admire it,' said Mr. Knightley. 'It is too small – wants strength. It is like a woman's writing.'
>
> This was not submitted to by either lady. They vindicated him against the base aspersion. 'No, it by no means wanted strength – it was not a large hand, but very clear and certainly strong. Had not Mrs. Weston any letter about her to produce?' No, she had heard from him very lately, but having answered the letter, had put it away.
>
> 'If we were in the other room,' said Emma, 'if I had my writing-desk, I am sure I could produce a specimen. I have a note of his. – Do not you remember, Mrs. Weston, employing him to write for you one day?'
>
> 'He chose to say he was employed' –
>
> 'Well, well, I have that note; and can shew it after dinner to convince Mr. Knightley.'
>
> 'Oh! when a gallant young man, like Mr. Frank Churchill,' said Mr. Knightley drily, 'writes to a fair lady like Miss Woodhouse, he will, of course, put forth his best.'[37]

A jealous Mr Knightley projects an emasculated character onto the hand of his imagined rival; he also sees handwriting as essentially performative, such that Churchill can adopt a different hand depending on whether he wishes to impress the addressee. For Austen, these gendered interpretations of handwriting are shown to be meaningless, serving the petty desires of the parties (Emma wishes to goad Mr. Knightley by praising Churchill; Mr Knightley wishes to undermine Churchill in Emma's eyes) rather than signifying anything objective about the hands themselves. In *Pride and Prejudice*, a similar scene produces the same conclusion, as the ingratiating Miss Bingley lavishes praise on Darcy's hand:

> The perpetual commendations of the lady, either on his hand-writing, or on the evenness of his lines, or on the length of his letter, with the perfect unconcern with which her praises were received, formed a curious dialogue, and was exactly in union with [Elizabeth's] opinion of each.[38]

Austen aligns herself with Darcy and Elizabeth, who understand the nonsensical nature of Miss Bingley's flattery. Austen's purpose in both examples (as well as at another moment in which Emma's praise of Jane Fairfax's handwriting is revealed to be utterly empty[39]) is to draw out the essential absurdity of attempts to assign meaning to handwriting: Churchill's hand presents as both 'wanting strength' and 'certainly strong', depending on what the viewer wishes to say about it/him; Miss Bingley's and Emma's praise of the handwriting of Darcy/Jane Fairfax is likewise hollow. For Austen, handwriting is largely a social performance, which can mask or distort character as much as it can reveal it.

Austen's suspicions about attaching meaning to handwriting were not unique to her. In 'Authoresses and Autographs', an article that appeared in the *New Monthly Magazine* for 1824 and that seems to respond directly to Disraeli's attempt to read character into handwriting, the author protests,

> in vain did I try to reconcile to the rules of system the delicate feeble strokes of Elizabeth Hamilton's pen, with the vigorous tone of her mind. In vain I seek to discover the type of delicacy and reserve in the masculine lines of Mrs. Brunton; and little was there of elegance or even vivacity in the long, meager, but regular characters of Mrs. Piozzi.[40]

The author's comments reveal that assigning meaning to handwriting was a commonplace, if controversial, pastime; they further reveal that handwritten documents of authors were being shown and examined for the purpose of engaging in these sorts of analysis.

Beyond attempts to reconcile an author's handwriting with her character, handwritten documents have also been valued as material traces of the human hand that created them. Aileen Douglas has written extensively about the growing belief that handwriting provided access to the body and mind of its creator. The retention, preservation and distribution by family members of many literary manuscripts, including Austen's own, were likely guided by these sentiments. Within her novels, however, Austen treats the sentimental response to handwriting satirically, much as she had ridiculed attempts to attach meaning to it. In *Sense and Sensibility*, Marianne finds Willoughby's inscription on her sheet music and his musical notations unbearable: she spends her time 'gazing on every line of music that he had written out for her, till her heart was so heavy that no farther sadness could be gained; and this nourishment of grief was every day applied'.[41] The description of Marianne nourishing her grief labels this activity as self-indulgent and destructive. In *Mansfield*

Park, even the sensible and dull Fanny swoons upon receiving a handwritten note from Edmund:

> she seized the scrap of paper on which Edmund had begun writing to her, as a treasure beyond all her hopes, and reading with the tenderest emotion these words, 'My very dear Fanny, you must do me the favour to accept' – locked it up with the chain, as the dearest part of the gift. It was the only thing approaching to a letter which she had ever received from him; she might never receive another; it was impossible that she ever should receive another so perfectly gratifying in the occasion and the style. Two lines more prized had never fallen from the pen of the most distinguished author – never more completely blessed the researches of the fondest biographer. The enthusiasm of a woman's love is even beyond the biographer's. To her, the hand-writing itself, independent of anything it may convey, is a blessedness. Never were such characters cut by any other human being as Edmund's commonest handwriting gave! This specimen, written in haste as it was, had not a fault; and there was a felicity in the flow of the first four words, in the arrangement of 'My very dear Fanny,' which she could have looked at for ever.[42]

In her brief appearance as a heroine of sensibility, Fanny's devotion to the perfection of Edmund's hand, 'independent of anything it may convey', demonstrates her conventional attachment to handwriting, which can make even a hastily written and very short note, uttering banal endearments ('My very dear Fanny'), seem precious. Fanny's treatment of the two lines, saved and locked up 'as the dearest part of the gift', at once rehearses and mocks the treatment of autographs as holy relics. Indeed, the passage evokes the fawning treatment of literary manuscripts by distinguished authors. Although the narrative treatment of Fanny is comic and satiric, we feel for Fanny even if Austen depicts her heroine's affective response as conditioned by her society's excessive attachment to handwritten papers.

This growing devotion to the handwriting of authors converges in a set of examples all pertaining to Lord Byron. John Murray, who was responsible for preserving so many of his most famous author's manuscripts, opined on his Lordships hand as follows:

> I believe it would be difficult to find a handwriting in which the character of a man and of his writings is more accurately reflected than is the case with Lord Byron. With Byron every mood seems to be reflected in his handwriting – the impulsive waywardness of the man can be seen on every page, whether of poetry or of his letters.[43]

As discussed in Chapter 4, Byron himself commented on his own handwriting. Shortly before his death in his Cephalonia Journal (NLS MS 43353), he claims that 'my handwriting is sufficient – it is that of one who thinks much, rapidly, – perhaps deeply – but rarely with pleasure . . .'. Byron's addressee in the journal is never made explicit, but he appears almost to be imagining a public reader/viewership for it, who could see his hand and agree with his judgement. Others also commented on Byron's handwriting and on the value it possessed. After Byron's death, Thomas Carlyle sent Jane Welsh a letter from Goethe and a fragment of a letter in Lord Byron's hand. Welsh replied: 'the autographs you have sent me, have all of them a value . . . but Byron's handwriting – my own Byron's – I esteem, not as a *curiosity* merely, but rather as a relic of an honoured and beloved Friend'.[44]

The sense of intimacy created by an autograph of a beloved author – 'my own Byron's' – was soon seized upon by publishers and transformed into a marketing gimmick that proved to be one of the period's great literary hoaxes. When Galignani's 1826 Paris edition of *Works of Lord Byron* first appeared, many readers were shocked to find a handwritten letter by the poet, dated 27 April 1819, tipped into the binding.[45] Many readers were convinced that the letter was authentic, though in fact it was engraved, and it is a misconception that continues to plague readers (and rare booksellers) to the present day. Such a stunt was not new, however; in 1811, Anna Seward's letters were published with an engraved letter leaving the copyright in her letters to her publisher, Archibald Constable (see Plate 14). Perhaps, then, it is Byron's celebrity that has engendered the response to the engraved letter. Byron's handwritten manuscripts would be reproduced not only through engraving, but as one of if not the earliest photographic images of an autograph. As Andrew Burkett has discussed in detail, in 1840 Henry Fox Talbot photographed four of five suppressed lines, and a signature, from the end of Lord Byron's manuscript copy of 'Ode to Napoleon Buonaparte' [277]. These lines, written to order by Murray (who needed to lengthen the poem to avoid paying stamp tax), were not in fact published when the poem first appeared in 1814 nor in subsequent editions, appearing only after Byron's death.[46] Talbot's choice of an unpublished fragment in Byron's hand as the subject of his new photographic art demonstrates the astonishing power that had come to reside in handwritten literary manuscripts.

The changing attitude towards literary manuscripts may also be detected in the economic value placed upon Byron's manuscripts, by Murray and even by Byron himself. Few publishers took the care to preserve the fair and press copies of poems, particularly after they were printed. Murray, however, saved many of Byron's fair copies, press copies and proofs, though likely without a thought of selling them. Byron, however, sensed that his manuscripts might possess not only literary but market value. In 1832, before his departure for Greece, he presented a bundle of manuscripts to Teresa Guiccioli. She recounts the scene in *Vie de Lord Byron en Italie*:

> 'Here are some of my scribblings,' he said, 'as they came out of my head – Murray has sent them back to me.' 'I will keep them for you until you come back,' she replied. 'Do what you like with them,' said he, 'unless you think they had better be burned. But perhaps,' he added, 'some day they may be prized!'[47]

This day was, however, somewhat slower to arrive than Guiccioli would have liked. When she brought the manuscripts with her to England in 1832, with the intention of selling them to raise money to erect a monument to Byron in Ravenna, she met with no success. In a letter to John Murray dated 24 October 1832, in which she solicited his advice, she expresses an understanding of their precarious market value:

> But though those manuscripts are so dear and valuable to me, I do not delude myself to think it any easy task to find a *purchaser*. They are but a *literary luxury*, and very few persons in the world will employ a large sum of money in such a luxury. However, my intention now is to make an *advertisement* that such and such original MSS. of Lord Byron are *to be sold* in order to raise a monument to him with the result. Before I do this, I wish to have your advice.[48]

In fact, she was unable to find a buyer, and the manuscripts were not purchased until 1900, when bought by J. P. Morgan (also the purchaser of many of Austen's letters and several fiction manuscripts). As Guiccioli observed, autograph literary manuscripts, even those by one the greatest poets of the period, like those of Scott which had gone on the auction block the year before, had not fully made the transition from relics, worthy of devotion and subject to reproduction in various media, to saleable commodities.

The Romantic Manuscript in Print

As we have seen, discussions of literary manuscripts found their way into the poems, novels, and essays of the period. Facsimiles of handwritten documents were also reproduced, as engraved (and later lithographed) signatures of authors, as well as longer samples of handwriting were printed, as with the page from Pope's draft of the *Iliad*. These signatures and samples had begun to appear in print with greater frequency during the later part of the eighteenth century.[49] The engraved facsimiles of Shakespeare's three known signatures, for example, were first reproduced in the 1788 edition of his plays.[50] The first four volumes of John Fenn's edition of the Paston letters, published as *Original Letters, written during the reigns of Henry VII, Edward IV, and Richard III*, appeared from 1787 to 1789, with a final volume appearing in 1823. In his edition, Fenn included numerous facsimiles engraved from the letters, including samples of handwriting, signatures, paper-marks, and seals of the letters. John Thane's *British Autography* (published 1788–93) included 269 engraved portraits embellished with autographs and occasionally longer samples of handwriting. This work helped to establish the visual convention that would become ubiquitous in frontispieces of author's works, namely the addition of the subject's signature at the foot of the engraved portrait.[51] A typical example may be found in Barbauld's 1825 works, adorned with a silhouette and an engraved signature (see Plate 15). David McKitterick has noted the rising interest in type facsimiles (i.e., facsimiles of early printed books) in the early nineteenth century; and Michael Twyman has observed the appearance of facsimiles of ancient scripts in the early nineteenth century, as 'interest was gradually awakened in the actual appearance of the letters and other symbols used'.[52] In these ways, manuscripts were remediated in print, using a variety of technologies including engraving, lithography and photography. They were thus made visually present to readers of the day, and established the importance of handwriting and handwritten documents to the understanding and appreciation of writers and their works.

As we have seen with Talbot's photographic facsimile of Byron's 'Ode to Napoleon', from 1840 onward it became possible to reproduce full manuscripts using photography. One of the first known photographic facsimiles of a complete manuscript was published in

1858, when Camille Silvy reproduced the *Manuscrit Sforza*.[53] Silvy asserted that photography could be a truly restorative medium: several passages in the manuscript, illegible to the human eye, were rendered visible, he claimed, through photographic reproduction.[54] Although photographic reproduction would become the standard mode of reproducing facsimiles of manuscripts in print, it remained a costly and, in most cases, compromised medium: image quality is almost always diminished rather than enhanced (colour images being prohibitively expensive, even today); images are rarely reproduced to the exact dimensions of the original; and, in most cases, neither the three-dimensionality of the original nor its materials can be replicated (though these effects are attempted in what are referred to as facsimile editions).[55] Photographic facsimiles of the manuscripts of modern authors, including those active in the Romantic period, did not begin to appear until the second half of the twentieth century, and then only rarely. Because of this, for those wishing to consult literary manuscripts throughout most of the nineteenth and twentieth centuries, there was only one option: to view the manuscript in person, whether by applying to the owner or collector, or visiting the institution in which it was held. From the 1930s onward, microform, a form of microphotography that shrinks image size (usually to 1/25 of the original), provided a cost-efficient means of delivering and storing large numbers of page images, was available for some manuscripts but not many modern ones.[56]

As a result, most of the literary manuscripts of Romantic authors were known exclusively through their textual manifestations in print. Unpublished writings by most authors were usually edited and reproduced typographically. The early deaths of the second generation of male Romantic poets – Keats in 1821, Shelley in 1822, Byron in 1824 – resulted in their literary executors inheriting a large quantity of unpublished poetry. According to Jack Stillinger, Keats published only forty-five of his total output of 150 poems; when Mary Shelley published the *Posthumous Poems of Percy Bysshe Shelley* in 1824, she included eighty-three poems, most of which had never been previously published;[57] and, as discussed in Chapter 4, a majority of Byron's poems were unprinted in his lifetime, and they began to appear shortly after his death, chiefly in Thomas Moore's *Letters and Journals of Lord Byron* in 1830. In addition to thorny editorial problems raised by the state of these manuscript remains, larger questions surfaced as to what was acceptable for print. Keats's unprinted poems were found in journal letters to family, commonplace books and notebooks – that is, material forms that imply an audience, but usually a confidential rather than a public one. According to Mary Shelley, many of her husband's poems were 'written on the spur of the occasion, and never retouched', with their unfinished state presenting a host of problems.[58] Eager to control the reputation of his celebrity author, John Murray responded cautiously to Byron's death, participating in the destruction of the poet's memoirs and publishing the more controversial poems in his authorised collections only after they had been printed by Moore or Galignani.

The deaths of several major female authors, all of whom left unpublished writing, presented similar though perhaps even greater challenges. William Godwin grossly miscalculated when, the year after his wife's death, he published *Memoirs of the Author of A Vindication of the Rights of Woman* with her previously unpublished, and seemingly autobiographical, fiction.[59] Austen's heirs were far more careful: after her death in 1817 they published a staid and brief 'biographical notice' with her two posthumous novels in 1818 and issued none of her unpublished fiction for over half century. After Anna Barbauld's death in 1825, Lucy Aikin was guarded, if not misleading, in her framing of her aunt's life and poetic career, and she held back some of her aunt's poems, as discussed in Chapter 3. These examples also illustrate differential practices respecting the preservation of literary manuscripts. Godwin apparently destroyed his wife's surviving literary manuscripts, though he kept many of his own, even after publication. Austen's family destroyed most of her letters but preserved (at least some of) the unpublished work; we do not know if there was other unpublished material that was destroyed by Austen herself or by the family. We do not know which of her aunt's manuscripts Aikin kept (we only know some survived to be destroyed in September 1940).

Scholarly editions of the period's major writers, which began to appear in 1965 with David Erdman's *The Poetry and Prose of William Blake*, provided the first reassessments of the manuscript record. Erdman's edition was followed in 1970 by the appearance of the first volumes in the Cornell Wordsworth. Over the next five decades, scholarly print editions of the major Romantic authors (all of the Big Six male Romantic poets; Walter Scott, the leading novelist of the day; and two exceptional female authors, Jane Austen and Mary Shelley) were published, some in editions that took over three decades to produce, many by editors who became leaders in the field of textual scholarship (see Table 6.1). The Romantics have proven to be fertile ground for editorial theory, due in part to the extensive archives of surviving manuscripts, in part to the textual complexities these manuscripts present. Table 6.1 collects these landmark editions, which have set the standard for decades, if not generations, to come, since 'the economics of publishing mean that relatively few works are ever accorded the luxury of being presented in competing scholarly editions'.[60] These scholarly editions provide the most sustained engagement with Romantic-period literary manuscripts since those of the first generation of editors, many of whom were family members or intimate associates of the authors. R. W. Chapman's editions of Jane Austen's novels and unpublished writing, dating from 1923, also bear mentioning, as the first to apply serious editorial methods to Austen's works, and indeed to the English novel.[61]

Table 6.1 Major scholarly critical editions of Romantic authors

Major author	Title/imprint	General editor	Dates	Volumes
William Blake	*The Poetry and Prose of William Blake*; *The Complete Poetry and Prose of William Blake* (University of California Press; Anchor Books/Doubleday)	David Erdman	1965, 1980, 1982	2
S. T. Coleridge	*Collected Works of S. T. Coleridge* (Princeton University Press)	Kathleen Colburn	1970–2002	23
William Wordsworth	*The Cornell Wordsworth* (Cornell University Press)	Stephen Parrish	1975–2007	21
John Keats	*The Poems of John Keats* (Belknap/Harvard University Press)	Jack Stillinger	1978	1
Lord Byron	*Lord Byron: Complete Poetical Works* (Oxford University Press)	Jerome McGann	1980–93	7
Walter Scott	*The Edinburgh Edition of the Waverley Novels* (Edinburgh University Press)	David Hewitt	1993–2015	30
Mary Shelley	*The Novels and Selected Works of Mary Shelley* (Pickering)	Nora Crook	1996	8
Percy Shelley	*The Complete Poetry of P. B. Shelley* (Johns Hopkins University Press)	Donald Reiman/ Neil Fraistat	2003–	3 (published to date)
Jane Austen	*Cambridge Edition of the Works of Jane Austen* (Cambridge University Press)	Janet Todd	2005–8	9

The process of editing often involved these editors in the interpretation and representation of original manuscripts; many of the poems were being published for the first time, or from suspect sources; and much of the fiction (including Scott's *Waverley* novels, Shelley's *Frankenstein*, and Austen's unpublished writing) had not been edited with attention to the surviving manuscript record. The representation of original manuscripts within critical editions inevitably effects a separation of the textual from the physical, or in McGann's terms, of the linguistic from the bibliographical. Hans Gabler has noted that all editorial processes necessarily effect this separation, for 'transmission and editing have always divorced text from documents: text can only be transmitted and edited by being lifted off one document and inscribed upon another. Traditional editing therefore leaves the documents as documents behind.'[62] The dynamics and temporality of manuscript writing are thus always necessarily lost, in the process of being 'lifted off one document and inscribed upon another'.[63] However absorbed by and faithful to the original manuscripts editors might be – and the scholarly editions of the works of Romantic authors do often exemplify fidelity to the manuscript record to a remarkable extent – critical editions by their very nature distance us from the original documents they remediate.

Of the print critical editions included in Table 6.1, the Cornell Wordsworth includes photographic facsimiles of a large number of manuscript pages of the major poems, underscoring the editors' commitment to the original documents in which we find Wordsworth's compositions. Published between 1975 and 2007, the original plan for the twenty-one-volume edition had been to create a set of facsimiles (and transcriptions) of entire notebooks, which would attempt to replicate Wordsworth's poetic notebooks.[64] However, this approach was ultimately rejected as unwieldy, as poems are often drafted across multiple manuscripts, and as the Wordsworth's manuscript notebooks often contain an heterogeneous mix of material, as we saw in Chapter 1. Instead, the emphasis was placed on the chronological development of individual poems, with the attempt to capture their textual development across multiple notebooks. The Cornell Wordsworth's particular devotion to the manuscript derives from an editorial strategy that accords early complete drafts, even of works printed and reprinted in the poet's lifetime, supreme textual authority. In most cases, the editors reject the tradition of honouring the final lifetime version or edition of a literary work as a means of discovering authorial intention, arguing that this editorial approach has not served Wordsworth's poetry well. In speaking of the state of the canon prior to the Cornell series, Jonathan Wordsworth noted that 'most great poets are known by the best versions of their works; Wordsworth is almost exclusively known by his worst'.[65]

The Cornell series aims instead to offer unencumbered reading texts in the 'earliest complete form' of the poems, 'to uncover the early versions of both long familiar and largely unknown poems and to trace and record the changes through the poet's lifetime in drafts, letters, journals, proofs, and print to the final lifetime edition of 1850'.[66] To do this, editors necessarily had to carefully scrutinise the manuscript record. The quantity and nature of surviving manuscripts meant, however, that the decision about the 'earliest complete form' of a poem was often a difficult one, given Wordsworth's lifelong process of revision, such that 'every major poem and nearly all of the shorter lyric and narrative poems of lesser length underwent a . . . transformative journey in the poet's hands'. As a result, most volumes include 'an *apparatus criticus* of all variant readings from all surviving manuscript and print forms over which the poet exercised control'.[67] By privileging the individual poetic work, many of which are developed across several notebooks and over long periods of time, attention is inevitably deflected from the material practices of verse making and manuscript production, as these collaborative and iterative processes are inscribed within the pages of the family's notebooks. The Cornell Wordsworth – like all the other editions surveyed here – presents a reading text for each poem, described as a version of the poem 'as it stood upon its completion, with all later revisions stripped away'.[68] These reading texts, which occupy the privileged position near the beginning of each volume following the prefatory material, make sacrifices for the sake of legibility, one of the ways in which critical editions inevitably strip away the temporality and, in Wordsworth's case, the communality, of the processes embodied in the manuscript pages and notebooks.

J. C. C. Mays, in his three-volume contribution of the *Poetical Works* to the *Collected Works of S. T. Coleridge*, acknowledges that textual variation is the norm for Coleridge, as different versions of his poems were written, copied and circulated amongst different readers, for different purposes, at different periods of time: 'poems which exist in several versions are likely to exist in forms which differ because Coleridge's intentions changed, and it is not obvious which – if any – version is representative'.[69] Although he orients the edition around individual poems, with volume 1 presenting reading texts and volume 2 collecting and displaying variants, Mays seeks to present the variants 'not as departures from a chosen norm' but as 'different versions (*Fassungen*), many of which have claims to authority'.[70] According to Mays, 'the recording of variants must make it evident how several versions or performances often exist side by side'.[71] Mays's ambition is to 'enable a reader to hold in mind a sense of the way the poems move, as they often do, simultaneously in several planes: that is, the way the poems move laterally, as a series of independent versions, and vertically, as one version overlays and succeeds another'.[72] Mays thus acknowledges that different versions – in Coleridge's case, the result of multiple manuscript copies prepared by him and others, sometimes over decades – have independent significance. Coleridge, as we have seen with 'Christabel', also continued revising his poems even after their first publication, correcting published copies and dispersing them to friends.[73] Unlike the Cornell Wordsworth, in which different versions are acknowledged but an editorial preference has been established for the earliest complete versions of all poems, Mays's edition endeavours, within the sequential bounds of the print edition, to offer a 'versioning' edition of Coleridge's poetry, one that respects the multiplicity of Coleridge's poetics. Although only a single version of the poem is elevated to the position of the reading text, Mays's second volume, as well as his headnotes for each poem in volume 1, attempts to present Coleridge's poetic output 'as a series of independent versions', in an effort to be faithful to the poet's habits of revision and dissemination, and, ultimately, to the manuscript record itself.

The canon of Coleridge's verse that Mays includes also displays a high regard for the original manuscripts and the social life they record. The edition includes for the first time approximately one hundred poems that had been previously excluded from all major editions. These are described as 'for the most part minor pieces: early poems, fragments, notebook, and album verses, metrical experiments, musings and notations that evolved in verse form'.[74] Mays argues against George Whalley's attempt to develop a poetic canon based only on the verse Coleridge chose to publish, designating those left unpublished by Coleridge and his early editors as insignificant.[75]

By offering an expanded notion of what counts as Coleridge's verse, including poems deemed juvenile or trivial or fragmentary, Mays reforms our understanding of the social processes of verse-making, resituating the poems within their original contexts, in which poetry need not be finished, polished, or otherwise important or major in order to have been shared with and enjoyed by others.

With the second generation of Romantic male poets, the manuscript record takes on a new urgency, as many of their works were left unpublished at their deaths. The intense study of these manuscripts has yielded influential theoretical insights. In editing Keats's poetic output, Jack Stillinger has placed enormous importance on the transmission history of the poems, which passed through and were changed by many hands, whether en route to print or not. The editor's task is a challenging one, for Keats was famously indifferent to his manuscripts and, according to Richard Woodhouse, 'impatient of correcting'.[76] Keats's friends stepped in; Woodhouse preserved and collected Keats's manuscripts so meticulously that he became, in Stillinger's words, 'a Keats *scholar* almost as early as Keats became a poet'.[77] Charles Brown kept four manuscript books with transcripts of Keats's poetry to protect the verse from being loaned to (and lost by) 'young blue-stocking ladies'.[78] Woodhouse, Brown and others therefore played a critical role in the production, circulation and publication of Keats's poetry, so much so that Stillinger developed his editorial theory to accommodate the collaborative practices by which most of Keats's poems were transmitted. As a result, Stillinger rejects using as his copy-text holograph versions, as doing so would purge the interventions of others from the texts of the poems. Instead, Stillinger uses either later transcriptions or printings in the three volumes published in Keats's lifetime, as additions made in the process of transcribing and publishing must 'be considered an essential element in the fulfilment of the poet's intentions, and it ought to be obvious that the publishers' and printers' additional refinements of minor details are simply further fulfilling those intentions'.[79] For Stillinger, the aim is not to strip the text of the contributions of others but to acknowledge them as central aspects of the creative process that enabled Keats's manuscripts to journey into wider circulation.

In *Multiple Authorship and the Myth of Solitary Genius* (1991), Stillinger draws upon his editorial findings to describe and theorise the thoroughly socialised process of writing, repudiating the theory of solitary genius in favour of one that acknowledges the compound nature of authorship in almost all cases. His appreciation of the actual conditions of authorship, and the nature of publication as an ongoing and complicated process usually involving different technologies and multiple individuals, also leads Stillinger to prefer an editorial policy that treats versions as evidence of a succession of collaborations. As with Mays's edition of Coleridge's poems, however, the material and economic constraints of the print codex limit the full realisation of this approach. The nature of scholarly editing seems structurally to forbid a comprehensive approach to the literary manuscript itself: to quote Gabler again, 'original documents possess features which no edition one might imagine could exhaust, since they are in truth unamenable to editing'.

Shelley's poetic canon has also proven extremely difficult to reconstruct: according to Stuart Curran, 'the embarrassing state of the Shelley texts, after so many years and so many editors, is legion'.[80] There are many reasons for this: the dispersal of his manuscripts to several repositories, their fragile condition, and 'the myriad of vexed textual problems' they pose.[81] The latest edition of Shelley's poems currently in production, by Donald Reiman and Neil Fraistat, promises an editorial model that will contribute another intervention in the field of textual theory. Like Mays's edition of Coleridge, the first volume begins with Shelley's earliest poetry, providing what Michael O'Neill claims will be 'a radical overhaul of a critical tradition that regards the [earliest] poems as worthless juvenilia'.[82] The editors do not discard or marginalise the unpublished material. In fact, in their commitment to representing Shelley's unpublished poems and his revision process, the editors demonstrate a strong fidelity to the manuscript evidence. Volume 2 reproduces *The Esdaile Notebook*, a cycle of fifty-eight early poems, according to Shelley's arrangement, thus enabling the integrity of the notebook to stand. Rejected passages of poems that circulated (whether in manuscript or print) are also included as supplements to those poems, whilst other poetic drafts that Shelley rejected or left incomplete at his death are to be grouped either according to their publication histories or the notebooks in which they survive, with diplomatic texts of his significant incomplete poetic drafts and fragments.

Given Reiman's editorial involvement, it is not surprising that this new edition makes a strong case for the importance of distinguishing poems according to Shelley's intentions respecting publication, a foundational element of Reiman's conception of modern manuscripts, as we have seen. Thus,

> [The *Collected Poetry of Percy Bysshe Shelley*] presents the poems that [Shelley] intended to publish, according to the groupings he arranged and in the chronological order in which he hoped to issue them. Within each such volume or gathering we place the individual poems, wherever possible, in the order that [Shelley] planned for their publication. Those poems that he released only privately to close friends, without attempting publication, are arranged chronologically in separate groupings according to defined periods of his life, and within those groups, in the order that he sent or gave them to friends.[83]

The editors justify this approach as follows:

> Readers will thus have before them discrete versions that reflect the author's creative thinking about a poetic whole that he intended to release to a historically identifiable audience, rather than a conflation of his judgments at different times, meant for different audiences. Each released poem, then, will appear in the version in which [Shelley] released it, following his preferred standards of grammar, pointing, and orthography as established by his MSS and published editions.[84]

Fraistat's and Reiman's groupings presume that the audience was reasonably determinate when Shelley was alive and that evidence exists to ascertain that intention now. As Michael O'Neill notes, this arrangement is different than in almost all previous editions of Shelley's verse, which have typically been organised chronologically, based on the date of composition. In the new edition 'published and unpublished material is not intermingled', but rather separated out.[85] Further, by separating unpublished poems into those Shelley intended to publish and those he did not, as O'Neill observes, 'the appeal to authorial intention is resolute'.[86] O'Neill suggests that '[a]ppropriate licence seems to be given the editors by "intended to publish" and "hoped to issue"';[87] nevertheless, as discussed in Chapter 1, intentionality may not always be transparent or fixed, particularly in the case of Shelley, who encountered significant resistance to the publication of his poems. Many of Shelley's individual poems also fall within multiple categories: 'Mont Blanc', for example, was released privately before making its public debut in *The History of a Six Weeks' Tour*.

Unfinished poetry presents yet another problem of divination. These poems are separated into another category, as these 'unfinished pieces are not part of [Shelley's] self-presentation to his contemporaries'.[88] For these unreleased fragments, a different editorial procedure is used: these are not edited as finished poems but as works in progress, so they are provided with full diplomatic transcriptions and are separated from both the public and released manuscript poems, and published in a 'supplement' section.[89] O'Neill notes that, adhering to their categories, the editors 'will consign *The Triumph of Life* ... to this category of "unreleased 'poetry,'"' though, according to O'Neill, Shelley likely harboured an intention to publish this and other 'unreleased fragments' upon completion, once again suggesting the difficulties involved in fixing intentionality.[90] The divisions insisted upon by the editors may also have the unintended effect of devaluing the poetry that Shelley released privately. Although the editors insist that they 'seek to avoid ... separating [Shelley] into two Shelleys – the private person whose inner feelings are documented in his unreleased poems and private letters and the public poet who, during a period of great social and ideological upheaval, was struggling with other writers for the hearts and minds of the British establishment and reading public',[91] it is hard to see how their arrangement does not, implicitly, support the view that print publication (or the desire for it) represents the ultimate achievement for a poet.

By including each released poem 'in the version in which [Shelley] released it', the editors give primacy to a concept of publication that captures the manuscript evidence at one moment in time, placing before readers 'discrete versions that reflect the author's creative thinking about a poetic whole that he intended to release to a historically identifiable audience, rather than a conflation of his judgments at different times, meant for different audiences'.[92] A particular manuscript witness thus stands in for the dynamic process of manuscript inscription and alteration. At the same time, the editors do include multiple versions of poems released to distinct audiences, thus helping readers to understand the ways in which different versions of Shelley's texts circulated.[93] Although they have not yet been published as part of the first three volumes, the editors promise that readers will be presented with both the public version of a poem like 'Mont Blanc' and the surviving unreleased versions.

One advantage of Fraistat's and Reiman's groupings is that it renders the fact of manuscript circulation explicit and gives to these poems an identity, acknowledging their social circulation. It is these distinctions that can be obscured in a chronologically arranged scholarly edition, such as Jerome McGann's monumental seven-volume edition of Byron's poetry, *Lord Byron: Complete Poetical Works*, published between 1980 and 1993. McGann follows a traditional chronological arrangement by date of publication (or composition, if unpublished), in almost all cases.[94] In many respects and for obvious reasons, given the quantity of celebrated poetry Byron printed while alive, it is of all the critical editions discussed in this chapter the least invested in presenting Byron as a manuscript writer. Unlike Shelley's and Keats's, nearly all of Byron's major poems were published; and unlike Wordsworth and Coleridge, Byron was not an inveterate reviser of his poems. With poems published before 1816, McGann includes as copy-text a print version, usually a later printing, as Byron supervised the printing of most of his poems until that date; after 1816, when Byron left England and was necessarily more distant from the publication process, an earlier version is usually preferred. The edition also conforms to the model of most critical print editions by supplying clean reading texts, annotated with select variants and with extensive commentary in the notes at the end of each volume.

McGann's achievement in this volume is to draw together (and choose between) the extensive manuscript and print witnesses that survive for nearly all of Byron's poetry. As is consistent with his purpose (of publishing a comprehensive and correct edition of all of Byron's poems), he consults only 'textually relevant' manuscripts, and where manuscript evidence is relevant, relies on the manuscript of highest authority.[95] Like many editions with reading texts, the variations made in the manuscript and proof stages (of which many survive uniquely through John Murray's forethought), as well as details about alterations of a manuscript from composition through copy editing, are collected in notes in a separate section of the edition and require considerable expertise on the part of the reader interested in reconstructing the flow of textual changes over time. While McGann provides variants he does not adopt procedures that 'attempt to describe the physical manner in which charges were made on manuscripts, for instance, whether they are interlinear insertions, or marginal'.[96] Information about a poem's actual circulation during the poet's lifetime is often contained in the extensive notes that accompany each poem, collected at the end of each volume. Therefore, a basic fact about each poem, whether it was published in the author's lifetime, remains obscured within the reading texts.

Since the release of the final volume of the edition, however, McGann has been critical of his own efforts and those of other textual critics, noting that the 'textual condition' conforms neither to the author's original creative intention (which rarely crystallises in a single moment in a manuscript), nor to a final print version, nor to the text as it might be reconstructed in an eclectic edition. Notwithstanding the enormous achievements of textual scholars working in the Romantic period, including McGann's own, he insists upon the shortcomings:

> Textual and editorial theory has heretofore concerned itself almost exclusively with the linguistic codes. The time has come, however, when we have to take greater theoretical account of the other coding network which operates at the documentary and bibliographical level of literary works.[97]

McGann has thus come to champion a theory of 'the socialization of texts' and a versioning model of editing. He readily acknowledges how difficult such a form of editing is within the traditional print realm. Critical print editions, he observes, are 'infamously difficult to read and use. Their problems arise because they deploy a book form to study another book form.'[98] For McGann, '[t]he Byron edition thus brought home the degree to which our scholarly instruments and institutions establish a horizon of critical possibilities', as they 'drive the resources of the codex to its limits and beyond'.[99]

Even working within these physical and to some extent conceptual limits, the critical editions surveyed in this chapter have been tremendously successful in excavating and theorising the Romantic literary manuscript: even when a manuscript version is not used as copy-text, its existence is usually noted and its variants often provided; and within each edition's editorial principles we encounter a thorough reckoning with the nature of the manuscript evidence and its significance. Through notes and variants, editors have sought to demonstrate the dynamic process of writing and circulation and have frequently drawn attention to the unpredictable and circuitous paths that texts traverse between writing and publication. Further, these editions, though emphasising different aspects of their author's manuscripts, have often worked to deconstruct the reading texts of the individual poem the editors themselves have provided, to better reflect that literary production and dissemination are far messier than the polished and finished world of print implies. Speaking about the Cornell Wordsworth, Kathryn Sutherland claims that the 'comprehensive facsimiles images' it includes 'effectively decompose its editorially inferred "Reading Texts"' such that, taken as a whole, 'the Cornell Wordsworth remains a landmark in its self-conscious questioning of the limits of print-based editing and the theories that underpin it'.[100] In different but equally compelling ways, all of the editions discussed in this chapter have used Romantic literary manuscripts to rethink editorial practice and reimagine the critical edition. Conversely, editorial practice has grappled with the period's literary manuscripts and with the literary culture in which they were embedded.

It has been argued that digital scholarly editions offer the potential to move beyond 'the limits of print-based editing', through greater storage capacity and the ability to more fully capture the material nature of manuscript materiality and textuality. Although Hans Gabler observes that 'original documents possess features which no edition one might imagine could exhaust', digital presentation offers the capacity to remediate many more of those original features than print. The final section of this chapter explores the digital remediations of the manuscripts of William Blake, Jane Austen, and Mary Shelley, as these critical digital editions have demonstrated how the study of Romantic period literary manuscripts can be reinvigorated through their presentation in a new medium. For the first time, it is possible to collect large numbers of photo-facsimiles of literary manuscripts held by different repositories into a single resource; at the same time, the use of the digital medium does not itself circumvent all of the problems that plague print editions, and it may raise some unique challenges of its own.

The Digital Romantic Manuscript

With the emergence of high-resolution digital photography, the robust storage capacity of computers and other hand-held devices, and the ease of transmission enabled by the internet, many of the long-standing difficulties involved in reproducing and disseminating copies of handwritten documents may be coming to a close. The potential benefits of digital media for the remediation of literary manuscripts are considerable: the ability to include a far larger number of documentary witnesses than is possible in print; to navigate and link to other sources with great ease; to reproduce high-quality colour images of the original manuscripts; and to correct and augment material over time. At the same time, it is important not to overestimate the affordances of digital media, nor to underestimate the time and resources needed to develop digital resources, nor to ignore the issues of reliability and sustainability that they present. Digital editions appear to be less durable than their print counterparts and have posed similar issues in terms of their usability, given the difficulties associated with screen reading. As Susan Schreibman, speaking of the first decade of digital editions (c. 1993–2003), observes: 'claims about technology's potential . . . while common in theory, were difficult and thus rarely implemented in practice'.[101] As we enter the third decade of the digital turn, few editions have been able to surpass the achievements of the print critical edition; nor have they become available in the profusion that was once thought inevitable. Both the technical and the economic barriers to the production of digital editions remain high, as digital publication does not circumvent the economics of print but simply transfers the cost from publishers and consumers to funding agencies and institutional libraries.[102] Finally, electronic editions have 'not [been] freed . . . from the layout economies invented for the printed page nor from the kinds of documentation and presentation of data agreed upon for the print format', and, as commentators have noted in relation to the number of textual witnesses digital media allows, more is not necessarily better.[103] According to Paul Eggert, the digital turn has brought about intensified scrutiny of print-based critical editions in part because 'we cannot but be aware of their material interface'.[104] At the same time, we must interrogate digital editions, to assess whether they have been successful in attempting to alleviate old problems, and whether in doing so they have created new ones.

Of all the major male Romantic poets, William Blake is the only one whose writing has been subject to rigorous methods of collection, digitisation and curation by scholars and technology experts. As one of the earliest digital editions – it launched in 1996 – *The William Blake Archive* fully exploits the digital medium to display Blake's uniquely integrated visual textuality. As a facsimile edition, it privileges the material artefact, showcasing Blake's plates, engravings, watercolours and manuscripts. Although digital remediations necessarily re-present the original, threatening distortions particularly in the rendering of colour and scale, the Archive has dedicated itself to the 'meticulous care of images and adherence to a strict set of established guidelines'.[105] The visual bias of web presentation is particularly suited to reproducing Blake's illuminated manuscripts, which are extremely difficult (and expensive) to produce faithfully in print. *The William Blake Archive* also provides transcriptions and image descriptions (enabling detailed text and image searches), annotations and detailed metadata about each archival object. It further enables a variety of ways to view and interact with the material. By providing tools for viewing the illuminated books, manuscripts and engraved commercial works, *The William Blake Archive* gives precedence to the visual elements of Blake's work in a way that is particularly aligned with web presentation.[106]

Now over twenty years old, the Archive has grown and changed over time, demonstrating the evolving nature of many digital projects:

> Digital editions are typically never complete: there is frequently no point that marks the end of a project, as with book publication. Rather, digital editions tend to be open-ended. The relative ease in adding new material as well as in correcting old content allows for an expansionary editorial model, much like hypertext itself, with shifting centers and nodes.[107]

As an open access site, the Blake Archive allows for unprecedented access to Blake's *oeuvre* and its emphasis on the unique copies of Blake's illuminated books supports side-by-side comparisons, digitally reunifying unique copies that are widely dispersed across various institutions across the world. *The William Blake Archive* promotes the independent significance of each copy, much in the same way that editors of scholarly print editions like Mays have sought to give attention to different manuscript and print versions of Coleridge's poems. In other words, *The William Blake Archive*, by refusing to elevate a single copy as representative, treats all copies as equally important and worthy of attention, a position that is challenging to implement in print. The profusion of copies, the open-endedness of the site, and its changeability (with upgrades and shifts in technology) can, however, pose problems of consistency and usability. As with print scholarly editions, constraints and trade-offs are inevitable.

The manuscripts of only two other authors of the Romantic period have been extensively edited for digital media, those of two of its major female authors, Jane Austen and Mary Shelley.[108] *Jane Austen's Fiction Manuscripts* collects photofacsimiles and displays them either independently or with transcriptions of the approximately 1,100 pages of fiction written in Jane Austen's hand.[109] The project gathers all of Austen's fiction manuscripts, most of which were dispersed after her death and subsequently sold to libraries and private collections in the United Kingdom and the United States. The manuscripts, discussed at length in Chapter 5, offer a unique glimpse into Austen's career, for, '[u]nlike the famous printed novels, all published in a short span between 1811 and 1818, these manuscripts trace Jane Austen's development as a writer from childhood to the year of her death; that is, from 1787 (aged 11 or 12) to 1817 (aged 41)'.[110] This collection demonstrates the power of digital media to harness a single author's literary manuscripts now scattered across continents, manuscripts that are, by their very nature, difficult to display in print. While some of these manuscripts have been digitised elsewhere, they exist isolated on various institutional webpages such as those of the British Library and the Bodleian. Often what is reproduced are selections from a manuscript (e.g., the British Library's digitised version of Austen's 'The History of England', which is contained within a larger juvenile notebook, 'Volume the Second'). All of these manuscripts have been transcribed and printed in modern editions of Austen's works, but print facsimiles are often expensive or out of print, and no single book contains all of the facsimiles of the fiction manuscripts.

The most recent student edition, *The Manuscript Works of Jane Austen*, provides reading texts of select juvenile pieces from her three manuscript compilations ('Volume the First', 'Volume the Second' and 'Volume the Third'), as well as *Lady Susan*, *The Watsons* and *Sanditon*, but not the cancelled chapters of *Persuasion*, which are included in Broadview's edition of that novel (again as idealised reading texts) and in the current Oxford World's Classics editions.[111] *The Cambridge Edition of the Works of Jane Austen* includes her manuscript works over three volumes: *Juvenilia* includes reading texts with insertions and deletions included in footnotes, and a photographic facsimile of 'The History of England', illustrated by her sister Cassandra; *Persuasion* includes a facsimile of the cancelled chapters 10 and 11, as well as a reading text of the same; and *Later Manuscripts* includes reading texts and diplomatic transcriptions for *The Watsons* and *Sanditon*, the two later manuscripts that are in draft form.[112] The facsimiles that are provided, particularly of the cancelled *Persuasion* chapters, are reproduced in grayscale; the manuscript images are illegible in places due to fading and overwriting. Currently no print edition, therefore, brings together all the manuscript material, and given the costs of doing so, one is unlikely to be forthcoming, at least not in an accessible format. Even if it were economically feasible, it is unlikely that print could compete with the detail provided by high-resolution colour photographic facsimiles.[113] In this way, *Jane Austen's Fiction Manuscripts* exceeds what exists and what is possible in print. Digital technology also provides additional functionality, such as magnification and side-by-side comparison of different pages, both practices that are not possible within a codex.[114]

Like *The William Blake Archive*, *Jane Austen's Fiction Manuscripts* is a purposefully object-based collection. Therefore, the only transcriptions provided are diplomatic, and they are

> faithful to Austen's spelling, paragraphing, and punctuation; to her abbreviations and other distinctive features of her writing hand: her long 's' (ʃ) and ampersand (&) are preserved, as is her use of underlining. Line and page breaks are carefully followed; all signs of revision and correction are transcribed as they occur in the body of the text.[115]

In keeping with the commitment to the manuscript artefact, the meticulous diplomatic transcriptions may be viewed only alongside the manuscript page images, not apart from them, meaning that no reading texts are provided. Of course, digital editions viewable on screens are not (yet) able to reproduce the three-dimensionality of material artefacts, and the sense of scale is inevitably lost. Nevertheless, there are significant differences between what is revealed by digital facsimiles as compared to their print analogues, to say nothing of the even wider gulf between digital facsimiles and regularised reading texts. Returning to Hamburger's understanding that '[o]ne does not necessarily have to be able to read a script in order to respond to it as a highly differentiated and expressive set of marks that provides one of the most immediate, recognisable physical traces of human presence, thought and activity', the viewing of digital surrogates online allows us to understand many of these non-linguistic aspects of literary manuscripts.[116]

Visibly represented for us in the Austen digital edition are a number of features unique to such manuscripts, including variations in Austen's use of the space of the writing page; the relative consistency of her handwriting within a single document and across documents, which might suggest shifts in tempo or starts and stops in writing; changes in ink, which can provide clues as to the sequence of revisions, and even pauses to refill a quill with ink; revision types, whether interlinear or via pasted or pinned additions; and contributions of other hands and how they appear on the page. Through detailed notes provided by the editor and the manuscript curators, it is possible to imaginatively recreate the precise nature of the support for the pages displayed, the size and construction of the materials, as well as conservation efforts. Of course, to these visual and physical elements must be added the textual and linguistic features, with one of the key ambitions of the project being to allow users to better understand the interactions between the textual and the material:

> A particular feature of this edition is the evidence provided for the relationship between the manuscripts as linguistic structures (as words, phrases, punctuation) and as the physical documents that support those structures (quires of paper, folded into homemade booklets or bought already bound into blank notebooks). It is an edition of a series of objects as well as of their texts. This more than any function of the digital medium sets it apart from previous Austen manuscript editions, changing its relationship to its materials. Information . . . in the Head Note attached to each manuscript is offered as an aid to the reconstruction of the physical objects and to strengthen our view of their importance to the texts inscribed upon them.[117]

The edition thus allows for careful study of Austen's material practices of composition and circulation, investigations that would be difficult to pursue with even the highest quality print facsimile. As the editors point out, the digital medium enables 'an edition of a series of objects as well as of their texts'. What *Jane Austen's Fiction Manuscripts* does not provide is access to the contextual editorial work that is present in the print editions of Austen's manuscript work. Although it unquestionably improves our access to the materiality of Austen's manuscripts, it does not provide the layers of information about a text's history and meaning available in most scholarly print editions.

The Shelley-Godwin Archive likewise provides exceptional access to the study of another collection of Romantic-era manuscripts, as the project's editors will eventually digitise and transcribe the handwritten legacy of the four central family members: William Godwin, Mary Wollstonecraft, Mary Shelley and Percy Shelley. The project was launched with Mary Shelley's *Frankenstein* notebooks and has since added several manuscripts of Percy Shelley. The digital editing of the *Frankenstein* notebooks relies upon Charles E. Robinson's magisterial print facsimile edition of *The Frankenstein Notebooks*.[118] Robinson worked valiantly in this edition to overcome many of the challenges of print: compensating for the grayscale facsimile reproductions with extensive notes at the foot of the page to describe physical features of the manuscript; using roman font for Mary's hand and italics for Percy's additions to separate out their contributions; attempting to replicate the irregular cancel lines that appear on the manuscript page; and using shading to signal other complex aspects of the manuscript. The typographical diplomatic transcriptions in print, which are for the most part highly legible, were produced after much trial and error using the word processing software of the 1990s.[119] The large format of the book, and the addition of the relevant passages from the first print edition in a third column – a feature that is unfortunately abandoned in the digital edition – render Robinson's facsimile highly functional for studying the compositional process and the genetic history of the novel. Despite the book's high scholarly value, the first edition is currently out of print; fortunately, a less expensive two-volume paper reissue was released by Routledge in early 2018, a testament to the enduring value of this facsimile edition.

The editors of *The Shelley-Godwin Archive* have attempted to augment the print edition in a number of respects.[120] By using Robinson's transcriptions and attributions for their mark-up, and by including his detailed accounts of the composition of the notebooks and their physical makeup in their site, the archive has moved us some way towards 'uniting the authority of the traditional print edition with the searchable multiple texts made possible by electronic publication'.[121] The editors of the Archive describe as its 'marquee feature' a tool that enables users to toggle between viewing those words on any given page which were written in Mary Shelley's hand, those in Percy Shelley's hand, or both. One can also filter word searches according to these attributions, as well as by added and deleted passages, and it is possible for readers to view both diplomatic and reading texts. As machine-readable and hence searchable texts, and as open source and freely available resource, the *Frankenstein* manuscripts are useable in ways impossible in the print medium. The site is designed to allow users to engage with the material in a variety of ways, either by examining all witnesses of a single text or individual notebooks on their own. This capability derives from the expertise of the project's editors, their knowledge of the source material and their awareness of the different ways in which scholars might wish to approach the material:

> The manuscript notebooks of Percy Shelley, in particular, are generally filled with a variety of material, with the drafts of individual poems scattered throughout on any available pages. While there is much valuable information to be gained by viewing these pages in their notebook order, being able to see in sequence all of the pages belonging to a particular work is also extremely valuable. Over time, we hope to present all known manuscripts for any given work of our four authors. Thus, for example, we will be uniting the fair copy of *Prometheus Unbound* with all of the known drafts for the poem, with the drafts themselves presented, as closely as possible, both in the linear sequence of the work and in the page sequence of the manuscripts in which they are found.[122]

The resource thus combines the ability to study the chronological development of poems and the material form and sequence of writing with individual notebooks; thus *The Shelley-Godwin Archive* seems to allow both what the Cornell Wordsworth produced (a work-focused edition) with what they originally desired to produce (a notebook-focused edition).

These three digital editions emerge from and rely upon the expert knowledge of their editors and their willingness to collaborate and experiment with digital humanists. The editions have drawn upon the innovations and successes of textual editors of Romantic literary manuscripts and their contributions to our understanding of Romantic literary textuality. The editors of these projects have sought to use digital media to advance their own understanding of the unique material features of the literary manuscripts (and, in Blake's case, his illuminating printings). Like the early antiquarians, collectors, publishers, literary friends and family members to whom we owe the survival of the profusion of literary manuscripts from the Romantic period, digital editors, like their print counterparts, are custodians of the manuscript record, and have done much to preserve and disseminate it, bringing a new level of scrutiny to handwritten documents and to the ways in which materiality shapes writing. And like those late-eighteenth-century collectors and bibliophiles who wished to share and save manuscripts from destruction and neglect, digital editors have continued the work of bringing manuscripts out of the archive, in the expectation that many will regard them as 'treasure[s] to be proud of' as well as to learn from.

Conclusion

As we have seen throughout this chapter, many literary manuscripts of the Romantic period have enjoyed a second life after they their creators had composed, revised, and shared them. As material artefacts, manuscripts been valued, preserved, and remediated since the eighteenth century. They were valued by family members and friends, and cherished and preserved for the traces they were felt to hold of the author's physical presence. They were traded, collected, and sometimes mutilated by their possessors. Manuscripts were saved from destruction by antiquarians and studied by scholars and biographers. Signatures and small samples of handwriting were remediated in print, as secondary portraits deemed useful aids to deciphering character. In the late nineteenth and early twentieth centuries, manuscripts of famous authors acquired economic value, a result of their uniqueness and textual significance, and of the belief that such artefacts possess and transmit the aura of their creator's personality and genius. For many subsequent generations, the literary manuscripts of the Romantic authors were consulted by literary scholars and textual editors, treated as essential witnesses in the construction of sound textual editions.

It is only more recently, with the emergence of sociological and bibliographical approaches, that scholars have come to more fully recognise McGann's claim that 'documents are far from self-transparent. They are riven with the multiple histories of their own making.'[123] The scholarly print and digital editions surveyed in this chapter have been attentive to these 'multiple histories', as they have endeavoured to reinstate the materiality of the original. But such an outcome has not been automatic and has certainly not been easy; instead, as Johns argues about early print culture, it has had 'to be *made*'.[124] Recently, scholarly editors have been deeply engaged in understanding digital textuality, as a means of revealing more about manuscripts than their 'linguistic codes' and 'the texts they preserve'. According to Kathryn Sutherland and Marilyn Deegan of *Jane Austen's Fiction Manuscripts*,

> There is a kind of allegiance, against print, between the digital environment and working manuscripts, both of which favour looser or hybrid expressive forms and resist the stability that print prefers. Representation in print tends to confer a solidity or finality on working materials that is not intrinsic: careful consideration of how to present manuscripts in electronic form should enable the preservation of their dynamic and axiological qualities.[125]

The three digital editions of Romantic manuscripts surveyed in this chapter have in large part risen to this challenge, representing literary manuscripts neither as copy-texts, nor as privileged portals into the personality of authors, but rather as witnesses to the practices of literary culture as they coalesce and unfold over time – as dynamic examples of the acts of composing, copying, revising and collecting that constitute the life of writing. The research for this book has been dependent on the consultation of original manuscripts, print editions and facsimiles, *and* digital editions; the handwritten, the published and the digital were all necessary aids to research.[126] And this makes sense, for we inhabit, as did our predecessors, a multimedia world, and its traces are inscribed in notebooks and loose sheets, in drafts and fair copies, as much as in the more fixed and final printed forms their writing often took, sometimes in their lifetimes, sometimes only posthumously, often with the assistance of editors. We should no more think of digital editions as replacing print editions than we should attempt to understand literary history according to a model of supersession, with one medium overtaking another. Rather, as Romantic literary manuscripts are given a digital life, our need to research within a mixed-media economy will persist, as will the inevitable draw back towards the original manuscripts.

Notes

1. Gioia, 'Magical Value of Manuscripts', p. 9.
2. Ibid. pp. 10–11.
3. Jerome McGann, *The Textual Condition*, p. 43.
4. Roger Chartier and Peter Stallybrass, 'What Is a Book?' p. 191.
5. Thomas Astle, *The Origin and Progress of Writing* (1784), p. i. Astle's work was regarded as an 'authoritative source for the history of writing well into the nineteenth century, and was last reprinted in 1876': see Nicholas Hudson, *Writing and European Thought 1600–1830* (1995), pp. 4, 33–4. See also Nigel Ramsay, 'Astle, Thomas (1735–1803)'.
6. Astle, *The Origin and Progress of Writing*, p. i.
7. Ibid. p. i.
8. Ibid. p. xxi.
9. Ibid. pp. ix–x.
10. John Fenn, *Original Letters, written during the reigns of Henry VII, Edward IV, and Richard III*, I: vii.
11. Anna Barbauld, *Miscellaneous Pieces in Prose* (1773), p. 92.
12. Ibid. p. 93.
13. Anna Barbauld, *Legacy for Young Ladies, Consisting of Miscellaneous Pieces, in Prose and Verse* (1826), pp. 77–8.
14. Isaac Disraeli, 'Recovery of Manuscripts', *Curiosities of Literature* (1807), p. 24.
15. Fenn, *Original Letters*, I: ix.
16. Ibid. III: ii.
17. Reiman, *The Study of Modern Manuscripts*, pp. 10–17, 36.
18. Walter Scott, *Chronicles of the Canongate*, pp. 3–4.
19. Thomas Frognal Dibdin, *Bibliophobia* (1832), pp. 8–11. Dibdin also lists prices for the sales of the various manuscripts, pp. 10–11.
20. Ibid. pp. 10–11.
21. Ibid. p. 11.
22. Ibid. pp. 11–12.
23. One of the most notorious examples of mutilation is Keats's autograph of 'I stood tiptoe on a little hill', which Charles Cowden Clarke cut up into thirteen pieces (containing twenty-two fragments of the poem on the rectos and versos) as mementoes for the poet's admirers and friends. Sarah Coleridge also cut up the Quarto Copy Book to satisfy requests for copies of Coleridge's handwriting samples in the 1840s (*The Collected Works of Samuel Taylor Coleridge: Poetical Works*, p. 1174.)
24. William Upcott, 'The Autobiography of a Collector', p. 476. See also 'The Late William Upcott', pp. 473–4.

25. Janet Ing Freeman, 'Upcott, William (1779–1845)' and see my discussion of Upcott in 'Do Women Have a Book History?'
26. A. N. L. Munby, *The Cult of the Autograph Letter in England* (1962), p. 79. An example of the rising commercial interest in autograph collecting can be found in how-to guides such as Henry T. Scott, *Autograph Collecting: A Practical Manual for Amateurs and Historical Students* (1894).
27. Jeffrey F. Hamburger, *Script as Image* (2014), p. 1.
28. Quoted in Douglas, 'Work in Hand: Script, Print and Writing, 1690–1840' (2017), p. 131.
29. Ibid. p. 130.
30. Disraeli, 'Autographs', p. 209.
31. Ibid. p. 210.
32. Dawson Turner, *Guide to the historian, the biographer, the antiquary, the man of literary curiosity, and the collector of autographs* (1848), p. viii.
33. 'Review of *Isographie des Hommes Célèbres* and *Autographs of Royal, Noble, Learned, and Remarkable Personages*', *Retrospective Review* 2 (1828): 352.
34. Isaac Disraeli, 'Autographs', II: 210.
35. Anna Barbauld, *Poems* (1773), p. 52.
36. Austen, *Persuasion*, p. 255.
37. Austen, *Emma*, pp. 321–2.
38. Austen, *Pride and Prejudice*, p. 51.
39. Austen, *Emma*, p. 168.
40. 'Authoresses and Autographs', *New Monthly Magazine* 11 (1824): 220.
41. Austen, *Sense and Sensibility*, p. 96.
42. Austen, *Mansfield Park*, pp. 307–8.
43. Cited in Andrew Burkett, 'Photographing Byron's Hand', p. 139.
44. Quoted in Reiman, *The Study of Modern Manuscripts*, p. 26.
45. *The Works of Lord Byron including the suppressed poems* (1828).
46. See Burkett, 'Photographing Byron's Hand', pp. 132–4; and *CPW*, III: 456.
47. *Poems 1807 to 1818. Poems in the Autograph of Lord Byron once in the possession of the Countess Guiccioli.*(1986), p. xiii.
48. Ibid. p. xiv.
49. On the historical rise of these facsimiles, see David McKitterick, *Old Books, New Technologies: The Representation, Conservation, and Transformation of Books since 1700* (2014), pp. 112–13; Munby notes that autograph collecting is not modern, but began long before attempts were made to engrave facsimiles of handwriting (*Cult of the Autograph Letter*, p. xii).

50. *The plays of William Shakespeare* (1778), I: 200.
51. This was a practice followed in extra-illustration, where portraits (or 'heads') were placed alongside biographical sketches: Marcia Pointon, 'Illustrious Heads', (1993).
52. See the index entry for 'type facsimiles' in *Old Books, New Technologies*, p. 286 and Michael Twyman, *Printing 1770–1970: an Illustrated History* (1998), p. 72.
53. McKitterick, *Old Books, New Technologies*, p. 120.
54. Scholars have made similar claims for digital photography: 'Even passages that had been deleted could be made legible': Grace Ioppolo, 'Switching on the World of Dramatic Manuscripts', p. 66.
55. For more on the facsimile edition, see Meg Roland, 'Facsimile Editions: Gesture and Projection'.
56. Though its discovery was coextensive with that of photography, its application as a means of storing and transmitting data was not realised until the 1920s, when the British Library began to microform its collections of manuscripts and rare books, a process that intensified in the 1930s in the lead-up to the Second World War. Whether reproduced in reels (microfilm) or sheets (microfiche), microforms enabled conservation by protecting fragile manuscripts and books from being handled. Their compactness also meant that they could be stored and distributed far less expensively than paper equivalents. Finally, microform is a stable archival format, predicted to last a minimum of 500 years.
57. Jack Stillinger, *The Poems of John Keats* (1978), p. 7; Mary Shelley reprinted *Alastor* because the first printing was extremely scarce; 'Mont Blanc' (also reprinted) had appeared only in the Shelleys' *History of a Six Weeks' Tour*, and a few other poems had appeared 'scattered in periodical works': Percy Shelley, *Posthumous Poems of Percy Bysshe Shelley* (1824), p. vii.
58. Shelley, *Posthumous Poems*, p. viii.
59. Ghislaine McDayter, 'On the Publication of William Godwin's *Memoirs of the Author of A Vindication of the Rights of Woman*, 1798'.
60. Paul Eggert, 'Apparatus, Text, Interface: How to Read a Printed Critical Edition', p. 99. Byron and Wordsworth are only being re-edited now. Jane Stabler is editing Byron for the Longman Annotated English Poets Series, with the last volume due to be submitted in 2037. Ruth Abbott and Michael Rossington are co-editing William Wordsworth, for the same series.
61. Janine Barchas's important essay, 'Why K. M. Metcalfe (Mrs Chapman) is "Really the Originator in the Editing of Jane Austen"', suggests that K. M. Metcalfe must be credited with first applying these principles to Austen's novels.

62. Hans Walter Gabler, 'The Primacy of the Document in Editing', p. 188.
63. Ibid. p. 198.
64. For more on the facsimile edition, see Roland, 'Facsimile Editions'. According to Roland, facsimile editions represent a 'complex and under-theorised editorial terrain' (abstract; p. 48).
65. Quoted in Curtis, 'The Cornell Wordsworth', p. 2.
66. Ibid. pp. 5, 3.
67. From flyleaf to William Wordsworth, *Last Poems, 1821–1850* (1999).
68. Quoted in Curtis, 'The Cornell Wordsworth', p. 2.
69. Coleridge, *Poetical Works*, I.I, p. lxxix. I have previously noted how Coleridge would reuse his love poems, substituting new names as his love interests shifted, a practice of recycling that is ubiquitous in his poetry: Levy, *Family Authorship*, p. 180, n. 8.
70. Coleridge, *Poetical Works*, I.I, p. lxxx.
71. Ibid. p. cxxi.
72. Ibid. p. cxxiii.
73. Ibid. pp. xcv, cxiv, cxvii, cxix.
74. Ibid. p. lxxxiii.
75. Ibid. p. cxviii.
76. Stillinger, *The Poems of John Keats*, pp. 3–4.
77. John Keats, *The Manuscripts of the Younger Romantics: John Keats, Poems, Transcripts, Letters* (1985), p. xiii.
78. Stillinger, *The Poems of John Keats*, p. 741.
79. Ibid. p. 13.
80. Stuart Curran, 'Review of the *Manuscripts of the Younger Romantics. Shelley. Volumes 1-III*', p. 214.
81. Ibid. p. 216.
82. Michael O'Neill, 'Review of *The Complete Poetry of Percy Bysshe Shelley*, Volume One', para. 3.
83. Percy Shelley, *The Complete Poetry of Percy Bysshe Shelley*, I: xxix. Volume 2 was released in 2004; volume 3 in 2012.
84. Ibid. I: xxix–xxx.
85. Michael O'Neill, 'Review of *The Complete Poetry of Percy Bysshe Shelley*, Volume One', para. 4.
86. Ibid. para 5.
87. Ibid. para. 4.
88. *The Complete Poetry of Percy Bysshe Shelley*, I: xxxii.
89. Ibid. I: xxxii.
90. O'Neill, 'Review of *The Complete Poetry of Percy Bysshe Shelley*, Volume One', para. 5.
91. *The Complete Poetry of Percy Bysshe Shelley*, I: xxxiii.
92. Ibid. I: xxix–xxx.

93. Ibid. I: xxxiii.
94. McGann publishes the early poems arranged as they appeared in *Hours of Idleness*, thus presenting many of the poems out of order of first publication. See Byron, *Complete Poetical Works*, I: xxviii.
95. Ibid. I: xxix, xli.
96. Ibid. I: xli.
97. McGann, *The Textual Condition* (1991), p. 43. This work appeared while McGann was completing his edition of Byron.
98. Jerome McGann, *Radiant Textuality: Literature after the World Wide Web* (2004), p. 56.
99. Ibid. pp. 80, 79.
100. Kathryn Sutherland, 'Anglo-American Editorial Theory', p. 256.
101. Susan Schreibman, 'Digital Scholarly Editing', para. 5.
102. Linda Bree and James McLaverty, 'The Cambridge Edition of the Works of Jonathan Swift and the Future of the Scholarly Edition', p. 129.
103. Marilyn Deegan and Kathryn Sutherland, 'Introduction', p. 5.
104. Eggert, 'Apparatus, Text, Interface', p. 98.
105. Morris Eaves, 'Picture Problems: X-Editing Images 1992–2010', para. 6.
106. For a thorough examination of *The William Blake Archive*'s features and usability, see Kendal Crawford and Michelle Levy, 'Review of "The William Blake Archive"' and 'Review of "The William Blake Archive (Upgrade)"'.
107. Schriebman, 'Digital Scholarly Editing', para. 41.
108. Keats's manuscripts held by the Houghton Library, Harvard University, have been digitised but not transcribed, and the same is true of manuscripts in the possession of the Wordsworth Trust. Unlike the *William Blake Archive*, however, which is free, the digital collection of Wordsworth's manuscripts is available only via subscription from Adam Matthew. Further, although the metadata are excellent, none of the manuscripts have been transcribed and there are no critical annotations. Eventually, the Shelley-Godwin archive will include the literary manuscripts that survive of Mary Wollstonecraft.
109. Kathryn Sutherland (ed.), *Jane Austen's Fiction Manuscripts: A Digital Edition*, <http://www.janeausten.ac.uk>.
110. Ibid. Introduction.
111. *Jane Austen's Manuscript Works*, ed. Bree, Sabor, and Todd.
112. See *The Cambridge Edition of the Works of Jane Austen: Persuasion*, ed. Todd and Blank; *Juvenilia*, ed. Sabor; *Later Manuscripts*, ed. Todd and Bree.
113. Matthew Driscoll and Elena Pierazzo, *Digital Scholarly Editing: Theories and Practices* (2016), p. 5.

114. For a detailed account of the edition's principle features, see my 'Review of "Jane Austen's Fiction Manuscripts"'.
115. Sutherland (ed.), Editorial Principles, *Jane Austen's Fiction Manuscripts: A Digital Edition*.
116. Hamburger, *Script as Image*, 1.
117. Sutherland (ed.), Editorial Principles, *Jane Austen's Fiction Manuscripts: A Digital Edition*.
118. Mary Shelley, *The Frankenstein Notebooks: A Facsimile Edition* (1996).
119. Ibid. p. xi.
120. *The Shelley-Godwin Archive*, ed. Neil Fraistat, Elizabeth Denlinger and Raffaele Viglianti. Available at <http://shelleygodwinarchive.org/>.
121. Deegan and Sutherland, 'Introduction', *Text Editing, Print and the Digital World* (2009), p. 6.
122. *The Shelley-Godwin Archive*, 'Project Introduction'.
123. Jerome McGann, *A New Republic of Letters: Memory and Scholarship in the Age of Digital Reproduction* (2014), p. 45.
124. Johns, *The Nature of the Book*, p. 2.
125. Deegan and Sutherland, 'Introduction', *Text Editing, Print and the Digital World* (2009), p. 8. Frederike Neuber, in his review of the *Shelley-Godwin Archive*, notes two weaknesses; the failure to include the first print edition for comparison purposes (as Robinson does in the print facsimile); and the failure to use a more robust genetic encoding model to provide 'further layers reconstructing the chronology of the writing process': see 'Review of "The Shelley-Godwin Archive: The edition of Mary Shelley's Frankenstein Notebooks"' (para. 22).
126. A fuller discussion of digital remediations of manuscripts, particularly in relation to women's manuscripts, may be found in Laura Estill and Michelle Levy, 'Evaluating digital remediations of women's manuscripts'.

Afterword: Blake's Digitised Printed Script

This coda brings *Literary Manuscript Culture in Romantic Britain* to a close with a short consideration of William Blake's 'Illuminated Printing', his practice of conjoined printing of word and image, which he describes as a 'method of Printing both Letter-press and Engraving in a style more ornamental, uniform, and grand, than any before discovered'.[1] Blake's unique process for printing manuscripts becomes emblematic of the connections between the two media that have been the subject of this book. By fusing the roles of author and publisher, illustrator and bookseller, Blake sought to collapse the communications circuit, consolidating it within a single agent – himself. As Michael Phillips notes:

> By writing his own text, making his own designs and etching them together in relief so that the entire page could be printed from the same surface, Blake placed himself in sole charge of each step in the creation, reproduction, pricing, and publication of his illuminated books, apart from making the paper.[2]

Blake's motivations for devising a method of printing and book production 'which combines the Painter and the Poet' points to his dissatisfaction with contemporary book production and to his desire to create a material form fusing script and drawing, letter-press and engraving.

As a visual artist and commercial engraver, Blake was intimately familiar with the separate processes used to reproduce and combine words and images within printed books. As Joseph Viscomi notes, 'the conventional illustrated book was the product of much divided labour',[3] and this division was readily apparent to any reader. If words and images were reproduced on a single page, they necessarily occupied separate regions of the page, reflecting the different process used for printing letterpress and engraving images: first, letterpress would be printed leaving a blank space in an area where the engraving was to be printed, and then the sheet would be printed by the engravers, who would impress the engraving into the blank.[4] Image and text could be further divided within the book itself, as when separate engraved leaves were tipped into letterpress books. In these cases, print and letterpress were usually printed on noticeably different paper, and, whereas letterpress would be printed on both sides, engraving would appear usually only on one side, visually enhancing the separation between the two: 'technically, such integration [of text and illustration] was possible in conventional (intaglio) etching . . . , but the economics of publishing had long defined etching as image reproduction and letterpress as text reproduction'.[5] Printing techniques of the day simply could not replicate the richly integrated world of the illuminated manuscript, in which words and images, black ink and coloured pigments, were combined.

Blake's attempt to reunite word and image, script and print, resulted in his experimental form of illuminated printing.[6] The plate from Copy T of 'The Little Boy Lost' (Plate 16), presents the horizontal separation between image and word often seen in letterpress pages with engravings, but as may be seen within this plate, Blake's new technique allowed for greater interpenetration of word and image, 'ventur[ing] well beyond existing practice and the physical constraints of letterpress'.[7] In the plate of 'Little Boy Lost', angels enfold the text of the poem and tendrils reach within it, repeating the poem's motif of the enveloping forest and the encroaching darkness in which the boy finds himself. Blake also uses a soft watercolour wash applied to the text area and a uniform colour scheme to wed word and image. This effect is even more apparent in other plates in Copy T of *Songs*, where the background (usually a mottled sky) becomes the shared ground and thus integrates words and image into a cohesive whole.[8] 'Infant Joy' (Plate 17) provides such an example.

By developing a form of printing that unified word and image, Blake achieved the 'integrality of the acts of writing and drawing'.[9] But Blake, by abandoning the use of letterpress and reproducing text not by the compositor's art of setting type, nor by using a burin, the engraver's tool, went further still in his effort to emulate and represent the human hand that writes letters and draws images. By writing directly on the copper plate with a quill or a brush – it is a subject of debate which implement he used, or if he used both at different times – he created texts that were written, not composed with type or etched by engraving.[10] Viscomi claims that 'with tools and materials properly made, Blake could write his texts as easily as manuscript'.[11] Blake did have to learn how to write in reverse, a form of mirror writing used by engravers that creates a mediated process for the reproduction of writing.[12] Nevertheless, both the processes Blake invented and the effect he produced emphasises the human hand as the originator of text.

Blake's unique style of printed script warrants attention. Plates 16 and 17 illustrate some of the complexity apparent in his reproduction of handwriting. In these plates, Blake uses a cursive hand for his title and a roman script, more evocative of typography, for the text of the poem itself. The typographical elements of the text of the poem are evident in the vertical orientation of the letters, the lack of joined up words, the use of serifs, and – perhaps most tellingly in Plate 16 – the double-story 'g', a clear marker of the period's print typography. Blake's double-story 'g' imitates the revived Carolingian of early humanist minuscule,[13] and also the typographic forms that descended from this script, reminding us that from its earliest days, print (as with incunabula) imitated manuscript. The handwriting reflected in Blake's illuminated books is decidedly not the regulated and ornamented copperplate script used by engravers of the period for title pages and captions in printed illustrations.[14] Rather, Blake's handwriting more closely approximates the ordinary fair-copy hand of the period. The result is handwriting that 'creates the intimacy of a personal, expressive voice precisely because it does not overwhelm readers with its style'.[15] In other words, Blake's hand offers some of the spontaneity and irregularity that informs the actual handwriting of his day, which, as we have seen in the last chapter, was believed to convey authenticity and individuality. At the same time, the minute size and compactness of the letters Blake used for his textual reproductions in the illuminating printings, the occasional blurring caused by printing, the encroachments of design and colouring, and the idiosyncrasies of the hand – all produce challenges of legibility, a distancing effect that might have estranged some of his readers.

These difficulties are apparent in Blake's plate for 'Infant Joy', with its overwhelming flower design, intense coloration, and text printed in a faint red ink.

Blake's emulation of the handwritten thus provides both an echo of the scribal medium and a departure from it. We are, of course, not reading Blake's actual handwriting – ink applied to the page with the use of a writing implement – but rather a printed impression of ink applied to plate onto which Blake has written and drawn, in reverse, with a chemical solution. Blake's efforts do, however, perhaps more than print, situate his productions within an artisanal framework, drawing his productions back to the making hand (and body) and thus emphasising the craftsmanship of bookmaking; at the same time, however, he separates us from the moment of composition and creation through the intervention of the printing plate, with its reproductive capacity mediating the connection between artist/poet and the reader/viewer. Furthermore, the 'manuscript' of the plate itself is both illegible, since the text is written in reverse, and inchoate, since it does not achieve its final form until it is printed. Further, Viscomi and Phillips believe that Blake did not compose directly onto the plate but worked from drafts of image and text, adding a further level of mediation, with the plate itself serving as the fair copy.[16] Our distance from the creative origins of Blake's productions is further eroded by his destruction of the copper plates and most of the manuscript drafts of his poems, thereby enacting the practices of the print shop, in which press copies were routinely discarded after use.[17]

Blake's remediation of handwriting and his attempt to replicate the visual potentiality of illuminated manuscripts could not escape his enmeshment in the world of print in other respects as well. He could have produced single copies of exquisite illuminated manuscripts, possibly with more ease than his illuminating prints, but he chose instead to use a complicated, experimental reproductive technique. He originally claimed that he could produce his illuminated printings 'at less than one-fourth the expense' of print. However, the promised efficiencies of his method proved unachievable: in thirty-eight years he produced fewer than twenty-five copies of *Songs*.[18] Blake was undoubtedly attracted to the creativity enabled by experimentation, and the artistic control made possible by taking over all aspects of production. At the same time, Blake's method in many ways replicated a model of print production. The investment he made creating plates (and the cost of the copper for the plates) meant that the texts themselves were more fixed and less malleable than a handwritten (and possibly even a letterpress) version. With his wife, he shared the labour of producing his illuminated books, dividing some of the production tasks and thus replicating the circuit model present within the book trades. He even experimented, around 1793, with colour printing, a further attempt to mechanise a process that was usually done by hand. The impressions were not printed and coloured one at a time but rather in sets, with individual books compiled in assembly-line fashion to 'indicate edition printing and coloring', rather than each book being printed and finished individually, one at a time.[19] After more than three decades, he claimed that '[t]he Few [illuminated books] I have Printed & Sold are sufficient to have gained me great reputation as an Artist which was the chief thing Intended', and indeed, most of his copies were given or sold to artists, who were both friends and patrons.[20]

Ultimately, however, Blake was no more successful in separating his own techniques and processes from the realm of print than he was in separating his artistic career from his work as a commercial engraver. Blake's work on his illuminated printings 'occup[ied] very specific, concentrated, and dateable periods' in his life,[21] and his remunerated engraving work for a public audience proved indispensable to financing the production of the illuminated books, the audience for which was necessarily far more limited. Scholars have generated new understandings of Blake's career, in which the handmade, illuminated books are part of his larger output of material, much of which was for the commercial market. Similarly, this study calls for an adjustment to our understandings of the careers of Barbauld, Austen and Byron, as authors whose involvement with print might also be described as 'very specific, concentrated'. Barbauld's career as a print poet, certainly in stand-alone publications, was highly focused, as was Austen's six-year stint as a published novelist. After 1809, Byron's career in print was characterised almost exclusively by the publication of long poems. In all three cases, the success these authors enjoyed in their engagements with print have overshadowed their persistent and extensive use of script. None of these authors, however, wrote exclusively for print; just as Blake moved between creative and commercial bookmaking, so did they move between different reproductive technologies, for different purposes, at different times.

Blake's 'illuminating printings' animate, both in the form of their manufacture and in their material appearance, the conjoined histories of the media of script and print, which are neither successive nor parallel in their development but rather simultaneous and intermingled.[22] Throughout this book, I have explored some of the many ways in which the culture of script was dynamically entangled with print, and Blake's illuminated printings, and the processes used to create them, demonstrate a similar complexity and interdependence. Phillips suggests that for Blake, motives of safety as much as of aesthetic desire encouraged his method of printing the illuminated books. Printing to a high standard kept costs high, thus ensuring that his purchasers were limited to an audience who could be trusted to sympathise with his radical views. In other words, as with many of the other authors examined in this book, manuscript (or in Blake's case, its simulacrum) provided an alternative space for cultural expression, one that always existed in relation to, but was never identical with, print.

The Songs of Innocence and of Experience aims at '[s]hewing the two contrary states of the human soul', representing the nature of innocence and experience as both cyclical and complementary, alternating and antagonistic. Blake, through his illuminated printings, sought to deconstruct the categories of media within which he and other authors and artists of his day worked, bringing forth their fundamental inseparability. He thus provides us with an exemplum of media interactivity, whether understood on the level of his career, his books or his plates. The *William Blake Archive*, an online repository of Blake's works, further positions Blake's material artefacts as objects of remediation. Morris Eaves, writing about his involvement in the Archive, addresses the opportunities and dangers of digitising Blake. On the one hand, he notes, '[a]fter centuries of image deprivation, we now bathe in a sea of pictures, most of them digitised at some stage'.[23] On the other hand, the reproduction of Blake's printed manuscripts in digital form, no matter how thoughtfully and rigorously performed, involves distortions, in size, colour and dimensionality.[24] The books that Blake printed and stitched together, and the sense of his works as unfolding sequentially within the bibliographical codes of the bound book, are also lost when viewed as discrete windows on screens. As Luisa Calè observes:

The archival logic of the page and the primacy of design has shaped the digital facsimiles uploaded on the Blake Archive, which privilege the printed area of the page, as if disbound, trimmed of its margins, and seen through a window. The dynamism of the book as a technology for turning the pages is left to the imagination.[25]

Just as Blake's illuminated books belie the complex technical means used to create them, the seeming transparency and immediacy of digital media must not blind us to the losses involved in translating a material form into a (more) immaterial one.

This book has focused on the material and cultural history of print and script and their intertwining through the late eighteenth and early nineteenth centuries. Whereas some authors, like Lamb, protested against the unsettled nature of manuscript, and its ability to record uncertainty and contingency for posterity, others living at the time, and for the two centuries that have followed, have valued it precisely for this reason. Most of the authors explored in this book, even some of the most celebrated, worked within a multimodal world, transitioning, whether seamlessly or with difficulty, between the realms of script and print. Literary reviews embraced and rejected writing printed from social manuscripts; and authors and collectors engaged with the meaning and value of handwritten documents. We are still grappling with the enormous manuscript legacy we have inherited, and how it impacts the interconnected textual, literary and bibliographical histories of the period. Concluding with Blake reminds us that print and script are inevitably part of a larger media ecology, one that involves visual as well as oral culture. *Literary Manuscript Culture in Romantic Britain* takes one step towards understanding the ongoing role that literary manuscripts played within this wider media landscape, leaving much more work to be done.

Notes

1. From his prospectus of 1793, quoted in Joseph Viscomi, 'Illuminated Printing', p. 41.
2. Michael Phillips, *William Blake: The Creation of the Songs, from manuscript to illuminated printing* (1987), p. 29.
3. Viscomi, 'Illuminated Printing', p. 42.
4. See Phillips, *Williams Blake*, pp. 29–30.

5. Viscomi, 'Illuminated Printing', p. 41.
6. Although Viscomi asserts that the combination of the word and image 'appears not to have been the impetus for the invention', it is clearly the result he achieves; and it is almost certain that his invention was the result of a constellation of forces and motivations: ibid. p. 41.
7. Michael Phillips, 'Printing Blake's *Songs*, 1789–1794', p. 221.
8. For example, 'Introduction' (Object 4), 'The Shepherd' (Object 5), and 'The Lamb' (Object 8) in *The William Blake Archive*, Morris Eaves, Robert Essick, and Joseph Viscomi (eds), 1996. Available at <http://www.blakearchive.org>.
9. Joseph Viscomi, *Blake and the Idea of the Book* (1993), p. 25.
10. Alexander S. Gourlay, 'Review of Viscomi, *Blake and the Idea of the Book*', p. 33.
11. Viscomi, *Blake and the Idea of the Book*, p. 60.
12. Ibid. p. 31.
13. Laurent Pflughaupt, *Letter by Letter: An Alphabetical Miscellany* (2007), pp. 71–3.
14. Philips suggests that this development was the result of Blake's growing accomplishment in mirror writing, *The Creation of the Songs*, p. 18.
15. Viscomi, *Blake and the Idea of the Book*, p. 59.
16. Ibid. p. 30; Phillips, *William Blake*, p. 1.
17. Viscomi believes that Blake did not compose his poems (as opposed to his designs) directly on the plate and provides the rationale described for why these were not preserved. According to Viscomi as well, 'Blake left virtually no manuscripts of the illuminated poems': *Blake and the Idea of the Book*, p. 30. Only two notebooks containing drafts for the illuminated poems have been preserved, with the most important being British Library Add MS 49460. This notebook was preserved by Blake almost certainly because its original owner was his brother Robert, who died at age seventeen in 1787: Phillips, *William Blake*, pp. 1, 32.
18. Phillips, 'Printing Blake's *Songs*', p. 206.
19. Viscomi, *Blake and the Idea of the Book*, pp. 112–13, 131, 142. Gourlay points out that we should be careful not to 'put undue emphasis on "editions" when they are as small and as various as these. Even uncoloured copies printed at the same time in the same ink on the same paper and bound in the same order will manifest differences that may be significant from an editorial point of view' ('Review of Viscomi', p. 34).
20. Viscomi, 'Illuminated Printing', p. 60; Philips, *William Blake*, p. 113.
21. Viscomi, *Blake and the Idea of the Book*, p. 156.
22. They also gesture idealistically to a past that never was, for throughout most of the period in which illuminated manuscripts were made, different aspects of production were specialised, with labour divided between scribes, illustrators, binders, and others.

23. Eaves, 'Picture Problems', para.1.
24. Eaves observes that human intervention is required at every stage to ensure compliance with 'a strict set of established guidelines' and requires 'the color correction of every image on calibrated equipment': ibid. para. 6.
25. Luisa Calè, 'Book Disorders: Composite Forms and the Alternative Possibilities of the Disbound Page', unpublished paper delivered at Harvard University, 14 May 2015, 23. A version of this paper has now been published: 'Blake, Young, and the Poetics of the Composite Page'.

References

Manuscript Collections Consulted

Beinecke Library
Bodleian Library, Oxford
British Library
Chawton House Library
Houghton Library, Harvard University
Huntington Library
John and Virginia Murray
King's College, Cambridge
National Library of Scotland
Pforzheimer Collection, New York Public Library
Wordsworth Trust

Additional Sources

Adams, John, *The Portable John Adams*, ed. John Patrick Diggins (New York: Penguin, 2004).
[Advertisement], *Annual Review* 3 (1804): [957–8].
'Advertisement', *Edinburgh Review* 1, no. 1 (October 1802): n.p.
'Advertisement', *Edinburgh Review* 3, no. 5 (October 1803): n.p.
Aikin, John, *Annual Register, or a View of the History, Politics and Literature, for the Year 1818* (London: Baldwin, Cradock and Joy, 1819).
Aikin, John, *Essays on Song-Writing* (London: J. Johnson, 1772).
Aikin, Lucy, 'Mrs Barbauld's MSS. To the Editor', *Monthly Repository and Review*, n.s., II (January–December 1828): 55.
Aikin, Lucy, 'Memoirs', in *Works of Anna Laetitia Barbauld*, ed. Lucy Aikin, 2 vols (London: Longman, Hurst, Rees, Orme, Brown, and Green, 1825).
Aikin, Lucy, 'Southey and "The Aikins": His Injustice Towards Mrs. Barbauld', *Gentleman's Magazine*, July 1850, 26–7.

Alexander, Meena, *Women in Romanticism: Mary Wollstonecraft, Dorothy Wordsworth, and Mary Shelley* (Basingstoke: Macmillan, 1989).
Allan, David, *Commonplace Books and Reading in Georgian England* (Cambridge: Cambridge University Press, 2010).
Allen, Reggie. 'The Sonnets of William Hayley and Gift Exchange', *European Romantic Review* 13 (2002): 383–92.
Anderson, Chris, *The Long Tail: Why the Future of Business Is Selling Less of More* (New York: Hyperion, 2006).
Astle, Thomas, *The Origin and Progress of Writing, as well Hieroglyphic as Elementary, illustrated by engravings taken from marbles, manuscripts and charters, ancient and modern, also, some account of the origin and progress of printing* (London: T. Payne, [1775] 1784).
Austen, Henry, 'Biographical Notice of the Author', in *Northanger Abbey: and Persuasion* (London: John Murray, 1818), pp. v–xvi.
Austen, Henry, 'Biographical Notice of the Author', in James Edward Austen-Leigh, *A Memoir of Jane Austen and Other Family Recollections*, ed. Kathryn Sutherland (Oxford: Oxford University Press, 2002), pp. 135–44.
Austen, Jane, *The Cambridge Edition of the Works of Jane Austen: Emma*, ed. Richard Cronin and Dorothy McMillan (Cambridge: Cambridge University Press, 2005).
Austen, Jane, *The Cambridge Edition of the Works of Jane Austen: Juvenilia*, ed. Peter Sabor (Cambridge: Cambridge University Press, 2006).
Austen, Jane, *The Cambridge Edition of the Works of Jane Austen: Later Manuscripts*, ed. Janet Todd and Linda Bree (Cambridge: Cambridge University Press, 2008).
Austen, Jane, *The Cambridge Edition of the Works of Jane Austen: Mansfield Park*, ed. John Wiltshire (Cambridge: Cambridge University Press, 2006).
Austen, Jane, *The Cambridge Edition of the Works of Jane Austen: Northanger Abbey*, ed. Barbara M. Benedict and Deirdre Le Faye (Cambridge: Cambridge University Press, 2006).
Austen, Jane, *The Cambridge Edition of the Works of Jane Austen: Persuasion*, ed. Janet Todd and Antje Blank (Cambridge: Cambridge University Press, 2006).
Austen, Jane, *The Cambridge Edition of the Works of Jane Austen: Pride and Prejudice*, ed. Pat Rogers (Cambridge: Cambridge University Press, 2006).
Austen, Jane, *The Cambridge Edition of the Works of Jane Austen: Sense and Sensibility*, ed. Edward Copeland (Cambridge: Cambridge University Press, 2006).
Austen, Jane, *Jane Austen: Minor Works*, ed. R. W. Chapman (Oxford: Oxford University Press, 1982).

Austen, Jane, *Jane Austen's Letters*, 3rd edn, ed. Deirdre Le Faye (New York: Oxford University Press, 1995).

Austen, Jane, *Jane Austen's Manuscript Works*, ed. Linda Bree, Peter Sabor and Janet Todd (Peterborough, ON: Broadview Press, 2012).

Austen-Leigh, James Edward, *A Memoir of Jane Austen: And Other Family Recollections*, ed. Kathryn Sutherland (Oxford: Oxford University Press, 2002).

'Authoresses and Autographs', *New Monthly Magazine* 11 (1824): 217–24.

Backscheider, Paula, *Eighteenth-Century Women Poets and Their Poetry: Inventing Agency, Inventing Genre* (Baltimore: Johns Hopkins University Press, 2008).

Backsheider, Paula, and Catherine Ingrassia (eds), *British Women Poets of the Long Eighteenth Century: An Anthology* (Baltimore: Johns Hopkins University Press, 2009).

Baillie, Joanna, *A Collection of Poems: Chiefly in Manuscript, and from Living Authors* (London: Longman, Hurst Reese, Orme, and Brown, 1823).

Barbauld, Anna, *Anna Letitia Barbauld: Selected Poetry and Prose*, ed. William McCarthy and Elizabeth Kraft (Peterborough, ON: Broadview Press, 2002).

Barbauld, Anna, *Eighteen Hundred and Eleven* (London: Joseph Johnson, 1812).

Barbauld, Anna, *Epistle to William Wilberforce, Esq. On the rejection of the bill for abolishing the slave trade* (London: Joseph Johnson, 1791).

Barbauld, Anna, 'Essay on the Origins and Progress of Novel Writing', in *The British Novelists* (London: Rivington, 1810).

Barbauld, Anna, *Legacy for Young Ladies, Consisting of Miscellaneous Pieces, in Prose and Verse*, ed. Lucy Aikin (London: Longman, 1826).

Barbauld, Anna, *Miscellaneous Pieces in Prose* (London: J. Johnson, 1773).

Barbauld, Anna, *Poems* (London: Joseph Johnson, 1773).

Barbauld, Anna, *Poems by Anna Laetitia Barbauld* (London: Joseph Johnson, 1792).

Barbauld, Anna, *The Poems of Anna Letitia Barbauld*, ed. William McCarthy and Elizabeth Kraft (Athens and London: University of Georgia Press, 1994).

Barbauld, Anna, 'A Thought on Death', *Christian Disciple* [Boston], n.s. 3 (November–December 1821): 440; '*Christian Disciple*, n.s. 4 (September–October 1822): 322–3; *Monthly Repository* 17 (October 1822): 636; *Monthly Repository* 17 (November 1822): 679; *New-York Literary Journal, and Belles-Lettres Repository* 3, no. 2 (June 15, 1820): 158.

Barbauld, Anna, *Works of Anna Laetitia Barbauld*, ed. Lucy Aikin, 2 vols (London: Longman, Hurst, Rees, Orme, Brown, and Green, 1825).

Barbauld, Anna and John Aikin, *Evenings at Home; or, the Juvenile Budget Opened*, 6 vols (London: J. Johnson, 1792–6).

Barchas, Janine, *Matters of Fact in Austen: History, Location, and Celebrity* (Baltimore: Johns Hopkins University Press, 2012).

Barchas, 'Why K. M. Metcalfe (Mrs Chapman) is "Really the Originator in the Editing of Jane Austen"', *Review of English Studies* 68: 125 (1 June 2017): 583–611, <https://doi-org.proxy.lib.sfu.ca/10.1093/res/hgw149>.

Barker, Hannah, 'England, 1760–1815', in Hannah Barker and Simon Burrows (eds), *Press, Politics and the Public Sphere in Europe and North America 1760–1820* (Cambridge: Cambridge University Press, 2002), pp. 93–112.

Barnard, Teresa, *Anna Seward: A Constructed Life: A Critical Biography* (Farnham: Ashgate, 2009).

Batchelor, Jennie, *Women's Work: Labour, Gender, Authorship, 1750–1830* (Manchester: Manchester University Press, 2010).

Beal, Peter, Jeremy Griffiths and A. S. G. Edwards (eds), *English Manuscript Studies 1100–1700* (New York: Oxford University Press, 1989).

Behrendt, Stephen C., *British Women Poets and the Romantic Writing Community* (Baltimore: Johns Hopkins University Press, 2009).

Bellanca, Mary Ellen, 'After-Life-Writing: Dorothy Wordsworth's Journals in the Memoirs of William Wordsworth', *European Romantic Review* 25 (April 2014): 201–18.

'Belles Lettres and Miscellanies', *Annual Review* 1 (1802): 629.

Bettany, G. T., 'Hunter, Anne (1742/3–1821)', revised by M. Clare Loughlin-Chow, in *Oxford Dictionary of National Biography* (Oxford: Oxford University Press, 2004).

Blake, William, *Milton: A Poem and the Final Illuminated Works*, ed. Robert Essick and Joseph Viscomi (Princeton: Princeton University Press, 1998).

Blake, William, *Songs of Innocence and Songs of Experience*, British Museum, copy T.

Bland, Mark, *A Guide to Early Printed Books and Manuscripts* (Malden, MA: Blackwell, 2013).

Blank, Antje, 'Charlotte Smith after 200 Years', *Women's Writing* 16, no. 1 (2009): 1–5.

Bree, Linda and James McLaverty, 'The Cambridge Edition of the Works of Jonathan Swift and the Future of the Scholarly Edition', in Marilyn Deegan and Kathryn Sutherland (eds), *Text Editing, Print and the Digital World* (Farnham: Ashgate, 2009), pp. 127–36.

Broadview Anthology of British Literature: The Age of Romanticism, ed. Joseph Black, 2nd edn, vol. 4 (Peterborough, ON: Broadview Press, 2010).

Burke, Edmund, *The Writings and Speeches of Edmund Burke. Vol. VIII: The French Revolution 1790–1794*, ed. L. G. Mitchell (Oxford: Oxford University Press, 1999).

Burkett, Andrew, 'Photographing Byron's Hand', *European Romantic Review* 26, no. 2 (2005): 129–48. doi:10.1080/10509585.2015.1004543.

Butler, James A., 'Poetry 1798–1807: *Lyrical Ballads* and *Poems, in Two Volumes*', in *Cambridge Companion to Wordsworth*, ed. Stephen Gill (Cambridge: Cambridge University Press, 2013), pp. 38–54.

Calè, Luisa, 'Book Disorders: Composite Forms and the Alternative Possibilities of the Disbound Page', unpublished paper delivered at Harvard University, 14 May 2015.

Calè, Luisa, 'Blake, Young, and the Poetics of the Composite Page', *Huntington Library Quarterly* 80(3) (2017): 453–79. Project MUSE, doi:10.1353/hlq.2017.0026.

Cameron, Sharon, *Choosing Not Choosing: Dickinson's Fascicles* (Chicago: University of Chicago Press, 1992).

Carlson, Julia S., *Romantic Marks and Measures: Wordsworth's Poetry in Fields of Print* (Philadelphia: University of Pennsylvania Press, 2016).

Chapman, R. W., 'Preface', in *Fragment of a Novel Written by Jane Austen: January–March 1817; Now First Printed from the Manuscript*, n.p. (Oxford: Clarendon Press, 1925).

Chartier, Roger and Peter Stallybrass, 'What Is a Book?', in *The Cambridge Companion to Textual Scholarship*, ed. Neil Fraistat and Julia Flanders (Cambridge: Cambridge University Press, 2013), pp. 188–204.

Chen, Anna, 'In One's Own Hand: Seeing Manuscripts in a Digital Age', *Digital Humanities Quarterly* 6.2 (2012) <http://www.digitalhumanities.org/dhq/vol/6/2/000138/000138.html> (accessed 30 April 2015).

Christie, William, *The Edinburgh Review in the Literary Culture of Romantic Britain: Mammoth and Megalonyx* (London: Pickering & Chatto, 2009).

Clery, Emma, *Eighteen Hundred and Eleven: Poetry, Protest and Economic Crisis* (Cambridge: Cambridge University Press, 2017).

Cochran, Peter (ed.), *Byron's Early Poems of Nottinghamshire and London* (Hucknall: International Byron Society, n.d.) <https://petercochran.files.wordpress.com/2009/03/poems_of_nottinghamshire_and_london.pdf>.

Coleridge, Samuel Taylor, *Biographia Literaria*, in *The Collected Works of Samuel Taylor Coleridge*, ed. James Engell and W. Jackson Bate, 23 vols, vol. 7 (Princeton: Princeton University Press, 1983).

Coleridge, Samuel Taylor, *Collected Letters of Samuel Taylor Coleridge*, ed. E. L. Griggs (Oxford: Clarendon Press, 1956).

Coleridge, Samuel Taylor, *The Collected Works of Samuel Taylor Coleridge: Poetical Works*, ed. J. C. C. Mays (Princeton: Princeton University Press, 2001).

Coleridge, Samuel Taylor, *Sibylline Leaves: A Collection of Poems* (London: Fenner, 1817).

Comitini, Patricia, '"More Than Half a Poet": Vocational Philanthropy and Dorothy Wordsworth's *Grasmere Journals*', *European Romantic Review* 14 (2003) 307–22.

Crawford, Julie, *Mediatrix: Women, Politics and Literary Production in Early Modern England* (Oxford: Oxford University Press, 2014).

Crawford, Kendal and Michelle Levy, 'Review of "The William Blake Archive"', *RIDE* 5 (2017). doi: 10.18716/ride.a.5.5 (accessed January 30 2019).

Crawford, Kendal and Michelle Levy, 'Review of "The William Blake Archive (Upgrade)"', *RIDE* 7 (2017). doi: 10.18716/ride.a.7.5 (accessed 30 January 2019).

Crick, Julia C. and Alexandra Walsham (eds), *The Uses of Script and Print, 1300–1700* (Cambridge: Cambridge University Press, 2004).

[Croker, John Wilson], 'Mrs. Barbauld's *Eighteen Hundred and Eleven*', *Quarterly Review* 7 (June 1812): 309–13.

Curran, Stuart, 'Review of the *Manuscripts of the Younger Romantics. Shelley*. Volumes I–III', *Keats-Shelley Journal* 36 (1987): 213–16.

Curran, Stuart, 'Women and the *Edinburgh Review*', in Demata and Wu, pp. 195–209.

Curtis, Jared, 'The Cornell Wordsworth: A History' (Cornell University Press, n.d.) <http://www.cornellpress.cornell.edu/html/WYSIWYGfiles/files/Cornell_Wordsworth_History.pdf> (accessed 30 April 2015).

Dallas, Robert Charles, *Recollections of the Life of Lord Byron* (London: Charles Knight, 1824).

Darnton, Robert, 'What Is the History of Books?', *Daedalus* 111, no. 3 (1982): 65–83.

Deegan, Marilyn and Sutherland, Katherine, 'Introduction', in *Text Editing, Print and the Digital World* (Farnham: Ashgate, 2009), pp. 1–9.

Demata, Massimiliano, 'Prejudiced Knowledge: Travel Literature in the *Edinburgh Review*', in Demata and Wu, pp. 82–101.

Demata, Massimiliano and Duncan Wu (eds), *British Romanticism and the Edinburgh Review: Bicentenary Essays* (Houndmills: Palgrave Macmillan, 2002).

Demata, Massimiliano and Duncan Wu (eds), 'Introduction', in Demata and Wu, pp. 1–12.

De Quincey, Thomas, 'William Wordsworth', in David Wright (ed.), *Recollections of the Lakes and the Lake Poets* (London: Penguin, 1970).

Dibdin, Thomas Frognal, *Bibliophobia* (London: Henry Bohn, 1832).

Disraeli, Isaac, 'Autographs', in *A Second Series of Curiosities of Literature*, 3 vols (London: John Murray, 1824), II: 207–14.

Disraeli, Isaac, 'Recovery of Manuscripts', in *Curiosities of Literature*, 5th edn (London: John Murray, 1807), pp. 24–34.

Doody, Margaret Ann, 'The Early Short Fiction', in Edward Copeland and Juliet McMaster (eds), *The Cambridge Companion to Jane Austen* (Cambridge: Cambridge University Press, 1997), pp. 72–86.

Douglas, Aileen, *Work in Hand: Script, Print and Writing, 1690–1840* (Oxford: Oxford University Press, 2017).

Driscoll, Matthew and Elena Pierazzo, *Digital Scholarly Editing: Theories and Practices* (Cambridge: Open Book, 2016).

Duguid, Paul, 'Material Matters: The Past and Futurology of the Book', in David Finkelstein and Alistair McCleery (eds), *Book History Reader* (New York: Routledge, 2006), pp. 494–508.

Dyer, Gary, *British Satire and the Politics of Style, 1789–1832* (Cambridge: Cambridge University Press, 1997).

Dyer, Gary, 'The Circulation of Satirical Poetry in the Regency', *Keats-Shelley Journal* 61 (2012): 65–73.

Eaves, Morris, 'Picture Problems: X-Editing Images 1992-2010', *Digital Humanities Quarterly* 3, no. 3 (2009).

Eggert, Paul, 'Apparatus, Text, Interface: How to Read a Printed Critical Edition', in Neil Fraistat and Julia Flanders (eds), *The Cambridge Companion to Textual Scholarship* (Cambridge: Cambridge University Press, 2013), pp. 97–118.

Enfield, William, *Hymns for Public Worship* (London: Warrington, 1772).

Erdman, David V. and David Worrall (eds), *The Manuscripts of the Younger Romantics: Childe Harold's Pilgrimage: A Critical, Composite Edition*, vol. VI. General Editor Donald Reiman (New York and London: Garland Publishing, 1991).

Erickson, Lee, *The Economy of Literary Form: English Literature and the Industrialization of Publishing, 1800–1850* (Baltimore: Johns Hopkins University Press, 1996).

Estill, Laura and Michelle Levy, 'Evaluating digital remediations of women's manuscripts', *Digital Studies / Le champ numérique*, 6 (2016), <http://doi.org/10.16995/dscn.12> (accessed 29 August 2017).

Ezell, Margaret J. M., 'The Laughing Tortoise: Speculations on Manuscript Sources and Women's Book History', *English Literary Renaissance* 38, no. 2 (2008): 331–55.

Ezell, Margaret J. M., *Social Authorship and the Advent of Print* (Baltimore: Johns Hopkins University Press, 1999).

Fairer, David, 'Coleridge's Sonnets from Various Authors (1796): A Lost Conversation Poem?', *Studies in Romanticism* 41, no. 4 (2002): 585–604.

Fairer, David, *Organising Poetry: The Coleridge Circle, 1790–1798* (Oxford: Oxford University Press, 2009).

Fay, Elizabeth, *Becoming Wordsworthian: A Performative Aesthetics* (Amherst: University of Massachusetts Press, 1995).

Feder, Rachel, 'The Experimental Dorothy Wordsworth', *Studies in Romanticism* 53, no. 4 (2014): 541–60.

Fenn, John, *Original Letters, written during the reigns of Henry VII, Edward IV, and Richard III*, 5 vols (London: G. G. J. and J. Robinson, 1787–1823).

Fergus, Jan, *Jane Austen: A Literary Life* (Basingstoke: Macmillan, 1991).

Fergus, Jan, 'The Professional Woman Writer', in Edward Copeland and Juliet McMaster (eds), *The Cambridge Companion to Jane Austen* (Cambridge: Cambridge University Press, 1997), pp. 12–31.

Ferris, Ina, 'The Debut of *The Edinburgh Review*, 1802', *BRANCH: Britain, Representation and Nineteenth-Century History*, ed. Dino Franco Felluga, <http://www.branchcollective.org/?ps_articles=ina-ferris-the-debut-of-the-edinburgh-review-1802?>.

Flint, Christopher, *The Appearance of Print in Eighteenth-Century Fiction* (Cambridge: Cambridge University Press, 2011).

Floyd, Daniel F., 'Anne Hunter's Poetry in Manuscript: a Rare Discovery', *Notes and Queries* 55, no. 4 (2008): 411–13.

Gabler, Hans Walter, 'The Primacy of the Document in Editing', *Ecdotica* 4 (2007): 197–207.

Gaillet-De Chezelles, Florence, 'Wordsworth, a Wandering Poet: Walking and Poetic Creation', *Études anglaises* 63, no. 1 (2010): 18–33.

Gallagher, Catherine, *Nobody's Story: The Vanishing Acts of Women Writers in the Marketplace, 1670–1820* (Oxford: Clarendon, 1995).

Gamer, Michael, *Romanticism, Self-Canonization, and the Business of Poetry* (Cambridge: Cambridge University Press, 2017).

Garside, Peter, 'The English Novel in the Romantic Era: Consolidation and Dispersal', in Garside, Raven and Shöwerling (eds), II: 15–103.

Garside, Peter, James Raven and Rainer Schöwerling (eds), *The English Novel, 1770–1829: A Bibliographical Survey of Prose Fiction Published in the British Isles.* 2 vols (Oxford and New York: Oxford University Press, 2000).

Gemmill, Katie, 'Jane Austen as Editor: Letters on Fiction and the Cancelled Chapters of Persuasion', *Eighteenth-Century Fiction* 24, no. 1 (2011): 105–22.

Gill, Stephen, 'Copyright and the Publishing of Wordsworth', in John O. Jordan and Robert L. Patten (eds), *Literature in the Marketplace: Nineteenth-Century British Publishing and Reading Practices* (Cambridge: Cambridge University Press, 1995), pp. 74–92.

Gioia, Dana, 'The Magical Value of Manuscripts', in Rodney Phillips (ed.), *The Hand of the Poet* (New York: Rizzoli, 1997), pp. 1–19.

Gordon, George (Lord Byron), 'Advertisement', in *Poems*, n.p. (London: John Murray, 1816).

Gordon, George (Lord Byron), *Byron's Letters and Journals*, ed. Leslie A. Marchand (Cambridge, MA: Harvard University Press, 1973–1982).

Gordon, George (Lord Byron), *The Complete Miscellaneous Prose*, ed. Andrew Nicholson (Oxford: Clarendon Press, 1991).

Gordon, George (Lord Byron), *The Complete Poetical Works*, ed. Jerome McGann, 7 vols (Oxford: Clarendon Press, 1986).

Gordon, George (Lord Byron), *English Bards and Scotch Reviewers* (London: James Cawthorn, 1809).

Gordon, George (Lord Byron), 'Fare thee Well' and 'A Sketch from Private Life', *The Champion* 172 (21 April 1816): 19.

Gordon, George (Lord Byron), *Hours of Idleness* (Newark: S. and J. Ridge, 1807).

Gordon, George (Lord Byron), *Poems* (London: John Murray, 1816).

Gordon, George (Lord Byron), *Poems 1807–1818: Poems in the Autograph of Lord Byron Once In the Possession of the Countess Guiccioli*, ed. Alice Levine and Jerome J. McGann (New York: Garland, 1986).

Gordon, George (Lord Byron), *The Works of Lord Byron including the suppressed poems* (Paris: A. & W. Galignani, 1828).

Gordon, George (Lord Byron), *The Works of Lord Byron: letters and journals*, ed. Rowland Edmund Prothero (London: John Murray, 1899).

Gourlay, Alexander S., 'Review of Viscomi, *Blake and the Idea of the Book*', *Blake: An Illustrated Quarterly* 29, no. 1 (1995): 31–5.

Graham, Peter, 'Byron and the Business of Publishing', in Drummond Bone (ed.), *The Cambridge Companion to Byron* (Cambridge: Cambridge University Press, 2004), pp. 27–43.

Grigson, Caroline, *The Life and Poems of Anne Hunter: Haydn's Tuneful Voice* (Liverpool: Liverpool University Press, 2009).

Groom, Nick, 'Chatterton, Thomas (1752–1770)', in *Oxford Dictionary of National Biography* (Oxford: Oxford University Press, 2004).

Gross, Jonathan David, *Byron: The Erotic Liberal* (New York: Rowman and Littlefield, 2001).

Hamburger, Jeffrey F., *Script as Image* (Paris: Peeters, 2014).

Harris, Jocelyn, 'Jane Austen's Unseen Interlocutor', in William McCarthy (ed.), *Anna Barbauld: New Perspectives* (Lewisburg, PA: Bucknell University Press, 2014), pp. 237–58.

Harris, Jocelyn, *A Revolution Almost beyond Expression: Jane Austen's Persuasion* (Newark: University of Delaware Press, 2007).

Haslett, Moyra, *Pope to Burney, 1714–1779: Scriblerians to Bluestockings* (Basingstoke: Palgrave Macmillan, 2003).

[Hazlitt, William], 'Review of "Christabel; Kubla Khan, a Vision; The Pains of Sleep"', *The Examiner*, 2 June 1816, 348–9.

Higgins, David, *Romantic Genius and the Literary Magazine: Biography, Celebrity and Politics* (London: Routledge, 2005).
Hogg, Thomas Jefferson, *The Life of Percy Bysshe Shelley*, 4 vols (London: Moxon, 1858).
Homans, Margaret, *Women Writers and Poetic Identity: Dorothy Wordsworth, Emily Brontë, and Emily Dickinson* (Princeton: Princeton University Press, 1980).
Hudson, Nicholas, *Writing and European Thought 1600–1830* (Cambridge: Cambridge University Press, 1995).
Hunter, Mrs John, *Poems* (London: T. Payne, 1802).
Index of Literary Manuscripts, vol. 4: 1800–1900, part I, ed. Barbara Rosenbaum and Pamela White (London: Mansell, 1982–93).
Ing Freeman, Janet, 'Upcott, William (1779–1845)', *Oxford Dictionary of National Biography* (Oxford: Oxford University Press, 2004), <http://www.oxforddnb.com/view/article/28005> (accessed 17 November 2010).
'Introduction', *Annual Review* 7 (1808): iii–xiv.
Ioppolo, Grace, 'Switching on the World of Dramatic Manuscripts', *Shakespeare Studies* 32 (2004): 66–72.
Jackson, Heather, *Marginalia: Readers Writing in Books* (New Haven, CT: Yale University Press, 2001).
Johns, Adrian, *The Nature of the Book: Print and Knowledge in the Making* (Chicago: University of Chicago Press, 1998).
Johnson, Claudia, 'Introduction', in Jane Austen, *Northanger Abbey, Lady Susan, The Watsons, Sanditon*, ed. James Kinsley and John David (Oxford: Oxford University Press, 2003) .
Johnson, Samuel, *The celebrated letter from Samuel Johnson, LL.D. to Philip Dormer Stanhope, Earl of Chesterfield; now first published, with notes, by James Boswell, Esq.* (London: Charles Dilly, 1790).
Justice, George, 'Introduction', in Justice and Tinker (eds), pp. 1–16.
Justice, George, '*Sanditon* and the Book', in Claudia L. Johnson and Clara Tuite (eds), *A Companion to Jane Austen* (Oxford: Wiley-Blackwell, 2009), pp. 153–62.
Justice, George, 'Suppression and Censorship in Late Manuscript Culture: Frances Burney's Unperformed *The Witlings*', in Justice and Tinker (eds), pp. 201–22.
Justice, George and Nathan Tinker (eds), *Women's Writing and the Circulation of Ideas: Manuscript Publication in England, 1550–1800* (Cambridge and New York: Cambridge University Press, 2002).
Keach, William, 'A Regency Prophecy and the End of Annd Barbauld's Career', *Studies in Romanticism* 33 (Winter 1994): 569–77.

Keats, John, 'Letter from John Keats to John Taylor on 27 February 1818', in *Selected Letters of John Keats*, ed. Grant F. Scott (Cambridge, MA: Harvard University Press, 2002), pp. 96–7.

Keats, John, *The Manuscripts of the Younger Romantics: John Keats: Poems, Transcripts, Letters, &c: Facsimiles of Richard Woodhouses's Scrapbook Materials in the Pierpont Morgan Library*, vol. 4, ed. Jack Stillinger (New York: Garland, 1985).

Keats, John, *The Poems of John Keats*, ed. Jack Stillinger (Cambridge, MA: Harvard University Press, 1978).

Keats, John, *The Texts of Keats's Poems*, ed. Jack Stillinger (Cambridge, MA: Harvard University Press, 1974).

Kelemen, Erick, *Textual Editing and Criticism: An Introduction* (New York: Norton, 2009).

Labbe, Jacqueline, *Charlotte Smith: Romanticism, Poetry and the Culture of Gender* (Manchester: Manchester University Press, 2003).

Lamb, Charles, 'Oxford in the Vacation', *The London Magazine*, 2 October 1820, 365–9.

Lamb, Charles, *Letters of Charles Lamb*, ed. Thomas Noon Talfourd (London: Moxon, 1837).

Lamb, Charles, 'On Garrick, and Acting; and the Plays of Shakspeare, considered with reference to their fitness for Stage Representation', *The Reflector* 2.4 (June 1811): 298–313.

'The Late William Upcott', *Gentleman's Magazine*, 2nd ser., 26 (1846): 473–4.

Le Faye, Deirdre (ed.), *Jane Austen's Letters*, 4th edn (New York: Oxford University Press, 2011).

Le Faye, Deirdre, '*Sanditon*: Jane Austen's Manuscript and her Niece's Continuation', *Review of English Studies* 38, no. 149 (1987): 56–61.

Levin, Susan M., *Dorothy Wordsworth* (New York: Pearson Longman, 2009).

Levin, Susan M., *Dorothy Wordsworth and Romanticism* (Jefferson, NC: McFarland & Co., 1987, revised 2009).

Levy, Michelle, 'Austen's Manuscripts and the Publicity of Print', *ELH* 77, no. 4 (2010): 1015–40.

Levy, Michelle, 'Do Women Have a Book History?', *Studies in Romanticism* 53, no. 3 (2014): 297–317.

Levy, Michelle, *Family Authorship and Romantic Print Culture* (Basingstoke and New York: Palgrave Macmillan, 2008).

Levy, Michelle, 'The Radical Education of *Evenings at Home*', *Eighteenth-Century Fiction* 19, nos. 1–2 (2006–7): 123–50.

Levy, Michelle, 'Review of "Jane Austen's Fiction Manuscripts"', *RIDE* 5 (2017). doi: 10.18716/ride.a.5.1 (accessed 30 January 2019).

Levy, Michelle, 'Women and Print Culture, 1750–1830', in Jacqueline Labbe (ed.), *The History of British Women's Writing, 1750–1830*, vol. 5 (Basingstoke and New York: Palgrave Macmillan, 2010).

Levy, Michelle, 'The Wordsworths, the Greens, and the Limits of Sympathy', *Studies in Romanticism* 42, no. 4 (2003): 541–63.

Levy, Michelle and Mark Perry, 'Distantly Reading the Romantic Canon: Quantifying Gender in Contemporary Anthologies', *Reassessing British Women Writers of the Romantic Period: A Special Issue of Women's Writing* 22, no. 2 (2015): 132–55.

Longman Anthology of British Literature, ed. David Damrosch et al., 5th edn, vol. 2a (Toronto: Pearson Education, 2012).

Lonsdale, Roger (ed.), *Eighteenth-Century Women Poets: An Oxford Anthology* (Oxford and New York: Oxford University Press, 1989).

Love, Harold, *The Culture and Commerce of Texts: Scribal Publication in Seventeenth-Century England* (Oxford: Clarendon Press, 1998).

Love, Harold, *English Clandestine Satire, 1660–1702* (Oxford: Oxford University Press, 2004).

Love, Harold and Arthur Marotti, 'Manuscript Transmission and Circulation', in David Loewenstein and Janel Mueller (eds), *The Cambridge History of Early Modern English Literature* (Cambridge: Cambridge University Press, 2002), pp. 55–80.

McCarthy, William, *Anna Letitia Barbauld: Voice of the Enlightenment* (Baltimore: Johns Hopkins University Press, 2008).

McCarthy, William, 'Introduction: Anna Letitia Barbauld Today', in William McCarthy and Olivia Murphy (eds), *Anna Letitia Barbauld: New Perspectives* (Lewisburg: Bucknell University Press, 2014), pp. 1–21.

McDayter, Ghislaine, 'On the Publication of William Godwin's *Memoirs of the Author of A Vindication of the Rights of Woman*, 1798', *BRANCH: Britain, Representation and Nineteenth-Century History*, ed. Dino Franco Felluga. Extension of *Romanticism and Victorianism on the Net*.

McGann, Jerome, 'Byron and "The Truth in Masquerade"', in Robert Brinkley and Keith Hanley (eds), *Romantic Revisions* (Cambridge: Cambridge University Press, 1992), pp. 191–209.

McGann, Jerome, 'Database, Interface, and Archival Fever', *PMLA* 122, no. 5 (2007): 1588–92.

McGann, Jerome, *Fiery Dust: Byron's Poetic Development* (Chicago: University of Chicago Press, 1968).

McGann, Jerome, *A New Republic of Letters: Memory and Scholarship in the Age of Digital Reproduction* (Cambridge, MA: Harvard University Press, 2014).

McGann, Jerome, 'Private Poetry, Public Deception', in *Byron and Romanticism*, by Jerome McGann, ed. James Soderholm (Cambridge: Cambridge University Press, 2002), pp. 113–40.

McGann, Jerome, *Radiant Textuality: Literature after the World Wide Web* (Basingstoke: Palgrave, 2004).

McGann, Jerome, *The Textual Condition* (Princeton: Princeton University Press, 1991).

Mack, Robert L., 'The Austen Family Writing: Gossip, Parody, and Corporate Personality', in Claudia L. Johnson and Clara Tuite (eds), *A Companion to Jane Austen* (Oxford: Wiley-Blackwell, 2009), pp. 31–40.

McKitterick, David, *Old Books, New Technologies: The Representation, Conservation, and Transformation of Books since 1700* (Cambridge: Cambridge University Press, 2014).

McKitterick, David, *Print, Manuscript and the Search for Order, 1450–1830* (Cambridge: Cambridge University Press, 2003).

McLane, Maureen, *Balladeering, Minstrelsy, and the Making of British Romantic Poetry* (Cambridge: Cambridge University Press, 2008).

Mandel, Anthony, *Jane Austen and the Popular Novel: The Determined Author* (Houndsmill: Palgrave, 2007).

Marchand, Leslie A., *Byron: A Biography*, 3 vols (New York: Alfred Knopf, 1957).

Marotti, Arthur, *Manuscript, Print, and the English Renaissance* (Ithaca, NY: Cornell University Press, 1995).

Mee, Jon, *Conversable Worlds: Literature, Contention, and Community, 1762 to 1830* (Oxford: Oxford University Press, 2011).

Mellor, Anne K., *Mothers of the Nation: Women's Political Writing in England, 1780–1830* (Bloomington: Indiana University Press, 2000).

Mellor, Anne K., *Romanticism and Gender* (New York: Routledge, 1993.

Miller, D. A., *Jane Austen, or the Secret of Style* (Princeton: Princeton University Press, 2003).

Mole, Tom, *Byron's Romantic Celebrity: Industrial Culture and the Hermeneutic of Intimacy* (Basingstoke and New York: Palgrave Macmillan, 2007).

Moore, Thomas, *Life of Lord Byron: with his Letters and Journals*, 6 vols (London: John Murray, 1854).

Morley, E. J., *Correspondence of H. C. Robinson with the Wordsworth Circle* (Oxford: Clarendon Press, 1827).

Moretti, Franco, *Distant Reading* (London: Verso, 2013).

Mr Thelwall's Reply to Observations on Mr. Thelwall's Letter to the Editor of the Edinburgh Review (Glasgow: W. Lang, 1804).

Multigraph Collective, *Interacting with Print: Elements of Reading in the Era of Print Saturation* (Chicago: University of Chicago Press, 2018).

Munby, A. N. L., *The Cult of the Autograph Letter in England* (London: University of London Press, 1962).

Neuber, Frederike, 'Review of "The Shelley-Godwin Archive: The Edition of Mary Shelley's Frankenstein Notebooks"', *RIDE* 2 (2014). doi:10.18716/ride.a.2.5.

Newlyn, Lucy, 'Dorothy Wordsworth's Experimental Style', *Essays in Criticism* 57, no. 4 (2007): 325–49.

Newlyn, Lucy, *William and Dorothy Wordsworth: 'All in Each Other'* (Oxford: Oxford University Press, 2013).

Nicholson, Andrew, *Letters of John Murray to Lord Byron* (Liverpool: Liverpool University Press, 2007).

Nicholson, Andrew, *The Manuscripts of the Younger Romantics: Lord Byron: Byron Poems 1807–1824, and Beppo*, vol. XXII (New York and London: Garland, 1998).

Norton Anthology of English Literature, 3rd edn, ed. M. H. Abrams (New York: Norton, 1974).

Norton Anthology of English Literature, 7th edn, ed. M. H. Abrams and Stephen Greenblatt (New York: Norton, 2000).

Norton Anthology of English Literature, 9th edn, ed. Stephen Greenblatt et al. (New York: Norton, 2012).

'Novels', *Annual Review* 7 (1809): xiii.

'Novels and Romances', *Annual Review* 1 (1803): 717.

'Novels and Romances', *Annual Review* 3 (1804): 542.

'Obituary of Mrs. Anna Laetitia Barbauld', *Monthly Repository* 20 [1825]: 185–6.

Observations on Mr. Thelwall's Letter to the Editor of the Edinburgh Review (Edinburgh: D. Willison, 1804).

O'Neill, Michael, 'Review of *The Complete Poetry of Percy Bysshe Shelley*, Volume One', *Romanticism on the Net* 20 (November 2000).

'On Watering-places', *Monthly Magazine* 2 (1796): 605–8.

Parker, Mark, *Literary Magazines and British Romanticism* (Cambridge: Cambridge University Press, 2000).

Pflughaupt, Laurent, *Letter by Letter: An Alphabetical Miscellany* (New York: Princeton Architectural Press, 2007).

Phillips, Michael, 'Printing Blake's *Songs*, 1789–1794', *The Library*, 6th series, 13, no. 3 (1991): 205–37.

Phillips, Michael, *William Blake: The Creation of the Songs, from Manuscript to Illuminated Printing* (Princeton: Princeton University Press, 1987).

Piper, Andrew, 'The Art of Sharing: Reading in the Romantic Miscellany', in Inna Ferris and Paul Keen (eds), *Bookish Histories* (Basingstoke: Palgrave, 2009), pp. 127–47.

Piper, Andrew, *Dreaming in Books: The Making of the Bibliographic Imagination in the Romantic Age* (Chicago: University of Chicago Press, 2009).

'Poetry', *Annual Review* 4 (1805): 535.

Pointon, Marcia, 'Illustrious Heads', in *Hanging the Head: Portraiture and Social Formation in Eighteenth-Century England* (New Haven, CT: Yale University Press, 1993), pp. 53–78.

Poovey, Mary, *The Proper Lady and the Woman Writer: Ideology as Style in the Works of Mary Wollstonecraft, Mary Shelley, and Jane Austen* (Chicago: University of Chicago Press, 1984).

Pratt, Willis W., *Byron at Southwell: The Making of a Poet* (New York: Haskell House, 1973).

'Preface', *Annual Review* 3 (1804): iii–iv.

'Prospectus of a New Work, the first Volume of which will be published in early 1803 to be entitled "The Annual Review, or Register of Literature"' (Paternoster-Row, London: T. N. Longman and O. Rees, n.d.) (bound with *Annual Review*, British Library shelf mark 250.k.1).

Ramsay, Nigel, 'Astle, Thomas (1735–1803)', *Oxford Dictionary of National Biography* (Oxford: Oxford University Press, 2004).

Raven, James, *The Business of Books: Booksellers and the English Book Trade 1450–1850* (New Haven, CT: Yale University Press, 2007).

Raven, James, 'Historical Introduction: The Novel Comes of Age', in Garside, Raven and Schöwerling (Oxford: Oxford University Press, 2000).

Reiman, Donald, *The Study of Modern Manuscripts: Public, Confidential, and Private* (Baltimore: Johns Hopkins University Press, 1993).

'Review of *A Series of Plays* by Joanna Baillie', *Annual Review* 1 (1802): 680–5.

'Review of *An Account of the Life and Writings of James Beattie. By Sir W. Forbes*', *Edinburgh Review* 10, no. 19 (April 1807): 171–99.

'Review of *An Account of the Life of Samuel Johnson*', *Edinburgh Review* 7, no. 14 (January 1806): 436–41.

'Review of *A Tour through Holland*', *Monthly Review, or, Literary Journal* 54 (September 1807): 29–38.

'Review of Augustus Von Kotzebue, *Travels through Italy*', *Edinburgh Review* 7, no. 14 (January 1806): 456–70.

'Review of *The Battle of Largs: a Gothic Poem*', *Annual Review* 4 (1805): 566–8.

'Review of *The Chaplet, a Collection of Poems*', *Annual Review* 4 (1805): 621.

'Review of *The Cottagers of Glenbournie* by Elizabeth Hamilton', *Annual Review* 7 (1808): 608–15.

'Review of Dugald Stewart's *Account of the Life and writings of William Robertson*', *Edinburgh Review* 2, no. 3 (April 1803): 229–49.

'Review of *Hours of Idleness* by Lord Byron', *Annual Review* 6 (1807): 529–31.

'Review of *Hours of Idleness*. By Lord Byron', *Edinburgh Review* 11, no. 22 (January 1808): 285–9.

'Review of Hours of Idleness', *Monthly Literary Recreations* (13 July 1807): 67–71.

'Review of *Isographie des Hommes Célébres* and *Autographs of Royal, Noble, Learned, and Remarkable Personages*', *Retrospective Review* 2 (1828): 351–2.

'Review of John Thelwall, *Poems written chiefly in Retirement*', *Edinburgh Review* 2 (April 1803): 197–202.

'Review of Kotzebue's *Travels to Paris*', *Edinburgh Review* 5, no. 9 (October 1804): 78–91.

'Review of *Life and Correspondence of Robert Southey*', *The Gentleman's Magazine* (June 1850): 611–19.

'Review of *The Life and Posthumous Writings of William Cowper*', *Edinburgh Review* 2, no. 3 (April 1803): 64–90.

'Review of *Love Letters to my Wife*. By James Woodhouse', *Annual Review* 3 (1804): 596.

'Review of *Lyric Poems* by James Mercer', *Annual Review* 3 (1804): 563–64.

'Review of *Lyric Poems. By James Mercer, Esq.*', *Edinburgh Review* 7, no. 14 (January 1806): 471–8.

'Review of *Marmion: a Tale of Flodden Field*. By Walter Scott', *Annual Review* 7 (1808): 462–73.

'Review of *Marmion: a Tale of Flodden Field*. By Walter Scott', *Edinburgh Review* 12, no. 23 (April 1808): 1–35.

'Review of *Memoirs of the Life of Mrs. Elizabeth Carter*', *Annual Review* 6 (1807): 386–7.

'Review of *Memoirs of Richard Cumberland: Written by Himself*', *Edinburgh Review* 8, no. 15 (April 1806): 107–28.

'Review of Mr Pratt, *Bread; or, the Poor. A Poem*', *Edinburgh Review* 1, no. 1 (October 1802): 108–12.

'Review of Mrs John Hunter, *Poems*', *Edinburgh Review* 1, no. 2 (January 1803): 421–6.

'Review of Northanger Abbey: and Persuasion', *British Critic*, n.s., 9 (March 1818): 293–301.

'Review of *Northanger Abbey; and Persuasion*', *Edinburgh Magazine and Literary Miscellany*, n.s., 2 (May 1818): 453–5.

'Review of *The Peasant's Fate: a rural Poem* by W. Holloway', *Annual Review* 1 (1802): 652.

'Review of *Poems and Tales* by Miss Trefusis', *Annual Review* 7 (1808): 524–5.

'Review of *Poems and Plays* by Mr. Jerningham', *Annual Review* 5 (1806): 529–30.

'Review of *Poems*, by Miss Aikin', *Monthly Review* 48 (January 1773): 54–9
'Review of *Poems*. By Mrs. John Hunter', *Annual Review* 1 (1802): 650.
'Review of *Poems. By the Rev. J. Mant*', *Edinburgh Review* 11, no. 21 (October 1807): 167–71.
'Review of *Poems, in Two Volumes*', *Monthly Literary Recreations* (July 1807): 65–6.
'Review of *Poems in Two Volumes*. By William Wordsworth', *Edinburgh Review* 11, no. 22 (October 1807): 214–31.
'Review of *The Poetical Register for 1804*', *Annual Review* 5 (1806): 532–4.
'Review of *Public Characters of 1801–1802*', *Edinburgh Review* 1, no. 1 (October 1802): 122.
'Review of Robert Southey, *The Curse of Kehama*', *Edinburgh Review* 17 (November 1810): 429–65.
'Review of Robert Southey, *Thabala, the Destroyer: A Metrical Romance*', *Edinburgh Review* 1, no. 1 (October 1802): 63–83.
'Review of *Sibylline Leaves*', *Monthly Review* 88 (January–April 1819): 24–38.
'Review of *Simple Tales*. By Mrs Opie', *Edinburgh Review* 8, no. 16 (July 1806): 465–71.
'Review of *Specimens of the Later English Poets, with Preliminary Notices. By R. Southey*', *Edinburgh Review* 11, no. 21 (October 1807): 31–40.
'Review of S. T. Coleridge's *The Statesman's Manual*', *Edinburgh Review* 27 (September 1816): 414–59.
'Review of *Travels from Berlin, through Switzerland, to Paris, in the year 1804*', *Annual Review* 3 (1804): 83–8.
'Review of *Travels Through Italy in the years 1804 and 1805*', *Annual Review* 4 (1805): 43–9.
'Review of *Verses, social and domestic. By George Hay Drummond*', *Annual Review* 1 (1802): 670–1.
'Review of *The Wanderer of Switzerland* by James Montgomery', *Edinburgh Review* 9, no. 18 (January 1807): 347–54.
'Review of Wordsworth's *The Excursion*', *Edinburgh Review* 24 (November 1814): 1–30.
'Review of the *Works of Anna Laetitia Barbauld*', *Monthly Repository* 20 (1825): 484–9; 558–62.
'Review of *The Works of Richard Owen Cambridge*', *Edinburgh Review* 3, no. 5 (October 1803): 56–60.
'Review of *The Works of the Right Honourable Lady M. W. Montagu*', *Edinburgh Review* 2, no. 4 (July 1803): 507–22.
'Review of *The Works of the Right Honourable Lady Mary Wortley Montagu*', *Annual Review* 2 (1804): 502–7.
Rodgers, Betsy, *Georgian Chronicle: Mrs. Barbauld and Her Family* (London: Methuen, 1958).

Roland, Meg, 'Facsimile Editions: Gesture and Projection', *Textual Cultures: Text, Contexts, Interpretation* 6, no. 2 (2011): 48–59.

Rutherford, Andrew (ed.), *Lord Byron: The Critical Heritage* (London and New York: Routledge, 1995).

Schellenberg, Betty, 'Bluestocking Women and the Negotiation of Oral, Manuscript, and Print Cultures', in Jacqueline Labbe (ed.), *The History of British Women's Writing, 1750–1830*, vol. 5 (Basingstoke and New York: Palgrave Macmillan, 2010), pp. 63–83.

Schellenberg, Betty, *Literary Coteries and the Making of Modern Print Culture 1740–1790* (Cambridge: Cambridge University Press, 2016).

Schellenberg, Betty, *The Professionalization of Women Writers in Eighteenth-Century Britain* (Cambridge: Cambridge University Press, 2005).

Schellenberg, Betty, 'The Second Coming of the Book, 1740–1770', in Laura Runge and Pat Rogers (eds), *Producing the Eighteenth-Century Book: Writers and Publishers in England, 1650–1800* (Newark: University of Delaware Press, 2009), pp. 30–52.

Schneider, Elisabeth, Irwin Griggs and John D. Kern, 'Brougham's Early Contributions to the Edinburgh Review: A New List', *Modern Philology* 42, no. 3 (1945): 152–73.

Schoenfield, Mark, *British Periodicals and Romantic Identity: The 'Literary Lower Empire'* (New York: Palgrave, 2009).

Schreibman, Susan, 'Digital Scholarly Editing', in *Literary Studies in the Digital Age: An Evolving* Anthology (2013, n.p.) <https://dlsanthology.mla.hcommons.org/>.

Scott, Henry T., *Autograph Collecting: A Practical Manual for Amateurs and Historical Students* (London: L. Upcott Gill, 1894).

Scott, Walter, *Chronicles of the Canongate*, ed. Claire Lamont (2000). Part of *The Edinburgh Edition of the Waverley Novels*, 30 vols, ed. David Hewitt (Edinburgh: Edinburgh University Press, 2015).

Scrivener, Michael, *Seditious Allegories: John Thelwall and Jacobin Writing* (University Park: Pennsylvania State University Press, 2001).

Shakespeare, William, *The plays of William Shakespeare. In ten volumes. With the corrections and illustrations of various commentators; to which are added notes by Samuel Johnson and George Steevens, second edition, revised and augmented* (London: C. Bathurst et al., 1778).

Shelley, Mary, *The Frankenstein Notebooks: A Facsimile Edition*, Manuscripts of the Younger Romantics, vol. IX, ed. Charles Robinson (New York and London: Garland, 1996).

Shelley, Mary (ed.), *Poetical Works of Percy Bysshe Shelley* (London: Ward, Lock & Co, 1839).

Shelley, Mary and Percy Shelley, *History of a Six Weeks' Tour* (London: Hookham and Ollier, 1817).

Shelley, Percy, *The Complete Poetry of Percy Bysshe Shelley*, vol. 1, ed. Donald H. Reiman and Neil Fraistat (Baltimore: Johns Hopkins University Press, 2003).

Shelley, Percy, *The Poems of Percy Shelley*, ed. Geoffrey Matthews and Kelvin Everest, 3 vols (Longman: London and New York, 1969).

Shelley, Percy, *Posthumous Poems of Percy Bysshe Shelley* (London: John and Henry Hunt, 1824).

Shelley, Percy, *Shelley's Poetry and Prose* (New York and London: Norton, 2002).

The Shelley-Godwin Archive, ed. Neil Fraistat, Elizabeth Denlinger and Raffaele Viglianti, <http://shelleygodwinarchive.org/>.

Sher, Richard, *The Enlightenment and the Book: Scottish Authors and Their Publishers in Eighteenth-Century Britain, Ireland, and America* (Chicago: University of Chicago Press, 2006).

Siskin, Clifford, *The Work of Writing: Literature and Social Change in Britain, 1700–1830* (Baltimore: Johns Hopkins University Press, 1998).

Smiles, Samuel, *A Publisher and his Friends: Memoir and Correspondence of John Murray, with an Account of the Origin and Progress of the House, 1768–1843*, 2 vols (London: J. Murray, 1891).

Smith, Charlotte, *Collected Letters of Charlotte Smith*, ed. Judith Phillips Stanton (Bloomington: Indiana University Press, 2003).

Smith, Charlotte, *The Poems of Charlotte Smith*, ed. Stuart Curran (Oxford: Oxford University Press, 1993).

Smith, Helen, *'Grossly Material Things': Women and Book Production in Early Modern England* (Oxford: Oxford University Press, 2012).

Smith, Nicholas D., *The Literary Manuscripts and Letters of Hannah More* (Farnham: Ashgate, 2008).

Southam, Brian, *Jane Austen: a Student's Guide to the Later Manuscript Works* (London: Concord Books, 2007).

Southam, Brian, *Jane Austen's Literary Manuscripts: a Study of the Novelist's Development through the Surviving Papers* (London: Athlone Press, 2001).

Southey, Robert, 'Wat Tyler', ed. Matt Hill. *Romantic Circles*, <https://www.rc.umd.edu/editions/wattyler/> (accessed 25 October 2004).

St Clair, William, *The Reading Nation in the Romantic Period* (Cambridge: Cambridge University Press, 2004).

Stauffer, Andrew, 'The Career of Byron's "To the Po"', *Keats-Shelley Journal* 57 (2008): 108–27.

Stauffer, Andrew, 'Hemans by the Book', *European Romantic Review* 22:3 (2011): 373–80.

Stauffer, Andrew, 'Lord Byron's *Fugitive Pieces*', unpublished essay.

Stauffer, Andrew, 'New Light on Byron's Regency in America', *Byron Journal* 28 (2000), 29–36.

Stauffer, Andrew, 'Sorting Byron's "Windsor Poetics"', *Shelley Journal* 51 (2002): 30–4.

Staves, Susan, *A Literary History of Women's Writing in Britain, 1660–1789* (Cambridge: Cambridge University Press, 2006).

Stillinger, Jack, *Coleridge and Textual Instability: The Multiple Versions of the Major Poems* (New York and Oxford: Oxford University Press, 1994).

Stillinger, Jack, *Multiple Authorship and the Myth of Solitary Genius* (New York: Oxford University Press, 1991).

Strachey, J. St Loe, 'In "Sanditon", Half of a New Novel by Jane Austen: Modernity of Her Outlook Again Evident in This Unfinished Work', *New York Times*, 5 April 1925, 13.

Sutherland, Kathryn, 'Anglo-American Editorial Theory', in Neil Fraistat and Julia Flanders (eds), *The Cambridge Companion to Textual Scholarship* (Cambridge: Cambridge University Press, 2013), pp. 42–60.

Sutherland, Kathryn, 'Chronology of Composition and Publication', in Janet Todd (ed.), *The Cambridge Edition of the Works of Jane Austen: Jane Austen in Context* (Cambridge: Cambridge University Press, 2005), pp. 12–22.

Sutherland, Kathryn, 'From Kitty to Catharine: James Edward Austen's hand in *Volume the Third*', *Review of English Studies* 66, no. 273 (2015): 124–43. doi:10.1093/res/hgu042.

Sutherland, Kathryn (ed.), *Jane Austen's Fiction Manuscripts: A Digital Edition* (University of Oxford and King's College, 2010), <http://www.janeausten.ac.uk>.

Sutherland, Kathryn, *Jane Austen's Textual Lives: from Aeschylus to Bollywood* (Oxford: Oxford University Press, 2005).

Sutherland, Kathryn (ed.), 'Sanditon: Diplomatic Display', in *Jane Austen's Fiction Manuscripts: A Digital Edition*.

Sutherland, Kathryn and Elena Pierazzo, 'The Author's Hand: From Page to Screen', in Marilyn Deegan and Willard McCarty (eds), *Collaborative Research in the Digital Humanities* (Farnham: Ashgate, 2012), pp. 191–212.

Thelwall, John, *A Letter to Francis Jeffray on certain Calumnies and Misrepresentations in the Edinburgh Review* (Edinburgh: Turnball, 1804).

Todd, Janet, *The Cambridge Introduction to Jane Austen* (Cambridge and New York: Cambridge University Press, 2006).

Todd, Janet and Linda Bree, 'Jane Austen's Unfinished Business', *Persuasions* 30 (2008): 222–34.

'To the Great Variety of Readers', *Mr. William Shakespeares Comedies, histories & tragedies, published according to the true originall copies* (London: Isaac Jaggard and Edward Blount, 1623).

Tuite, Clara, '*Sanditon*: Austen's pre–post Waterloo', *Textual Practice* 26, no. 4 (2012): 609–29.

Turner, Dawson, *Guide to the historian, the biographer, the antiquary, the man of literary curiosity, and the collector of autographs, towards the verification of manuscripts, by reference to engraved fac-similes of handwriting* (Yarmouth: C. Sloman, 1848).

Twyman, Michael, *Printing 1770–1970: An Illustrated History of Its Development and Uses in England* (London: British Library, 1998).

Upcott, William, 'The Autobiography of a Collector', *Gentleman's Magazine*, 2nd ser., 26 (1846): 474–6.

Virgil, *The Works of Virgil, Translated into English Prose*, 4th edn (London: Fuller et al., 1793).

Viscomi, Joseph, *Blake and the Idea of the Book* (Princeton: Princeton University Press, 1993).

Viscomi, Joseph, 'Illuminated Printing', in Morris Eaves (ed.), *The Cambridge Companion to William Blake* (Cambridge and New York: Cambridge University Press, 2003), pp. 37–62.

Waters, Mary, '"Slovenly Monthly Catalogues": The *Monthly Review* and Barbauld's Periodical Literary Criticism', *Nineteenth-Century Prose* 31, no. 1 (2004): 53–81.

Wells, John Edwin, 'De Quincey and *The Prelude* in 1839', *Philological Quarterly* 20 (1941): 1–24.

Werner, Marta L., '"Reportless Places": Facing the Modern Manuscript', *Textual Cultures: Texts, Contexts, Interpretation* 6, no. 2 (2011): 60–83.

Whelan, Timothy, *Other British Voices: Women, Poetry, and Religion, 1766–1840* (New York: Palgrave, 2015).

The *William Blake Archive*, ed. Morris Eaves, Robert Essick, and Joseph Viscomi (1996), <http://www.blakearchive.org>.

The Writings of Thomas Jefferson, ed. H. A. Washington, 9 vols (New York: Riker, Thorne, 1853–5).

Wimsatt, W. K., Jr and Monroe C. Beardsley, 'The Intentional Fallacy', in *The Verbal Icon: Studies in the Meaning of Poetry* (Lexington: University Press of Kentucky, 1954), pp. 3–20.

Wollstonecraft, Mary, *Vindication of the Rights of Woman*, ed. Miriam Brody (London: Penguin, 2004).

[Woodfall, William], 'Review of *Poems*, by Miss Aikin', *Monthly Review* 48 (January 1773): 54–9, 133–7.

Woof, Pamela, 'The Uses of Notebooks: From Journal to Album, from Commonplace to Keepsake', *Coleridge Bulletin: The Journal of the Friends of Coleridge* 31 (2008): 1–18.

Woolf, Virginia, 'Jane Austen', in *The Common Reader, First Series*, ed. Andrew McNeillie (Orlando: Harcourt, 2002), pp. 137–8.

Wordsworth, Christopher, *Memoirs of William Wordsworth* (Boston: Ticknor, Reed, and Fields, 1851).

Wordsworth, Dorothy, *Journals of Dorothy Wordsworth*, ed. Ernest de Selincourt, 2 vols (Hamden, CT: Archon Books, 1970).
Wordsworth, Dorothy, *Journals of Dorothy Wordsworth*, ed. William Knight (London: McMillan, 1897).
Wordsworth, Dorothy and William Wordsworth, *The Early Letters of William and Dorothy Wordsworth (1787–1805)*, ed. Ernest de Selincourt (Oxford: Clarendon Press, 1935).
Wordsworth, Dorothy and William Wordsworth, *Letters of William and Dorothy Wordsworth*, 2nd edn, Shaver, Chester L., et al. (Oxford: Clarendon Press, 1967).
Wordsworth, William, 'Essay, Supplementary to the Preface', in *Poems, Including Lyrical Ballads, and the Miscellaneous Pieces of the Author. With Additional Poems, a New Preface, and a Supplementary Essay*, 2 vols (London: Longman, 1815).
Wordsworth, William, *Last Poems, 1821–1850*, ed. Jared Curtis (Ithaca, NY: Cornell University Press, 1999).
Wordsworth, William, *Lyrical Ballads, and Other Poems, 1797–1800*, ed. James Butler and Karen Green (Ithaca, NY: Cornell University Press, 1992).
Wordsworth, William, *The Poetical Works of William Wordsworth*, 8 vols, ed. William Knight (London: Macmillan, 1896).
Wordsworth, William, 'Preface to *Lyrical Ballads*, 1800', in *Lyrical Ballads and Other Poems, 1797–1800*, ed. James Butler and Karen Green (Ithaca, NY: Cornell University Press, 1992).
Wordsworth, William, *The Prelude: 1799, 1805, 1850*, ed. M. H. Abrams, Stephen Gill and Jonathan Wordsworth (New York: Norton, 1979).
Wordsworth, William, 'The Prelude', *Tait's Edinburgh Magazine*, ed. Thomas De Quincy (January, February and April 1839).
Wordsworth, William, *The Prose Works of William* Wordsworth (London: Moxon, 1876).
Wordsworth, William, *Prose Works of William Wordsworth*, ed. W. J. B. Owen and Jane Worthington Smyser, 3 vols (Oxford: Clarendon, 1974).
Wright, Gillian, *Producing Women's Poetry, 1600–1730: Text and Paratext, Manuscript and Print* (Cambridge: Cambridge University Press, 2013).
Zimmerman, Sarah M., 'Smith, Charlotte (1749–1806)', *Oxford Dictionary of National Biography* (Oxford University Press, 2004), <http://www.oxforddnb.com/view/article/25790> (accessed 7 September 2015).
Zionkowski, Linda, *Men's Work: Gender, Class, and the Professionalization of Poetry, 1660–1784* (New York: Palgrave, 2001).

Index

Adams, John, 11, 131
Aikin, Arthur, 68, 87
Aikin, John, 120–1, 133
   Barbauld's poems to and about, 105–7
   Evenings at Home; or, The Juvenile Budget Opened, 65, 111
Aikin, Lucy
   review of Byron, 78–9
   work for *The Annual Review*, 68, 82, 87
   The Works of Anna Laetitia Barbauld, 18, 102, 105–6, 108, 110, 122, 232
Allen, Reggie, 41
Anderson, Chris, 99n
Annual Review, 66–93
   criteria for reviews, 72–3
   hints to writers, 86–7
Astle, Thomas, 21, 217–18
Austen, Cassandra, 18, 210n, 211n, 220, 246
Austen, George, 186
Austen, Henry, 29
Austen, Jane, 6, 18, 20–1, 28–9, 42, 182–213, 190, 233, 263
   'amateur' and 'professional' writing, 185–6
   Cambridge edition, 246
   circulation of unpublished work, 184, 189, 220
   clandestine satire, 189–90, 198
   Emma, 14, 187, 189–91, 197–8, 224–5
   on handwriting, 224–7
   'The History of England', 183, 246
   Jane Austen's Fiction Manuscripts (digital archive), 246–8, 252
   juvenilia, 4, 18, 182–5, 198, 202, 246
   Lady Susan, 18, 186–9, 194, 198, 202–3, 246
   Mansfield Park, 187, 190–1, 197–9, 212n, 222–7
   Northanger Abbey, 17, 22, 188, 197, 205
   Persuasion, 135n, 197, 205, 207, 224
   cancelled chapters, 187–8, 191, 191–4, 246–7
   'Plan of a Novel', 184, 186–7, 189, 198–200, 204
   posthumous reviews, 205–6
   praised for restraint and control, 205–6
   Pride and Prejudice, 13, 182, 197, 199, 202, 225–6
   Sanditon, 18, 186, 188, 191–208, 246
   bears signs of Austen's physical deterioration, 196
   stylistic experimentation, 203

self-censorship, 184
Sense and Sensibility, 182, 197
small booklets used for secrecy, 191, 207
surviving manuscripts, 135n, 183–4, 207, 220; showing stages of work, 182–3, 104, 182–3, 191–205, 207–8
takedown of marriage plot, 199
three-volume notebook, 183–5
The Watsons, 186–7, 191–6, 198, 202, 205, 210n, 246
'When Winchester Races', 187
Austen-Leigh, Edward, 185, 196
autographs, 36, 221, 223, 226, 251, 253n, 254n

Backsheider, Paula, 101
Baillie, Joanna, 118, 127
Barbauld, Anna Laetitia, 14, 56, 68, 101–39, 203, 230, 232, 263
drawings, 111, 114
manuscript circulation, 101–2, 110–12
pamphlet publication, 120
personal and intimate poems, 105–7, 109, 111
poems for Mary and Joseph Priestley, 113–16, 118, 119, 137n
poems to and about John Aikin, 105–6, 111–13
political poems, 118–26, 128
preference for manuscript over print, 6, 117–18
published poems, 108–9; unauthorised, 11–12
quoted by Thomas Jefferson, 131
radicalism, 120–1
reviews, 98n
revisions to work, 105
surviving manuscript record, 104–5, 112–13, 219–20
unpublished work, 18–19, 101
use of inscription, 107
use of irony, 126
use of manuscript for sociability, 107–8, 129
Wedgwood cameo, 101
writing process, 107–8
POEMS AND OTHER WRITING:
'The Apology of the Bishops, in Answer to "Bonner's Ghost"', 119
British Novelists, 74
'The Caterpillar', 104
'Characters', 111, 115
'On the Classics', 218
'On the Death of Princess Charlotte', 123, 127, 129
'Dialogue in the Shades', 126
Eighteen Hundred and Eleven, A Poem, 120–6
Epistle to William Wilberforce, 120, 126
Evenings at Home; or, The Juvenile Budget Opened, 65, 111, 124
'To a Great Nation', 119
'The Groans of the Tankard', 109
'The Invitation', 109
'On a Lady's Writing', 224
'Life', 104
'To a little invisible Being who is expected soon to become visible', 104–5
'To Miss Kinder', 123–6
'On Monastic Institutions', 217–18
'The Mouse's Petition', 107, 109, 115
'To Mr. Barbauld, November 14, 1778', 105
'To Mr. Barbauld, with a Map of the Land of Matrimony', 105–6

Barbauld, Anna Laetitia (*cont.*)
  Poems, 101–2, 108–10, 114
  'The Rights of Women', 126
  'A Summer Evening's Meditation', 115, 124
  'A Thought on Death', 11, 129–32
  'Verses Inscribed on a Pair of Screens', 106
  'Washing Day', 71
  The Works of Anna Laetitia Barbauld, 101, 105–6, 110
Barchas, Janine, 206
Beardsley, Monroe, 31–2
Beckford, William, 157
Birmingham riots, 118
Blake, William
  engraving work, 23, 260
  illuminated manuscripts and printing, 5, 53, 245, 250, 259–65
  'Infant Joy', 260, 262
  'The Little Boy Lost', 260
  scholarly and critical editions of his work, 232–3
  Songs of Innocence and Experience, 3, 262, 264
  The William Blake Archive (digital archive), 244–5, 257n, 264
Bland, Mark, 1–2, 34, 39
Blank, Antje, 43
Bluestocking circle, 25n, 73
Bonner, Edmund, 119
booksellers, 99n
Bowles, William, 25n
Brawne, Fanny, 15
Bree, Linda, 188
British Museum, 217, 219
Brougham, Henry, 150–2
Broughham, Henry, 64, 68, 78
Brown, Charles, 237
Burkett, Andrew, 228
Burney, Frances (Fanny), 187
Burns, Robert, 42

Byron, Lord, 14, 17–18, 140–81, 263
  commonplace book, 170
  control over distribution of his work, 154, 163–6, 189
  criticism in Edinburgh Review, 150–1
  criticism of William Wordsworth, 152
  death, 231
  disguising identities in his poems, 147–9, 174n
  early verse collections, 143–52
  handwriting, 227–9, 230
  letters and journals, 171–2, 231
  manuscript circulation, 5, 163–70
  manuscripts showing stages of work, 104
  Murray's control over Byron's poetry, 165–7, 232
  poems to Augusta Leigh, 165
  political commentary in his poems, 161–2, 168–70
  presents himself as a youthful amateur, 150
  privately printed work, 145–6, 153
  publication during his lifetime, 141–2, 143–5; unauthorised, 167–8
  satires and lampoons, 4, 166
  self-censorship, 158
  sexually risqué and erotic poems, 146–8
  surviving drafts and revisions, 155–60, 220, 227, 229
  POEMS, COLLECTIONS AND OTHER WRITING:
  'Answer to Some Elegant Verses', 148
  'To Caroline', 147, 149
  Cephalonia Journal, 171, 228
  Childe Harold's Pilgrimage, 20, 143, 153–62, 188

'Childish Recollections', 148–9, 175n
Complete Poetical Works, 241
'Condolatory Address', 168–9
The Corsair, 169
Curse of Minerva, 153, 168
Don Juan, 122, 138n, 177n
English Bards and Scotch Reviewers, 88, 142, 153–5, 159–60
'An Extract from a Parish Register', 166
Fugitive Pieces, 144–8, 151, 168
Hebrew Melodies, 163
Hints from Horace, 142, 153
Hours of Idleness, 64, 144, 149–54
  criticised by *Edinburgh Review*, 77–8
'To a Knot of Ungenerous Critics', 147–8
'To a Lady who presented to the author a lock of hair', 147
'The Lament of Tasso', 142
'Lines to a Lady Weeping', 169
'To Mary', 146–7
'Ode to Napoleon Buonaparte', 228, 230
'To the Po. June 2nd 1819', 166
Poems, 152, 163
Poems, Original and Translated, 144, 151
Poems on Various Occasions, 144
The Prisoner of Chillon and other Poems, 165
'To the Rev. J. T. Becher', 148–9
A Selection of Hebrew Melodies, 163
'To the Sighing Strephone', 147
Various, 147–8, 155
'The Vault'/'Windsor Poetics', 169–70

Cadell, Thomas, 186
Calé, Luisa, 264–5
Cameron, Sharon, 56–7
Carlyle, Thomas, 228
Carr, Sarah, 127
Carr, Sir John, 84, 86, 160–1
Carter, Elizabeth, 84
Castlereagh, Viscount, 125, 138n
Chandler, Mary, 101
Chapman, R. W., 185, 196, 233
Chatterton, Thomas, 22, 122, 138n
Chen, Anna, 30
'Christabel' (Coleridge), 5, 12–13, 236
Christie, William, 88
Clarke, Charles Cowden, 253n
Clarke, J. S., Austen's attack on, 189–90
Clarkson, Catherine and Thomas, 52
Coleridge, Samuel Taylor, 3, 52, 233
  'Christabel', 5, 12–13, 34–5, 236
  handwriting, 253n
  publication of *Sonnets from Various Authors*, 10–11
  Sibylline Leaves, 17, 163–4
  textual variation, 235–7
  unpublished work, 236–7
Comitini, Patricia, 46
communications circuit, 9
Condell, Henrie, 28
Cowper, William, 43, 97n
Crosby, Benjamin, 194
Curran, Stuart, 238

Darnton, Robert, 9
de Quincey, Thomas, 12
Deegan, Marilyn, 252
Demata, Massimiliano, 84
Dibdin, Thomas Frognall, 220
Dickinson, Emily, 30, 56–7

digital media
  challenges of reproducing literary manuscripts, 264–5
  cost of developing, 244
  digital editions/collections, 21–3, 103, 182, 216, 243–52, 264
  durability and sustainability, 244
  forces re-examination of print, 216
  opportunities of new technology, 92, 252
Disraeli, Isaac, 28, 30
  interest in handwriting, 223–4
  'Recovery of Manuscripts', 218
Doody, Margaret, 185, 206
Douglas, Aileen, 223, 226
Drummond, George Hay, 79
Duguid, Paul, 92

East India Company, 30
Eaves, Morris, 264
Eddleston, John, 156
Edgeworth, Maria, 91
Edinburgh Review
  derisive reviews, 71–4, 81–2, 87–8; of Byron, 77–8, 150–2, 159; of William Wordsworth, 71, 82–3
  on manuscripts and publication, 66–93, 144
  on memoirs and travel writing, 82–6
  on suitability for publication, 71–82, 88–9, 144
  on social verse, 108
Egerton, Thomas, 186
Eggert, Paul, 244
Elgin, Lord, 161, 176n
Emma (Austen), 14, 187, 189–91, 197–8, 224–5
engraving, 260
epistolary writing, 5, 188
Erdman, David, 161, 232
Ezell, Margaret, 6, 46, 102, 103–4

Feder, Rachel, 46
Fenn, John, 217–19, 230
Fergus, Jan, 185
Flint, Christopher, 208n
Fraistat, Neil, 238–40
French Revolution, 117–18

Gabler, Hans, 234, 238, 243
Gagging Acts, 125, 128
genius, 28–9, 31, 238, 251
  and multiple authorship, 237–8
Gentleman's Magazine, 87
Gifford, William, 72, 166–7
Gioia, Dana, 214–15
Godwin, William, 232
  Shelley-Godwin Archive (digital archive), 249, 257n, 258n
Grigson, Caroline, 95n
Groom, Nick, 138n
Guiccioli, Teresa, 166, 171, 229

Hamburger, Jeffrey, 222, 247
Hamilton, William, 161
handwriting, 4, 7–8, 21, 30, 52, 53, 214–15, 222–9, 251
  antagonism to, 29–30
  autograph collecting, 21–22, 221–2, 228, 253n, 254n
  considered to reveal character, 30–1, 115, 171, 215, 222–8
  and digital archiving, 243–50
  as an instrument of enlightenment, 215–17
  reproducing in other media, 22, 228, 230, 247, 252
  as technology, 216–17
  value placed on, 228–9
Harris, Jocelyn, 192, 203
Harrow School, 149
Haydn, Franz Joseph, 73
Hayley, William, 41
Hazlitt, William, 13
Heminge, John, 28
Hobhouse, John, 151

Hodgson, Frances, 162
Hogg, T. J., 154
Holland, Lord, 128, 161
Holloway, W., 74
holographs, 36, 108, 214, 220
homosexuality, 157
Hope, Thomas, 161
Horner, Francis, 68
Hunt, Leigh, 154
Hunter, Anne, 73–4, 77
Hutchinson, George, 52
Hutchinson, Sarah, 52

illness, 51
Ingrassia, Catherine, 101

Jefferson, Thomas, 11, 131
Jeffrey, Francis, 68, 71, 73, 88
   criticism of Walter Scott,
     75–6
Jerningham, Edward, 97n
Jersey, Lady, 168–9
Johns, Adrian, 14, 65, 252
Johnson, Claudia, 194
Johnson, Joseph, 120
Johnson, Samuel, 39–40, 98n

Keats, John, 122, 233
   autograph, 253n
   digital archive, 257n
   The Jealousies, 4
   'This living hand, now warm
     and capable', 3–4, 15–16
   manuscript transcripts, 237
   'Ode to a Nightingale', 28
   on poetic inspiration, 29
   transmission history, 237–8
   unpublished poems, 5, 231–2
Kinnaird, Douglas, 166
Knight, William, 48–9
Kotzebue, August von, 84–5, 88
Kraft, Elizabeth, 101, 109

Lady Susan (Austen), 18, 186–9,
   194, 198, 202–3, 246

Lamb, Charles, 29–30, 215
   attack on Barbauld, 59n
   disgust at Milton's corrected
     draft of 'Lycidas', 29–31, 58,
     219, 222
   'Oxford in the Vacation',
     28–30, 58
   on Shakespeare, 59n
Lamb, Lady Caroline, 164–5
Leacroft, Julia, 147
Leigh, Augusta, 165, 170
letters, preservation, 219, 221
Levin, Susan, 45–6
literary reviews, 66–93
lithography, 21, 22, 230
Lloyd, Martha, 13
London Corresponding Society,
   88
Longman, Susan Levin, 48
Love, Harold, 2, 10, 32,
   104, 189

McCarthy, William, 101, 109,
   111, 116, 127
McGann, Jerome, 22, 140–1,
   215–16, 234, 241
   socialisation of texts, 242
McKitterick, David, 2, 230
Mansfield Park (Austen), 187,
   190–1, 197–9, 212n, 222–7
Mant, Revd J., 77
manuscripts (literary)
   'archival reading', 46, 188
   archives of, 1, 18–19, 44, 104,
     110, 135n, 164, 217, 219–20,
     233, 251
   authorial control over, 4, 9,
     11–14, 35, 39, 44, 65, 146,
     152, 154, 163–6, 169,
     189, 235
   categorising, 15, 32–3, 35–7,
     103, 214, 238–40
   chosen over print publication,
     1–2, 4, 6, 46, 104, 140,
     236

manuscripts (literary) (*cont.*)
confidential, 15–17, 32–6, 38, 49: Austen's, 20–1, 184, 186–208, 232; Barbauld's, 107, 123, 126, 131, 232; Byron's, 140, 143, 155–6, 171–2, 176n
digital and photographic reproduction, 21, 182, 223, 228, 230–2, 243–51
drafts: difficult to distinguish and transformed from fair copies, 53, 57; meanings of, 29–31, 36–7, 182, 197–8, 204, 222–3, 234; showing stages of work and textual variation, 29–31, 36–7, 104–5, 191–7, 235–6
economic value, 18, 35, 215, 220–2, 228–9
functions/uses of, 214
engraved facsimiles of handwriting and manuscripts, 21, 52, 228, 230, 254, 49
fair copies, 53, 104, 111, 127, 155, 158, 164, 166, 169, 184, 184, 185–6, 188, 239–40, 262
illustration of, 2–3, 16–17, 45, 47, 52, 145, 183, 259–61
intentionality regarding readership, 15–16, 31–8, 41, 45, 49, 51, 59, 64, 89–90, 129, 153, 156, 164, 189, 234–5, 239–40, 242
meanings attached to, 2, 22, 29–31, 214–52, 265
as a means of sociability, 1–2, 8–10, 32–4, 37–8, 56–8, 93, 103–4, 111, 113, 124, 128–9, 146, 164, 166, 170–2, 187–91, 202–8, 214, 236–7, 240–1: for domestic/family audiences, 4, 14, 19, 45–8, 52, 64–5, 73, 77, 106–8, 124, 183–5

destruction or loss, 16, 19, 38, 44, 134n, 146, 187, 207, 220, 232, 251; by printers, 110, 135, 179n
operating outside of, but impacted by, the market economy, 9–10, 14, 16, 38–9, 41, 44, 64, 67, 92
preservation, 1, 7–8, 18, 20–1, 103–14, 123–4, 141, 164, 166, 179n, 191, 216–20, 229, 237, 241, 257n; by authors and their family or associates, 18, 41, 44, 46–7, 49, 56–7, 111, 184, 219–20, 135n; by collectors, 36, 214–15, 22—1, 229, 251
private, as distinct from or transitioning to social/confidential, 2, 13–14, 15–16, 19, 31–6, 38, 41, 43–6, 48, 58, 65, 105, 111, 127, 151, 163, 166, 172, 189, 207, 239–40
and public readership, 44–5
reverence for, 214–15, 217
as a vehicle of dissent, 4, 113, 119, 148, 158–60, 162, 189, 193, 195–6, 198, 200, 202, 204–6
Marotti, Arthur, 2, 10, 32
Mays, J. C. C., 235–8, 245
Melbourne, Lady, 164–5, 170
Mercer, James, *Lyric Poems*, 81
microforms, 231, 255n
Miller, D. A., 196
Milton, John
'Lycidas', 215, 219; Lamb's disgust at corrected manuscript, 28–31, 58, 219, 222
Montagu, Lady Mary, 72–3
Montgomery, James, 78
Monthly Repository, 121
Monthly Review, 64, 109
Moore, Thomas, 28, 223, 231
More, Hannah, 13, 14, 119
Moretti, Franco, 141

Morgan, J. P., 229
Murray, John, 7, 18, 143, 158–9, 162
  control over Byron's poetry, 165–7, 232
  preserved Byron's manuscripts, 220, 227, 229

Nathan, Isaac, 163
Newlyn, Lucy, 49
Nicholson, Mary Anne, 123–4
Northanger Abbey (Austen), 17, 22, 188, 197, 205
Norton Anthology of English Literature, 45, 47–8

O'Neill, Michael, 239–40
Opie, Amelia, 91
oral culture, 3, 34–5
Owen, Richard, 97n

Paston letters, 230
patronage, 39–40
Peninsular War, 158, 161
Perdita Manuscripts, 1500–1700, 103
Persuasion (Austen), 135n, 197, 205, 207, 224
  cancelled chapters, 187–8, 191, 191–4, 246–7
Phillips, Michael, 259, 262
Phillips, Richard, 118
photography, 228, 230–1, 243
Pierazzo, Elena, 213n
Pigot, John and Elizabeth, 146
Piper, Andrew, 2–3
plagiarism, 12–13
The Poetical Register, and Repository of Fugitive Poetry for 1804, 79
poetry, social, 107–9
Poole, Tom, 10
Pope, Alexander, 223, 230
Pratt, Samuel Jackson, 71
Pratt, Willis, 145

The Prelude (Wordsworth), 4–5
Pride and Prejudice (Austen), 13, 55, 182, 197, 199, 202, 225–6
Priestley, Elizabeth Rayner, 123
Priestley, Joseph, 109
Priestley, Mary, 113–14
Prince Regent (George IV), 14, 123, 128, 168–9, 189
print culture
  Blake's illuminated printing, 5, 259–65
  commercial practices and norms associated with, 9–11, 35, 39, 41, 43–4, 58, 83–6, 91–2, 144, 263
  contentious nature of print, 1, 14, 64–93
  demands and constraints of print, 148, 155–62, 165–6, 169–70, 182, 185, 188, 196, 206–8
  destruction of manuscripts in print process, 30, 192, 229
  engraved facsimiles of handwriting and manuscripts, 21, 52, 228, 230, 251, 254n
  fixing the fluidity of manuscript textuality, 29–30, 38–9, 58
  as a fluid medium itself, 11, 40, 58, 145
  as an intimate or social medium, 10–11, 33–34, 79, 89–90, 92
  private printing, 5, 10–11, 38, 83–4, 119, 141–2, 144–7, 153, 167–8, 173n, 180n
  as public medium, 2, 18, 85, 89–90, 147–52
  rapid expansion of, 1, 7, 12, 17, 22, 33, 66–7, 88, 90, 92–3, 215–16
  regularisation of manuscript in print, 197, 231, 249
  separates textual from physical, 234, 243

print culture (*cont.*)
  textual migration from private to public, 8, 11–13, 15, 30, 33–4, 49, 64–6, 68–88, 73, 129–32, 158, 184, 192–4, 206–8
  unauthorised print publication, 36, 38, 43–4, 102–3, 108, 119, 129–32, 141, 170
  values ascribed to/assumptions about, 14–15, 21, 46, 59, 66–7, 189
  as vehicle of enlightenment, 215–18
  withholding from print, 4, 35, 101–3, 112–18, 147, 162–70

quantitative humanities, 15, 19–20, 69, 102, 140–1, 144

Radcliffe, Ann, 61n
Reiman, Donald, 15, 32–3, 107, 184, 219, 238–40
review publications, 66–93
Ridgeway, Samuel, 25n
Robinson, Charles E., 249
Robinson, Henry Crabb, 119
Rodgers, Lady, 110, 111
Rogers, Samuel, 166–7
Romantic period
  afterlives of manuscripts, 21, 251–2
  cultural meanings of manuscripts, 2, 22, 29–31, 214–52, 265
  differences from earlier periods, 9–10
  manuscripts occupied middle ground, 64
  origins of, 41
  and poetic genius, 28–9, 31, 150, 207, 237–8, 251
  reassessment of manuscript records, 232–3
  second generation, 237

  textual scholars/editors of Romantic literary manuscripts, 1, 8, 15, 21–2, 31–2, 37, 185, 216, 230–52
  ubiquity of print, 33, 92
Rosetta Stone, 21
Rowe, Elizabeth Singer, 109
Rutherford, Andrew, 151

Sabor, Peter, 184
St Clair, William, 2, 11
Samuel, Richard, 'The Nine Living Muses of Great Britain', 101
Sanditon (Austen), 18, 186, 188, 191–208, 246
  bears signs of Austen's physical deterioration, 196
  stylistic experimentation, 203
satire, 154, 160, 167, 173n
  clandestine, 189–90, 198
Schellenberg, Betty, 3
Schreibman, Susan, 244
Scott, Walter, 91, 154
  Chronicles of the Canongate, 220
  on Austen's *Emma*, 205
  Marmion, 75–6, 82, 207
  plagiarism of Coleridge, 12–13
  preserved and auctioned his own manuscripts, 220, 229
  Waverley novels, 233–4
Scrivener, Michael, 88, 90
Selincourt, Ernest de, 45, 52, 55
Sense and Sensibility (Austen), 182, 186, 197
Seward, Anna, 228
Shakespeare, William, 28, 219, 230
Sharpe, Lucy Reid, 123
Shelley, Mary, 13, 166, 232, 233
  Frankenstein Notebooks, 249–50
  History of a Six Weeks' Tour, 65–6, 70, 85
  Shelley-Godwin Archive (digital archive), 249–50

Shelley, Percy
  Adonais, 122
  difficulty of reconstructing texts from manuscripts, 238–9
  The Esdaile Notebook, 238
  grouping of poems for publication, 238–41
  History of a Six Weeks' Tour, 65–6, 70, 85, 239
  'Masque of Anarchy', 125
  'Mont Blanc', 66, 239–40
  poems circulated in manuscript form, 5
  Poetical Works, 13
  'released' manuscripts, 33–5
  Shelley-Godwin Archive (digital archive), 249–50, 258n
  'Stanzas Written in Dejection, Near Naples', 40
  The Triumph of Life, 240
  unfinished work, 240
  unpublished work, 231–2
Sher, Richard, 100n
Sibylline Leaves, 64
Siskin, Clifford, 205
Smith, Charlotte, 16, 58, 161
  abusive and dissipated husband, 42–3
  Elegaic Sonnets, 38–44, 91, 143
  The Emigrants, 43
  income, 12
  manuscripts burned, 38, 58
  politicisation of her oppression, 43
  unauthorised publication of her work, 6, 12, 38, 65
  writes to support family, 43
Smith, Sydney, 68
social authorship, 103–4, 107, 154
Songs of Innocence and Experience (Blake), 3, 262, 264
Southey, Robert, 68
  Life and Correspondence, 87
  Specimens of the Later English Poets, 80–1
  Thalaba, 70, 85–6
  Wat Tyler, 12, 25n

Staël, Madame de, 165
Stauffer, Andrew, 145, 166
Stewart, Dugald, 83
Stillinger, Jack, 231, 237–8
subscription, as beggary, 60n
Sutherland, Kathryn, 183–4, 185–6, 192, 196, 213n, 243, 252

Talbot, Henry Fox, 228, 230
Tanner, Tony, 202
Thane, John, 230
Thelwall, John, 88–90
Todd, Janet, 188
Tuite, Claire, 202
Turner, Dawson, 220, 223
Turner, William, 114
Twyman, Michael, 230

Unitarianism, 130
Upcott, William, 221

Vallon, Annette, 51
A Vindication of the Rights of Woman (Wollstonecraft), 43
Viscomi, Joseph, 259, 262

walking, as an acceptable female activity, 55
Warrington, 108–9
Waters, Mary, 74
The Watsons (Austen), 186–7, 191–6, 198, 202, 205, 210n, 246
Werner, Marta, 30–2, 48
West, Lady Mary, 109
Whalley, George, 236
Whelan, Timothy, 6–7
Wilberforce, William, 120
Wimsatt, W. K., 31–2
Wollstonecraft, Mary, 14, 119, 126
  Shelley-Godwin Archive (digital archive), 249, 257n
  unpublished manuscripts, 232
  A Vindication of the Rights of Woman, 43

women
  acceptable behaviour/discourse, 43–4, 55, 91, 112–14, 119, 194–5, 225
  economic dependency and distress caused by, 42–4, 194–5, 198–200, 208
  importance of the study of manuscripts to, 5–7, 25n, 46, 104
  pressures of print culture, 6–7
  professional and social restrictions, 113
  representation of in anthologies, 47, 101, 103
Woodfall, William, 109, 110, 132
Woodhouse, James, 84
Woodhouse, Richard, 237
Woof, Pamela, 47–8
Woolf, Virginia, 194
Wordsworth, Dorothy, 6–7, 16, 44–59, 45–6
  accounts of her walks, 51, 55
  assumptions made about lack of print publication, 45–7
  brother accused of appropriation and stifling her work, 49
  depersonalisation of manuscripts, 48–9, 55
  family and domestic life, 46
  Grasmere Journals, 47–51
  journals, 7, 48
  multiple versions of her poems, 56–7
  Narrative of the Life of George and Sarah Green, 62n
  notebooks inspired brother's writing, 49–51
  poetry, 56
  Recollections of a Tour in Scotland, 52–6, 161
  revisions to her work, 53–6, 105
  selections of work chosen for publication, 48–9
  surviving manuscripts, 44
  tour notebooks, 51–2
  work published in the *Memoirs of William Wordsworth*, 48
  writings on the natural world, 48
Wordsworth, Jonathan, 235
Wordsworth, Mary (Hutchinson), 51
Wordsworth, William, 122
  accused of appropriating and stifling sister's work, 49
  affair with Annette Valon, 51
  'To a Butterfly', 50
  Cornell edition, 232–6, 243
  criticised by *Edinburgh Review*, 71, 82–3
  criticised by Byron, 152
  digital archive, 257n
  inspired by sister's notebooks, 49–51
  manuscript notebooks, 234
  marriage, 51
  Memoirs of William Wordsworth, 48
  'Michael', 49
  natural genius, 28
  Poems in Two Volumes, 71, 152
  on poetic inspiration, 29
  poetry in sister's journals, 47–8
  on poets, 40
  The Prelude, 4–5, 12, 34–5
  'The Thorn', 49
  understood value of manuscripts, 219
  writing process revealed by sister's journals, 51
writers, advice to, 86–7

Zimmerman, Sarah, 43

EU representative:
Easy Access System Europe
Mustamäe tee 50, 10621 Tallinn, Estonia
Gpsr.requests@easproject.com

www.ingramcontent.com/pod-product-compliance
Lightning Source LLC
Chambersburg PA
CBHW070818250426
43672CB00031B/2787